Military Aviation

in

Malta G.C.

1915-1993

A comprehensive history

John F. Hamlin

First published 1994
by GMS Enterprises
67 Pyhill, Bretton
Peterborough
England
PE3 8QQ

Tel & Fax 0733-265123

ISBN 1 870384 25 3

The main text of this book
has been set in 10pt 'Times'
on an Apple Macintosh DTP system

Printed and bound for
GMS Enterprises by
Woolnough Ltd
Express Works
Irthlingborough
Northants

Contents

Appendices

Bibliography

The following books may be of interest to readers wishing
to study the history of military aviation in Malta in greater detail:

Night Strike For Malta (830 Squadron, Fleet Air Arm) by Kenneth Poolman
Jane's Publishing Co., 1980
ISBN 0 7106 0003 8

The Cross and The Ensign -- a naval history of Malta 1798-1979 by Peter Elliott
Grafton Books (Collins Publishing Group), 1982
ISBN 0 586 05550 9

The Air Battle of Malta
HMSO 1944

Warburton's War by Tony Spooner DSO DFC
William Kimber, 1987
ISBN 0 7183 0661 9

Wings In The Sun by Air Chief Marshal Sir David Lee
HMSO, 1989
ISBN 0 11 772620 6

Faith, Hope and Malta GC by Tony Spooner DSO DFC
Newton Publishers, 1992
ISBN 1 872308 50 3

The Unconquered Isle: Malta by Ian Hay
Hodder & Stoughton, 1943
no ISBN

The Air Battle for Malta by James Douglas-Hamilton
Airlife Publishing Ltd., 1990
ISBN 1 85310 067 6

The Squadrons of the RAF and Commonwealth by James J. Halley
Air Britain, 1989
ISBN 0 85130 164 9

The Squadrons of the Fleet Air Arm by R. C. Sturtivant
Air Britain, 1984
ISBN 0 85130 120 7

Introduction

Situated as they are at a 'crossroads' for shipping in the central Mediterranean, the islands of Malta have for centuries been of the greatest military importance. It is not surprising, therefore, that it was realised, early in the First World War, that Malta could be the base from which flying-boats of the fledgling Royal Naval Air Service would help keep the shipping lanes open. By the end of the war such a base was well-established, but during the inter-war period landplanes gradually ousted the water-borne aircraft in importance.

After a very slow start in 1940, The Royal Air Force and Fleet Air Arm built up considerable facilities on Malta, with some involvement by the US Army Air Force at the time of the invasion of Sicily. No less than five airfields were then active on Malta, and a temporary airstrip was busy on the neighbouring island of Gozo. The siege of Malta in 1941/42, which took a terrible toll of lives, buildings and equipment, was overcome in great part by the heroic efforts of British and Commonwealth aircrews and of course by the tenacity of the Maltese people. It must also never be forgotten that without the efforts of the RAF and FAA ground crews, often underfed and working in conditions of extreme danger, no aircraft would have left the ground, and the battle would have been lost.

Post-war, the RAF suffered a period of retrenchment in Malta as elsewhere, but the FAA tended to become more active. Added to the FAA, US Navy aviation activity increased for several years in the 'fifties. Eventually, political considerations caused a gradual reduction in all British military forces in Malta, and well before the final departure of the RAF in 1978 all but one airfield had been closed. During the same period, the Maltese Government was building up its own small but efficient military aviation arm, which forms part of the islands' defensive capability today.

This book is an attempt to record concisely the history of all the hundreds of flying units which have spent time on Malta over the years, with the deliberate ommission, due to restricted space, of the very numerous short-term disembarkations of FAA squadrons. Non-flying units have been mentioned in the narrative where appropriate, but while it is not suggested that such units are of lesser significance, efforts to keep this book to a reasonable size preclude the inclusion of their detailed histories.

Sincere thanks are given to the many individuals and organisations who contributed information and illustrations, in particular members and officers of the George Cross Island Association and Mr Fredrick Galea of the National War Museum Association, whose help was invaluable.

John F. Hamlin
Newmarket

Abbreviations

AA	Anti-Aircraft		EVT	Educational & Vocational Training
AACU	Anti-Aircraft Cooperation Unit		F	Fighter [e.g. F.8]
A&AEE	Aircraft & Armament Experimental			[not applicable to early flying boats]
	Establishment		FAA	Fleet Air Arm
A-B	Augusta-Bell		FASRON	Fleet Aircraft Service Squadron
ACM	Air Chief Marshal			[US Navy]
AEW	Airborne Early Warning [e.g. AEW.3]		FAW	Fighter All Weather [e.g. FAW.21]
AFC	Air Force Cross		FB	Fighter-bomber [e.g. FB.5]
AFM	Armed Forces of Malta		FG	Fighter Group [USAAF]
AHQ	Air Headquarters		FGA	Fighter/Ground Attack [e.g. FGA.2]
AI	Airborne Interception [radar]		Fg. Off.	Flying Officer
Air Comm.	Air Commodore		Flt.	Flight
AMES	Air Ministry Experimental Station		Flt. Lt.	Flight Lieutenant
	[a euphemism for radar station]		Flt. Sgt.	Flight Sergeant
AMWD	Air Ministry Works Directorate		FR	Fighter/Reconnaissance [e.g. FR.47]
AOC	Air Officer Commanding		FR	Fleet Reconnaissance
AOC-in-C	Air Officer Commanding in Chief			[e.g. 440(FR)Flight]
APC	Armament Practice Camp		FRU	Fleet Requirements Unit
AS	Anti-submarine [e.g. AS.4]		FS	Fighter Squadron [USAAF]
ASR	Air-Sea Rescue		ft.	feet
ASR&CF	Air-Sea Rescue & Communication		FTS	Flying Training School
	Flight		Fw.	Focke-Wulf
ASV	Air to Surface Vessel [radar]		GCA	Ground Controlled Approach
AVM	Air Vice Marshal		GCB	(Knight) Grand Cross of the Bath
BABS	Beam Approach Beacon System		GCI	Ground Controlled Interception
Bf.	Bayerische Flugzeugwerke AG		GCMG	(Knight) Grand Cross of the Order of St.
	(Messerschmitt)			Michael & St. George
BG	Bombardment Group [USAAF]		GOC	General Officer Commanding
BOAC	British Overseas Airways Corporation		Gp. Capt.	Group Captain
Br.	Breda		GR	General Reconnaissance
BS	Bombardment Squadron [USAAF]		HAS	Helicopter/Anti-submarine [e.g.HAS.22]
C	Transport (aircraft) [e.g. C.20]		He.	Heinkel
CBE	Commander of the Order of the British		HE	His Excellency
	Empire		HF	High Frequency [radio]
C-in-C	Commander-in-Chief		HMS	His/Her Majesty's Ship
CF	Communications Flight		HQ	Headquarters
CO	Commanding Officer		HR	Helicopter/Rescue [e.g. HR.5]
COD	Carrier On-board Delivery [e.g. COD.4]		HRH	His/Her Royal Highness
Col.	Colonel		JG	Jagdgeschwader [Luftwaffe fighter unit]
CR	Fiat		Ju.	Junkers
C&TTS	Communications & Target Towing		KBE	Knight Commander of the Order of the
	Squadron			British Empire
CR/DF	Cathode ray direction finder		KCB	Knight Commander of the British
det.	detachment			Empire
D/F	Direction finder		km.	kilometres
DFC	Distinguished Flying Cross		LAC	Leading Aircraftsman
DH	De Havilland		LARAF	Libyan Arab Republic Air Force
Do.	Dornier		lb.	pound [weight]
DSC	Distinguished Service Cross		LCT	Landing Craft: Tank
DSO	Distinguished Service Order		LST	Landing Ship: Tank
DZ	Dropping Zone		LG	Landing Ground [in the Western Desert]
ECM	Electronic Counter-Measures [e.g.		Lt.	Lieutenant
	ECM.22]		Lt.(A)	Lieutenant (Air)

Lt. Cdr.	Lieutenant Commander	RNAMY	Royal Naval Aircraft Maintenance Yard
m.	metres	RNA Sqdn.	Royal Naval Air Squadron
MAEE	Marine Aircraft Experimental Establishment	RNAS	Royal Naval Air Service
		RNVR	Royal Naval Volunteer Reserve
MC	Macchi (aircraft type)	RNZAF	Royal New Zealand Air Force
MC	Military Cross	S	Strike [e.g. S.4]
MCU	Marine Craft Unit	SAAF	South African Air Force
MEDME	Mediterranean & Middle East	SANA	(An Italian airline)
Met.	Meteorological	SM	Savoia-Marchetti
MFA	Maltese Facilities Agreement	SNAFU	Situation normal: all fouled up!
MiG	Mikoyan-Gurevich	SNCO	Senior Non-Commissioned Officer
Mk.	Mark		[i.e. Sgt., Flt. Sgt. and Warrant Officer]
MLF	Malta Land Force	SP	Staging Post
MRAF	Marshal of the Royal Air Force	Sq. or Sqdn.	Squadron
MT	Motor transport	Sqdn. Cdr.	Squadron Commander [a pre-1918 rank]
MU	Maintenance Unit	Sqdn. Ldr.	Squadron Leader
NAAFI	Navy, Army and Air Force Institute	SR	Strategic Reconnaissance
NATO	North Atlantic Treaty Organisation	SS	Steamship
navex	navigation exercise	SSQ	Station Sick Quarters
NCO	Non-commissioned officer	Stn.	Station
NF	Night Fighter [e.g. NF.13]	T	Trainer [e.g. T.7]
NWMA	National War Museum Association [Malta]	TF	Task Force [of Malta]
		TT	Target Tug or Target Towing [e.g. TT.10]
OATS	Officers' Advanced Training School		
OBE	Order of the British Empire	U	Unmanned [drone aircraft, e.g. U.10]
OCU	Operational Conversion Unit	UAE	United Arab Emirates
OTU	Operational Training Unit	UK	United Kingdom
P&MG	Photographic & Mapping Group [USAAF]	USAAF	United States Army Air Force
		USAF	United States Air Force
PR	Photographic reconnaissance	USN	United States Navy
PRU	Photographic Reconnaissance Unit	USS	United States Ship
Pt. Off.	Pilot Officer	VE	Victory In Europe
RA	Regia Aeronautica (Italian Air Force)	VHF	Very High Frequency [radio]
RAF	Royal Air Force	VIP	Very Important Person
RAuxAF	Royal Auxiliary Air Force	VJ	Victory Over Japan
RAAF	Royal Australian Air Force	Wg. Cdr.	Wing Commander
RCAF	Royal Canadian Air Force	WOp	Wireless operator
RE	Reggiane	W/T	Wireless Telegraphy
Regt.	Regiment	yds.	yards
RN	Royal Navy		

MILITARY AVIATION IN MALTA G.C. 1915-1993

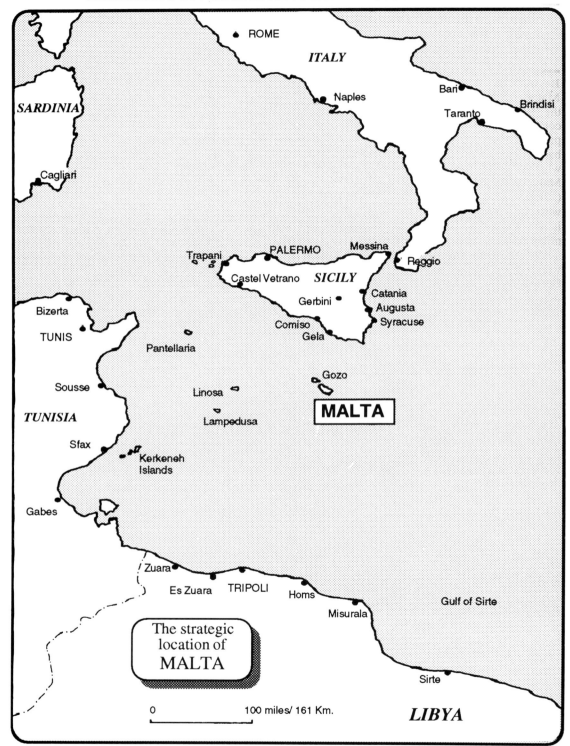

The strategic
location of
MALTA

0   100 miles/ 161 Km.

Chapter 1
THE UNSINKABLE ISLAND

Beginnings

Malta, located near the central lengthwise point of the Mediterranean Sea, has inevitably been considered, over many centuries, a highly valuable piece of territory, and its recorded history goes back to about 1500 BC. Two main islands make up what the modern holidaymaker thinks of as Malta: Malta itself, about 17 miles (27km.) by 8 miles (13km.) and Gozo, which lies just off the north-west end of Malta and is very much smaller. Malta is about 60 miles (95km.) from Sicily and 200 miles (320km.) from both Libya and Tunisia.

When war was declared in 1914, the opponents were Great Britain and France on one side and Germany and Austria, and possibly Italy, on the other. It was agreed that the British fleet would guard the North Sea while French ships looked after the Mediterranean, where the Italian fleet was active. Germany had other plans, however, and had in 1912 despatched a battle cruiser and a light cruiser with orders, in the event of war, to inflict maximum damage on targets of opportunity, including Malta, before retreating or, in all probability, being destroyed. Before the outbreak of war, Britain had sent three battle cruisers and a cruiser to the Mediterranean, and there were four light cruisers at Alexandria and three submarines at Malta. As it turned out, early naval conflict was in the Dardanelles area rather than around Malta.

During the latter half of 1915, Germany had 15 submarines in the Mediterranean, mainly in the Aegean Sea, where they were positioned against Allied forces in the Dardanelles, and in the Adriatic. This concentration of enemy activity created an urgent need for counter-measures, particularly after the battleships HMS *Triumph* and HMS *Majestic* were sunk by submarine U21. On 20 December the senior British naval officer in Malta suggested the use of a small airship to be based on the island to scout for enemy submarines. Their Lords of the Admiralty, however, being foresighted for once, considered seaplanes a better proposition and Sqdn. Cdr. Bowhill, on his way to Mesopotamia, was told to advise the senior naval officer on the best location for a seaplane base on Malta.

The position chosen was near the torpedo depot at Calafrana (then spelt with a C) and the anticipated completion date was May 1916. The 6900-ton seaplane carrier HMS *Ark Royal II* (later renamed *Pegasus*) was already in the Mediterranean, and while the seaplane base was being built a second carrier, HMS *Manxman,* a converted Isle of Man packet, arrived to join her. Construction of the Calafrana base was duly completed, and a number of flying boats arrived from the UK in July 1916 to begin operations.

In May 1917 it was proposed that flying boats should be built in Malta dockyard to alleviate the incapacity of other manufacturers. Work began in June on a batch of Felixstowe F.3 aircraft but was delayed by a shortage of engines, the first of which did not arrive until November, when the first few aircraft were completed.

Another scheme was mooted in August 1917, involving the use of kite balloons on ships, with shore bases for servicing and re-charging. Accordingly, six sheds and a gas-making plant were built at the head of Lazzaretto Creek, Ta'Xbiex.

A plan for reorganisation was submitted to the Admiralty in January 1918. The Mediterranean Sea would be divided into five self-contained areas: Malta, Italy, the Aegean Sea, Port Said and Gibraltar, and the Senior Air Staff Officer would be based in Malta. All aircraft sent by sea were to be allocated to Malta for redistribution and the main stockpile of stores and equipment would be kept on the island. Four additional carriers would be required to distribute seaplanes to the other areas and to act as forward bases where no shore facilities existed. A major extension to Calafrana to handle the F.3 flying boats and reserve seaplanes would be necessary. Production of the F.3s would be increased from 12 to 50 and given priority with a view to basing 12, plus three reserves, at Calafrana. In addition, the number of seaplanes for use on the carriers and in reserve was to be 36.

On formation of the Royal Air Force on 1 April 1918 Calafrana became part of the Malta Group, the other Stations in the Group being No.1 Kite Balloon Base and the Dockyard Construction Unit.

A Training Camp was then set up at Spinola, targetted with training 2000 Maltese recruits, and by August 1918 700 men had been dealt with.

The establishment of aircraft for Malta was now set at twelve F.3 flying boats and two Flights of six Shorts seaplanes with a reserve of seaplanes for the carriers. Twelve F.3s had been completed by August 1918 but four were sent to the Adriatic area, leaving five airworthy examples in Malta, two being under repair and one apparently written off. Shortage of storage space meant that only four of the Shorts seaplanes could be kept erected at any one time.

The first land-based aircraft operated by the RAF in Malta appeared at a temporary airstrip on Marsa racecourse in September 1918. These were two DH.9As, with large wings and flotation gear, used by 562 (Malta Anti-Submarine) Flight, for which personnel were attached from Calafrana. A much larger and potentially more significant aircraft, J1936, the third prototype of the Handley Page V/1500, named *"Old Carthusian"*, arrived at Marsa on 21 December 1918 on a stage of a pioneering 7000-mile (11200km.) flight from Martlesham Heath to Karachi. After its overnight stay, the large aircraft, fully loaded with fuel, only just succeeded in clearing a stone wall at the end of the take-off run, but did so, only to force-land eight hours later 50 miles (80 km.) west of Mersa Matruh.

In August 1918 268 Squadron was formed at Calafrana to take over the Short seaplanes, followed by 267 Squadron in September to operate the F.3 flying boats. Malta Group was downgraded and retitled 17 (Malta) Wing, and this then controlled 267 and 268 Squadrons at Calafrana; 562 Flight at Marsa; No. 1 Kite Balloon Base;

Stores Park; Construction Unit at Zabba Camp; Training Depot at Spinola; and the Repair Depot.

During the first half of 1919, 562 Flight, the Kite Balloon Base, the Training Camp and the Stores Park all disbanded, and the two squadrons were reduced to one Flight each. After the disbandment of 268 Squadron in October 1919, all that remained of the RAF in Malta were 267 Squadron, a disposal depot and a newly-opened meteorological station. Of the attendant ships, HMS *Manxman* left in April 1919, HMS *Vindex* in June, HMS *Riviera* in August and HMS *Empress* in September. HMS *Ark Royal* left in December 1919, leaving only HMS *Engadine* in the Mediterranean, but this vessel was relieved by *Ark Royal* between February and September 1920.

The nineteen twenties and thirties

Flying boats from Calafrana continued to operate during the early 1920s on such naval cooperation duties as photographic reconnaissance, aerial gunnery, torpedo spotting, and bombing sea targets. However, the tide was turning in favour of more versatile land-based aircraft, and in January 1923 a new airfield, Malta's first apart from the temporary one at Marsa racecourse, was opened at Hal Far for use by carrier-based aircraft.

Alterations to the disposition of the Fleet in the spring of 1924, in which the main British naval force was concentrated in the Mediterranean, brought about a corresponding increase in aerial activity. In June HMS *Eagle* arrived off Malta, and its aircraft were taken ashore at Calafrana and Hal Far. They were the vanguard of a large number of Flights and Squadrons to use Malta's growing facilities for short or long periods over the next several years.

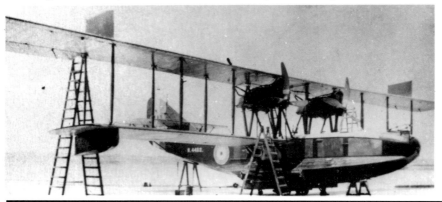

Early flying boats based in Malta included Felixstowe F.2A aircraft such as N4488 of 267 Squadron at Calafrana
[P. H. T. Green collection]

Left: The tented RAF detachment's camp at Ghain Tuffiena, close to Golden Bay, in 1929. The reason for the camp's presence there is unknown.

Right: HMS *Argus* in Grand Harbour on the way home from the China Station.

A varied selection of aircraft types from Hal Far seen airborne c.1931 near Mosta racecourse (the home of 562 Flight in 1919) *[P. H. T. Green collection]*

MILITARY AVIATION IN MALTA G.C. 1915-1993

Right: Two visitors from the Aeronavale (French Navy). Farman F.168 floatplanes of Escadrille 4B2, Karouba, at Calafrana in August 1930.
[D. R. Neate]

Left: A picture evocative from the 1930s: Flycatcher floatplane taxying on slightly choppy water at Calafrana.
[D. R. Neate]

Right: HMS *Courageous* in Grand Harbour.
[G. W. Jordan]

Left: A fine picture of HMS *Glorious* sailing into Grand Harbour in 1933, its aircraft probably having flown off to Hal Far.
[J. W. Parsons]

THE UNSINKABLE ISLAND

The flight deck of HMS *Glorious* in 1935 with Nimrods of 408 Flight and the Ripons of 461 Flight. *[J. W. Parsons]*

In 1924 a defence scheme for Malta was drawn up, and was tried out on 30 August by means of a dummy attack by aircraft flying off HMS *Eagle*. Anti-aircraft guns were manned on ships in Grand Harbour and by the army, and ten aircraft from Hal Far were detailed as defenders, each aircraft patrolling a sector. The trials were regarded as successful in that Eagle was located, the AA guns notified and the attacking aircraft repulsed. How realistic the defence plans were is another question!

Hal Far was organised as a permanent RAF Station in April 1929 and a Flight formed there for communications and other duties. Carrier-based Squadrons and Flights made use of Hal Far's facilities during the early 'thirties, but in 1935 when the crisis in Abyssinia came to a head the usual peaceful routine changed. Two squadrons of aircraft were sent out from the UK as a precautionary measure and the Fleet was reinforced by the carriers HMS *Glorious* and HMS *Courageous*. Malta's anti-aircraft defences at the time totalled twelve guns, but now extra artillery was sent out.

Fear of an Italian poison gas attack led to a dummy raid on Valletta in October 1935 which

turned out to be quite a bizarre event. Vans from which thunderflashes were thrown toured the streets, the church bells were rung and searchlights were illuminated, all to the cheers of the Maltese population. In December of that year the Prime Minister of Malta visited London and pleaded in the House of Commons for rapid construction of more airfields on the island, but the opinion of Army and RAF senior officers was that in the event of an attack Malta could not be defended, a point of view which, a few years later, was to prove almost fatal.

Meanwhile, in the late 'thirties, mock air raids were staged regularly. The Abyssinian war ended and the two squadrons attached to Hal Far went home. Carrier-based squadrons of the recently re-formed Fleet Air Arm continued to use Hal Far, and Calafrana was also active with water-borne aircraft. At both locations pilotless aircraft began flying in 1936 as targets for ships' gunners, but otherwise little thought seems to have been given to the question of the island's defences until 1938. At that time, with war with Germany almost inevitable, the Committee for Imperial Defence agreed to a long-term scheme for Malta, involving four fighter squadrons and 172 AA guns. In

This picture of Fairey IIIF S1510 of 823 Sqdn., coded 805, shows the primitive accommodation for the pilot and observer. Below is part of the Mediterranean Fleet in Grand Harbour. *[J. W. Parsons]*

October 1938 work started on an all-weather airfield at Luqa in a move to overcome the difficulties caused by poor wet-weather conditions at Hal Far, but by the outbreak of war in September 1939 Luqa was far from complete. Malta's small civil airport at Takali, which was used by the Italian airline Ala Littoria for services to Sicily and Libya, was now available for use by the RAF if required, but suffered from the same waterlogging problems as Hal Far.

The early war years, 1940 to 1942

By January 1940, when Air Commodore F. H. M. Maynard arrived to take over as AOC, there were still no RAF fighter aircraft based on Malta. Progress was being made at Luqa, however, and this new airfield, with paved runways, was opened as an RAF Station on 1 April 1940. An ominous quietness hung over Malta, but everything changed on 10 June, when Italy, riding on the success of Germany's assault on France, declared war on Great Britain, prompting the seizure of Italian ships in Grand Harbour and the rounding-up of Italian citizens on the island. Only two days before, Italian airliners had been using Luqa, which

had succeeded Takali, for scheduled services.

The total number of aircraft on the island on this date was five Swordfish used by the FAA for target-towing, one Queen Bee pilotless drone and eight Sea Gladiators which were stored in packing-cases at Kalafrana, having been left there by HMS *Glorious* when the carrier was on the way to Norway in May. Four of the Gladiators were released to the RAF on Admiral Cunningham's orders, hurriedly assembled at Kalafrana, and taken on charge at Hal Far as a Fighter Flight. Soon after the Gladiators entered service, a signal from the Admiralty was received in Malta; it asked why Fleet Air Arm property had been turned over to the RAF, as the aircraft were earmarked for HMS *Eagle* on her next visit. Such was the attitude of those in command at a distance who did not understand the seriousness of the situation.

The first raid on Malta was not long in coming. At 06.45 on 11 June 1940 ten SM.79 bombers of Regia Aeronautica (the Italian Air Force) attacked Grand Harbour and Hal Far airfield from a height of 14000 feet (4250m.) Waiting in readiness were the four Gladiators and the island's AA guns. During that first week of raids on the island the

Gladiators took off time and again to fend off superior numbers of Italian aircraft; this forced the enemy into providing fighter escort for his bombers, but Air Comm. Maynard reported at the time that the high speeds of the enemy aircraft made interception by the Gladiators difficult, and he pressed for more modern aircraft to be provided in quantity.

After two weeks the Regia Aeronautica sent a solo SM.79 on a photo-reconnaissance mission to back up German claims that the naval base in Grand Harbour had been totally destroyed. One of the Gladiators was successful in shooting down this aircraft just off Valletta, and the Italian crew was captured and brought ashore.

Relief, in a small way, came at the end of June, when four Hurricanes on passage to Egypt were appropriated by Air Comm. Maynard, an officer who by now had built up a reputation for holding on to any useful equipment which came his way. So the main fighter defence was taken over by the Hurricanes, the forerunners of hundreds of the type which in the months ahead would form the mainstay of the islands' defence until the arrival of Spitfires. The Gladiators were not forgotten, especially by the civilian population, and one of the aircraft, *'Faith'*, would be presented to the people of Malta at a later date as a symbol of the resistance put up during those early weeks of conflict.

At sea in June 1940 the threat against Malta came from the powerful Italian Navy fleet commanded by Admiral Angelo Iachino. Responsible for the naval defence of Malta was Admiral Sir Andrew Cunningham from his headquarters at Alexandria in Egypt. The Mediterranean Fleet comprised the aircraft carrier HMS *Eagle*, three battleships, six cruisers and twenty destroyers. The loss of the French fleet following the capitulation of France in June 1940 necessitated the formation of another naval force in the western Mediterranean, so on 28 June 'Force H' was created, with headquarters at Gibraltar. To the new fleet HMS *Eagle* transferred. In opposition were the six battleships, twenty-one cruisers and over fifty destroyers, but no aircraft carriers, of the Italian Navy, based on Sicilian ports or on mainland Italy.

At this stage of the war, Malta was still receiving convoys carrying supplies, and Malta-based Swordfish aircraft of the FAA were beginning to repay the Italians in kind by striking oil refineries in Sicily. In July the sole fighter defence of the island still rested on the Fighter Flight; other units on the island included a W/T Station at Kalafrana, a meteorological office at Valletta, Station Flight at Hal Far, 3 Anti-Aircraft Cooperation Unit at Hal Far and Kalafrana and a D/F Station and 241 and 242 Transportable Radio Units (in reality Type 6 radar units installed recently to provide early warning of enemy aircraft) at Fort Ta Salvatur.

It is now clear that the Italians anticipated overwhelming Malta within a few months, but somehow the Fighter Flight's Gladiators and Hurricanes managed to stave them off. Valuable time was thus gained to enable the Fighter Flight to be further expanded, and early in August, as Operation 'Hurry', twelve more Hurricanes were flown off the carrier HMS *Argus* to Luqa. This injection enabled the Fighter Flight to be given squadron status as 261 Squadron, which promptly took over the new Hurricanes.

HMS *Eagle* in
Grand Harbour
[G. W. Jordan]

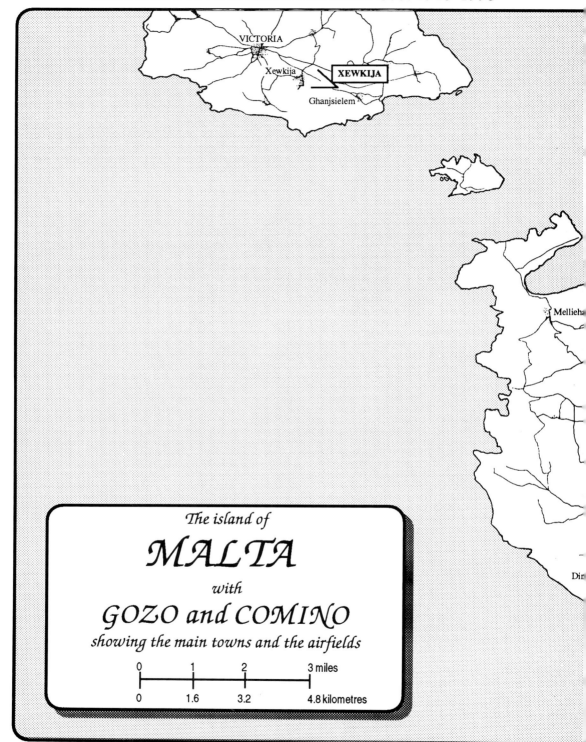

VICTORIA

Xewkija

XEWKIJA

Ghanjsielem

Mellieha

Din

The island of

MALTA

with

GOZO and COMINO

showing the main towns and the airfields

0	1	2	3 miles
0	1.6	3.2	4.8 kilometres

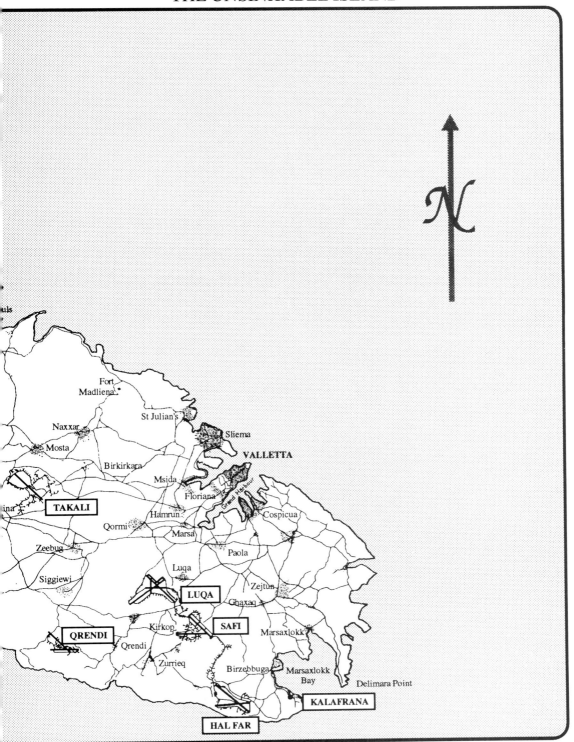

MILITARY AVIATION IN MALTA G.C. 1915-1993

During August 1940 the enemy changed his main target from the dockyard, which he believed he had destroyed, to the airfields on Malta. Most of the raids were now made at night, and Luqa experienced its first heavy raid. On 15 September 1940 (a significant date for those who had been experiencing the Battle of Britain) twenty Ju.87 Stuka dive-bombers of the Regia Aeronautica, with fighter escort, attacked Hal Far.

Of great value from September 1940 onward was the wide-ranging ability of Malta-based reconnaissance aircraft. Over a period of about eighteen months, these aircraft, initially mainly Martin Marylands, flew constant PR sorties over the whole central Mediterranean area, bringing back vital information on the deployment of enemy naval and ground forces under the most adverse conditions. Not even during the heaviest air raids did the PR aircraft falter, but later the Marylands were replaced by much faster PR versions of the Spitfire, which could evade the enemy fighters which were always looking for a 'kill'.

In November 1940 the FAA mounted a very successful attack on the Italian port of Taranto, following a reconnaissance by Malta-based aircraft. Several Italian battleships and cruisers were disabled, so securing, once again, breathing space for the military and civilian inhabitants of Malta. Soon after this, two convoys from Egypt and one from the UK arrived safely, and the RAF and FAA were both able to step up offensive operations from the island. Of twelve more Hurricanes which flew off HMS *Argus* in November, however, only four arrived on the island, due to a navigational error. The failure of Britain to provide adequate air defence was proving a major problem. At the same time, the Italian airborne effort was significantly reduced, due in some part to the heavy losses sustained by the Regia Aeronautica. This state of affairs was not acceptable to the German High Command, which promptly transferred Fliegercorps X from Norway to Sicily to carry out attacks on British shipping, a task for which it was well experienced, and to neutralise Malta. Equipped with Ju.87s, Ju.88 bombers and Bf.109 fighters, Fliegercorps X was ordered to put Malta into a state of siege by eliminationg the British fleet, particularly the aircraft carriers. To the British Prime Minister, Winston Churchill, in London and to Admiral Cunningham in Alexandria, Malta was an island which had to be defended at all costs as the only base from which heavy damage could be inflicted on the enemy supply convoys sailing between Italy and North Africa. Even during this defensive period, it was possible to mount small-scale raids by Malta-based Blenheims and Wellingtons on targets in Sicily and Libya, a fact which greatly cheered everyone on the island.

The erstwhile civil airport at Takali, taken over by the RAF in October 1940, soon began to play its part in the defence of the island. The Luftwaffe build-up in Sicily continued and on 9 January 1941 nine Ju.87s escorted by nine CR.42s of the RA attacked shipping in the bay of Marsa Scirocco, dive-bombed flying boats at their moorings at Kalafrana and attacked the three airfields, making three Wellingtons at Luqa unserviceable. Several reconnaissance flights over Malta followed, and a sense of impending disaster pervaded the island. During the evening of 10 January the aircraft carrier HMS *Illustrious,* listing badly after being attacked by Ju.87s and 88s while protecting a Malta-bound convoy, entered Grand Harbour. From her deck seven Fairey Fulmars and seven Swordfish were able to fly off to Hal Far to augment Malta's solitary fighter squadron, which stood by, ready for the worst. It came on 16 January. In the front line were Luftwaffe Ju.88s with RA CR.42s acting as escort, and bringing up the rear were Ju.87 dive-bombers, a total of more than seventy aircraft against which the RAF's small force of Hurricanes and four FAA Fulmars took off to do battle. This time, the enemy was aiming for *Illustrious;* an intense barrage was put up by the AA batteries and by guns of the various ships in harbour, and five enemy aircraft were shot down by this means. Another five were claimed by the fighters, which jumped on the intruders as they left Grand Harbour. HMS *Illustrious,* hit by only one bomb, survived, and repair work on her began.

Two days later, on 18 January, over eighty enemy aircraft raided Luqa and Hal Far in an attempt to eliminate the fighters which had caused so much trouble, and this breathing space enabled work on the *Illustrious* to be completed. Luqa airfield was put out of action for a time but was quickly repaired, and eleven enemy aircraft were destroyed by ground or air fire during the raid. The Luftwaffe then reverted to raiding Grand Harbour, and on 19 January the opposing force of six Hurricanes, a Gladiator and a Fulmar brought down no less than eleven of the eighty raiders, the AA gunners adding another eight, in all about a quarter of the enemy force. Repairs to HMS *Illustrious* were completed, and she sailed for Alexandria on 23 January, although the Italian radio had broadcast that she was so badly damaged that she would never re-enter service.

By late January 1941, although a great increase in the number of aircraft had been seen, the RAF and FAA presence on Malta was still much weaker than it should have been. Apart from the nine Swordfish of the FAA's 830 Squadron, there were sixteen Wellingtons of 148 Squadron, seven Marylands of 431 Flight and sixteen Hurricanes of 261 Squadron, the latter still being in sole charge of the aerial defence of the island. These meagre forces were supplemented as circumstances allowed by carrier-borne Swordfish and Fulmar aircraft. To give added early-warning facilities, two COL (Chain Overseas Low) radar installations had been set up, the first at Ta Silch at the end of December 1940 and the second at Fort Madliena three weeks later.

Even under the intensive assault from the air being suffered by Malta, leisure activities were still possible. During January 1941 a football match to raise money for the RAF Benevolent Fund was played with great success, and soon afterwards a concert party, the 'Raffians', was organised, made up of RAF personnel and civilian girls who worked at Air Headquarters. The producer, Fg. Off. Cyril Roche, had been a professional player, and under his direction the 'Raffians' toured the island to entertain the troops and airmen at every Station and camp, bringing much-needed respite from the day-to-day stress suffered by everyone on Malta.

To the people of Malta, the 'Illustrious Blitz' marked the beginning of the main siege of the island. Malta stood between Italy and Gen. Erwin Rommel's campaign in North Africa, and at long last the importance of the island was becoming recognised. The enemy was now carrying out an intensive mine-laying campaign in the waters surrounding Grand Harbour, and mine-sweeping became essential. Though air raids were a nightly occurence, the harbour was not put out of action, and convoys continued to arrive from time to time. Winston Churchill, very much aware of the

situation, sent a message to the Governor on 21 January for relaying to the people of Malta:

"The eyes of all Britain and indeed the whole British Empire are watching Malta in her struggle day by day, and we are sure that success as well as glory will crown your efforts."

The Air Ministry Works Directorate (AMWD), better known as the 'Works & Bricks', was by now stretched to the limit in its task of repairing airfields and other installations, the only machinery available for this purpose being a few antiquated rollers and some non-tipping lorries. The work went ahead, though, on a strict priority basis during the latter part of 1941. Apart from reconstruction of the most important buildings, it was found possible to construct bulk petrol chambers underground at Wied Dalam, with an 8-inch (20cm.) pipeline from Birzebbuga 1000 yards (915m.) away; main underground bomb stores at Luqa; and eight small underground direction-finder and radar stations. Largest and possibly most important of the projects carried out at this time was, however, the widening and consolidation of the road-cum-taxiway between Luqa and Safi and from there to Hal Far. This was now widened to 40ft. (12m.), and continuous aircraft dispersal areas and bomb dumps were built along its length. In June, the main wireless transmitter station at Siggiewi and receiver station at Kalafrana, both of which had been started in December 1938, came into use.

Provision of aircraft dispersal pens formed another high priority job for the AMWD staff. It had been decided that every aircraft on the island had to be given protection, and three different designs of pen (or revetment) were adopted. For aircraft of the size of Wellingtons the pens were 90ft. (27.5m.) square by 14ft. (4.25m.) high; those for smaller twin-engined aircraft were 75ft. (29m.) square by 12ft. (3.6m.) high; and for single-engined aircraft two intricate layouts giving an area 44ft. (13.5m.) square by 10ft. (3m.) high were chosen. To form the walls of the pens, three types of construction were used. Most successful was the use of masonry blocks as outer skins, the void filled with rubble. Secondly, petrol tins filled with rubble could be used to form slightly sloping walls, while the third method was to construct a framework of scaffolding tubes, line with corrugated sheeting and fill with rubble. Generally, the width of all

To build a blast-pen large enough to hold a Wellington took 60000 rubble-filled tins. On this one, sailors are helping the RAF men put up the walls.
[Tony Spooner]

walls was 8ft. (2.4m.) at the base, tapering to about 3ft. (90cm.) at the top.

An acute shortage of labour to carry out all the necessary work led to the setting up by the civil Government of an organisation under the Director of Manpower to conscript workers. The RAF, via the AMWD, was given top priority in using such conscripts. Even so, conflicting demands led in 1942 to the cancellation of all work on public shelters and rehabilitation and to the curtailing of all work for the Army and Navy so that absolute priortity could be given to the needs of the islands' aerial defenders.

Most of the horses and carts on the islands were commandeered to work three days a week on airfield repair and construction, while on the other days they carried out their normal work on the farms and in the streets. The rate paid was between 1/8d (about 8p or £M0.04) and 1/10d (about 9p or £M0.045) per hour, with a minimum daily rate of 10/- (£0.50 or £M0.27). At one time, no less than 850 such horse-and-cart combinations were at work.

Also in short supply were the materials needed for the repair and construction work. Bitumen, for example, a vital product for runways, became non-existent on Malta, until some salvaged from the wreck of a ship in Kalafrana Bay was obtained. When that had been exhausted, the sludge from oil tanks was used. Finally, when even that poor substitute had gone, 200 tons of condemned cement was used to grout taxiways by hand using petrol tins, and afterwards the surface was rolled.

Much pressure was now being put upon those in command to send more Hurricanes to Malta to bolster the island's defences, but the Battle of the Atlantic, then raging, effectively prevented carriers from delivering the vital aircraft. Meanwhile, the Luftwaffe was still building up its strength in Sicily and was able to carry out heavy dive-bombing attacks and fighter sweeps over Malta virtually every day. Luqa and Hal Far airfields bore the brunt of the attacks and became unserviceable for short periods of time. In addition, very valuable aircraft were destroyed on the ground. The enemy, slowly but surely, was gaining air superiority and the situation was becoming desperate. Different methods had to be used to get fighters to Malta, and in March 1941 twenty-one Hurricanes, with RAF personnel and stores, were loaded onto a cargo steamer, HMS *Parracombe,* in the UK for passage to the island. It never reached its destination: instead it was sunk, with heavy loss of life. However, on 3 April twelve Hurricanes Mk.IIa, more of a match against Bf.109s than the earlier Mk.I, were flown off HMS *Ark Royal* at a point between Gibraltar and Malta, and were escorted by a Sunderland flying boat to Takali. Some were piloted by men who had fought in the Battle of Britain and who were now being asked to take part in a battle which promised to be just as intense. Another twenty-three Hurricanes flew in by the end of April and on 21 May 47 more arrived after flying off HMS *Furious.* These aircraft enabled two more squadrons to be formed for the defence of the island. Winston Churchill's resolve was as strong as ever, and he stated on 10 May that Malta, Egypt and Gibraltar would be defended

Hurricanes on the deck of HMS Argus ready to fly off to Malta. *[James Pickering]*

with the full strength of the Empire.

More mining of Grand Harbour took place in May, but at the end of that month, after securing virtual command of the skies around Malta and limiting the striking power of the Malta-based bombers, the Luftwaffe began to pull out of Sicily and transfer Fliegercorps X to the eastern front. After nearly a year of sustained raids by day and night, the people of Malta and the thousands of service men and women based there were able to give thanks that they had survived, and Malta entered a period of relative quietness. The opportunity of sending more Hurricanes to the island was taken, and 43 arrived on HMS *Ark Royal* on 7 June and another four on HMS *Victorious* on 15 June. The Governor, Sir Charles Bonham-Carter, now resigned due to ill health and was succeeded by Maj. Gen. Sir William Dobbie KCB GCMG DSO, who had been the acting Governor. In June another change of RAF

command came when AVM Sir Hugh Pughe Lloyd CBE took over as Air Officer Commanding Malta.

With the departure of the Luftwaffe from Sicily, air attacks on Malta, now carried out by the Italian Air Force alone, became less frequent. The Italians seemed nervous about their sole responsibility, and at times few of their aircraft actually crossed the Maltese coast, preferring to drop their bombs in the sea rather than meet the challenge of the Hurricanes which now formed a much more potent defence force. Offensive raids from Malta's airfields were now stepped up, Wellingtons and Blenheims of the RAF and Swordfish of the FAA taking part. During the first half of July 1941 a record 122 bomber sorties were mounted from Malta, including raids by the FAA on Tripoli harbour and the ships it contained and on shipping at sea. Much work was done on the three airfields on Malta to prepare them for bomber

Fairey Fulmars, probably of 800X Flight, on the deck of a carrier with Hurricanes destined for Malta. *[Topham via R. C. Sturtivant]*

operations, including the provision of many more dispersal areas.

Activity in the night skies over Malta became intense during the summer of 1941, caused by the RAF bomber force's missions, aircraft being ferried to or from the island, FAA aircraft on strike missions or by the small night-fighter force which had been set up as the Malta Night Fighter Unit to work in close cooperation with the army. The island was divided into two parts, east and west of Valletta, with one or more Hurricanes allocated to patrol each area when a raid was imminent. Each Hurricane located the intruders and was able to intercept at the moment when the army's searchlights, acting on radar plots, illuminated the enemy aircraft. The scheme, on average, was responsible for the destruction of 28% of the intruders.

In the early hours of 26 July 1941, the Italians launched an attack on Grand Harbour, and the newly-arrived convoy and submarines it contained, by a number of E-boats. For Italy, this operation, though bravely carried out, was a total disaster, and three of a number of Macchi fighters sent to cover the retreat of surviving E-boats were shot down by RAF Hurricanes for the loss of one whose pilot baled out. Every E-boat was then destroyed.

During the autumn of 1941, Malta-based Blenheims increased their attacks on enemy shipping, but by November had sunk only about 50000 tons since April. More successful were the FAA Swordfish aircraft from Hal Far, which in a similar period destroyed 110000 tons of shipping by the use of torpedoes and mines. Bomb-carrying Hurricanes were also active, raiding, for instance, Comiso airfield in Sicily to deter Italian aircraft from attacking a supply convoy which was approaching Malta. Wellingtons based at Luqa, meanwhile, mounted missions against both ends of the enemy lines of supply to North Africa — Naples and Tripoli. For the first time, 4000lb. (1800kg.) bombs were dropped by these Wellingtons. The Malta-base Blenheims now began a period of intense activity against targets in Libya prior to the advance of the 8th Army into the Cyrenaica area. Things appeared to be going the Allies' way, and the Axis powers could not let this state of affairs continue, particularly as 63% of all cargo shipped to Libya in November 1941 had

failed to reach its destination due to the activities of Malta-based aircraft. So in December 1941 the Luftwaffe returned to Sicilian airfields with a view to destroying Malta as a military base and achieving control of the Mediterranean Sea.

The spring of 1942 was the period in which the heaviest air offensive was mounted by the enemy against Malta. The strategy employed was to use overwhelming numbers of aircraft carrying heavy bomb-loads, and this ploy very nearly succeeded. To add to the horror of heavy bombardment, the weather that spring was very poor, gales, thunderstorms and heavy rain being common. Although these conditions hampered the enemy, Malta's fighters were prevented from carrying out their defensive task to any great extent. To make matters worse, Takali and Hal Far airfields were waterlogged in January, causing the fighters to be moved to an already overcrowded Luqa, where, given a break in the weather, enemy aircraft could inflict the maximum damage. Bomber formations of up to forty aircraft raided Malta by day and night, and single aircraft made opportunist attacks. At the same time, offensive raids by RAF aircraft diminished, partly due to the impossibility of accurate weather forecasting and lack of diversion airfields.

However, raids by aircraft based on Malta that did take place were effective. Attacks were made early in January by Blenheims on Castel Vetrano airfield in Sicily, destroying thirty-five or so Ju.52s

Code LE signifies 242 Squadron, which, while on the way to the Far East, off-loaded its Hurricanes to Malta on 12 November 1941 to be absorbed by 126 Squadron. This one seems to have overshot, but looks repairable. *[NWMA]*

Ground transportation during the seige was very much a problem, so local horses and carts were commandeered into service for three days a week!

on the ground and Wellingtons followed by putting more out of action. In the opposite direction, Marylands, Beauforts and Beaufighters of the RAF and Swordfish and Albacores of the FAA raided Tripoli as many times as possible. At the same time the defence of the island by the limited number of Hurricanes became more difficult and they were hard-pressed to defend a convoy carrying much-needed supplies which reached the island in January. Still the enemy onslaught against Malta intensified, and in a five-week period in January and February 1942 almost two thousand bomber sorties were mounted against the island. On 7 February there were sixteen raids in twenty-four hours, during which bombers in dispersal at Luqa, again the only operational airfield, were destroyed. Even so, a reduced number of bomber sorties were flown by the RAF squadrons during this period against targets in Sicily and Libya.

The constant raids on the island became so serious early in March 1942 that AVM Lloyd reported a growing number of aircraft being put out of action while on the ground, and he pressed hard for fighter reinforcements. A massive campaign of extension and construction was therefore started, mainly by the army. Apart from rapid repairs to the landing areas, the soldiers, up to three thousand at any one time, built, in three months, 27 miles of taxi-tracks, 14 heavy bomber pens, 170 fighter pens, 70 pens for reconnaissance aircraft and 31 pens for the FAA, the pens being built, as before, from earth-filled oil drums or stone. All this work was carried out regardless of frequent air raids. AVM Lloyd remarked afterwards that the RAF's job would have been impossible without such help from the army, whose men later went a stage further by helping RAF ground crews with such

jobs as re-arming and refuelling aircraft.

Almost a thousand tons of bombs had fallen on Malta in February, but in March 2170 tons were dropped, and the Luftwaffe, with a little help from the Regia Aeronautica, was gaining air superiority. Their fighter-bombers began to be able to attack at low level with some confidence, and the three airfields on Malta suffered even more damage. Even so, until early in March the Wellingtons from Luqa managed to mount counter-offensive missions against enemy shipping and harbours. In addition, aircraft being ferried from the UK to the Middle East continued to use Malta as a staging post, mainly at night when darkness gave some sort of protection from enemy fighters. Between November 1941 and July 1942 almost 750 aircraft passed through Malta in this way, and even BOAC aircraft reached the island with supplies, often unloading during air raids. 24 Squadron, based at Hendon in north London, began VIP and mail flights to Malta under the auspices of Ferry Command in April 1942, using Hudson aircraft, a service which would be greatly expanded over the next few years.

Early in March, the first fifteen Spitfires to take part in the battle arrived via Gibraltar, after being flown off the carriers HMS *Eagle* and HMS *Argus*. They went into action on 10 March, after which a spell of bad weather enabled airfield repairs to proceed without interruption.

A convoy of four merchant ships with heavy naval escort left Alexandria on 20 March and was within sight of Grand Harbour when Bf.109s struck, sinking one of the supply ships and damaging another. The enemy forces then did everything within their power to prevent the unloading of the ships, dropping 1870 tons of

A nice picture of DH.86B N6246 of 24 Squadron, based at Hendon, seen on a visit to Malta. This aircraft was destroyed in a hangar fire on 5 May 1942. *[NWMA]*

bombs on the harbour between 24 March and 12 April and doing a vast amount of damage. Against this onslaught, the RAF's Hurricanes and Spitfires put up as strong a resistance as their still limited numbers allowed, but at the end of March the enemy turned once again to the airfields, a move which, while allowing the unloading of supply ships to proceed, did nothing to help the RAF and the soldiers who still laboured long and hard to maintain useable landing areas.

Without vast amounts of supplies, the enemy forces in North Africa could not advance eastward towards Egypt, and, to the Axis powers, Malta was the stumbling-block. Large numbers of Luftwaffe aircraft were based in Sicily with the sole task of eliminating Malta (the Regia Aeronautica having now faded into the background), and on average 170 bombers attacked the island every day, usually in three raids, which at least allowed the RAF and army cooks time to serve some meals. Against the Luftwaffe were ranged the Hurricanes and Spitfires which remained after many had been destroyed on the ground during raids. By the middle of April 1942 it was sometimes possible to put up only six aircraft to repel the raiders — four to attempt to shoot down enemy aircraft and two to defend the airfields.

Two more batches of Spitfires arrived in Malta in March and April, this time flown off the American carrier USS *Wasp*. The second batch, 47 aircraft on 20 April, was intercepted between the carrier and the airfield and as soon as the Spitfires

The Torpedo Section at Hal Far during 1942's heavy raids. Although the roof has caved in, a sign painted on the wall reports 'Business as usual'. The Hurricane, though, is a write-off. *[R. A. Powell]*

landed a fierce attack was made on them. In one day 306 Luftwaffe aircraft concentrated on trying to destroy the new aircraft, dropping 985 tons of bombs on Takali and 485 tons on Luqa, and within three days these two airfields were ruined and 30 of the 47 Spitfires destroyed. By the end of April 1942 the defending forces, while having shot down a large number of the raiders, had lost twenty-three Spitfires and eighteen Hurricanes in action during the month, with another eighty-seven aircraft damaged, many of them on the ground. On occasion, the RAF force virtually went out of existence, a bleak situation indeed. However, at the end of the month there was a lull, due partly to the Luftwaffe's own stretched resources in Sicily and partly to the enemy's need to transfer part of his strength to other fronts.

At this time, fears of an invasion of Malta came to the surface, prompted by the discovery near Gerbini in Sicily of three new airstrips which it was thought could have been for the assembly and operation of troop-carrying gliders. The RAF reconnaissance aircraft based on Malta maintained a close watch on these sites, but in the event they were not used.

The quieter period at the end of April 1942 gave the defenders of Malta vital breathing space and allowed a further sixty-two Spitfires to fly off USS *Wasp* and HMS *Eagle* on 9 May, although four of them did not make it to the island. This deluge of new aircraft and the arrival of a cruiser carrying ammunition, provoked the enemy into mounting renewed constant raids on the airfields and harbour. However, the opposition put up by the newly-arrived aircraft and by the ground gunners was sufficient to discourage the Luftwaffe, which then mounted only small-scale raids and fighter sweeps by day but increased raids by night. These were beaten off by Beaufighters from Luqa, which had taken over the night defence task from Hurricanes. Another 17 Spitfires arrived from HMS *Eagle* on 18 May, 27 out of 31 on 3 June and 32 on 9 June. Air superiority was gradually being regained by Malta-based squadrons, and offensive sorties were now being made once more from the island against ports and airfields and particularly against enemy convoys bound for North Africa.

A new Governor-General, Lord Gort, arrived in a Sunderland flying boat of 10 Squadron, RAAF, at Kalafrana on 7 May during a raid. Bombs fell nearby as the party came ashore, and Lord Gort was told that without reinforcements and supplies Malta could last only another six weeks.

In June 1942 two Allied convoys sailed for Malta, one from Gibraltar and the other from Alexandria, in a concerted attempt to deliver vital supplies to the island. The westbound convoy, code-named Vigourous, was attacked so fiercely that it had to return to Alexandria, but part of the other convoy, Harpoon, succeeded in reaching Grand Harbour to unload valuable cargo. During the voyages, Beaufighters from Malta, USAAF

Hoisting Spitfires on board a Malta-bound aircraft carrier at King George V Dock, Glasgow, in April 1942. *[NWMA]*

Wellington VIII
HF857 of 38
Squadron seen on 17
June 1942 being
rescued from a small
hole by a group of
soldiers. *[IWM]*

B-24s from Egypt and carrier-borne fighters had played their part in the air battles overhead.

The superior, and still increasing, number of fighters based on Malta now allowed a more positive posture to be made. On 1 July the enemy began yet another attempt to neutralise the squadrons and to compel Malta to submit. During the first eleven days of that month Malta-based fighters shot down 78 enemy aircraft and ground gunners another five, but twenty-one fighters and twelve pilots were lost. The losses suffered by one Ju.88 Geschwader based in Sicily were so heavy that it had to be withdrawn from operations. Interception before the raiders reached Malta now became the watchword.

The AOC Malta, AVM H. P. Lloyd, was posted on 14 July 1942 and was succeeded by AVM Sir Keith Park, a veteran of the Battle of Britain. AVM Lloyd was Knighted on 31 July, a fitting reward for his steadfast services in the face of almost insuperable odds. Before he left, he remarked that

"...But for the army we should have been out of business. The aerodromes were in such a frightful state that rollers had to be used continuously for twenty-four hours on end; the army was magnificent."

The incoming AOC issued a special Order of the Day in an effort to boost morale in the month when the island's population was nearest to starvation. There were 188 raids in July, but 153 enemy aircraft were shot down. By the end of the month, however, air superiority was back in Allied

hands, due partly to better radar coverage allowing more effective forward interceptions to be made and partly to rapidly-increasing numbers of aircraft. A further 31 Spitfires had flown off HMS *Eagle* on 15 July, one more, EP117, having crashed into the aircraft carrier's bridge and gone over the side, and yet another 32 on 21 July.

By this time, Malta had become of strategic importance for the bombing of southern Italy, Sicily and Sardinia and was continuing to serve as a staging post for the increasing numbers of aircraft bound for Egypt and points east. Ensuring that Malta was provisioned, however, was more difficult than ever, as convoys had to pass through the Sicilian narrows, which could be covered easily by aircraft based in Sicily or Pantellaria. To give some defence to the convoys, they were escorted by aircraft carriers during the critical period, and this ploy succeeded in minimising damage.

During July 1942 plans were made to send a very large convoy to Malta carrying absolutely vital supplies of food for the malnourished civilian population and military personnel, there now being food and fuel for only another three weeks. As it had been impossible for the June convoy from Alexandria to reach Malta, it was decided that the convoy now planned would sail from the UK via Gibraltar. It was inevitable that the enemy would learn of the plan, and he reacted by building up his air and sea forces in Sardinia and Sicily. The convoy, Operation 'Pedestal', consisted of two battleships, three aircraft carriers, three cruisers

Probably photographed on board HMS *Victorious*, part of a Malta-bound convoy in August 1942, these Sea Hurricanes are from 885 Squadron Fleet Air Arm. *[NWMA]*

and fourteen destroyers making up Force Z, which would turn back at Gibraltar, and a number of close escort ships known as Force X which would see the cargo vessels to Malta. Another aircraft carrier, HMS *Furious,* carrying 38 Spitfires for Malta, and numerous other ships, would sail with the main convoy. There were eleven British and five American merchantmen, including the tanker USS *Ohio.* The convoy left the river Clyde in Scotland on 2 August 1942 and began to meet enemy resistance on 11 August near Ibiza, attacks on the ships increasing by the hour. HMS *Furious* launched her load of Spitfires before massive German and Italian attacks were made, causing very severe damage and loss to merchant ships and escorts alike, one major casualty being the carrier HMS *Eagle,* which was sunk by submarine U-73. Of the fourteen cargo vessels, only five reached Grand Harbour on 13 August, and the crippled tanker *Ohio* was towed in two days later, but at least the supplies they brought enabled the population to survive for a further four months or so. The Navy was so impressed that it sent a message of praise to the RAF squadrons involved, which had, the message said, greatly contributed to reducing the scale of the attack.

This vital convoy had been given air protection by Malta-based Spitfires and Beaufighters as soon as it was within their range, and Wellingtons had attacked the Italian fleet in an attempt to prevent its participation. With the same purpose in mind, Beaufighters had strafed airfields in Sicily to try to neutralise the enemy air forces. Strangely enough, little attempt was made by the enemy to disrupt the unloading of the five cargo vessels in Grand Harbour, and the enterprise could be regarded as successful notwithstanding the considerable loss of life and shipping.

With the newly-arrived supplies safely stored, Malta in general and the RAF and FAA in particular began to feel much more optimistic. The number of offensive sorties against enemy convoys making for Tripoli increased, torpedo-carrying Beauforts and Beaufighters making considerable impact. The enemy shipping now tended to use a more easterly route to North Africa to avoid Malta-based aircraft, a tribute to the squadrons there. It was also possible to mount, on 20 August, the first offensive sweeps (Rodeos) over southern Sicily by Spitfires of 229 and 249 Squadrons, and, a week later, the first night intruder missions over that island. But as time passed the supplies of fuel, ammunition and, in particular, food, delivered in August were running down as no replenishments had arrived.

The first trained Flying Control officers arrived in Malta in August 1942 and were followed by NCO airfield controllers to take over the task from untrained personnel. Proper control towers were then provided at Luqa, Takali and Hal Far, as were runway control caravans.

Early in October 1942 yet another campaign against Malta was started by the Luftwaffe, which was re-grouping in Sicily. During the first week of that month 1400 sorties were flown against Malta, for the loss of no fewer than 114 enemy aircraft and only twenty-seven Spitfires. On 11 October, fifty-eight escorted bombers raided Malta, losing eight bombers and seven fighters in the process. This was the beginning of an eight-day blitz in which some 600 enemy aircraft took part. The defending Spitfires shot down 132 of them, and the ground gunners another eight, while sixty-four more never reached their bases in Sicily, presumably coming down in the sea; all this for a loss of thirty-one RAF aircraft. Malta's forward interception system, now fully proved, ensured that fewer raiders reached the islands, but even so 80 people were killed and considerable damage was done to buildings. While this blitz was taking place there was only one night on which Malta-based bombers were unable to make attacks on enemy shipping. No Maltese airfield was made unserviceable for more than a few minutes.

On 23 October 1942 the 8th Army made its historic attack at El Alamein, and the people and forces on Malta felt that at last permament relief was in sight. Soon afterwards, a message ordering a convoy of five ships to carry desparately-needed supplies to enemy-held North Africa was intercepted. Twenty Beauforts took off from Luqa and Hal Far and sank four of the ships off Tobruk, the other vessel being destroyed by USAAF B-24s before being unloaded. Six of the Beauforts did not, unfortunately, return to base.

By now, raids on Malta had declined to little more than token efforts. The enemy realised that Malta could not now be beaten, even though the population was still living in conditions of great hardship. On 10 November the situation was again eased by the arrival, unscathed, of four supply ships, and on the same day the 8th Army entered

Benghazi. This breakthrough consolidated the Allied landings on 7 November in French North Africa, the preparation for which had been aided by photographic sorties flown by Malta-based aircraft. The RAF Wellingtons and Beaufighters then began to concentrate on a massive bombing campaign on targets in Tunisia, particularly the airfield at El Aouina and on shipping in Tunis harbour. In this the Wellingtons were assisted by Albacores of recently-arrived 821 Squadron, which was adept at target illumination. Another new tactic put into action at this point was the use of Spitfires as light bombers. These aircraft, escorted by other Spitfires, were successfully used against Sicilian airfields, enemy resistance being minimal. To add to the facilities on Malta, the new airfield at Qrendi was occupied by its first squadron, which moved over from Takali at the end of November, a second squadron following early in December.

The convoy which finally ended the siege of Malta set sail as Operation 'Stoneage' from Alexandria on 16 November 1942. Although attacked by enemy aircraft on the voyage, it reached the island without loss, escorted for the last part of the journey by Spitfires and Beaufighters. No attempt was made to attack the ships on arrival, and to the enormous delight of the brave people of Malta and servicemen, unloading took place without interference.

The islands of Malta had sustained almost unbelievable damage and horrific casualties during the thirty months since raids began, but now the tables had been turned, and Malta-based squadrons were about to increase greatly their offensive operations against the enemy in Italy and North Africa. Even now, vigilance had to be maintained, as a few raids still took place; for example, thirty enemy aircraft raided Luqa on 18

Based in the UK, Hudson AE62• of 206 Squadron at rest on a Maltese airfield.
[NWMA]

A nice shot of an unidentified Malta based Beaufighter taking to the air.
[NWMA]

December, destroying nine Wellingtons and four Spitfires on the ground.

Further supply convoys arrived in December 1942, bringing a great deal of seasonal cheer and adding to Malta's hopes for a much less arduous year to come.

The later war years (1943 to 1945)

1943 was destined to be the year in which the tables turned for Malta and a major offensive, the invasion of Sicily, was launched. While spasmodic air raids did continue, the now considerable fighter force was generally able to fend off any attackers. Sometimes a few got through, however, as on 21 May, the first raid of the year, when thirty-six Fw.190s escorted by Bf.109s raided Hal Far and Takali and destroyed three Albacore aircraft on the ground. There were 30 raids that month — nothing compared with the 248 in May 1942.

On the credit side, the 1000th aircraft shot down by Malta-based aircraft was claimed on 10 May by Sqdn. Ldr. J. J. Lynch, an American from California, when he destroyed three of four aircraft

shot down off Sicily: two Cants and a Ju.52 troop-carrier.

By 1942, following the liberation of North Africa, a network of direction-finding and fixer stations had been set up on Malta. Early in 1943 a control tower was built at Qrendi airfield, fitted with VHF and HF radio, duplicate sets being installed in a bomb-proof dugout nearby. At much the same time, a regional flying control centre was established, on 10 June, to handle all flights in the vicinity of Malta and to control air-sea rescue operations. Close liaison was established with fighter controllers, maritime controllers, airfields and the other control centres in the Mediterranean area. Malta Control's area was eventually extended from 0° to 20°E and from North Africa to Corsica and southern Italy.

Preparations for the invasion of Sicily.

To prepare for the planned invasion of Sicily, in which Malta would feature very strongly, a new priority list of work to be done was drawn up. Early in 1943 5051 (Airfield Construction) Squadron

Hectic activity as a Beaufighter is readied for another sortie. Note that a Bren gun carrier is in use as a trolley tug.
[NWMA]

This Luftwaffe Bf.109, seen here under intense scrutiny by interested parties, crash-landed at Luqa in May 1943.
[B. Tonks]

was drafted in from the Middle East, and began work at Safi. In addition, a Tunnelling Company of the Royal Engineers arrived, with four Pioneer Companies, three from Mauritius and one from Basutoland. A large consignment of mechanical plant was received with open arms on 15 February and consisted of about sixty small tipper trucks and fifteen dumpers, much of which was put to work without delay. The timing of the arrival of this equipment was just right, as without it the considerable work to be done could not have been completed in time.

Also in use during 1943 was a temporary narrow-gauge railway system, powered by three 25/30 hp Whitcombe diesel locomotives, though where they worked is not recorded. At the same time, the labour force was expanded greatly by the addition of shelter construction and ARP personnel (whose original tasks were now almost redundant), 300 miners and 900 general labourers. About 2300 soldiers and 150 convicts were also employed, the latter building aircraft pens under the watchful eyes of the police force! By the end of June 1943, considerable work had been completed in extensions and repairs at Hal Far, Luqa and Takali.

Administratively, AHQ Malta was placed under the operational control of the C-in-C Mediterranean, ACM Sir Arthur Tedder, on 15 February 1943, although for matters of supply and administration AHQ Malta continued to be controlled by HQ Middle East at Cairo. On the mail flights made by 24 Squadron from the UK, Dakotas replaced the Hudsons from April 1943, and Yorks took over the VIP function in May.

Malta was favoured on 20 June 1943 by a visit from His Majesty King George VI, who had expressly asked for such a visit to be arranged while he was in North Africa. It was only a year since Malta had been 'on its knees', but it was now safe for such a visit to be made. The King arrived in HMS *Aurora*, escorted by four destroyers, and was received at Customs House Steps by the Governor, Lord Gort, and the Lieutenant Governor, Vice-Admiral Arthur Power. His Majesty then made a tour of Malta's bombed towns and talked with many Maltese citizens before leaving for Tripoli in the evening.

Planning for the forthcoming invasion of Sicily was now well under way, with Malta's position in the forefront as a jumping-off point and base for fighter aircraft. Admiral Sir Andrew Cunningham moved his HQ from Algiers to Malta on 3 July, and Generals Alexander and Eisenhower arrived a few days later to take part in the final planning, followed by General Montgomery. Before the invasion could take place, three small Italian islands had to be captured to prevent their use during the invasion. Accordingly, Pantellaria was taken on 11 June, Lampedusa next day and Linosa soon afterwards.

For the invasion of Sicily, a massive build-up of RAF squadrons got under way. As part of the invasion preparations, a fifth airfield had been constructed at Safi, along the taxi-track linking Luqa with Hal Far, and was ready by March 1943. Three fighter squadrons took up residence there early in June, and no less than eighteen squadrons arrived at Luqa from North African bases for a short stay pending transfer to airfields which would be captured in Sicily, with a further eleven squadrons at Hal Far and nine at Takali. This influx

Joint efforts: two sailors and a soldier re-arm a Kittyhawk.
[via Tony Spooner]

of aircraft and about 6000 personnel clearly put enormous strains on RAF resources. Some of these squadrons did not operate from Malta during the short time they were on the island, but some, including 1437 (Strategic Reconnaissance) Flight, which flew Mustangs from Luqa (the only Mustangs ever to operate from the island), proved very useful. To provide additional airfield facilities, a temporary airstrip was hurriedly constructed at Xewkija on Gozo for the use of a USAAF Fighter Group flying Spitfires, and was ready at the end of June.

On 10 July 1943 the invasion of Sicily, Operation 'Husky', was launched, hundreds of landing craft and other vessels making their way to the beaches carrying sixteen thousand troops of the British 8th and US 7th Armies. The naval presence consisted of no less then 750 warships, small and large, of the Royal Navy and US Navy. The weather was poor, but the element of surprise was complete. Resistance was light, as the Axis had not been aware of the planned location of the assault, but the 85-mile (136km.) long stretch of landing craft off the Sicilian beaches was a prime target for Luftwaffe forces in Sicily, Sardinia and southern

Italy should they have attacked in force.

Although they did not use Maltese airfields, two huge fleets of allied aircraft used Delimara Point as a landmark on the way from airstrips in the Kairouan area of Tunisia to Sicily. The first wave (Operation 'Ladbrooke') comprising 108 Dakotas, 22 Albemarles and seven Halifaxes, each towing a glider packed with troops, passed Delimara Point at about 21.20 on 9 July at altitudes of between 250ft. (75m.) and 350ft. (105m.), and the second wave (Operation 'Fustian'), consisting of C-47s of the USAAF 51st Troop Carrier Wing carrying paratroops, with more gliders towed by RAF aircraft made the same journey three days later.

Five squadrons of Malta-based Spitfires gave protection from a few minutes after dawn over the beach-heads of Avola, Pachino and Scogliatti, while Spitfires of the USAAF from Xewkija protected Gela. During the day only 57 enemy fighters were sighted during nearly 1100 Allied sorties, the enemy concentrating on trying to repel the bomber forces flying from North Africa.

By 12 July a firm foothold had been established in Sicily and airfields were being captured. The HQ of the Western Desert Air Force was established at

Seen on a visit to Malta, probably in 1943, is P-38G 42-12759 of the 96th FS, 82nd FG, US 12th Air Force, coded BK.
[NWMA]

The combined efforts of men from all three services were employed to re-arm this Spitfire.
[Tony Spooner]

Pachino on 13 July with the three Spitfire squadrons of 244 Wing which now moved in from Malta, and on 15 July the USAAF's 31st Fighter Group moved from Xewkija to operate from Ponte Olivo and Licata. The Kittyhawks of 239 Wing also moved from Malta to Pachino and the Spitfires of 324 Wing to Comiso, and within days the huge influx of aircraft and men which had crowded Malta's airfields had moved on.

Malta then became uncharacteristically quiet, and by the beginning of September 1943 there were only 184 RAF aircraft on the island. On 3 September Gladiator *'Faith'* was presented to the people of Malta by AVM Park in a ceremony in Palace Square, Valletta, and on the same day Italy signed an armistice with the Allies. Very soon, the Italian fleet sailed from Genoa, La Spezia and Taranto for Malta, Spitfires from the island

escorting the ships as far as their range allowed. 27 ships arrived in Grand Harbour on 11 September, and many more later.

There were, as might be expected, great celebrations on the island, and a number of roads and squares were named to celebrate the armistice. VIPs visiting the island before the year's end included President Roosevelt of the USA, who arrived on 10 December to pay his tribute to the people of Malta.

The opportunity was now taken to begin a rectification programme on all the airfields and other RAF installations to remove all traces of war damage and to prepare some of them for use by larger and faster aircraft. Hal Far and Kalafrana in particular received attention in this way. To overcome the dust problem, grass was sown for the first time at Luqa and Hal Far, using seed of grass

USAAF A-20B 41-3364 [18], possibly of the 47th BG, flying along the south coast of Malta
[R. G. Harrington]

Seafires Mk.III ranged on the deck of an anonymous aircraft carrier in Grand Harbour late in 1944. On the nearest aircraft, NF539, the markings K:W can be seen, illustrating the aircraft's previous use by 899 Squadron on board HMS Khedive. The squadron disembarked to Hal Far for a few days at the end of July 1944. The second aircraft is NN339.
[NWMA]

types selected for their hard-wearing features.

The next year, 1944, was a year of recession for the airfields of Malta. The war had, in effect, moved on, leaving little for the RAF and FAA in Malta to do. By mid-February, when Luqa's long-serving 69 Squadron left, only one squadron remained on that airfield, and this departed at the end of June.

A major change of use was planned for Luqa, however, and by the end of March 64 Staging Post had become established to deal with the increasing number of aircraft and their crews and passengers in transit. Hal Far was similarly quiet, and Takali

was home to just one FAA squadron. Qrendi's last squadron had left in September 1943, and Safi's final resident in October, although Safi remained open as a Maintenance Unit.

A rare raid alert was sounded on 28 April 1944 when a lone Ju.88 crossed Malta at 28000 feet (8500m.+). A Beaufighter was scrambled from Luqa and heavy AA fire was opened up, but to no avail.

During the almost five years of hostilities against Malta enormous damage had been done. A summary of wartime activities is appropriate at this point:

Typical of the high-speed rescue launches based in Malta during and after the Second World War was HSL128, seen here at Kalafrana.
[J. S. Houghton]

MILITARY AVIATION IN MALTA G.C. 1915-1993

Enemy sorties against the islands:	approx. 26000
Tonnage of bombs dropped on Malta:	14154
Maltese civilians killed:	1192
Maltese civilians injured:	3713
RAF losses in the air:	547
RAF losses on the ground	160
Enemy aircraft destroyed:	1252

The late nineteen-forties

When hostilities in Europe came to a successful conclusion on 8 May 1945, the RAF and FAA in Malta were at a very low ebb. Luqa airfield was extremely active as 64 Staging Post, while at Hal Far only an ASR squadron equipped with Warwicks and Walrus amphibians and the AHQ Malta Communications Flight were resident. Takali housed the FAA's Fleet Requirements Unit, and Kalafrana was in use only as a staging post for flying boats on the way to or from the Far East.

However, a large number of RAF and FAA personnel were still on the island, and were making themselves extremely useful in clearing debris remaining from the war years and providing technical expertise in rebuilding essential services. AHQ Malta still administered RAF units as far away as Sardinia, Sicily, Corsica and Algeria, although rapid contraction was taking place.

Before long, the political situation in both Palestine and Egypt began to give cause for concern, and it was decided that operational squadrons would be deployed to Malta once more. First to arrive, in July 1945, was a squadron of Spitfires which moved into Hal Far and a Warwick and Wellington-equipped squadron which came to take up residence at Luqa. Mosquitos returned to

Hal Far in September and one of the FAA's few Wellington squadrons followed a month later. By mid-October 1945, therefore, Malta was home to five operational squadrons and two support units. Luqa's main task remained the provision of staging post facilities for many of the large number of aircraft bringing home to the UK up to twelve thousand troops each month from south-east Asia. A newly-installed direction-finder ('homer') system with master Station at Dingli and 'slaves' at Gozo, Salma Bay and Dingli was now working well for Transport Command, whose aircraft found such facilities essential to poor-weather operation.

During 1946 the Egyptian government carried on with its attempt to rid the country of the British military presence, which as far as the RAF was concerned comprised two squadrons of Tempests, one of Mosquitos and five of Dakotas, housed on three airfields in the Canal Zone. However, RAF and FAA units on Malta were again depleted during that year, the Mosquitos leaving in January, the Warwick squadron disbanding in March and the FAA Wellington squadron in April, and another Warwick squadron going to Palestine in September. By the end of 1946, after a 'shunt round' of the three remaining units, a squadron of Spitfires was at Takali, the Fleet Requirements Unit was at Hal Far, which had become a Naval Air Station in April 1946, and the Communications Flight was at Luqa. Kalafrana, without any resident units, was passed to FAA control in June 1946.

1947 saw the troubles in Palestine at their most intense, and Malta was used for refuelling and servicing of aircraft carrying out long and tedious

A post-war picture of a Sea Otter of the FAA, with a shy-looking RAF airman wearing 'best blue' standing by.
[J. Betts]

Halifax VI RG876 (?) of 224 Squadron, based at Gibraltar, on a visit to Malta. [C. Ashworth via P. Porter]

sea searches for illegal immigrants making for Palestine. That year, control of three major airfields in Libya — El Adem, Benina and Castel Benito — was inherited by AHQ Malta, but Elmas in Sardinia passed out of Malta control on closing down. The wartime airstrip at Safi again became an RAF Station in its own right as the home of 137 MU, dedicated to the repair of aircraft, and 397 MU, a storage unit. Kalafrana continued to offer services to flying boats passing along the Mediterranean Sea.

In 1947 an element of self-government was given to the people of Malta. By the end of that year the FAA was rather more prominent on the island than the RAF, having Fireflies and several other types at Hal Far and Seafires at Takali, while the RAF's presence remained the Vampire squadron at Takali and the Communications Flight at Luqa, with the Maintenance Units at Safi.

The final episode of the Palestinian problem was played out during the first half of 1948 and involved the movement of two squadrons of Lancasters from Ein Shemer to a safer base at

Luqa. The massive and protracted airlift from south-east Asia of homeward-bound troops dwindled, and Luqa became a joint military and civilian airfield providing facilities for BOAC and BEA as well as RAF aircraft. At the end of 1948, to relieve a chronic shortage of RAF personnel and to provide a more tangible association with the citizens of the islands, recruitment locally into the RAF began, the new element being known as the RAF (Malta). Maltese people could join on a three- or five-year commitment, and the scheme appears to have contributed to the well-being of the RAF on Malta, as no squadron movements took place during 1949. The two FAA fighter squadrons, however, left the island in March 1948.

The fifties...

As the nineteen-fifties began, the importance of Malta as a strategic base began to lessen. Many British Colonial countries were now securing their independence, thus removing the need for guaranteed lines of communication with them, and Great Britain, a member of NATO, felt that

Boston IV, BZ473, was previously used by 88 Squadron in England and France and is recorded as crashing on a ferry flight to the Middle East on 9 August 1945. However, it is seen here on a Maltese airfield, presumably just before its final flight. Note the Mustang in the background. [NWMA]

MILITARY AVIATION IN MALTA G.C. 1915-1993

Lancasters of 38 Squadron airborne off the western end of Malta, with the small island of Comino below and Gozo on the extreme left. *[F. D. Sheppard]*

reliance could be placed on fellow NATO members for mutual security in times of trouble. However, a perceived shortage of airfield facilities prompted the consideration in July 1951 of building a new airfield on Gozo, but of course nothing came of this idea, and it would probably have been quite impracticable. The situation as far as the RAF and FAA were concerned was static: no movements of squadrons on Malta took place between April 1948 and July 1952, when two Royal Australian Air Force squadrons arrived at Hal Far for a five-month stay. They returned during 1953, and a flight of Skyraiders, the first to be based on the island, arrived at Hal Far in October.

The United States Navy, which had, for several years, used Hal Far as a land base during exercises and as a staging post, opened a full-scale servicing and maintenance base there in 1953, known as FASRON 201. Many types of carrier-borne and land-based patrol aircraft were to be seen at Hal Far for the next six years or so, but as the US Fleet in the Mediterranean contracted the need for such a facility also waned, and it disbanded in June 1959.

When, on 26 July 1956, President Nasser of Egypt nationalised the Universal Suez Canal Company and transferred all its assets to the State of Egypt, British and French reaction was severe. Trade with Egypt was quickly stopped and the nationalisation of the canal was referred, after a series of diplomatic failures, to the United Nations Security Council. Plans for military intervention

had been drawn up immediately after the take-over of the canal, and initially involved the despatch of several RAF squadrons from the UK to Cyprus during August.

Malta's part in 'Operation Musketeer', as the campaign became known, began early in October 1956, when the Air Staff decided that further bomber squadrons would be required if a short and effective operation was to be won. Akrotiri airfield, the only viable one on Cyprus, was already overloaded, and it was therefore decided to base the extra aircraft, long-range Valiants and Canberras, 53 aircraft in all, on Malta, as shown below:

Sqdn.	UK base	Aircraft	Qty	Location
9	Binbrook	Canberra B.6	7	Hal Far
12	Binbrook	Canberra B.6	7	Hal Far
101	Binbrook	Canberra B.6	8	Hal Far
109	Binbrook	Canberra B.6	7	Hal Far
138	Wittering	Valiant B.1	8	Luqa
148	Marham	Valiant B.1	6	Luqa
207	Marham	Valiant B.1	6	Luqa
214	Marham	Valiant B.1	4	Luqa

The aircraft arrived at their temporary Maltese bases between 22 September and 30 October 1956. Phase 1 of a revised plan of campaign was the elimination of the Egyptian Air Force; Phase 2 covered sustained air attacks on key targets and Phase 3 was for an attack on Port Said. Continuing diplomatic efforts came to nought, and 'Operation Musketeer' was put into effect on 31 October 1956. After a false start in which the Luqa-based Valiants and some Canberras bombed Cairo International

On the flight deck of HMS *Eagle* as she enters Grand Harbour during her cruise in the spring of 1953 are Skyraiders of 849 Squadron, Attacker FB.2s of 803 Squadron, Sea Hornet NF.21s of 809 Squadron and Firefly AS.6s of 814 Squadron. The aircraft are not recorded as having disembarked to Hal Far on this occasion.
[P. Porter collection]

Airport in error, the offensive quickly got under way, the Valiants raiding Cairo West, Fayid and Kasfareet airfields (which during the Second World War had been RAF bases!) and the Canberras additionally attacking Luxor, where many Egyptian IL-28 bombers had been dispersed. Within 48 hours the EAF was effectively neutralised, and Phase 1 was complete. Attention was then given to strategic targets such as roads and railways, armoured vehicles and gun emplacements by both types of aircraft in conjunction with Cyprus-based squadrons.

The invasion, Phase 3 of the plan, took place on 5 November 1956, but did not involve participation by Malta-based squadrons. On the following day, however, political considerations brought a sudden end to the fighting, and a rapid evacuation took place. The Canberra and Valiant squadrons departed for their UK bases over the next few weeks, bringing an end to Malta's involvement in this unsatisfactory episode. During the period 20 to 24 December 1956, 350 RAF and 35 French transport aircraft used Luqa as a staging post, the most concentrated airlift in which Luqa had ever

been involved, after which activities at the airfield returned to normal.

The late fifties was a period of steadily reducing British defence commitment and Malta, where about a quarter of the labour force was employed by the Services, was not unaffected. At the end of 1956 the deployment was similar to that of a year before, except that a squadron of photo-reconnaissance Meteors had replaced Venoms at Takali and a squadron each of Sea Hawks and Sea Venoms were at Hal Far. The Armament Practice Camp at Takali had not received any RAuxAF squadrons for some time, at least one such attachment, 604 Squadron, having been cancelled due to the Suez crisis. In fact there would be no more, as the RAuxAF was disbanded in March 1957.

Over the next few years, the three airfields on Malta, particularly Luqa, continued to maintain a strong presence. Canberras appeared in 1958 to be based at Luqa, as did Whirlwind helicopters at Hal Far, which also continued to provide shore facilities for carrier-based squadrons. Luqa also continued to act as an important staging post for aircraft of RAF Transport Command and chartered civilian aircraft carrying troops to and from points east. At times this task became very intensive, as in June 1958, when an airlift to Cyprus was mounted. During the eleven-day period, 119 Transport Command aircraft made use of Luqa's facilities, many of the troops they carried staying overnight. Attachments of Canberras and V-bombers also continued, as did Long-Ranger navigation exercises from UK bases.

During 1957 Malta maintained one maritime reconnaissance squadron, with varied tasks including air-sea rescue, anti-submarine patrols and searches in the eastern Mediterranean for vessels trying to take guns to Cyprus. Meteor night-fighters were responsible for air defence, while the perennial FRU provided facilities for the Mediterranean Fleet, as did the Malta Communications and Target Towing Squadron for the Royal Air Force.

The sixties and seventies.

Little change took place in the status quo in Malta during the early nineteen-sixties, except that with the introduction of longer-range transport aircraft the use of Luqa as a staging post began to diminish.

Fleet Air Arm carrier-based squadrons continued to use Hal Far's facilities until the end of 1962, but political tension on the island began to be felt, relations between the Maltese and British governments becoming strained. It was stated by Britain that a military base in the central Mediterranean was no longer absolutely necessary, and this confirmed the Maltese desire for complete independence. Full responsibility for its own affairs was achieved by Malta on 21 September 1964, and at the same time a ten-year agreement with Great Britain for the continued use of the bases in exchange for help in equipping and training Maltese forces was signed.

Hal Far airfield was returned to the RAF in September 1965 after twenty years and 38 Squadron was subsequently based there in addition to the Fleet Air Arm's 728 Squadron, a very long-term resident. The airfield was finally placed on Care & Maintenance status in September 1967.

After the agreement had run for only three years, the British government, in one of its cost-cutting moods, decided to reduce the forces in Malta again, explaining to the Maltese government that reinforcement could, if necessary, be made from the UK. By the end of 1967 only two

Canberra PR.9 XH169 of 39 Squadron flies low over two more Canberras parked on the apron. The location is uncertain. *[P. H. T. Green collection]*

Canberra squadrons were present, both at Luqa, and in February 1968 Takali, latterly used as an armament practice camp, closed down. In June AHQ Malta followed suit, overall control of the RAF in Malta then passing to HQ Near East Air Forces in Cyprus.

In 1969 some expansion took place when a squadron of Shackleton aircraft joined the RAF element in Malta and the Near East Communications Squadron was formed. Political problems between the two governments again arose, the Maltese Prime Minister, Dom Mintoff, making ever-greater demands in an attempt to compensate for the loss of revenue caused by the general reduction of British forces on the island. The British government, meanwhile, was concerned that other countries might step in to fill the void which would be caused by Britain's possible departure from the area. Plans to do just that were, nevertheless, drawn up, and on 28 December 1971 the Maltese government decreed that British forces were to leave the island within three days, obviously an impossibility. Eventually the date was agreed to be 31 March 1972.

One of the first decisions made by the new Maltese Government was to set up a coastal defence arm of the Malta Land Force. Helicopters were envisaged to supplement a number of patrol boats acquired from the USA, and the West German Government provided help in setting up the Helicopter Flight, as it was originally known. After an eight-month training course, eight Maltese pilots returned to Malta in May 1972, and soon four Bell 47 helicopters were in place. The

A vertical shot taken in February 1956 of Luqa and Safi airfields, one runway at Safi still being extant.
[P. H. T. Green collection]

operating base was St. Patrick's Barracks.

Meanwhile all training flights from the UK and other non-essential flying by the RAF from Luqa had been stopped, and a comprehensive withdrawal plan, Operation 'Mature', drawn up, the Station Commander of Luqa being responsible for detailed arrangements. Dependent families were flown to the UK in January 1972. Luqa's Canberra squadron left for Akrotiri in Cyprus and the other squadron, which was in the process of converting from Shackletons to Nimrods, moved to Sigonella in Sicily, leaving Luqa, and indeed Malta as a whole, devoid of military aircraft.

The withdrawal had the effect of convincing the Maltese government that British forces were still economically very useful to the island, and a change of heart prompted the signing, on 26 March 1972, of the Maltese Facilities Agreement, which allowed Britain the use of the airfields and other installations until 1979. Britain, for its part, agreed to increase financial aid to Malta. The new agreement brought some respite to British strategists, who were justifiably concerned about the possible use of the Malta dockyard by Russian ships, a move which would now be impossible.

Shortly after the signing of the Agreement, the two squadrons which had recently left returned to Luqa, and they remained there for the next several years. Britain finally decided, however, to withdraw completely from the island at the end of the MFA term, and began a long-term programme toward that end. The Nimrod squadron disbanded in December 1977, its commitment being taken over by UK-based squadrons using Gibraltar or Cyprus.

The year 1978 marked sixty years of RAF presence on the island (apart from the two years of RNAS activity before the formation of the RAF), and it was decided to celebrate the event by sending the Red Arrows aerobatic team to Malta from 25 to 29 September, together with many operational aircraft for display purposes. The Central Band of the RAF and the Queen's Colour Squadron of the RAF Regiment also took part in the celebrations, which were very popular with the people of Malta.

The end of the RAF's presence in Malta was now in sight, and 13 Squadron, the last one based on the island, left for the UK in October 1978. Luqa airfield was to become Malta's civil airport, and was to be handed over complete with all facilities. The locally-enlisted Maltese RAF men were sufficiently well-trained to operate most of the equipment there, and many of them transferred to

Her Majesty the Queen speaking at the dedication of the Siege Bell. On the extreme left is Admiral of the Fleet Lord Lewin, KG GCB LVO DSC (President of the George Cross Island Association), with Prince Phillip on his left, while on the right is the President of Malta, Dr. Censu Tabone. *[Tony Spooner]*

Maltese Government service at that time. In anticipation of the RAF withdrawal, the AFM Helicopter Flight moved temporarily to Hal Far in September 1978, eventually settling at Luqa the following March. Steady reductions in RAF personnel continued during the first three months of 1979.

In March an altar front was presented to St. Paul's Cathedral, Valletta, by the officer in charge of the withdrawal, Air Comm. H. D. Hall. His penultimate task was to take a farewell parade at Luqa on 31 March 1979, the day when the life of the Royal Air Force on the island of Malta finally came to an end. Next day, the 61st anniversary of the founding of the Royal Air Force, Air Comm. Hall piloted a lone Nimrod aircraft from Luqa, over Grand Harbour, dipping the aircraft's wings in salute before making a final circuit of the island and flying away to Gibraltar.

Today, the Air Squadron of the Armed Forces of Malta continues to operate from Luqa, its stock of aircraft having been increased in February 1992 by the arrival of five Bird Dog light aircraft supplied from surplus Italian Air Force stocks.

To commemorate the valiant efforts of all who took part in the siege of Malta, 1940-1942, a memorial, financed by public subscription, was erected in 1991/92 at a point overlooking the entrance to Grand Harbour. The memorial takes the form of a 12-ton bell, hanging in a stone cupola reached by a flight of steps. At the end of May 1992 Her Majesty the Queen dedicated the Siege Bell Memorial during a ceremony opened by the President of the George Cross Island Association, Admiral of the Fleet Lord Lewin KG GCB LVO DSC and attended by many hundred veterans of the siege. Prominent among the guests of honour was HE the President of Malta, Dr. Censu Tabone, whom Her Majesty knighted during her visit.

In addition, a Book of Remembrance was placed in the Malta War Museum. In this book are the names of over 7000 men and women who lost their lives while defending or supplying the islands between 1940 and 1943.

The Maltese Government, in generous recognition of the events of fifty years ago, has arranged for a commemorative Malta Medal to be struck and awarded to those who made the award of the island's own George Cross possible, an idea inspired by King George VI himself in 1942.

ORDERS OF BATTLE

ORDER OF BATTLE 31.12.40

148 Sqdn.	Wellington	Luqa
228 Sqdn.	Sunderland	Kalafrana
261 Sqdn.	Hurricane	Takali
431(GR)Flt.	Maryland	Luqa
830 Sqdn.	Swordfish	Hal Far

ORDER OF BATTLE 30.6.41

69 Sqdn.	Maryland	Luqa
126 Sqdn.	Hurricane	Takali
185 Sqdn.	Hurricane	Hal Far
249 Sqdn.	Hurricane	Takali
800X Flt.	Fulmar	Hal Far
830 Sqdn.	Swordfish	Hal Far

ORDER OF BATTLE 31.12.41

2 PRU det.	Beaufighter	Luqa
21 Sqdn.	Blenheim	Luqa
40 Sqdn.	Wellington	Luqa
69 Sqdn.	Maryland	Luqa
104 Sqdn. det.	Wellington	Luqa
107 Sqdn.	Blenheim	Luqa
126 Sqdn.	Hurricane	Takali
185 Sqdn.	Hurricane	Hal Far
249 Sqdn.	Hurricane	Takali
828 Sqdn.	Albacore	Hal Far
830 Sqdn.	Swordfish	Hal Far
1435 Flt.	Beaufighter	Takali

ORDER OF BATTLE 30.6.42

39 Sqdn. det.	Beaufort	Luqa
69 Sqdn.	Baltimore/Spitfire	Luqa
126 Sqdn.	Spitfire	Luqa
217 Sqdn. det.	Beaufort	Luqa
185 Sqdn.	Hurricane	Hal Far
221 Sqdn. det.	Wellington	Luqa
603 Sqdn.	Spitfire	Takali
1435 Sqdn.	Hurricane	Takali
RNA Sqdn.	Albacore/Swordfish	Hal Far

ORDER OF BATTLE 31.12.42

23 Sqdn.	Mosqutio	Luqa
40 Sqdn.	Wellington	Luqa
69 Sqdn.	Baltimore/Spitfire/Wellington	Luqa
104 Sq. det.	Wellington	Luqa
113 Sq. det.	Wellington	Luqa
126 Sqdn.	Spitfire	Luqa
185 Sqdn.	Hurricane	Hal Far
227 Sqdn.	Beaufighter	Takali
229 Sqdn.	Spitfire	Qrendi
249 Sqdn.	Spitfire	Qrendi
272 Sqdn.	Beaufighter	Takali
821 Sqdn.	Albacore	Hal Far
828 Sqdn.	Albacore	Hal Far
1435 Sqdn.	Spitfire	Luqa

ORDER OF BATTLE 10.7.43

1 Sqn. SAAF	Spitfire	Luqa
3 Sqn. RAAF	Kittyhawk	Takali
23 Sqdn.	Mosquito	Luqa
31st FG	Spitfire	Xewkija
40 Sqn.SAAF	Spitfire	Luqa
43 Sqdn.	Spitfire	Hal Far
69 Sqdn.	Baltimore	Luqa
72 Sqdn.	Spitfire	Hal Far
73 Sq. det.	Hurricane	Luqa
79th FG	P-40	(not known)
81 Sqdn.	Spitfire	Takali
92 Sqdn.	Spitfire	Luqa
93 Sqdn.	Spitfire	hal far
108 Sqdn.	Beaufighter/ Mosquito	Luqa
111 Sqdn.	Spitfire	Safi
112 Sqdn.	Kittyhawk	Safi
113 Sq. det.	Wellington	Luqa
126 Sqdn.	Spitfire	Safi
145 Sqdn.	Spitfire	Luqa
152 Sqdn.	Spitfire	Takali
154 Sqdn.	Spitfire	Takali
185 Sqdn.	Spitfire	Qrendi
221 Sqdn.	Wellington	Luqa
229 Sqdn.	Spitfire	Qrendi
232 Sqdn.	Spitfire	Takali
242 sqdn.	Spitfire	Takali
243 Sqdn.	Spitfire	Hal Far
249 Sqdn.	Spitfire	Qrendi
250 Sqdn.	Kittyhawk	Hal Far
256 Sq. det.	Mosquito	Luqa
272 Sqdn.	Beaufighter	Luqa
417 Sq. RCAF	Spitfire	Luqa
600 Sqdn.	Spitfire	Luqa
601 Sqdn.	Spitfire	Luqa
683 Sqdn.	Spitfire/Mosquito	Luqa
815 Sqdn.	Albacore	Takali
826 Sqdn.	Albacore	Takali
828 Sqdn.	Albacore	Hal Far
1435 Sqdn.	Spitfire	Safi
ASR&CF	(various)	Hal Far

ORDER OF BATTLE 31.12.43

69 Sqdn.	Baltimore	Luqa
108 Sqdn.	Beaufighter/Mosquito	Luqa
185 Sqdn.	Spitfire	Hal Far
221 Sqdn.	Wellington	Luqa
229 Sqdn.	Spitfire	Hal Far
256 Sq. det.	Mosquito	Luqa
728 Sqdn.	(various)	Takali
ASR&CF	(various)	Takali

ORDER OF BATTLE 31.12.44

255 Sq. det.	Beaufighter/Mosquito	Hal Far
283 Sqdn.	Warwick	Hal Far
728 Sqdn.	(various)	Takali
AHQ Malta CF	(various)	Hal Far

ORDER OF BATTLE 31.12.45

38 Sqdn.	Warwick	Luqa
73 Sqdn.	Spitfire	Hal Far
255 Sqdn.	Mosquito	Hal Far

728 Sqdn.	(various)	Takali
765 Sqdn.	Wellington	Hal Far
RN Com. Flt.	(various)	Takali
AHQ Malta CF	(various)	Hal Far

ORDER OF BATTLE 31.12.46

38 Sqdn.	Lancaster	Luqa
73 Sqdn.	Spitfire	Takali
728 Sqdn.	(various)	Hal Far
AHQ Malta CF	(various)	Luqa

ORDER OF BATTLE 31.12.47

38 Sqdn.	Lancaster	Luqa
73 Sqdn.	Spitfire	Takali
728 Sqdn.	(various)	Hal Far
802 Sqdn.	Seafire	Takali
814 Sqdn.	Firefly	Hal Far
Stn. Flt.	Harvard	Hal Far
AHQ Malta CF	(various)	Luqa

ORDER OF BATTLE 31.12.48

37 Sqdn.	Lancaster	Luqa
38 Sqdn.	Lancaster	Luqa
73 Sqdn.	Vampire	Takali
728 Sqdn.	(various)	Hal Far
Stn. Flt.	Harvard	Hal Far
AHQ Malta CF	(various)	Luqa

ORDER OF BATTLE 31.12.53

37 Sqdn.	Shackleton	Luqa
38 Sqdn.	Shackleton	Luqa
75 Sq. RAAF	Vampire	Takali
76 Sq. RAAF	Vampire	Takali
728 Sqdn.	(various)	Hal Far
849C Sqdn.	Skyraider	Hal Far
FASRON 201		Hal Far
Stn. Flt.		Hal Far
AHQ Malta CF	(various)	Luqa

ORDER OF BATTLE 31.12.58

USN VW-2	WV-1	Hal Far
USN VR-23	P2V	Hal Far
38 Sqdn.	Shackleton	Luqa
39 Sqdn.	Canberra	Luqa
728 Sqdn.	(various)	Hal Far
728B Sqdn.	Firefly/ Meteor/ Canberra	Hal Far
848 Sqdn.	Whirlwind	Hal Far
Stn. Flt.		Hal Far
Malta C&TTS	Beaufighter etc.	Takali

ORDER OF BATTLE 31.12.63

38 Sqdn.	Shackleton	Luqa
39 Sqdn.	Canberra	Luqa
728 Sqdn.	(various)	Hal Far
750 Sqdn.	Sea Venom	Hal Far
Stn. Flt.		Hal Far

ORDER OF BATTLE 31.12.73

13 Sqdn.	Canberra	Luqa
203 Sqdn.	Nimrod	Luqa

Chapter 2
LUQA

Origins.

Luqa airfield, by far the longest-lasting of the five airfields on the island of Malta, had its origins in a grass landing field of about 2450ft. (735m.) in diameter which had been formed before 1938 by incorporating a number of terraced fields. Stone rubble walls and quarried stone were used as filling material, in some places 5'0" (1.5m.) thick after removing such topsoil as there was. This soil was then replaced and seeded.

In 1938 the construction of four paved runways was commenced. Considerable quantities of limestone pitching 6" to 12" (150 - 300mm.) thick were required to level the strips, and on top of this 2.5" (65mm.) of bitumen macadam was laid, blinded with pea gravel. Runway lengths, including over-runs, were: 14/32 3150ft. (960m.); 06/24 2950ft. (900m.); 09/27 3150ft. (960m.); and 00/18 2400ft. (732m.). All this made Luqa very modern by the standards of the day, and a trial landing was made by Flt. Lt. George Burges in June 1939. When completed Luqa came into use as

Malta's civilian airport, the Italian airline moving its operation from Takali, which was subject to waterlogging.

As part of the heightened awareness of possible attack by Germany and/or Italy, Luqa became an RAF Station on 1 April 1940, although Italian airlines continued to use it. By the end of June the strength was 19 officers, 61 other ranks and 43 civilians, but by mid-July most of the civilians had left. One of the first aircraft to visit the new Station was brand-new Flamingo transport R2764, carrying the photo-reconnaissance expert Dr. Cotton from England via Marseilles and Ajaccio on 8 April.

It was September 1940 before the first operating unit was in position at Luqa. This was 431(General Reconnaissance) Flight, formed on 19 September to operate Maryland aircraft in a photo-reconnaissance role. Heavier aircraft arrived on 9 November in the shape of the Wellingtons of a hastily-organised unit known temporarily as the Malta Wellington Flight, which

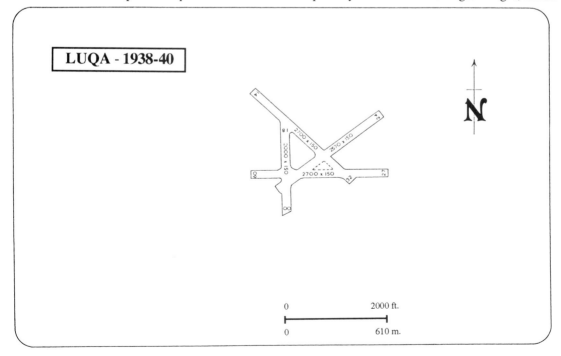

LUQA - 1938-40

N

0	2000 ft.
0	610 m.

Luqa from the air in 1940. One hangar has been destroyed.
[After The Battle magazine]

Inside a sandbag-protected hangar at Luqa in August 1940 a badly-damaged Hurricane of 261 Squadron awaits its fate.
[James Pickering]

became 148 Squadron on 1 December. More Wellingtons arrived from Feltwell on 9 November 1940, when 37 Squadron carried out a few operations before moving on to Fayid.

Luqa in the firing line.
By the end of 1940 air raids on Luqa were frequent and severe. On 18 January 1941, for example, the warning sounded at 13.10 and five minutes later Luqa was at the receiving end of about 24 1000lb (450kg.) bombs which hit four hangars, badly damaging two of them and destroying by fire an aircraft inside. Two ground crew sheltering in a trench were killed in this incident. Next day all available personnel were working hard to fill craters on the airfield, and with the help of the Royal Engineers, the West Kent Regiment and Maltese workers the runways were serviceable by dusk. Worse was to come on 28 January, when two bombs dropped on the domestic area, one being a direct hit on one of the sergeants' blocks. Four NCOs were killed and nine injured in this raid. Next day there were three raids, one during the approach of six Hurricanes and two Wellingtons from Bardia.

431 Flight had become 69 Squadron on 10 January 1941, and this squadron was destined to spend the next three years on the island. A detachment of Whitleys flew in on 8 February from Dishforth in Yorkshire to take part in Operation

What a way to treat a Wimpey! Even the geodetic construction, noted for its strength, could not save this one (probably T2838 of 148 Squadron, which came to grief on 7 December 1940).
[B. Tonks]

Left: Raids by the Italian Air Force on Luqa early in 1941 destroyed all the metal-built hangars and many of the aircraft in them, including this Maryland.
[W. D. Roberts]

Below: A Wellington blazing away at Luqa after a raid in 1941.
[W. D. Roberts]

The control tower at Luqa in less than pristine condition in May 1941.
[J. Arthur Heath]

'Colossus', a special mission to southern Italy, but returned to the UK after eight days.

The raids on Malta continued, but Maltese rock proved its worth. Three barrack blocks were badly damaged on 4 February, the Officers' Mess was destroyed and a shelter received a direct hit, but those inside suffered only a covering of dust. Towards the end of February six Wellingtons of 148 Squadron were destroyed in a dive-bombing attack by Ju.87s and Ju.88s, and in March and April there were a number of night-time attacks on the airfield, causing damage to aircraft and buildings. 148 Squadron became so depleted that its remnants left for Kabrit in March.

Between May and November 1941 a temporary respite allowed the extension of the northwest/southeast and northeast/southwest runways to 4200ft. (1280m.) to be carried out, and at the same time temporary taxi-tracks and extensive dispersal areas were provided. Airfield

In a grass-grown sandbagged revetment, Wg. Cdr. Warburton prepares for yet another 69 Squadron sortie. He appears to be signing the Form 700, accepting the aircraft as serviceable.
[F. Mowlam]

After flying off from the USS *Wasp*, some of the Hurricanes which reached Luqa were destroyed on the ground soon after arrival.
[D. N. Enser]

lighting was installed, aircraft pens were built and a underground power station and operations room was constructed.

Even when all this work was going on, a build-up of strength at Luqa took place, if only on a temporary attachment basis. During May and June, Blenheims of 139 Squadron were present, as were Beaufighters of 252 Squadron. July and August saw Blenheims of 105 and 110 Squadrons operating from Luqa. So far, all attachments had been from UK-based squadrons, but in early August 1941 Wellingtons of 38 Squadron from Egypt arrived for a lengthy stay. Also more permanent were the Blenheims of 107 Squadron, which arrived from Great Massingham on 20 August, and 40 Squadron, whose Wellingtons moved in from Alconbury on 31 October 1941. Two Whitleys, Z9158 and Z9159, arrived from Newmarket in England via Gibraltar on 3 December 1941 and on 6 December one took off with a Serbian co-pilot to drop containers over Yugoslavia. Other than that they appear not to have left the ground before leaving for home on 15 December. Immediately after Christmas 1941 the

Blenheims of 21 Squadron arrived from the UK and a detachment of 2 Photographic Reconnaissance Unit, flying Beaufighters, flew in from Heliopolis in Egypt. By the end of 1941, therefore, the squadrons in residence at Luqa were:

21 Squadron	(Blenheim)
40 Squadron	(Wellington)
69 Squadron	(Maryland)
104 Sqdn. det.	(Wellington)
107 Squadron	(Blenheim)
2 PRU det.	(Beaufighter)

Responsible for the rapid servicing, re-fuelling and turn-round of aircraft in transit through Luqa to the Middle East were the thirty or so men of the Delivery Flight (later renamed Transit Flight). By the end of 1941, the work was carried out at night so that the aircraft could be on their way before dawn to avoid the inevitable raids on the airfield. Aircraft of many types were dealt with, from single-engined light aircraft to heavy bombers such as Fortresses. The ground crews of the Delivery Flight initially worked a week of days and a week

This picture of a Wellington burnt out during one of the many air raids on Luqa shows clearly the geodetic construction of the aircraft.
[D. N. Enser]

Navy personnel wheeling a 'tin fish' to a waiting Beaufort of 69 Squadron at Luqa.
[K. Chinn]

of nights, but the system was later changed to 24 hours on and 24 off. One of the airmen, Mr. V. H. Taylor, recalls working at Luqa for a full four weeks, only going to his billet once a week, on a Sunday, to have a shower, a shave and a change of underwear! Otherwise, he and his colleagues took cat-naps when they could. Originally, Mr. Taylor had been billeted in stone-built barracks on the Station, but after they were blitzed the men had resorted to living (if that's the word) in slit trenches until space was found in the Poor House. There, hundreds of three-tier bunks had been erected from steel tubes which had been earmarked for use as airfield obstruction material, and at the end of the huge high-ceilinged building were the toilets, all open to the main area.

The early part of 1942 was significant for the constant air raids suffered by those at Luqa. The airfield itself was often out of use due to heavy cratering of the runways, and many aircraft in dispersals or hangars were written off by enemy action. On 25 February, for example, thirty Ju.87s (Stukas), ten Do.215s, ten He.111s and twelve Ju.88s, escorted by more than twenty fighters, raided Luqa at 13.00 hours, resulting in the airfield being out of action for 48 hours and 148 Squadron being reduced to two aircraft. A week later, on 4 March, when 14 enemy aircraft attacked Luqa, two billets were demolished and two Maryland aircraft severely damaged. 8 March was one continuous alert, and many buildings were destroyed. A Wellington aircraft was destroyed by fire and three more damaged, while six airmen in a bus were injured. On the same night, two Wellingtons of 37 Squadron, then based at Shallufa in Egypt, collided on the airfield at Luqa, with the loss of five crew members and injuries to eight more.

107 Squadron was disbanded in January 1942 and the 104 Squadron detachment left for Egypt. In March 21 Squadron also disbanded, while in April the 2 PRU Beaufighters returned to Egypt. On the credit side, 126 Squadron's Spitfires moved over from Takali in May. Joining them in June were the Beauforts of 39 Squadron detachment from the

Serious damage to one of Luqa's hangars during the siege period. On the extreme right an airman can be seen attempting to salvage engine components.
[via Tony Spooner]

MILITARY AVIATION IN MALTA G.C. 1915-1993

BOAC Lockheed Lodestar G-AGEH on a visit to Luqa in 1942, possibly on the UK to Cairo run. This aircraft was also allocated the RAF serial HK851 and was formerly USAAF 41-29635.
[K. Chinn]

Middle East, so that the status of Luqa squadrons at the end of June 1942 was thus:

39 Sqdn. det.	(Beaufort)
69 Squadron	(Maryland)
126 Squadron	(Spitfire)
217 Sdn. det.	(Beaufort)
221 Sqdn. det.	(Wellington)

Accidents to aircraft at Luqa, even without enemy action, were not unknown. A Hudson, V9025, on a delivery flight to the Middle East via Gibraltar and Malta, stalled on the approach to Luqa's long runway on 31 March 1942 and spun in, the four crew members sadly losing their lives in the ensuing fire. A few nights later, on 4 April, two Wellingtons, BB512, being delivered by OADU, and Z8575 of 1443 Flight from Harwell in the UK, collided on the flarepath.

Very early the next morning another Wellington ran into the wreckage at the side of the runway while taking off and was burnt out, but nobody was hurt. Five days later, another Hudson on its way to the Middle East, AE524, crashed on take-off. A civilian aircraft, Lodestar G-AGCR of BOAC (formerly AX718), crashed on take-off from Luqa on 13 April.

The Station Armoury, the Main Stores, the NAAFI and the Ration Stores were all destroyed in a raid on 7 April 1942. Luckily, the rations had been removed from the stores after a raid the previous day, so nobody starved. More destruction that month included the officers' quarters and part of the airmens' quarters on 25 April, half of Station Sick Quarters and many other buildings on 28 April. A number of men, RAF and Army, were inevitably injured in these raids, but there were no fatalities. The airfield itself was again frequently cratered.

Gp. Capt. C. Riley DFC became Station Commander on 17 April 1942, in place of Gp. Capt. J. S. Chick MC DFC, who had been in command during much of the hardest part of the siege of Malta. By mid-June 1942 the personnel strength of RAF Luqa had risen to 2000, the highest so far. Gp. Capt. Riley's stay was very short, as he was relieved by Gp. Capt. J. E. Thomas DFC on 18 June 1942.

During the summer of 1942, when air attacks on Luqa were less intense. 39 Squadron, with Beauforts, which had come from the Middle East as a detachment on 22 June, became a full Squadron in August, while 1435 Flight was re-formed in July, also becoming a full Squadron within a few weeks. 227 Squadron, flying Beaufighters, was also formed in August.

The Secretary of State for Air visited Luqa on 3 August 1942, presumably to boost morale. It was probably not his influence, but for a time there were no raids, and such activities as concerts and film shows could be held in the camp cinema. Between 13 and 20 August, however, all entertainment was stopped and there was intense activity due to the arrival of an important convoy of ships at Valletta. The personnel strength was now 2783, and the cinema had to be used as accommodation, although it was very cramped and there was a shortage of beds. Following an attack on an enemy convoy on 17 August the AOC sent a congratulatory message to the Luqa-based squadrons, praising a fine example of team-work between the Beaufighters, Beauforts and Spitfires. That month, regular freight and passenger flights from Bilbeis to Luqa began, operated by 117 Squadron Dakotas.

Gp. Capt. Thomas left on 14 September 1942 and was replaced by Gp. Capt. W. R. Le May OBE. Luqa remained strangely quiet and untouched until

After a nose-dive into the quarry at the end of Luqa's main runway this Wellington is somewhat the worse for wear.
[W. D. Roberts]

11 October, when over thirty unescorted Ju.88s dropped their bombs on the airfield. Although five of the aircraft were shot down and two more damaged, they succeeded in destroying a Beaufighter on the ground. Following this raid the AOC Mediterranean sent a message to all fighter pilots and ground crews, telling them *"where you have worked hard you must work harder"*. This was apparently intended to boost morale!

The transportation of freight from the UK to Malta by air became a regular feature in October 1942. For this purpose, 511 Squadron, based at Lyneham in the UK, sent a detachment of two Liberators to Gibraltar on 17 October. The initial target was to be some 35 tons per month, and the return flights would carry wounded personnel on the first stage of their journey home. Freight-bearing wooden floors were installed in the two Liberators, and their noses were metalled and fitted with loading hatches. This nucleus developed into a considerable enterprise as time went by, and by August 1943 was supplemented by a Hendon to Luqa service flown initially by Albemarles and later by Dakotas. 39 and 227 Squadrons left Luqa in November 1942 but were replaced by three Wellington squadrons from the Middle East — 40,

A 4000-pounder about to be loaded onto a Wellington under the shade of a temporary hangar at Luqa in 1942.
[K. Chinn]

Well dug in: the
entrance to Luqa's
wartime Sick
Quarters and
Armament section
carved out of the soft
rock of Malta.
[W. D. Roberts]

148 and a detachment of 104, and just after Christmas Luqa's first Mosquito squadron, 23 Squadron from Bradwell Bay in Essex, arrived.

RAF strength at Luqa at the end of November 1942 was 2974, comprising 230 officers, 665 SNCOs and 2079 other ranks. The Poor House was the scene that Christmas of a huge dinner, for which the newly-renovated kitchens were used. The officers served, between 11.00 and 15.00, over 3500 meals, and the AOC and HE the Governor visited during the day. Afterwards, there were free concerts for all.

On the offensive

Although by the end of 1942 the worst was over, a raid on Luqa on 18 December by about thirty enemy aircraft succeeded in destroying seven Wellingtons and damaging three more, only one attacker being shot down. However, the RAF had taken up the offensive, and at the end of the year the following squadrons were in residence at Luqa:

23 Squadron	(Mosquito)
40 Squadron	(Wellington)
69 Squadron	(Baltimore, Spitfire, Wellington)
104 Sqdn. det.	(Wellington)
113 Sqdn. det.	(Wellington)
126 Squadron	(Spitfire)
1435 Squadron	(Spitfire)

Lengthening of the two main runways was carried out in 1942, runway 06/24 being extended at its south-west end to 4320ft. (1317m.) and runway 14/32 at its south-east end by about 650ft. (200m.). Further extensions of the same runways in the same directions were built in 1943, 06/24 then becoming 5880ft. (1793m.) and 14/32 becoming 5320ft. (1623m.) in length. At the same time, a 50ft. (15m.) wide perimeter track connecting the runway ends to two aprons on the north side of the airfield was provided.

Transit aircraft were now increasing in number: during December 1942 163 such flights arrived and 128 departed. One might ask what happened to the balance of 35 aircraft! Sadly, one of them must have been a Halifax with a Polish crew and sixteen time-expired men on board which crash-landed after being recalled from its journey to the UK. By now, Hudson aircraft of 24 Squadron, based at Hendon, were operating a shuttle service between Gibraltar and Luqa, sometimes taking in Maison Blanche in Algeria.

The start of the year 1943 marked the beginning of a new era in the history of Malta in general and Luqa specifically, with those based there metaphorically, and in some cases actually, licking their wounds. More squadrons arrived — 458 Squadron, a RCAF unit, and 221 Squadron, both flying Wellingtons, and 39 Squadron (which had left Luqa only a few weeks previously) all came in

from Shallufa in January. The 104 Squadron detachment and 40 Squadron, together forming 238 Wing, left for the Western Desert, however. A new squadron formed at Luqa in February was 683 Squadron, which was issued with Spitfires and Mosquitoes for reconnaissance purposes in view of the need for information for the impending invasion of Sicily.

A further change of Station Commander took place on 28 January 1943, when Gp. Capt. W. H. Merton relieved Gp. Capt. Le May. The number of RAF personnel was still growing: at the end of February there were 340 officers, 649 SNCOs and 2655 other ranks, a total of 3644, with 485 soldiers and 650 civilians.

Further reconnaissance capability arrived towards the end of April 1943 in the unusual shape of a detachment of F-4 and F-5 Lightnings of the USAAF's 3rd Photographic and Mapping Group. Over the next eight weeks the detachment flew regular sorties over Sicilian harbours and airfields, often in conjunction with 683 Squadron. April was also a busy month for aircraft in transit through Luqa, 253 arriving and 218 departing. Among them were B-24Ds of the 98th Bomb Group from Benina, Libya, and of the 376th Bomb Group from Solluch, also in Libya, which put down at Luqa on the way home from operations. The service run by 117 Squadron was operating from Castel Benito by April 1943, using Hudsons instead of Dakotas. On the other hand, Dakotas began to take over from Hudsons on 24 Squadron's Gibraltar to Luqa shuttle service, the first such sortie being flown by Dakota I FD772 on 3 April, via Maison Blanche. Within a few weeks, other points of call included Casablanca, Oran and Biskra.

By the end of June 1943 a great deal of construction work had been completed in readiness for greatly expanded activity to come. Runway 06/24 had been extended to 5850ft. (1784m.), and there were now taxi-tracks around 60% of the airfield. Three large aprons for aircraft parking and a number of pens had also been completed.

June and July 1943 were the busiest of months at Luqa, just before and after Operation 'Husky', the invasion of Sicily. Some of the arriving squadrons, however, do not appear to have flown any missions while at Luqa, merely awaiting movement to newly-captured ports and airfields. Following 458 Squadron's departure on 17 May and 39 Squadron's move to Tunisia on 1 June, 108 Squadron Beaufighters arrived on 3 June, 272 Squadron's Beaufighters next day, five squadrons of Spitfires forming 244 Wing (92, 145 and 601 Squadrons RAF, 1 Squadron SAAF and 417 Squadron RCAF) between 7 and 14 June, 40 Squadron SAAF with Spitfires on 23 June and 600 Squadron with Beaufighters on 25 June. 126 and 1435 Squadrons left for Safi on 7 June to relieve the congestion a little. July saw another spate of movements: a detachment of 256 Squadron Mosquitoes arrived from Ford in the UK on 5 July, but 244 Wing's five squadrons began to leave on 1 July, completing their exit on 13 July. The air party of 272 Squadron left on 4 July, to return later.

To handle wounded and sick troops taking part in the invasion of Sicily an Air Evacuation Centre was set up at Luqa on 9 July 1943. The invasion was launched on 10 July, and Luqa-based Spitfires mounted 861 sorties that day to protect landing-craft off the Sicilian beaches, as well as 59 sorties

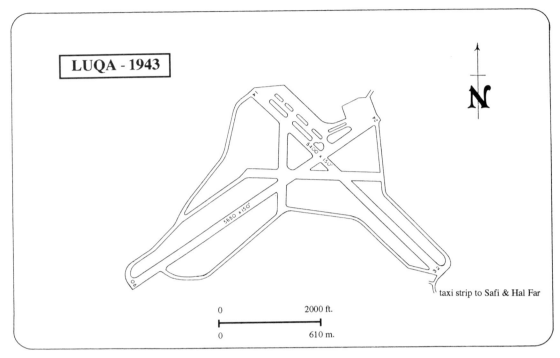

LUQA - 1943

N

taxi strip to Safi & Hal Far

| 0 | 2000 ft. |
| 0 | 610 m. |

in escorting bombers attacking Gerbini, Biscari, Comiso and Naples. Next day a further 714 protection sorties and 224 bomber escort sorties were flown, with a similar number on 12 July. During the next few days, the number of trips, while still substantial, dropped a little. The 73 Squadron Hurricanes left for North Africa on 13 July, but next day 239 Wing, comprising four squadrons of Kittyhawks, 259 and 260 Squadrons

RAF, 450 Squadron RCAF and 3 Squadron SAAF, arrived from various Stations. It is doubtful whether these Kittyhawks carried out any missions while at Luqa.

Very soon a great exodus got under way, 40 and 417 Squadrons leaving over the period 15 to 19 July, 239 Wing squadrons on 17/18 July and 600 Squadron on 26 July. Present at Luqa between 16 and 31 July, however, were the Mustangs of 1437

This Mustang I, seen in a typical fighter pen, is likely to have been a visitor to Malta, as the only Mustang-equipped unit to have been based on the island, 1437 (SR) Flight, used Mk.III aircraft, which sported a different (Malcolm) cockpit canopy.
[NWMA]

Shortly after the invasion of Sicily in 1943 a captured Bf.109 was flown to Malta for pilots to evaluate. Resplendent in 'training yellow', it is seen here in a sandbagged revetment at Luqa. *[W. D. Roberts]*

(Strategic Reconnaissance) Flight, which did carry out a few operations while on the island. These few Mustangs seem to have been the only ones ever based on Malta. The two squadrons of 232 Wing, 55 and 223, flying Baltimores, were next to arrive, on 20 July, and, finally, 219 Squadron's Beaufighters came in from Algeria on 30 July. The July figures for aircraft in transit through Luqa were impressive — 702 arrivals and 782 departures — but some of the most mobile of the squadrons already mentioned may have been included in these figures. In either case, the difficulties experienced by such personnel as catering staff, movements clerks and those whose job it was to arrange accommodation can be imagined.

From the end of July 1943 things at Luqa were infinitely more static, though the Station was still extremely busy. The eleven squadrons present on 31 July were:

23 Squadron	(Mosquito)
55 Sqdn. det.	(Baltimore)
69 Squadron	(Baltimore)
108 Squadron	(Beaufighter, Mosquito)
113 Sqdn. det.	(Wellington)
219 Sqdn. det.	(Beaufighter)
221 Squadron	(Wellington)
223 Sqdn. det.	(Baltimore)
256 Sqdn. det.	(Mosquito)
272 Squadron	(Beaufighter)
683 Squadron	(Spitfire, Mosquito)

On 13 August 1943, the Melita Bay Hotel and the United Services Hotel in Sliema, occupied by 69 and 683 Squadrons' personnel for some months, were vacated, as was the Modern Imperial Hotel ten days later, the officers moving to the Meadowbank Hotel. Aircraft transiting through Luqa were still numerous — 573 arrivals and 640

On detachment to Luqa in July/August 1943 were the Baltimores of 223 Squadron; this one, FA342 [P], appears to be landing, with battle damage evident to the fuselage. *[via A. Thomas]*

Seen at Luqa in 1943 was this captured Fw.190; the crosses and swastika seem to have been outlined in chalk.
[F. E. Wattam]

departures in August and 471 arrivals and 491 departures in September. Personnel figures remained high, and on 1 October 1943 billets at Siggiewi were taken over from RAF Qrendi, the ground crews of 23 Squadron moving there from the Poor House. Several premises at Ta'Xbiex and Sliema were de-requisitioned during October.

A new Station Commander in the shape of Gp. Capt. F. H. Tyson took over from Gp. Capt. Merton on 29 October 1943. By the end of that month nearly all operations from Luqa were reconnaissance sorties by 69 and 221 Squadrons. 683 Squadron began to move out on 20 November, followed on 29 November by 23 Squadron, leaving 69, 108, 221 and 256 Squadrons as the only occupants at the end of the year. Personnel figures dropped accordingly: at the end of 1943 the total was 2754, comprising 203 officers, 443 SNCOs and 2108 other ranks. Early in November, RAF Safi became a satellite of Luqa, losing its self-accounting status.

The year 1943, another hectic one for those at Luqa, came towards a conclusion on 8 December, when Franklin D. Roosevelt, the President of the USA, arrived from Cairo. He flew in a C-54 Skymaster, escorted by nine P-38 Lightnings, with four Spitfires of 229 Squadron from Hal Far providing top cover and 185 Squadron, also from Hal Far, carrying out standing patrols. At Luqa the RAF Regiment provided a guard of honour.

A year of fundamental change at Luqa, 1944 began with the attachment of 185 and 229 Squadrons for a couple of days while runway repairs were carried out at Hal Far. At the end of the

month the cave-dwellers of Station HQ, who had been working underground for years, came out into the sunlight, blinked, and set to work in new offices at ground level. By this time, most of the domestic tradesmen were Maltese members of the RAF, which allowed UK personnel to be repatriated more rapidly.

The transport era.

Far-reaching changes, however, were being planned, involving the use of Luqa as a staging post for aircraft flying along or across the Mediterranean, a function which the airfield had in fact been carrying out unofficially for almost its entire period of existence. Now, staff officers of Transport Command and BOAC who visited on 31 January were making plans to provide proper overnight accommodation and facilities for passengers and crews involved in large-scale aircraft movements. The squadrons currently based at Luqa would move out, and after some new construction all efforts would be directed to handling transit aircraft. At this time personnel on the Station numbered 2794, but this was set to decline rapidly.

Dakotas began moving the ground crews of 69 Squadron (resident at Luqa since September 1940, originally as 431 Flight) to Monte Corvino on 7 February 1944, and the rear party left by sea three days later. On 12 February a detachment of 221 Squadron left for Grottaglie, followed by the rest of the squadron on 22 March.

By the end of January the control tower was being rebuilt and enlarged and new Station workshops completed. For safety reasons, some of the dispersal pens used by fighter squadrons in the dark days of the siege were now removed, as they were too close to the runways for comfort.

There was a raid alert on 8 March 1944, a most unusual event by now, and four Beaufighters were scrambled. No contact was made, but one of the Beaus crashed on take-off, killing the crew.

After the departure of 256 Squadron's Mosquitoes to La Seina on 30 March, the strength of the Station had been reduced to 2041. By the end of the month, 64 Staging Post was in existence, and was handling an average of fifteen transit aircraft per day. It was fortunate that the figure was low, as civilians with sheep and goats were causing a great deal of alarm by trespassing on the airfield.

By May 1944 the AMWD (the 'Works & Bricks') was handling a considerable increase in work in connection with 64 Staging Post, and twenty junior airmen were allocated to form a pioneer squadron. Station personnel in general were encouraged to spend off-duty hours at the Rest Camp at St. Paul's Bay, to where a 'liberty' bus ran three times a week, and there was a daily bus to Sliema. All SNCOs housed in Balluta Buildings were moved to the Sergeants' Mess and Balluta Buildings was derequisitioned. At the end of May Station strength was 1409, but a month later it was les than 1000.

RAF Luqa's last based squadron (for the time being), 108 Squadron, left for Hal Far on 1 July 1944 and the Station Commander, Gp. Capt. Tyson, followed, to be replaced by Wg. Cdr. J. R. N. Gaynor. That month was a significant one for anyone interested in aircraft. First notables to arrive were ten Russian Air Force Li-2s (Russian-built C-47 Dakotas) which came in on 14 July carrying 120 officers, the first large batch of people that 64 SP had had to deal with. They stayed overnight and left for Bari next day. On 16 July it became known that squadrons of the US Navy and Fleet Air Arm would be arriving for short stays, and airmen housed in the Poor House were hurriedly moved to Safi Camp to enable the Poor House to be used by the visitors. At 06.30 on 19 July F6F Hellcat aircraft of USN Squadrons VF-74 and VOF-1 flew into Luqa from the carriers USS *Kaasan Bay*(CVE-69) and *Tulagi*(CVE-72) while taking part in Operation 'Dragon'. More aircraft arrived than were expected, but all were allocated space. The Americans returned to their carriers on 24 July and next day 879 Squadron's Seafires from HMS *Attacker,*an assault/escort carrier, arrived at 07.00. How long they stayed is not recorded, but probably only a few days.

The much-desired accommodation for 64 SP was now well advanced. In the officers' compound 21 Nissen huts were nearly finished, as were sixteen barrack blocks in the north camp area. Apart from this, all personnel still living in the Poor House were moved to Safi Camp on 27 August, and the building was at last de-requisitioned. Personnel strength at the end of July was 788, a further reduction.

Things were quiet in October, 64 SP handling 72 aircraft inbound and 80 departures. By then, a weekly UK to Malta service (Route HK) was being flown by 525 Squadron, using Warwicks and then Dakotas, and this became a twice-weekly event during October. In November things became much busier, as a large reinforcement programme of men and supplies to the Far East was under way under the title Operation 'Refors'. That month, 579 transit aircraft arrived and 499 left. On 25 November two more Russian Dakota 'clones' arrived from Moscow on the way to Paris carrying two Generals. Before leaving next day, they demanded fighter escort between Naples and Paris, but didn't get it! 64 SP was now so busy that the staff complained about *"stray aircraft lobbing in in search of leave, women, wine or vegetables"* (probably in that order!).

On 6 December a large new Officers' Transit Mess was opened and proclaimed as the best in the Mediterranean area. The Staging Post's facilities were said to be still too small, however. December's throughput of transit aircraft totalled 462 arrivals and 470 departures. One, a Wellington being ferried by a Yugoslavian crew from the UK to India, swung on take-off, hit one of the old pens, crashed into a quarry and burnt out, but the crew managed to escape with burns.

Towards the end of January 1945 there was much activity in connection with the tripartite conference to be held at Yalta in the Crimea. On 26 January one Col. Pfennig of the USAAF arrived with Detachment 'X' from the air traffic control centre at Casablanca to set up a signals office, and next day an RAF detachment from Bari came in for ground duties. Minor VIPs arrived in a C-54 on 28

January, and on 30 January no less than 33 P-38 Lightnings flew in for escort duties. Mr. Winston Churchill and President Franklin D. Roosevelt arrived on 31 January, and the whole circus left for Yalta on 3 February. A week later, some of the VIPs returned, but Churchill and Roosevelt proceeded to Cairo, there to discuss plans for the war in the Far East. Sixteen P-38s arrived at Luqa between 15 and 18 February, as did five Wellingtons of 38 Squadron from Foggia, all for 'special escort' duties, and on 19 February some were vectored onto the C-54 carrying the Prime Minister and President from Cairo. Whether the aircraft landed at Luqa or not is unclear.

By March 1945 the personnel at Luqa had risen to over 900 in number, and that month they dealt with 604 inbound transit aircraft and 601 departures. A Station badge, carrying the motto 'An Airfield Never Beaten', was received from the UK after approval by HM King George VI, and was accepted at a ceremonial parade on 4 May. Four days later came VE-Day, when there was a stand-down, followed by a Victory Parade in Valletta in which Luqa airmen took part.

Luqa's post-war life.
In June 1945 parties of 284 Wing personnel began to arrive, and it was learnt that 38 Squadron would move in early in July for ASR duties, the squadron personnel to be housed at Safi Camp. An advance party did arrive on 2 July, just after an outbreak of bubonic plague in Malta had been confirmed. Fortunately, restrictions on movement lasted only

a few days. The main party of 38 Squadron was delayed until 19 July, as no serviceable aircraft were on hand! By that time, the decision had been taken to close the domestic accommodation at Safi Camp, and the airmen and SNCOs there moved to Luqa.

Transit aircraft attended to during July totalled 809 arrivals and 826 departures, a busy month indeed. VJ-Day on 15 August was marked by a two-day stand-down, after which 64 SP's work continued as normal. A new Station Commander, Gp. Capt. K. F. Pickles, took over from Gp. Capt. Bisdee on 26 October. At the end of a very busy year, the Luqa personnel strength stood at 926, plus 336 civilians, but the number of transit aircraft now began to drop.

Three new units appeared at Luqa early in 1946. First came 728 Squadron of the Fleet Air Arm, which arrived on New Year's Day from Takali, and on 4 January the AHQ Malta Communications Flight moved in from Hal Far, as that Station was shortly to be taken over by the Fleet Air Arm. On 1 February 1357 (PAMPA) Flight was formed at Luqa to carry out meteorological sorties, but as no aircraft arrived for the new unit it was disbanded on 10 April. Among the many visiting aircraft in the early part of 1946 was Lancaster 'Aries', on the way home on 2 February after breaking the UK to South Africa record.

Problems with the unevenness of the NW/SE runway made the airfield unserviceable to four-engined aircraft from 11 April to 7 September

The RAF passenger reception building at Luqa, built for the many transit passengers handled by 64 Staging Post, looks more like a redundant barn!
[J. A. Brown]

Right: York MW185 during a stopover at Luqa on the way to the Far East. Note the code BP on the nose; this is part of the aircraft's radio call-sign, probably MOYBP. It is interesting to note that this machine finally finished it's days on Malta; in another guise it was registered as G-AMUT and is shown on page 72
[via J. Mounter]

Left: Viking VL232 of the Queen's Flight on a visit to Luqa.
[R. Robinson]

Avro York MW102 of ACSEA Communications Squadron staging through Luqa. Note the badge of Lord Louis Mountatten, C-in C South East Asia Command and the Governor General of India on the nose. *[R. A. Waller]*

Prototype Avro Tudor II VX202 sinks onto the Luqa runway at the end of a trial flight. *[R. A. Waller]*

1946, with a consequent reduction in accommodation and messing problems. The runway was resurfaced during that period, at the end of which the number of transit aircraft handled was down to about a quarter of the March figure. No sooner had the runway reopened than an outbreak of typhoid at Castel Benito in Libya caused all York aircraft which normally used that airfield to stage through Luqa instead. To assist with servicing these aircraft, a party of airmen came from Castel Benito, having presumably been checked for any signs of the disease!

By 1946 the two shortest runways were out of use, and the two main runways were resurfaced with asphalt varying between 1" (25mm.) and 5.5" (90mm.) thick in order to take up the irregularities.

Organisational changes in 1946 included the absorbtion of 64 Staging Post into Luqa HQ on 1 June and the opening of a new Air Traffic Control Centre to replace the original one at Lacaris Ditch on 16 September. Other improvements were the installation in October of an electric flarepath to replace the gooseneck system and the commissioning of a BABS Mk.II approach aid.

By the autumn of 1946 Lancasters from UK bases were staging through Luqa on their way to Shallufa in Egypt to take part in Exercise 'Sunbronze', a regular task for Bomber Command units, enabling crews to acquire tropical experience. One of these Lancasters, PA450 of 49 Squadron, Upwood, 'ran away' at Luqa on 18 December, but appears not to have come to any great harm, as it returned to service later. Had it

been at Luqa on 23 December it might have been damaged in a sudden violent storm. The runway caravan was blown over, a Spitfire was lifted and thrown into a wall and various buildings were damaged, and the airfield had to be closed while empty oil drums and sheets of corrugated steel were retrieved from the runways.

Notable visitors during the early days of 1947 included HRH The Duke of Gloucester, who arrived in York MW140 from Habbaniya on 22 January on his way from Sydney to London. He was met by the Governor of Malta, Mr. F. C. R. Douglas, and AVM K. B. Lloyd, and continued his journey next day. A Viking of the King's Flight, one of four to be used on the Royal tour of South Africa, arrived, carrying press men, on 5 February and stayed overnight before leaving for Cairo.

Life at Luqa had now settled down to a fairly routine pattern, the Station consisting in March of the 38 Squadron detachment, the Area Air Traffic Control Centre, the Central Meteorological Section, the Staging Post element of HQ and domestic support staff. Transit aircraft handled that month were 111 arrivals and 110 departures. By 16 April rebuilding of the passenger terminal had been completed, providing less spartan conditions for the transients being handled. Airliners of BOAC had become very prominent, although many of the airline's flights were switched to Castel Benito from the last week of June. Apart from the BOAC aircraft, many other civilian aircraft used Luqa as a convenient stopping-off place. By July, however, it was remarked that the flow of aircraft recently had been above the level for which the Station was established. In August the number of transit passengers increased further, while in September the evacuation of British families from India added further to the workload at Luqa.

For the opening of the Malta Legislature on 10 November 1947 a Viking of the King's Flight brought the Duke and Duchess of Gloucester to Luqa. Two officers and a hundred other ranks from Luqa represented the Royal Air Force by lining the streets of Valletta during the ceremonial parade that day.

Mosquito aircraft based in Germany were by now frequent visitors to Malta on Exercise 'Roundabout', a regular navigation and deployment exercise. Other visitors included Lincoln RF523 *'Thor II'* from the Empire Air Armaments School at Manby with a lecture team on 22 January 1948; a B-29 of the USAF on its way to Bahrain on 1 February; a SM.79 of the Italian Air Force on 12 February; and a Greek Air Force Dakota from Hassani on 24 February.

By 1 February 1948, RAF Luqa provided the following facilities:

Servicing for 205 transit aircraft per month.
Administration for the 38 Squadron detachment.
Malta Air Traffic Control Centre.
Central Meteorological Section.
Support for civilian operators.
AHQ Malta Communications Flight.
Administration for 8 Sector Operations Room.
Central Equipment Section.
Medical facilities for Malta-based units except AHQ.
Servicing facilities for 73 Squadron.

The main part of 38 Squadron returned to Luqa from Palestine on 1 April 1948 along with a similar squadron, 37 Squadron, although a few Lancasters were left behind pending final British withdrawal from that country in May. Transit traffic began to decline steeply at this time, largely due to the effects of the Berlin airlift, to which the greatest part of Transport Command resources were devoted. During the spring, on 11 March, one of the first Hastings transport aircraft to enter service arrived from Lyneham carrying the first air-portable sectional ramp for loading vehicles through the side cargo door; from Luqa the Hastings went on to Habbaniya in Iraq and thence to Sydney, where it arrived on 18 March. Summer visitors to Luqa included a Tudor IV, a Lincoln

with a Theseus engine, another B-29 and a lifeboat-carrying B-17. On 18 July HM the Shah of Persia arrived on a two-day visit to the island; he flew in York MW140, which used radio call-sign MOYDK, and left for Northolt to visit the British Royal family.

In July Exercise 'DXM '48' was held to test Malta's defences, and 37 and 38 Squadrons took part. The Station Operations Room was in action for the first time in this exercise. Transit traffic included a number of Lincolns returning from Shallufa to Hemswell after a period of training in the sun, and Mosquito TJ141 of 14 Squadron at Wahn in Germany; this aircraft, on a 'Roundabout' sortie, came to grief when it crashed into the sea off Gozo. During November, 56 aircraft of the Italian Air Force were handled, and between 16 and 18 November fifteen F-47s, veteran Thunderbolts from wartime days, with two A-26 target-tugs and two C-47 support aircraft, were present at Luqa on their way from Germany to Wheelus Field, Tripoli. The American influence was again felt on 15 to 18 December and on 19/20 January 1949, when sixteen F-47s, a C-47 and a B-17 'mother ship' were detached to Luqa for gunnery training, and again several more times during the early months of that year.

January 1949 was also a busy month at Luqa for the personnel handling aircraft in transit; on the peak day no less than 56 such flights staged through the airfield, which put a severe strain on all concerned. New building work was proceeding, and during the month additional barrack blocks for airmen were completed and married quarters were almost ready.

By April the intensity of transit aircraft using Luqa had, if anything, increased. In all, 1631 visiting aircraft were handled that month, comprising 416 British civilian, 700 American, 20 French, eight Dutch, four Rhodesian, 52 Italian, nine South African and six Pakistani. Among the RAF visitors were four Lancasters and a Lincoln from Shawbury on a 'navex' with Cranwell cadets and four USAF F-80 Shooting Stars which arrived from Germany to assess Luqa for gunnery training by jet aircraft. Having decided in the affirmative, 12 Shooting Stars arrived from Furstenfeldbruck on 29 April for a ten-day stay, the first of several such visits over the next few months.

During the summer of 1949, Lincolns from

A more unusual visitor to Luqa was this Italian Air Force SM. 82 serialled SM-2.
[R. Robinson]

various UK bases transited through Luqa on the way to Shallufa as part of Exercise Sunray, while in July Exercise 'Convex 1' brought detachments of maritime Lancasters from St. Eval. By November the flow of transit aircraft had further increased, with a maximum of 75 being dealt with in one day, an enormous effort. Among the visitors was HRH Princess Elizabeth, who arrived on 20 November in Royal Flight Viking VL246 to be met by the Duke of Edinburgh and numerous dignitaries. The Princess stayed in Malta until 28 November and on leaving congratulated all the Luqa personnel on the excellent arrangements which had been made.

The busy 'fifties.

During 1950, RAF Luqa, under the command of Gp. Capt. L. F. Brown since 17 September 1949, continued to be used by large numbers of transit aircraft and was a favourite destination for RAF aircraft on navigation exercises. Egyptian Air Force Sea Fury 703, piloted by Sqdn. Ldr. Neville

Duke, arrived on 16 February from Blackbushe on its UK to Cairo record attempt, and a week later 203 Squadron's Lancasters returned to take part in a two-week training exercise. Six elderly Wellingtons and two Lancasters from the CNCS at Shawbury appeared on 20 March and left two days later. During August, Exercise 'DXM'50' was held, and seven Mosquitoes from Fayid in Egypt arrived to take part, operating with the Mediterranean Fleet and US 6th Fleet.

1951 followed much the same pattern of activity, sometimes steady and at other times very intense. The largest exercise to test the defences of Malta was held in August 1951, entitled Exercise 'Beehive'. Taking part were the Mediterranean and US 6th Fleets, French and Italian naval units and aircraft from the four nations. A special feature was the prevention of passage of 'enemy' shipping through the Straits of Sicily. Operating from Luqa were, among others, night-fighter Mosquitoes of 219 Squadron from Kabrit, and Lincolns and a

Mosquito PR.34 VL618 of 13 Squadron at Luqa c.1950. This aircraft crashed into the Great Bitter Lake, Egypt, on approach to its home base, Kabrit, on 13 March 1951.
[D. Lister via P. Porter]

Left: The then new domestic site at Luqa, c.1951. *[D. Lister via P. Porter]*

Below: An oblique aerial shot of Luqa , taken sometime in the early 'fifties. The view is looking north-east, and towards the foreground can be seen 37 and 38 Squadrons' Lancasters in dispersal.
[F. D. Sheppard]

A F2H-2 Banshee of the US Navy, 123351, visiting Luqa c.1951. *[D. Lister via P. Porter]*

Mosquito from the Central Signals Establishment at Watton. During the exercise, two US Navy Banshees collided in mid-air, but the pilots were successfully rescued by high-speed launch.

Wellingtons and Valettas from Shawbury continued their navigational visits during the autumn of 1951, and between 18 and 31 October eight Consolidated PB4Y Privateers of US Navy squadron VP-24, coded HA, operated from Luqa.

HRH Princess Elizabeth at Luqa in 1951, accompanied by AVM De'Ath.
[F. D. Sheppard]

Visitors during January 1952 included four Lancasters of 210 Squadron from St. Eval which took part in Exercise 'Oversticks 2' with 37 and 38 Squadrons. Another St. Eval aircraft, Lancaster RF210, operating from Luqa on 23 January, had the misfortune to ditch, but all except one crew member were picked up.

Airfield activity at Luqa varied considerably from month to month, but in March the highest figure recorded was reached: 2002 movements. There were no accidents that month, but in April there were two. On the first day of the month (some might say it was an appropriate date!) Hastings TG609, which used radio call-sign MOGAY, undershot and suffered a collapsed undercarriage, while on 29 April Meteor NF.11 WD626 of the Central Fighter Establishment (call-sign Dynamite 2) overshot, but was repairable.

As the wartime runways and taxiways had, by 1952, developed excessive waviness, cracking and settlement, runway 06/24 was closed and a complete reconstruction programme was put in hand. A 60-ton roller was used as a means of determining the areas to be dealt with, and about 35% of the paved areas were found to be faulty. Repairs were carried out using compacted graded stone and new surfacing. Runway 14/32 was dealt with in 1953 and the taxiways in 1954/55.

As a further project, fourteen spectacle-type hardstandings were built in 1952, partly in concrete and partly in asphalt and a number of disused shallow quarries in the area were filled in. The new hardstandings eased the parking problem for the Venoms of 185 Squadron which arrived from Hal

Right: A Supermarine Attacker on a delivery flight to the Pakistan Air Force, staging through Luqa c.1951. [D. Lister via P. Porter]

Left: A French-built Ju.52/3m, this AAC.1 of the Armee de l'Air, serialled 355, is seen on a visit to Luqa about 1952. [R. Robinson]

Right: Mosquito NF.36 RL235 of either 39 or 219 Squadrons staging through Luqa c.1952. [R. Robinson]

Left: A most unusual machine -- Avro Ashton Mk.I prototype WB490, visiting Luqa. Note the US Navy P2Vs in the background. [R. Robinson]

Right: Hastings TG603 of 99 Squadron after being blown off Luqa's runway on 16 June 1952. The radio call-sign (MO)GAQ is prominent.
[R. Robinson]

Left: Luqa's airmens' mess and NAAFI shortly after completion in 1952.
[D. Lister via P. Porter]

Left: 'Dumbo' a Martin PBM Mariner amphibian of the US Navy, coded RD and thus probably from Squadron VP-47, was an example of the large number of more exotic aircraft types which visited Luqa over the years.
[D. Lister via P. Porter]

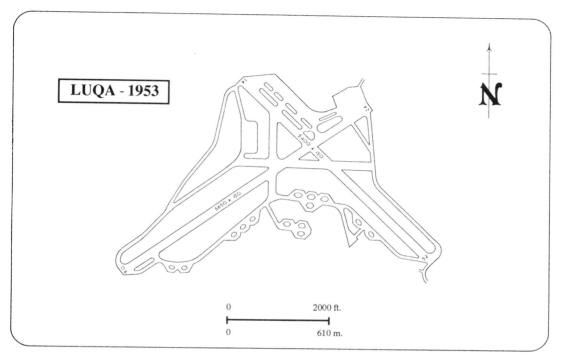

LUQA - 1953

N

0	2000 ft.
0	610 m.

Far on 23 July, although they moved on after about three weeks.

The first Shackletons seen at Luqa arrived on 1 November from 224 Squadron at Gibraltar to take part in Exercise 'Longstop', and returned after two weeks. More of the same type were four of 42 Squadron's aircraft from St. Eval which were present between 2 and 21 January 1953; four from 120 Squadron, Aldergrove, from 13 February to 4 March, and four from 206 Squadron at St. Eval at the same time. These groups of aircraft were taking advantage of the regular 'Fair Isle' detachment scheme then operated by Coastal Command to allow fair-weather training of long-range maritime crews, and this arrangement continued, using Luqa as the base, for a number of years.

A serious accident on Luqa's runway occured on 8 October 1952, when P2V-5 Neptune 127724 of the US Navy crash-landed and was destroyed by fire. Yet another nasty incident took place on 17 May 1953 as Valetta VW810 of 70 Squadron, Fayid, using call-sign MORKK, force-landed on

Not much remains of Valetta C.2 VW810 of 70 Squadron after colliding with the runway control caravan at Luqa on 17 May 1953.
[R. Robinson]

Left: Visiting Luqa from Topcliffe about 1953 was Neptune MR.1 WX516 [L:T] of 210 Squadron. This aircraft eventually found its way to the Argentine Navy.
[R. Robinson]

Right: Hastings TG537 seen at Luqa unloading the first batch of former prisoners of war from Korea, c.1953.
[R. Robinson]

Left: 29 Squadron Meteor NF.11s, based at Tangmere, visiting Luqa c.1953. WD722 [E] is in the foreground, WD792 [U] and another behind it.
[R. Robinson]

Right: Italian Air Force C-119G Boxcar 26009 at Luqa c.1953.
[R. Robinson]

grass next to the runway when its aileron jammed, hit the runway control caravan and burst into flames, with the loss of two lives.

Movements at Luqa increased steadily during 1953, from 2326 in July to 3232 in November. Included in the figures were a number of Neptunes of 36 Squadron which arrived on 6 November from Topcliffe and detachments of US Navy Squadron VP-21 and FASRON 104, which should in theory have gone to Hal Far.

More small construction projects were carried out in 1953, involving an aircraft readiness platform and a new taxiway running north and south between the end of runway 14 and the west end of the disused east/west runway. The Government of Malta built the Civil Terminal Apron along the east taxiway in 1955, but, apart from running repairs, it was 1961 before any further major work was undertaken.

1955 was marked by the arrival from Kabrit early in January of the Meteor night fighters of 39 Squadron to take up part of the commitment to the defence of the island. Visiting aircraft were still very much in evidence at Luqa, their arrival facilitated by new CR/DF (cathode ray direction finding) equipment installed during the previous year, although some of them had problems. A pair of USAF F-84s, taking off on 11 March, failed to clear a wall and struck a BABS hut, causing one of them to crash-land at Luqa and the other one at Hal Far. Visiting from Abu Sueir on 13 April, Meteor FR.9 VZ604, using call-sign Critic 27, crash-landed but survived to fly again.

During August 1955, eight Canberras from 40 Squadron at Wittering and eight from 44 Squadron at Honington arrived to take part in Exercises 'Blue Trident' and 'Lake Major', followed by eight Hunters of the Day Fighter Leaders' School. Business at Luqa that month was the best ever, a record 3264 movements being recorded. More exotic aircraft, Saab J-29s of the Royal Swedish Air Force, 24 of them with three support aircraft, were present between 3 and 8 September with officers and cadets of the RSAF Flying College, adding to the number of different types of aircraft seen at Luqa over the years.

The year 1956 began badly, with the collapse of the undercarriage of Neptune MR.1 WX547 of 1453 Flight, Topcliffe, which was using call-sign Sterile Y. This aircraft never flew again, and was sold for

A trio of F-86A Sabres of the USAF, with 49-1228 carrying 'buzz number' FU-228 in the foreground, seen at Luqa.
[R. Robinson]

Masquerading under the RAF serial XD670, this York was in fact G-AGNU of Air Charter or British Eagle and is seen here staging through Luqa on a trooping flight.
[J. Betts]

filming purposes in May 1957. Infinitely worse, however, was the crash after take-off on 18 February of civilian York G-ANSY of Scottish Aviation (Prestwick) in which 45 people lost their lives. This aircraft, originally MW193 of the RAF, had lately been carrying out trooping flights bearing the temporary RAF serial number XG929 but had recently reverted to its civil registration.

Other interesting visitors in 1956 included an SO.30 of the French Air Force, using call-sign FRAFU when it brought the French Secretary of State for Air on 18 August; US Navy R4D-5 17165 on 20 August; similar aircraft 12439 two days later; a French Navy Neptune with call-sign FYAGB on 12 September; and a NC.701 using call-sign FYCDO of the same owners on 15 September.

With the onset of political tension in the Middle East and particularly in the Suez Canal Zone, Luqa began to receive detachments of aircraft to bolster the RAF presence on the island. Four Hunters of 111 Squadron arrived from North Weald on 17 September to take up duties as the day fighter element for the defence of Malta, referred to as Operation 'Challenger', alongside resident 39 Squadron's night-fighter commitment. Five days

later, 25 Canberras flew in from Binbrook as part of a preliminary deployment of bomber aircraft, Operation 'Albert', but moved on a couple of days later to Hal Far, and four Valiants arrived from Marham on 24 September. Due to the tense situation, deployments of maritime aircraft from the UK under Exercise 'Fair Isle' were discontinued at this point. Yet more Valiants arrived at the end of October to reinforce Operation 'Albert'. However, the emergency was quickly resolved, sighs of relief were breathed by everyone, the tension eased and on 17 November the eighteen Valiants left for home. What a sight that must have been!

The 'Fair Isle' detachments of Coastal Command aircraft resumed early in 1957, and aircraft of other nationalities re-appeared at Luqa. An unusual one was a C-118 of the Royal Canadian Air Force, 425, which staged through on 10 January on its way from Beirut to Gibraltar. On 25 January USAF C-54D 42-72748 brought Maj. Gen. O'Keefe, the Commanding General of the US 17th Air Force, on a tour of inspection. Notwithstanding the end of the Suez emergency, the RAF continued to send detachments of bomber aircraft to Luqa under Exercise 'Goldflake',

USAF C-47B 44-77167 of MATS on a visit to Luqa. *[R. Robinson]*

US Navy R5D-3 Skymaster (C-54Q) 56549 undergoing some attention to an engine at Luqa; date unknown. *[J. Betts]*

Canberras of 12 Squadron from Binbrook and 15 and 44 Squadrons from Honington, with Valiants of 138 Squadron, Wittering and 148 Squadron, Marham, being very much in evidence during the first quarter of 1957. In April, Canberras of 9 Squadron at Binbrook and 35 Squadron at Upwood took their turn in 'Goldflake'.

May 1957 was another record month in terms of aircraft movements, the total being 3590. Two of them were Harpoons of the Portuguese Air Force, which by this time were rare aircraft indeed. A milestone was reached on 23 May, when the last aeromedical flight from the Far East by Hastings aircraft touched down at Luqa; thereafter Comets were to be used. The Swedish Air Force sent a Dakota (call-sign SAFTA) carrying its C-in-C from Nice to El Adem on 5 June.

One of Luqa's resident units, 37 Squadron, left on 21 August 1957, after nine years, taking its Shackletons to Aden/Khormaksar, where its services were needed on Red Sea area patrols. After the 'Shacks' had left, only 39 Squadron and the Malta Communications & Target Towing Squadron remained, and no doubt the characteristic growl of the contra-rotating Griffon engines was missed, although visiting Shackletons were still quite common.

A Battle of Britain display was held at Luqa in September 1957, and taking part were six Hunter F.6s from Odiham, five Canberras from 231 OCU at Bassingbourn and a Shackleton MR.3 from the A&AEE at Boscombe Down. At the end of the month, however, the main runway was closed for a week while resurfacing at an intersection took place, and aircraft not able to use the shorter runway migrated to other airfields meantime.

Luqa's visitors during the latter part of 1957 included a Royal Canadian Air Force C-118, 10000, on 18 October while on the way from the Azores to Basra in Iraq; Greek Air Force C-47 086 on 12 November flying to Naples; Conway-engined Vulcan VX770 from Rolls Royce at Hucknall for fair weather tests on 12 November; and three on 14 November — French Air Force SO.20 using call-sign FYAGC, from and to Bizerte; Italian Air Force Dakota I.1815 from and to Naples; and USAF C-54E 49099, also from and to Naples. Luqa was still a fine place for an aircraft enthusiast!

Canberra and Valiant detachments continued to use Luqa under Exercise 'Goldflake' during 1958, and Valettas on navigation exercises from

Standing in front of Transit Flight's buildings at Luqa is SA-16B Albatross 51-7163 of an air-sea rescue unit. *[R. Robinson]*

Vickers type 610 Viking VK.500 of the Arab Legion Air Force, seen at Luqa, was originally G-AJDK of BEA and then spent time with Eagle Airways before being sold to the Royal Jordanian Air Force.
[R. Robinson]

Topcliffe and Thorney Island began to put in appearances. On the debit side, the Malta Communications & Target Towing Squadron, long-term residents of Luqa, left on 25 February for the quieter pastures at Takali. A civilian airline involvement at Luqa was now growing rapidly, and one aircraft, Dan-Air's York G-AMUT came to grief on 20 May when it failed to stop after landing on runway 06, finally over-running and being badly damaged, but fortunately without casualties. Visitors on a typical May day were a SO.30P of the French Navy, using call-sign FYEBA and flying from and to Bone; C-121A 80615 of the USAF visiting from Paris/Orly; and a Greek Air Force C-

47 from Athens, SVVFB. A Scimitar prototype from Farnborough was flown to Luqa on 17 June by Lt. Cmdr. Robbins, who used call-sign MJURA.

39 Squadron, a Luqa resident for over three years, was disbanded on 30 June 1958 but was re-formed on the same day to take over the Canberras of 69 Squadron from Germany, so preserving continuity.

In August 1958 the month's aircraft movements totalled only 1404, about 40 per cent of the maximum reached some time before. But exotic visitors still arrived, and included an Indian Air Force Canberra, 973, on delivery on 13

Down in the weeds at the end of Luqa's runway 06 is Dan-Air's York G-AMUT. Wrinkling of the skin aft of the flight-deck windows is indicative of the damage - the aircraft was a write-off.
[Dan-Air Staff Association]

September; Greek Navy Dakota SVVRN from Athens on 21 September; Victor XA932 of 232 OCU, piloted by Wg. Cdr. D. Iveson on 14 October on a flight from Farnborough which took exactly two hours to cover the 1310 miles (2100km.); Convair I.1833, carrying the Italian Air Force C-in-C from Rome on 25 October; and a Lincoln using call-sign MFDAA from the Royal Air Force Flying College at Manby on 6 December.

1959 began fairly quietly at Luqa, Valiants and Canberras on 'Sunspot' detachments and Shackletons on 'Fair Isle' contributing to a total of 1781 movements during January. The activity then increased, building up to 2224 movements in May, including the arrival of eight Javelins of 85 Squadron, based at Stradishall, for Exercise 'Maltex'. More Javelins appeared in October, when 29 Squadron flew in from Leuchars in Scotland to take part in Exercise 'Sambar', involving interception of bombers over Malta. During December, two Canberra squadrons, 16 and 88, were attached from Germany, adding to the considerable work-load.

During 1959, no less than 2553 aircraft of 52 types were handled by the Luqa ground crews, apart from the based aircraft. Most common were Canberras, of which 583 were dealt with, and Hastings, of which 468 passed through Luqa. Beverleys accounted for another 370, and there were 251 Hunters. The remainder of the total was made up as follows: Varsities 88; Javelins 88; Comets 62; Valettas 61; Dakotas 61; Valiants 55; Shackletons 53; Expeditors 50; Devons 50; Shooting Stars 49; Meteors 48; Skymasters 25; Venoms 24; Lincolns 19; Bretagnes 16; Britannias 15; Vampires 12; Pembrokes 10; Whirlwinds 7; 8 each of 'Boxcars', Skyraiders, C-131s, and

Trackers; Harpoons 6; Neptunes 6; 4 each of L-23s, Bristol Freighters and Constellations; 3 each of Globemasters, Providers, Bird-Dogs and Otters; 2 each of Beaufighters, Gannets and Siebel 204s; and one each of Fokker S-14, Albatross, Sea Venom, Heron, Victor, Vulcan, Ambassador, Mariner, Avenger, Anson, SM.82, Ju.52 and L-16. The busiest single day was 12 November, when 28 visitors were handled. An interesting place indeed for an aviation enthusiast to be based!

The sixties: a period of routine.

Just as busy during 1960, the Station managed to stage a Battle of Britain display on 27 August featuring all units at Luqa plus the Hunters of 92 Squadron from Middleton St. George in the north of England. Included was Chipmunk WP987, a type rarely seen in Malta, which had been flown in in a Beverley for the event.

April 1961 saw the Trackers of 87 Gruppo of the Italian Air Force attached to Luqa from Sigonella for Exercise 'Medflex Invicta', a fleet support and anti-submarine exercise. During the period when Javelin night-fighters were being ferried to the Far East in June 1961, Valiant tankers operated from Luqa, and Javelins re-appeared in November for Exercise 'Maltadex', the annual defence exercise. Also taking part were 38 Squadron, the Valiants of 7 Squadron from Wittering, Canberras of 16 and 88 Squadrons from German bases and a French Navy Neptune squadron. Hard on the heels of this exercise came Exercise 'Solinus', for which 800 paratroops arrived in Britannias, while nine Hastings and five Beverleys brought in freight. The troops were then dropped from the Hastings and Beverleys on a DZ near El Adem.

A Whirlwind coded 977:C visiting Luqa from HMS *Centaur* in 1964.
[via R. C. Sturtivant]

Left: An RAF Beverley about to touch down at Luqa, while a USAF C-130 waits. Shackletons are parked in the background. *[J. Betts]*

Right: Visiting Luqa in 1970 was this Shackleton MR.2c, WL798, from 205 Squadron at Changi, Singapore. *[via R. C. Sturtivant]*

Above: XR724, a Lightning F.6 of 5 Squadron from Binbrook, almost ready for departure from Luqa. *[J. Betts]*

5 Squadron Lightning F.6 XR747 [P] from Binbrook about to take to the air from Luqa in the hands of Flt. Lt. D. Moss. Note the squadron's maple leaf emblem. *[Terry Brown via S. A. Scott]*

Runway 06/24 was extended yet again in 1961, to 7850ft. (2378m.). In addition, a new taxiway 60ft. (18m.) wide was built parallel to the runway, a new hardstanding was provided alongside the north taxiway and an apron in front of a new hangar. During the course of the contract a large cavern found under the site had to be filled in before work could proceed.

Little happened to disturb the routine at Luqa over the next few years, but civilian air traffic steadily increased. The Canberras of 13 Squadron moved in from Cyprus in September 1965, displacing the Shackletons of 38 Squadron, which moved to Hal Far when that airfield reverted to RAF 'ownership'.

By 1966 extensive areas of undulation had again developed in the oldest paved areas, and these and other sections had to be reinforced with varying thicknesses of asphalt. The work took a considerable time, not being completed until 1971, probably the last work carried out at Luqa under RAF stewardship apart from routine maintenance.

Following the departure of the Fleet Air Arm from Hal Far, FAA squadrons disembarked from ships to Luqa instead, and there was a steady procession of fixed-wing aircraft and helicopters between November 1968 and April 1977. Buccaneers of 800 Squadron were present in November 1968, followed by the Wessex

The first Blue Steel detachment of Vulcan bombers from Scampton at Luqa c.1970. *[P. Porter collection]*

Above: Luqa airfield from the air in 1973, showing work in progress on the passenger terminal.
[P. H. T. Green collection]
Below: The area between runways 14/32 and 06/24 seen from the air in 1975. The original north/south and east/west runways have completely disappeared. Four Canberras and an Argosy are seen on the apron.
[After The Battle magazine]

The concrete base of Luqa's wartime control tower as seen c.1975. A small control room made from timber and corrugated metal once graced the top of the structure. *[NWMA]*

helicopters of 845 Squadron in the following July. October 1969 saw quite a deluge: the Gannets of 849D Squadron, Sea Vixens of 899 Squadron and Buccaneer S.2s of 800 Squadron.

Shackletons returned to be based at Luqa in February 1969, when 203 Squadron moved in from Ballykelly. Later that year the Near East Communications Squadron arrived to provide a service for the area, but in September 1970 long-term resident 39 Squadron moved its Canberras back to the UK, its photographic reconnaissance facility being surplus to requirements.

A decline begins

More Gannets, this time from 849A Squadron, arrived at Luqa in February 1970 for a short attachment, with the Sea Vixens of 893 Squadron, Buccaneers of 801 Squadron and the Wessex helicopters of 814 Squadron. All left within about three weeks but, apart from the Wessexes, returned in April for a further short stay. More Buccaneers, this time from 809 Squadron, arrived in October 1970 and again in November. Then, in March 1971, the Buccaneers of 800 Squadron were back, in company with 826 Squadron's Sea Kings, 849D Squadron's Gannets and the Sea Vixens of 899

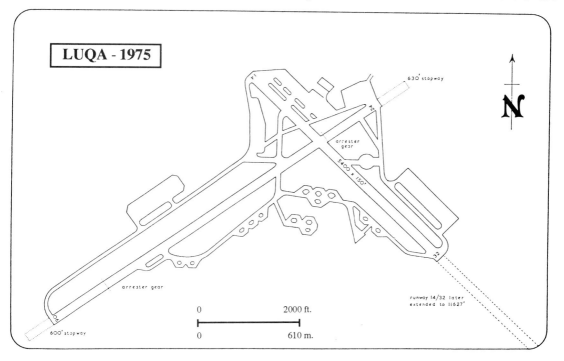

LUQA - 1975

Squadron. For Christmas 1971 the Wessexes of 820 Squadron were in temporary residence, returning the following May for a few days.

By January 1972 two resident squadrons remained at Luqa — 13 Squadron with Canberras and 203 Squadron, busy converting from Shackletons to Nimrods. It was at this time that political problems caused the RAF to begin evacuating its personnel, and 13 Squadron left for Cyprus and 203 Squadron for Sigonella in Sicily, leaving Luqa devoid of based units for the first time since 1945. The signing of an agreement two months later, however, enabled the two squadrons to return, the Nimrods in April and the Canberras in October.

Fleet Air Arm units did not stay away for long; the 809 Squadron Buccaneers were back in February/March 1973 with 824 Squadron's Sea Kings, 849B Squadron's Gannets and 892 Squadron's Phantoms. In April and May 1974 814 and 845 Squadrons' helicopters were once more in evidence, followed by the Sea Kings of 820 Squadron in June and 809 Squadron's Buccaneers in October. This was probably the last Fleet Air Arm detachment of fixed-wing aircraft to Malta.

The pattern of life at Luqa resumed, though with the inevitability of a withdrawal and handover to the Maltese Government always in the minds of those concerned. Military aircraft still visited on navigation exercises and for refuelling while on the way to or from points east. It was while attempting to land at Luqa on 14 October 1975 that Vulcan B.2 XM645 of the Waddington Wing exploded on an overshoot and crashed at Zabbar.

There seems to have been a gap between the departure of the 809 Squadron Buccaneers in October 1974 and the next, and probably the last, appearance of the Fleet Air Arm. That was in May 1977, when the Sea Kings of 814 Squadron were present for two weeks from HMS Hermes, bringing to an end, when they left, almost sixty years of marine aircraft operation from the island of Malta.

The end of the RAF presence at Luqa, and in Malta, was gradually approaching, and 203 Squadron disbanded at the end of 1977, leaving 13 Squadron's Canberras the sole residents. After a series of celebrations in 1978 (see Chapter 1), 13 Squadron left for Wyton in October 1978 and a long period of withdrawal began, culminating in the official closure of RAF Luqa on 31 March 1979.

This was, however, not the end of military flying at Luqa, for the Helicopter Flight of the Armed Forces of Malta moved into the former 13 Squadron premises in March 1979. Fourteen years later, the unit, renamed Task Force in April 1980 and Air Squadron, Armed Forces of Malta, in July 1992, continues to operate its small fleet of aircraft from Luqa.

Flying Units at Luqa

Summary						
Unit	**From**	**Date in**	**To**		**Date out**	**Aircraft Types**
431 (GR) Flt.	(formed)	19.9.40	(became 69 Sqdn.)		10.1.41	Maryland I; Blenheim; Skua
Malta Well. Flt.	Marham/Mildenhall	10.40	(became 148 Sqdn.)		1.12.40	Wellington
37 Sqdn. det.	Feltwell	9.11.40	Fayid		21.11.40	Wellington Ic
148 Sqdn.	(formed)	1.12.40	Kabrit		15.3.41	Wellington Ic
69 Sqdn.	(formed ex 431 Flt.)	10.1.41	Takali		31.10.41	Maryland I; Beaufort; Hurricane IIa
78 Sqdn. det.	Dishforth	8.2.41	Dishforth		16.2.41	Whitley V
139 Sqdn. det.	Horsham St. Faith	5.41	Horsham St. Faith		6.41	Blenheim IV
252 Sqdn. det.	Aldergrove	2.5.41	Aldergrove		21.5.41	Beaufighter I
110 Sqdn. det.	Wattisham	1.7.41	Wattisham		15.8.41	Blenheim IV
105 Sqdn. det.	Swanton Morley	28.7.41	Swanton Morley		9.41	Blenheim IV
38 Sqdn. det.	Shallufa	6.8.41	Shallufa		26.10.41	Wellington Ic
107 Sqdn. det.	Great Massingham	20.8.41	(disbanded)		12.1.42	Blenheim IV
113 Sqdn. det.	Bagush	23.9.41	Bagush		30.9.41	Blenheim
104 Sqdn. det.	Driffield	18.10.41	Kabrit		2.1.42	Wellington II
18 Sqdn. det.	Horsham St. Faith	10.41	Helwan		1.42	Blenheim IV
40 Sqdn.	Alconbury	31.10.41	Abu Sueir		5.42	Wellington Ic
69 Sqdn.	Takali	29.11.41	Montecorvino		7.2.44	Maryland I; Spitfire; Beaufort; Wellington Ic, VIII
21 Sqdn.	Watton	26.12.41	(disbanded)		14.3.42	Blenheim IV
2 PRU det.	Heliopolis	29.12.41	Heliopolis		4.42	Beaufighter
221 Sqdn. det.	LG.39	8.1.42	(into 69 Sqdn.)		26.8.42	Wellington VIII
126 Sqdn.	Takali	1.5.42	Safi		7.6.43	Spitfire Vc
217 Sqdn. det.	Leuchars	10.6.42	(absorbed by 39 Squadron)		20.8.42	Beaufort II
39 Sqdn. det.	LG.86	22.6.42	(re-formed as full squadron)		20.8.42	Beaufort I
1435 Flt./Sqdn.	(re-formed)	7.42	Safi		10.6.43	Spitfire Vb, Vc
227 Sqdn.	(formed)	20.8.42	Takali		25.11.42	Beaufighter VI
39 Sqdn.	(re-formed)	20.8.42	Shallufa		9.12.42	Beaufort I
113 Sqdn. det.	Bilbeis	9.42	Benina		3.9.43	Wellington
104 Sqdn. det.	Kabrit	6.11.42	LG.237		21.1.43	Wellington II (note A)
40 Sqdn.	LG.104	26.11.42	LG.237		20.1.43	Wellington III (note A)
148 Sqdn.	LG.167	7.12.42	(disbanded)		14.12.42	Wellington Ic
23 Sqdn.	Bradwell Bay	27.12.42	Alghero		7.12.43	Mosquito II, VI
458 Sqdn. RCAF	Shallufa	7.1.43	Protville		22.5.43	Wellington
39 Sqdn.	Shallufa	21.1.43	Protville 2		1.6.43	Beaufort I
221 Sqdn.	Shallufa	22.1.43	Grottaglie		28.2.44	Wellington XI
683 Sqdn.	(formed)	8.2.43	El Aouina (Tunis)		20.11.43	Spitfire IV, IX; Mosquito IV
3rd PR&MG, USAAF	Algiers	3.43	La Marsa		c.20.6.43	F-4; F-5
108 Sqdn.	Bersis	3.6.43	Hal Far		1.7.44	Beaufighter; Mosquito VI
272 Sqdn.	Takali	4.6.43	Borizzo		11.9.43	Beaufighter
92 Sqdn.	Ben Gardane	7.6.43	Pachino		13.7.43	Spitfire Vb, Vc, IX (note B)
145 Sqdn.	Ben Gardane	7.6.43	Pachino		13.7.43	Spitfire Va, Vb, IX (note B)
601 Sqdn.	Ben Gardane	7.6.43	Pachino		14.7.43	Spitfire Vb, Vc (note B)
1 Sqdn. SAAF	Ben Gardane	7.6.43	Pachino		13.7.43	Spitfire (note B)
417 Sqdn. RCAF	Ben Gardane	7.6.43	Cassibile		16.7.43	Spitfire (note B)
40 Sqdn. SAAF	Ben Gardane N.	23.6.43	Pachino		15.7.43	Spitfire
600 Sqdn.	Setif	25.6.43	Cassibile		26.7.43	Beaufighter VI
256 Sqdn. det.	Ford	5.7.43	La Senia		7.4.44	Mosquito XII
73 Sqdn. det.	La Sebala 2	8.7.43	La Sebala 2		13.7.43	Hurricane IIc
250 Sqdn.	Hal Far	14.7.43	Pachino		18.7.43	Kittyhawk III (note C)
260 Sqdn.	Zuara	14.7.43	Pachino		18.7.43	Kittyhawk III (note C)
3 Sqdn. RAAF	Takali	14.7.43	Pachino		18.7.43	Kittyhawk (note C)
450 Sqdn. RAAF	Zuara	14.7.43	Pachino		18.7.43	Kittyhawk (note C)
1437 (SR) Flt.		16.7.43	Lentini		31.7.43	Mustang
223 Sqdn.	Reyville	20.7.43	Monte Lungo		10.8.43	Baltimore III, IV (note D)
55 Sqd. det.	Reyville	20.7.43	Monte Lungo		10.8.43	Baltimore IIIa, IV (note D)
219 Sqdn. det.	Bone	30.7.43	La Sebala 2		27.8.43	Beaufighter VI
38 Sqdn.	Falconara	11.7.45	Hal Far		30.10.65	Wellington XIV; Warwick I; Lancaster III; Shackleton
728 Sqdn.	Takali	1.1.46	Hal Far		5.5.46	(various)
AHQ Malta CF	Hal Far	4.1.46	(became Malta Comm. & TT Sqn.)		6.54	(various)

MILITARY AVIATION IN MALTA G.C. 1915-1993

Unit	From	Date in	To	Date out	Aircraft Types
1357(PAMPA) Flt.	(formed)	1.2.46	(disbanded)	10.4.46	(none received)
37 Sqdn.	Ein Shemer	1.4.48	Khormaksar	21.8.57	Lancaster MR.3; Shackleton MR.2
185 Sqdn.	Hal Far	23.7.52	Idris	14.8.52	Vampire FB.5
Malta Comm. & TT Sqdn.	(ex AHQ Malta CF)	6.54	Takali	25.2.58	Dakota; Valetta
39 Sqdn.	Kabrit	10.1.55	(disbanded)	30.6.58	Meteor NF.13
Valiant Wing	Marham/Wittering	24.9.56	Marham/Wittering	17.11.56	Valiant B.1
39 Sqdn.	(re-formed)	1.7.58	Wyton	30.9.70	Canberra PR.3, PR.9
13 Sqdn.	Akrotiri	1.9.65	Akrotiri	6.1.72	Canberra PR.9
203 Sqdn. MR.1	Ballykelly	1.2.69	Sigonella	12.1.72	Shackleton MR.3; Nimrod
NECS		9.69			Valetta; Pembroke; Argosy
203 Sqdn.	Sigonella	23.4.72	(disbanded)	31.12.77	Nimrod MR.1
13 Sqdn. Station Flight	Akrotiri	10.10.72	Wyton	3.10.78	Canberra PR.9

Note A: these squadrons comprised part of 238 Wing.   Note B: these squadrons comprised 244 Wing

Note C: these squadrons comprised 239 Wing.   Note D: these squadrons comprised part of 232 Wing

431 (General Reconnaissance) Flight

At North Coates on the coast of Lincolnshire, eastern England, 'C' Flight of 22 Squadron received three Martin Maryland aircraft in August 1940 with orders to train three crews for service in Malta. The training was completed with some difficulty, and the aircraft were flown out to Malta via Thorney Island and across occupied Europe, arriving on 6 September at Luqa. There, on 19 September 1940, 431(GR) Flight was formed with the three Marylands and crews, absorbing the personnel of 3 AACU, which disbanded at Hal Far the same day.

With the three Marylands and a Blackburn Skua (L2911) which had been appropriated after escorting six Hurricanes to Malta from HMS *Argus,* 431 Flight began its task of photographic reconnaissance over Sicily, Libya (Tripoli in particular), Corfu and Albania. 431 Flight, in spite of a shortage of experienced navigators and trained ground crews, was able to produce vital photographs of all the major harbours and airfields in these areas for the use of both the Navy and the army. One of the Marylands, AR712, crashed on landing on 26 September and the following day was hit by an incendiary bomb, thus becoming a complete write-off. In October, however, two Blenheims, T2115 and T2164, were impressed for 431 Flight's use while they were on their way to Egypt, thus adding to the Flight's capabilities. They left early in November, but another Skua, L2882, arrived. The two Skuas stayed with 431 Flight until December 1940, when they were taken on board an aircraft carrier by their 'real' owner, the Fleet Air Arm.

During October 1940 the Navy showed great interest in the activities of the Italian fleet, which seemed to be concentrating at Taranto. On 10 October, Maryland AR705 made a reconnaissance of the harbour there and reported the presence of five battleships, two cruisers and two submarines, with more naval vessels at Brindisi. Further sorties to Taranto followed, and on 2 November the 431 Flight Maryland was attacked by three CR.42 fighters and a Cant Z.506 floatplane, which the Maryland crew succeeded in shooting down with their aircraft's four forward-firing machine guns. Another Italian aircraft, a Macchi C.200, shot down by 431 Flight on 7 November, was one of four which attacked the Maryland while it was operating again over Taranto. The Italian fleet was still building up there, as discovered by a 431 Flight sortie on 10 November which found five battleships, fourteen cruisers and twenty-seven destroyers. That night, HMS *Illustrious* launched its torpedo-carrying Swordfish aircraft against this large fleet, and an immediate damage-assessment sortie flown by 431 Flight revealed that several of the large Italian vessels had been sunk and others severely damaged. Much of the success of the historic Taranto raid went, rightly, to the efficient photo-reconnaissance work carried out by 431 Flight, whose aircraft carried, at Admiral Cunningham's insistence, Navy observers.

The versatility of the Maryland was again demonstrated on 24 December 1940, when one of 431 Flight's aircraft shot down a three-engined SM.79 bomber of the Regia Aeronautica (Italian Air Force). By now, however, the Flight had to contend with the Luftwaffe, which was building up its strength in Sicily, where its airfields were being closely watched by the ubiquitous Marylands. A few more aircraft had now arrived at Luqa, and the decision was taken to give the Flight squadron status, although, as was remarked at the time, this expansion was in name only and was not going to mean the provision of any more aircraft or spare parts. But, on 10 January 1941, 431 (GR) Flight became 69 Squadron in readiness for much greater activity once the supply position improved.

Malta Wellington Flight

In October 1940, twelve crews drawn from 75 and 149 Squadrons at Mildenhall and 38 and 115 Squadrons at Marham were detailed at very short notice to fly their Wellington aircraft to Malta, from where they were to attack a 'special' target. A return to the UK, it was implied, would be made after about ten days. The necessary airmen for servicing the aircraft left at once by sea and arrived in Malta after a week.

As soon as they arrived at Luqa after a long flight over enemy-occupied France, the aircrews were ordered to raid oil tanks in Naples harbour. Being the first bomber element on the island, the ad-hoc unit was obliged to make use of any and every person, whatever service they were in, to load, arm and refuel the Wellingtons, but the mission was a great success and a repeat was planned for the following night. Only three of the aircraft took off safely next time, however, the fourth one crashing near Rabat and the fifth in a quarry soon after take-off.

The unit did not return to England as intimated, as its services were too valuable to lose. Instead, raids were made on targets in Sicily, southern Italy and Yugoslavia and the Flight took part in the successful attack on the Italian fleet in Taranto harbour by dropping flares.

A raid on a large number of Italian Air Force aircraft at Castel Benito in Libya was then mounted, and a PR reconnaissance next day indicated that over 100 of the enemy aircraft had been destroyed or damaged. Night raids on Naples continued, and attacks on concentrations of Ju.87 Stukas on Sicilian airfields were also made, with some losses to the Flight.

In order to regularise the situation, the Malta Wellington Flight was given new status as 148 Squadron on 1 December 1940.

37 Squadron detachment

Following a period of involvement in night operations against European targets, 37 Squadron, equipped with Wellingtons, was detailed to move from its UK base at Feltwell in Norfolk to Fayid in Egypt. Six aircraft left on 8 November 1940 but one turned back. The others, fitted with extra fuel tanks, landed at Luqa during a raid soon after dawn next day after a nine-hour flight.

The crews were instructed to rest and then to refuel the aircraft before continuing the journey to Fayid, but on returning to their aircraft found that the fuel tanks had been removed and bombs loaded. The AOC Malta had decreed that any suitable aircraft passing through Malta was to be used for two operations from the island, regardless of how urgently its services were required elsewhere. In the event, the first such operation by 37 Squadron was abandoned, but on 13 November, an hour or so after the Fleet Air Arm had carried out their attack on Taranto harbour, the 37 Squadron aircraft were able to stir things up again with some 250lb. (110kg.) bombs. While the five crews were away on this mission, another seven aircraft, one flown by the CO, had arrived. He was most surprised to find the 37 Squadron presence still at Luqa!

Eventually, on 21 November, 37 Squadron was allowed to continue its interrupted journey to Egypt.

148 Squadron

After three previous existences, 148 Squadron was re-formed at Luqa on 1 December 1940 from the somewhat nebulous Malta Wellington Flight. On the day after reorganisation air tests were flown and a briefing was held for a raid on an oil refinery and railway yard at Naples. The outcome of this raid was uncertain due to poor weather, but three aircraft were able to bomb through gaps in the cloud, starting fires, while a fourth attacked an airfield at Catania in Sicily instead, claiming one aircraft destroyed on the ground.

148 Squadron's first notable success came on 7 December during a raid on Castel Benito airfield in Libya by six aircraft. Although two of the Wellingtons were badly damaged, two hangars on the airfield were made unusable and an administrative building and a fuel dump were also hit. Next came a raid on Valona in Albania on 13 December by four aircraft, but ten-tenths cloud

Three 148 Squadron
Wellingtons at Luqa,
the nearest being
T2746 [U]. Also seen
is a Blenheim of 21
Squadron, coded
YH:N.
[FAA Museum]

forced three to return with their bomb-loads.

Following a raid by nine of 148 Squadron's aircraft on naval vessels in Naples harbour on 14 December came a message from the AOC — *"You have been born and also reached years of discretion at the same time. Your prenatal activities indicate a healthy child. Good luck to you all and may 148 Squadron and its association with Malta prove of ever-increasing benefit to the Empire"*. These words of encouragement were taken to heart, as two more raids on Castel Benito were made before Christmas. On 20 December nine aircraft attacked with great effect, hitting nineteen enemy aircraft, of which five were destroyed by fire, and severely damaging buildings. Two days later, only two of ten Wellingtons found Castel Benito, which was obscured by a sandstorm, so the others bombed the secondary target, Tripoli. where the power station and customs house were hit.

After a brief respite at Christmas, further raids were mounted against Naples and Taranto and, early in January 1941, three raids on Tripoli by all ten of the squadron's Wellingtons. Widening its scope a little, 148 Squadron then attacked Messina harbour, where a battle cruiser was hit, and, on 12 January, Catania airfield. On this raid, one Wellington crashed into the sea alongside a trawler, HMS *Jade*, and another failed to return to base. Ten enemy aircraft were claimed as destroyed on the ground and others damaged, while the HQ building and a hangar were also destroyed. Three days later the good work was carried on, another ten aircraft at Catania being claimed as destroyed and a further hangar

damaged. Still more raids on this vital target were made before January was out, and the AOC once again signalled his congratulations.

During February 1941 raids on Castel Benito and Tripoli continued, notwithstanding the Luftwaffe's intense attack on Malta which had begun on 17 January. Three replacement Wellingtons arrived from the UK on 5 February, but one overshot on landing. To give the hard-pressed crews a rest, five aircraft took off for Heliopolis and two for Ismailia in Egypt, these two not being due to return as their crews had been posted.

Meanwhile, 148 Squadron Wellingtons carried on with raids on Catania, Tripoli and Comiso under ever-increasing difficulties caused by the German attacks on Malta. A particularly heavy raid on 25 February reduced the number of serviceable Wellingtons on 148 Squadron to two, six having been destroyed by fire, another one struck off charge and four needing several weeks' work to make them fit for further service.

On 13 March 1941 148 Squadron received a signal ordering an immediate move to Egypt, although some personnel were to be left behind as a detachment for refuelling and rearming the squadron's aircraft which would use Luqa as an advanced landing ground. Two days later the Wellingtons were ferried to their new base at Kabrit, and on 23 March 79 airmen left for Alexandria aboard HMS *Bonaventure*. At 16.00 that day Ju.87s and 88s dive-bombed the ship, without causing any casualties, and thirteen of them were shot down by 261 Squadron Hurricanes from Hal Far. The ship arrived safely at Alexandria on 25 March.

148 Squadron returned to Luqa from LG.167 on 7 December 1942 to be disbanded on 14 December.

69 SQUADRON

Brought up to squadron status from 431 (GR) Flight on 10 January 1941, 69 Squadron's official allotment was set at twelve Maryland and ten Beaufort aircraft. In fact on this date there were no Beauforts at all and only five Marylands, one of which was shot down the following day by Italian fighters while over Taranto. Nevertheless, the squadron pressed on with its vital task of photographing as many enemy installations as possible. Of five replacement Marylands which arrived in February and March, one was lost on 7 March when it was shot down by enemy fighters over Malta, to crash one and a half miles north of the village of Dingli. On the same day, another aircraft, short of fuel on yet another trip to Taranto, was obliged to make a forced landing at Medini in Greece.

In April a Hurricane arrived for the squadron for short photographic sorties, with another for training purposes. Two more Marylands were lost that month, one of them crash-landing after being set upon by the trigger-happy pilot of a Hurricane, but in May three more replacement aircraft arrived. Another one, belonging to the Free French Air Force, arrived at Luqa from Gibraltar on 8 June, and had a similar aircraft not crashed there it too would have been added to 69 Squadron's fleet.

The expertise of 69 Squadron was again required for a special mission on 20 June 1941, when the task was to photograph the entire 250-mile (400km.) coastal road from Benghazi to Tripoli, along which enemy supplies to the front line were moved. Although it was considered likely that this job would require several sorties it was in fact completed in one by the squadron's most expert pilot, Fg. Off. Adrian Warburton DFC, who took hundreds of shots which were later joined to provide a lengthy picture of the whole area. During the same sortie, time was even found to check an airfield near Misurata, where' Warby' shot up and destroyed three SM.79s.

69 Squadron's original CO, Sqdn. Ldr. E. O. 'Tich' Whiteley, left on 4 June 1941 and was succeeded by Sqdn. Ldr. R. D. Welland. He, however, was promoted to Wg. Cdr. on 28 July and handed over to Sqdn. Ldr. E. Tennant. Shortage of Marylands was still a problem, although two more had arrived early in June, with a further Hurricane, fitted with long-range tanks for PR work. But by the end of August only one Maryland was operational, with two long-range Hurricanes.

The first two long-awaited Bristol Beauforts arrived on 19 August for shipping patrols, although they were only on loan from 39 Squadron, which claimed them back on 1 October. Yet another CO, Wg. Cdr. J. H. Dowland, took over on 21 September, and within days the famed Adrian Warburton and his crew destroyed two more enemy aircraft — a Cant Z.506 and a Macchi 200. During October six more Marylands arrived, and at the end of that month the squadron moved to Takali. Its stay there was very short, however, airfield conditions making operations impossible, and a return to Luqa was made on 29 November 1941. The squadron's strength was now eleven Marylands, of which seven were serviceable, and two Hurricanes, one of them the training aircraft. By the end of December, however, the situation had worsened, only three Marylands being operational. Due to this shortfall, two Beaufighters of 2 Photographic Reconnaissance Unit were sent from Heliopolis in Egypt as an attachment to 69 Squadron. Replacement Marylands even included two South African Air Force aircraft, 1624 and 1639.

Maryland I AR735 of 69 Squadron belly-landed at Luqa on 14 April 1941 after being attacked by a Hurricane!
[K. Chinn]

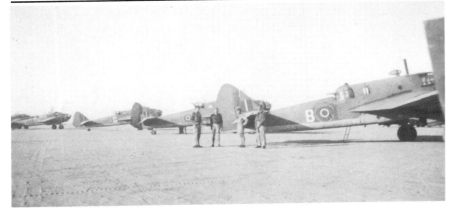

A line-up pf 69
Squadron Beauforts
at Luqa in 1942
[via R. C. Sturtivant]

January 1942 was not a happy month for 69 Squadron. On 13 January the CO was shot down in Maryland AR721 while returning from a patrol, his aircraft crashing into the sea off Tigne Point. One of his two attackers, Bf.109s, was then dealt with over the island. To replace Wg. Cdr. Dowland, Sqdn. Ldr. Tennant returned as a Wg. Cdr. Then, on 15 January, Flt. Lt. E. J. Williams DFC taxied SAAF Maryland 1624 into a stack of bombs on the airfield, killing himself and a number of ground-crew. At the end of a nasty month, on 28 January Hurricane Z3123 failed to return from a PR sortie over Italy, but it was later learned that the pilot had been taken prisoner. At this point, fourteen Marylands were on 69 Squadron strength, but only four were serviceable and another four were about to be struck off charge.

The situation did not improve during February 1942, and in March flying hours were very low due to losses and unserviceability. That month, however, a radical change of equipment for the squadron began, with the arrival of the first Spitfire. By the end of April the last Maryland, the type which had served 69 Squadron and its precursor, 431 Flight, well, had been withdrawn.

During May 1942 Plt. Off. Foster took over as CO of a much depleted squadron. In mid-June the first six Baltimore aircraft arrived, but one was almost at once destroyed on the ground when a Beaufort parked nearby caught fire and its torpedoes exploded. At the end of the month the squadron strength is recorded as three Baltimores and three Spitfires. More aircraft arrived in July, and in August it was possible to split the squadron into three Flights: 'A' Flight comprising the Baltimores; 'B' Flight the PR Spitfires; and 'C'

The badge, not officially approved, of 69 Squadron. Note the signatures of many of the unit's members underneath!
[G. E Carter via A. Thomas]

Wellingtonic T2818
of 69 Squadron's
Wellington Flight
[via R. C. Sturtivant]

Flight, a special duties flight equipped with Wellingtons Mk.VIII carrying ASV radar.

69 Squadron was taken over by Adrian Warburton, now a Squadron Leader, as CO in the middle of August 1942, and on 26 August a detachment of 221 Squadron was absorbed. On 25 August the first mission by the squadron's Wellingtons was mounted, with the intention of setting fire to a tanker stranded off Corfu. The CO began a series of what were euphemistically termed 'special flights' on 21 September, a low-level appraisal of the southern coast of Sicily, claiming a Do.24 flying boat as 'damaged' on the way. By November the ASV-equipped Wellingtons, bristling with aerials, had become known as 'Goofingtons', while those carrying torpedoes were called 'Fishingtons'.

In October 1942 Sqdn. Ldr. Warburton, known to one and all as 'Warby' and highly respected by everybody except perhaps the 'top brass', who did not always relish his unconventional methods, received a second Bar to his DFC. By now, photo-reconnaissance missions were being flown over Tunisia to prepare for the forthcoming invasion of North Africa, which took place successfully on 7 November. A week later, on 15 November, 'Warby' was shot down over Cape Bon by a Bf.109, and Capt. Clark, SAAF, was made temporary CO. 'Warby', however, had crash-landed without injury on Allied-held territory, and two days later obtained a ride on a Halifax to Gibraltar. There, after being arrested as a suspected spy, he found a Spitfire which he flew via Algiers and Bone to Malta. On the way, near the point where he had been shot down, he destroyed a Ju.88, thus avenging himself. He was then promoted to Wing Commander, and took up his work as though nothing had happened.

January 1943 was a month of heavy casualties for 69 Squadron, as two Spitfires, two Baltimores and a Wellington failed to return from operations. In February major reconstitution of the squadron took place. 'C' Flight, the special duty Wellington element, was transferred to 458 Squadron on 1 February and on 6 February 683 Squadron was formed from 'B' Flight, the Spitfire-equipped section, and Wg. Cdr. Warburton left with the Spitfires. This left only the Baltimores, which were replaced by more up to date Mk.IV aircraft over the next few months. By 31 July twelve were on

69 Squadron crews pose for a photograph in 1942. [G. E. Carter via A. Thomas]

Blenheim IV V5872
[XD:V] of 139
Squadron seen over
Malta during the
Squadron's
detachment to the
island in May 1941
[W. Hepworth]

strength, and the squadron's PR work continued in the less frantic atmosphere which now pertained.

By the early days of February 1944 69 Squadron found that it was too far from the action, and a move was therefore made to Montecorvo in Italy. Dakotas carried the squadron's stores and ground equipment from Malta to the new base, and the five Baltimores Mk.IV and five Mk.V flew to their new home on 7 February 1944 at the end of a most significant period in the squadron's life.

78 Squadron detachment

After modification at the Parachute Training School at Ringway, just outside Manchester, eight Whitleys of 78 Squadron, based at Dishforth, left via Mildenhall on the long journey to Luqa, where they landed on 8 February 1941. Their task was to be to mount Operation 'Colossus', the first active service by Allied paratroops, and the aircraft also carried stores containers and were fitted with long-range tanks.

Watched by the AOC Malta, the eight aircraft, six containing troops and two to act as a diversion, took off on the night of 10 February for the Pugliese aquaduct at Tragino in southern Italy. Having dropped the troops, mostly close to the target, all but one aircraft, T4167 [EY:S], returned from the mission at 02.00 next morning. The troops were less lucky, as they were captured some miles from the coast, where they were to be picked up by submarine. The seven surviving Whitleys left for home on 16 February.

139 Squadron detachment

Based at Horsham St. Faith in Norfolk, seven Blenheims of 139 Squadron took off on 11 May 1941 for Luqa via the staging post of St. Eval in Cornwall. No record of their activities in Malta, if any, exists, however. The detachment began the homeward journey after a few weeks on the island, arriving in England on 11 June 1941.

252 Squadron detachment

The first Bristol Beaufighters to operate from Malta were those of 252 Squadron, which was detached to Luqa from Aldergrove in Northern Ireland in May 1941. Fifteen aircraft left the staging post at St. Eval on 1 May bound for Gibraltar, although one aircraft, T3243, returned with engine trouble. Another aircraft, T3229, became lost and landed at Lisbon in Portugal, where the crew was interned. By 6 May these two aircraft had been replaced by others and all 15 had arrived at Luqa. For the next two and a half weeks they took part in shipping patrols, operated over Allied convoys, strafed enemy airfields in Sicily

Beaufighter T3317 of
252 Squadron
carrying a ? as a
code sits on a Luqa
dispersal.
[J. Arthur Heath]

and raided targets in Greece from forward airfields in Crete. During the period of attachment to Luqa, four Beaufighters were destroyed on the ground and three were lost in combat, one of them in Greece.

Of the remaining aircraft, four were sent to Egypt for further detachment and the other four left Luqa on 21 May for Gibraltar and home. Only two reached Aldergrove, however, one crashing in Mounts Bay, Cornwall and another one (T3235) in the Irish Republic.

110 Squadron detachment

Based at Wattisham in Suffolk, seventeen of 110 Squadron's Blenheims set course on 29 June 1941 for Luqa, where they arrived on 1 July. A week later, seven of them raided Tripoli harbour, destroying a warehouse and hitting three large ships, but from this mission only three Blenheims returned, a heavy toll indeed. On 13 July, a convoy off Tripoli was attacked by six aircraft of 110 Squadron quite successfully, as a three-masted schooner, apparently carrying ammunition, was hit and exploded, and a tanker was set on fire.

Next, on 14 July, came a raid by two aircraft on a Libyan coastal airfield, where a Ju.52 was destroyed. At the same time, three of the Blenheims attacked traffic on the Benghazi road and strafed a barracks.

Further attacks on shipping followed on 17 and 22 July, when two of five escorted merchant vessels were destroyed and another damaged. Tripoli power station was raided on 20 July, but on the way home the aircraft piloted by the CO, Wg. Cdr. Hunt, was hit by fire from an Italian fighter and crashed into the sea. The final major attack by the 110 Squadron Blenheims was on 23 July, when three of them strafed merchant ships in Trapani harbour, Sicily. On this occasion two ships were destroyed, but in doing so the formation leader's aircraft skimmed the water and although it was able to carry on it eventually crash-landed, the crew being captured. One of the three aircraft also raided an airfield on which torpedo-carrying aircraft were dispersed.

Little is recorded of activities between 28 July and the detachment's return to its home base on 15 August 1941, but those taking part had certainly added their contribution to the offensive effort being made at the time.

105 Squadron detachment

Twelve Blenheims of 105 Squadron left their base at Swanton Morley in Norfolk on 25 July 1941 and ten arrived safely at Luqa three days later via Gibraltar, one being delayed there and one having landed in Portugal in error.

The detachment got down to business without delay, mounting a raid by six aircraft on 31 July on a convoy fifty miles from Pantellaria, but on finding four CR.42 fighters covering the convoy the Blenheims returned to Luqa. An attempt was

On detatchment at Luqa in July 1941, 110 Squadron's Blenheims sometimes suffered air raid damage, as did this example coded VE:X.
[via Tony Spooner]

Blemheim IV V6014
[GB:J] of 105
Squadron in
dispersal at Luqa.
[IWM]

made next day to locate a convoy of four merchant vessels and five destroyers, but without success. Later that day Lampedusa harbour was raided by three aircraft, two of which scored hits, while one jettisoned its bomb-load. One of the three was shot down and crashed into the harbour.

Then came attacks on barracks in Libya and ships in Tripoli harbour, with some success, a direct hit on a 12000-ton merchant ship causing a huge explosion. Shipping at sea was also attacked, but the squadron decided not to molest such a convoy on 6 August when seeing that it was protected by three CR.42s. Similarly, a raid on Catania harbour by five aircraft on 8 August was called off when thirty of the Italian fighters were sighted, discretion being the better part of valour. Later in the month, raids on shipping were again successful, as were attacks on power stations and chemical works in Sicily.

September 1941 saw a continuation of sorties against enemy shipping until the detachment returned to its UK base at the end of the month.

38 Squadron detachment

On 5 August 1941 nine of 38 Squadron's Wellingtons, then based at Shallufa in Egypt, were ordered to proceed as a detachment to Luqa, where they arrived before dawn next day. Two days later, six of the aircraft mounted a very successful two-hour raid on Tripoli, and followed it that night with another attack on that city, using GP, incendiary and anti-personnel bombs to good effect. The large fire caused by the 38 Squadron aircraft could be seen forty miles (64km.) away, but this was nothing compared with the results of the raid on Tripoli power station on 11 August by all nine aircraft, each carrying six 500lb. (225kg.) bombs.

For several days the Wellingtons raided targets in Tripoli, then switched their attention to Catania harbour in Sicily, where considerable damage was done. Then came two more weeks of raids on Tripoli before docks, shipping and ferry terminals at Palermo and Messina, where another large fire was started, became 38 Squadron's targets during September. At the end of that month the squadron cooperated with 830 Squadron, FAA, whose Swordfish were busy laying mines in Tripoli harbour, and early in October worked with the Wellingtons of 69 Squadron in a number of attacks on convoys.

Naples was the target on the night of 16/17 October for 38 Squadron's Wellingtons, now

A Wellington Ic of 38
Squadron airborne
over the
Mediterranean early
in 1942.
[via A. Thomas]

sixteen in number. In raiding a torpedo factory, an aircraft factory and the Royal Arsenal, 36000lbs. (16360kg.) of bombs were dropped, including three of 4000lbs. (1800kg.). Another raid on Naples on the night of 21/22 October by eleven aircraft with thirteen of 104 Squadron caused great damage over a five-and-a-half hour period.

Its task complete, the 38 Squadron detachment returned to Shallufa on 25/26 October 1941.

107 Squadron detachment

To help in the campaign of attacks on targets in Libya and Sicily then being mounted from airfields in Malta, part of 107 Squadron, based at Great Massingham in Norfolk, flew out via Portreath and Gibraltar between 17 and 20 August 1941. Nothing is recorded of the squadron's first three weeks at Luqa, but by 15 September the detachment's Blenheims were hard at work. On 17 September the target for five aircraft was Licata, where 5000lbs. (2275kg.) of bombs were dropped from an altitude of fifty feet (fifteen metres). Two days later ships in Tripoli harbour were attacked, and on 2 September barracks and supply dumps at Misurata were bombed by five Blenheims. Transport on the road from Misurata to Benghazi was attacked on 24 September, one of the two 107 Squadron aircraft being lost that day. This target was visited again the following day, while on 26 September three aircraft went on a shipping sweep and also had another go at Libyan roads, successfully encouraging a petrol tanker to blow up. Six Blenheims made yet another assault on motor vehicles near Tripoli, causing very large explosions there and at a W/T station and barracks. For the time being, the final attack on roads in Libya was made on 30 September, when four aircraft which had not found anything to deal with on a shipping sweep diverted inland and caused damage to a petrol station and two busloads of Italian troops.

Then back to Sicily. Eight aircraft made a surprise attack on Marina de Catanzara on 3 October, during which warehouses and factories were bombed from low level against little opposition. Next day a 6000-ton (6110-tonne) motor vessel off Tripoli was the appointed target, but being unable to locate the ship, the 107 Squadron Blenheims attacked Zuara under intense AA fire. On the way back to Luqa a CR.42 of the

Italian Air Force made persistent attacks, and Sgt. Hamlin's aircraft was forced down into the sea. The crew managed to scramble into a dinghy and eventually rejoined the Squadron.

One Blenheim, searching at night for enemy shipping to deal with, found a motor vessel and attacked. Before returning to base, the 107 Squadron crew noted that the ship's stern was under water and it would probably sink. Results of a sweep by four aircraft off the southern coast of Italy on 9 October were not so good, as two Blenheims returned to base with engine trouble and the other two did not return at all.

For the rest of 1941 this pattern of operations continued, even on Christmas Day, and a number of aircraft were lost to enemy action, including that of the CO, Wg. Cdr. F. A. Harte, who was killed in action. Targets raided included railways in Sicily, various points in the Calabria province of Italy, airfields in Sicily and Libya, the inevitable roads carrying military vehicles in Libya and ships off the coast.

By the first week of January 1942 107 Squadron's task in Malta was regarded as complete and on 12 January the depleted detachment was disbanded and the three remaining original crews began the journey home. The nucleus of the squadron back at Great Massingham had meanwhile begun to re-equip with Boston aircraft, effectively becoming a new squadron.

18 Squadron detachment

Fifteen specially-modified Blenheims of 18 Squadron, then based at Horsham St. Faith in Norfolk, flew to Portreath in Cornwall on 10 October 1941 on the first leg of their trip to Malta for what was to be a 3- or 4-month attachment. Over the next few days the arduous stretch of the journey, over the Bay of Biscay to Gibraltar, was made by groups of three aircraft, but all safely arrived. The final leg, along the western Mediterranean, was flown at very low level, and most of the Blenheims were short of fuel when they arrived at Luqa. The first things the crews saw were the burning remains of several aircraft destroyed in an air raid which had just finished.

No records appear to have been kept of the squadron's activities while detached to Malta, but losses of aircraft and crews are known to have been high, and it was decided that no further useful

This 40 Squadron Ic Z1079 [BL:F] was destroyed by a strafing enemy aircraft on 3 January 1942, only minutes after this photograph was taken!
[via A. Thomas]

purpose would be gained by staying there. The remaining Blenheims were therefore fitted with long-range tanks and departed for Helwan in Egypt in mid-January 1942.

104 Squadron detachments

Based at Driffield in Yorkshire, fifteen of the Wellingtons of 104 Squadron began leaving for Malta on 15 October 1941 via either Portreath or Stanton Harcourt. They arrived at Luqa safely on 18 October, and next day joined with 38 Squadron in a successful raid on Tripoli. Two days later thirteen of the Wellingtons again made a joint raid with 38 Squadron, this time on Naples.

Attacks on Tripoli harbour, Palermo, Castel Benito airfield, Naples, Brindisi, Catania and Benghazi followed during the rest of October and November, culminating in a very successful raid on the Royal Arsenal at Naples on 27 November. December's activities were similar, until on 2 January 1942 the detachment moved to Kabrit in Egypt, to become a full squadron, the element remaining in England being renumbered.

104 Squadron sent a further detachment to Luqa from Kabrit on 6 November 1942, and this detachment's six Wellingtons quickly began a series of raids on Elmas and Decimomanu airfields in Sardinia and El Aouina airfield in Tunisia. Five more aircraft arrived on 22 November from LG. 104, to which the squadron itself had moved ten days earlier, and the enlarged detachment then concentrated on harbours at Tunis and Bizerta, other targets in Tunisia, and on Tripoli. A replacement Wellington, arriving on 7 December, unfortunately hit the ground too hard, bounced 50 feet into the air, stalled, crashed into a revetment and burst into flames, killing four crew members.

A message of congratulation for a job well done arrived from the AOC on 21 January 1943, and the detachment left Luqa for LG.237 the same day.

40 Squadron

The personnel of 40 Squadron, a Wellington-equipped unit based at Alconbury, were warned of an impending move to Malta on 17 October 1941. Plans were made for eight of the aircraft to leave on 23 October and eight on the following day. All were fitted with long-range fuel tanks and as many servicing staff as possible were to be carried aboard the aircraft.

On 23 October the AOC of 3 Group, Bomber Command, spoke to the crews and wished them luck, and the first eight Wellingtons took off, led by the CO, Wg. Cdr. Stickley. Next day a signal was received recording the arrival of seven of the aircraft at Luqa, but the eighth never turned up. The weather at Alconbury had deteriorated meanwhile, so departure of the second batch was delayed. Eventually, on 25 October, they took off for the Berkshire airfield of Hampstead Norris, but one aircraft was damaged on landing and continuing bad weather kept them there. At 03.00 on 26 October the Wellingtons began to take off for Portreath in Cornwall, but the third aircraft crashed and burst into flames, killing the five crew and four passengers on board and preventing further take-offs. The first two aircraft proceeded to Portreath and thence to Gibraltar, but it was 29 October before the remaining five aircraft left for Portreath and 30 October before they arrived at Gibraltar on the way to Luqa. While all this was going on, a squadron nucleus remained at Alconbury.

Once settled in at Luqa, 40 Squadron began bombing targets such as Benghazi and Naples, losing a few aircraft in the process. Accidents also occurred; on 30 November, for example, bombs on board Wellington X9662 on the ground exploded, killing two airmen and injuring three more.

At the end of December the squadron personnel in Malta learned that their unit would be renumbered 156 Squadron, but on 10 February

1942 this order was rescinded, and the nucleus back at Alconbury became 156 Squadron instead. Operations were hard on 40 Squadron, and in May 1942 the squadron left Luqa for Abu Sueir in Egypt, there to be reinforced and built up to full strength for further service.

By November 1942 40 Squadron was based at LG.104 in North Africa, although some of its Wellingtons had used Luqa as a temporary base during the autumn. On 26 November nine aircraft, each carrying four ground crew members, moved to Luqa on a more permanent basis.

The first sorties were carried out on 2 December, and consisted of attacks by eight aircraft on Bizerta and seven on Tunis and La Coulette. Subsequently raids were made on Catania airfield, Ragusa and Palermo, but Tunis remained a favourite target. By the end of December, 244 tons (248 tonnes) of bombs had been dropped in 160 effective sorties.

While the main section of 40 Squadron was at Luqa, a rear party had moved to LG.237 (Kilo 40), with a short period at Heliopolis. The Luqa element completed its task in January 1943 and on 22/23 January flew to LG.237 to rejoin the rear party as a complete squadron.

21 Squadron

Well-experienced in attacking coastal targets and shipping, 21 Squadron left Watton on Christmas Day 1941 and arrived at Luqa next day. The squadron's Blenheims began their service in Malta by carrying out a series of shipping sweeps off the coast of Tunisia, unfortunately losing two aircraft which failed to return from such a mission off Kerkenna Island on 14 January 1942. More aggressive tactics were employed from 19 January, when two Blenheims took off for a dawn attack on Catania in Sicily, although both returned to Luqa with bombs still aboard, unable to complete their mission.

Next day two aircraft were able to carry out an attack on petrol dumps and stores at Homs while two more mounted an attack on a petrol station at Zuara, both locations on the Libyan coast. This pattern of small-scale sweeps and raids continued over the next two months. Palermo harbour was attacked by six aircraft on 2 February, but only two returned safely. Three were lost to flak and the fourth, Z9812, crashed and the pilot was captured trying to destroy the aircraft; the other crew

members lost their lives. During 21 Squadron's period of duty in Malta at least seven Blenheims were destroyed in air raids apart from those which failed to return from missions, so it was an ill-equipped squadron that disbanded on 14 March 1942, to be re-formed in England next day.

2 Photographic Reconnaissance Unit detachment

Two Beaufighters of 2 PRU, specially fitted for photographic reconnaissance work, flew from Heliopolis in Egypt on 29 December 1941, bound for Luqa to augment 69 Squadron. One of them was piloted by Adrian Warburton, who had recently been 69 Squadron's most experienced pilot. As soon as the first aircraft, T4705, arrived, it was sent out on PR sorties over the harbours at Tripoli, Taranto and Palermo and over the Sicilian airfields from which it was expected that an invasion of Malta would shortly be launched. The second Beaufighter, T3301, joined in this task, but on 7 February 1942 was strafed by two Bf.109s while landing at Luqa after a sortie. The ensuing fire was put out by the camera operator, who was not qualified as aircrew, and he was quickly awarded the DFM. The aircraft, was struck off charge.

Meanwhile, two Mosquitos had arrived, and although allocated to 69 Squadron operated as part of the 2 PRU detachment. The first, W4062, had been on the way to 2 PRU in Egypt, but after being damaged by flak over Pantellaria crash-landed at Luqa. There it was repaired and joined in 2 PRU detachment's work. The second, W4063, flew in safely on 17 January 1942 and took part in operations before crash-landing on fire at Hal Far on 31 March after being attacked by two Bf.109s. By early April 1942 the 2 PRU detachment appears to have returned to Heliopolis.

221 Squadron

After a period of operation in Iceland in 1941, 221 Squadron returned to the UK at the end of the year and soon learned that a move to the Middle East was imminent. Ground and air parties left Docking in Norfolk on 8 January 1942, some of the aircraft, Wellingtons Mk.VIII, going to LG.39 in North Africa and some as a detachment to Luqa. There the detachment operated until being absorbed into 69 Squadron on 26 August 1942. The main part of the squadron, after several moves, was based at

MILITARY AVIATION IN MALTA G.C. 1915-1993

The detatchment of
221 Squadron at
Luqa during 1942
operated this
Wellington X, HZ979
[X:2]
[via R. C. Sturtivant]

Shallufa in Egypt by January 1943, flying Wellingtons of the 'Goofington', or search-and-shadow type. Orders came to the effect that the squadron was to move to Malta to fly torpedo-carrying Wellingtons ('Fishingtons') as well.

The eleven Wellingtons, led by Wg. Cdr. Hutton, left Shallufa loaded with aircrews, some ground crews, equipment and torpedos on the night of 21/22 January 1943 and reached Luqa safely. Remaining ground personnel travelled in a Dakota and a Hudson and found accommodation in the Poor House. Aircrews were billeted in Sliema, the officers at the Imperial Hotel and the SNCOs at Balluta Buildings. The severe shortage of food was a problem after the relative plenty of Egypt, but everyone survived.

221 Squadron's first sorties from its new base were flown on the night of 23/24 January against a convoy moving along the north-west coast of Sicily. One tanker was torpedoed and sank and another, plus an escorting destroyer, was damaged. Later missions were concentrated in the Sicilian narrows, with others over an area from Naples to Sardinia, Taranto and Bari. The radar carried by the squadron's aircraft was by now being jammed by the enemy, but this problem was soon overcome by the arrival of a later Mark of equipment not so susceptible to interference. In April small-scale raids on Porto Empodocle were carried out and in May the squadron was making searches off the west coast of Italy.

On 20 June the squadron had the honour of escorting His Majesty the King in HMS *Aurora* to the entrance of Grand Harbour and next day shadowing the King's departure from the island.

Seven of the Wellingtons were detached to Protville in Tunisia in July 1943, and from there they carried out patrols to the west and north of Sicily just before the invasion of that island. September tasks included the shadowing of two

battleships and three cruisers of the Italian Navy, which had by then surrendered, to Grand Harbour on 10 September, and the escort of the damaged HMS *Warspite*, which was being towed to Malta, on 19 September. Convoy escort work occupied most of October. On 2 October one Wellington missed Malta altogether in very bad weather; Sicily, now in Allied hands, was located, but as there were no night landing facilities there the aircraft, MP397, had to ditch 8 miles (13km.) south-east of Syracuse.

Over the next few months anti-submarine escort work was the routine for 221 Squadron, until in February 1944 it was ordered to move to Grottaglie in Italy, where it arrived on the last day of the month.

126 Squadron

After arriving officially from Takali on 1 May 1942, 126 Squadron's Spitfire pilots continued their arduous task of combating enemy raids on the island. By June, however, the squadron was called upon to carry out convoy escort duty, and had some success. On 15 June, while covering a 'Harpoon' convoy, an Australian pilot destroyed three enemy aircraft: a Fiat, an SM.84 and a MC.200. The squadron also played a part in guarding the major convoy which succeeded in reaching Malta in August.

Interception work continued at high intensity until the end of the siege of Malta in December 1942, and to a reduced extent afterwards, the squadron finally moving to newly-opened Safi airfield on 7 June 1943.

217 Squadron detachment

After leaving Leuchars in Scotland in May 1942, the HQ and groundcrew party of 217 Squadron sailed for South Africa, where a short time was spent before the final part of the voyage to Ceylon

This Beaufort Ia, DD959 [Q] of 217 Squadron, was shot down during a shipping strike on 20 June 1942.
[via A. Thomas]

was begun. The aircraft, meanwhile, flew the first leg of the journey, landing at Luqa. There the crews were prevailed upon to remain for a time to take part in a number of missions against enemy convoys. Although records of the detachment's activities at this period are virtually non-existent, it is known that nine of the squadron's Beauforts attacked a convoy off Tripoli on 21 June, losing three aircraft, including AW342, of which the sole survivor, the navigator, was picked up from the sea by an Italian destroyer. Another aircraft, L9799, reached Malta badly damaged and with an injured captain.

The Malta detachment was absorbed into 39 Squadron on 20 August 1942.

39 Squadron

A detachment of five Beauforts of 39 Squadron arrived at Luqa from LG.86 in North Africa on 22 June 1942 and next day began operations by participating with other squadrons in an attack on a convoy east of the toe of Italy. Hits were made on one motor vessel, but two of the 39 Squadron aircraft were shot down. The remaining three Beauforts took off on 3 July with eight aircraft of other units to search for a convoy, but failed to find it. Later the same day the Beauforts flew to the

south-west coast of Greece to attack another convoy, and during the rest of July and August the detachment carried on with its small campaign of shipping strikes, with varying degrees of success.

On 20 August 1942 the Malta detachment combined with the remnants of two depleted squadrons, 86 Squadron, which brought Beauforts out from Thorney Island in England, and the Luqa-based detatchment of 217 Squadron. The new unit became 39 Squadron, while the original detachment's HQ in Egypt merged into 47 Squadron. The CO of the new 39 Squadron was Wg. Cdr. R. P. Gibbs DFC+Bar, and the squadron now had sixteen operational Beauforts, with another four in reserve, all fitted to carry torpedos.

Twelve of the Beauforts attacked a convoy off the toe of Italy on 20 August, and on this, the squadron's first day of existence in its new form, two aircraft were lost. Similar missions were mounted in the next ten days, the most significant being on 30 August, when nine aircraft persuaded a tanker to explode. During the combat which took place over the convoy of which the tanker was a part, an Me.210 was destroyed, another one and a Cant CZ.500 were damaged and a Ju.88 was

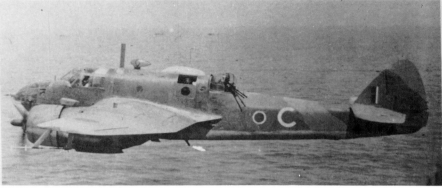

Beaufort II DD906 of
39 Squadron low
over the sea in 1943.
[via R. C. Sturtivant]

probably destroyed, for the loss of one Beaufort.

September 1942 was not a happy month for 39 Squadron. On 6 September twelve aircraft took off to attack a southbound convoy but three aborted; the other nine found the target and attacked, without recorded success, and two were shot down. Most of the remaining seven aircraft were damaged, and several crash-landed on returning to Luqa. Later in September orders were received that 39 Squadron was to relinquish all its remaining aircraft and equipment for transfer to 47 Squadron in Egypt, and so on 1 October the Beauforts left Malta. However, on 7 October came fresh orders: 39 Squadron was to be reconstituted at Luqa. By 11 October eleven Beauforts were ready to return, but a series of heavy raids on the island delayed them, and it was not until 1 November that they reached Malta. Three more aircraft and crews arrived at Luqa on 6 November, although these men were not trained for torpedo operations.

Missions by 39 Squadron began anew on 12 November with a mine-laying operation by five aircraft off Tunis harbour, but three of the Beauforts aborted and one crash-landed on return. A similar effort next day was more successful. Further mining missions followed in an attempt to close Palermo and Bizerte harbours before the first days of December, when the squadron was on standby for an attack on the Italian fleet, which in the event failed to materialise.

On 9 December 1942 ten of the squadron's aircraft and some ground personnel, under the command of Wg. Cdr. M. K. Gaine AFC, left Luqa for Shallufa in Egypt. Sqdn. Ldr. L. V. Worsdell DFC then assumed command of the six aircraft and personnel remaining behind, this party then becoming known as the 39 Squadron Detachment.

As such, small-scale anti-submarine and shipping patrols continued from Luqa.

The ten aircraft at Shallufa returned to Luqa on 21 January 1943, but several ground crews were left behind for temporary redistribution to other squadrons. Minelaying continued during February's indifferent weather and through the spring. To overcome the shortage of ground personnel at Luqa, the Beauforts were now sent to Heliopolis in Egypt for major servicing.

At the end of May 1943 squadron personnel learned that they were to move to Protville in Tunisia, and on 1 June the move was made. Crews were not pleased when they arrived at Protville to find that SNAFU had intervened — no arrangements had been made to accommodate them!

1435 Flight/Squadron

After an earlier period of existence at Takali, 1435 Flight was reformed in July 1942 at Luqa and received a number of Spitfires Mk.Vc and pilots from 603 Squadron, then in the process of disbandment. The Flight's CO was Sqdn. Ldr. A. D. Lovell DFC, a Battle of Britain veteran. By 2 August the new Flight had expanded to squadron size and was therefore given squadron status while retaining the number 1435, the only RAF squadron ever to carry a four-digit number.

Some action was seen during the last few days of July, and a 'probable' in the shape of a Bf.109 was claimed on 23 July. Next day two confirmed kills were made, both Bf.109s. Sad to say, 'friendly fire' from gunners on HMS *Dorset* shot down 1435 Squadron Spitfire EP197 on 13 August.

The late autumn of 1942, the final throes of the siege of Malta, was a busy and successful period for 1435 Squadron. On one day five Ju.88s were destroyed and three damaged, a Bf.109 claimed as a 'probable' and five damaged. The final tally at the end of October was 39 enemy aircraft destroyed, ten of them by Flt. Lt. H. W. McLeod, a Canadian pilot formerly with 603 Squadron who was awarded the DFC and Bar for his efforts.

The main effects of the siege having been overcome, fighter squadrons in Malta went over to offensive missions at the end of November 1942, and 1435 Squadron directed its attention to enemy transport aircraft flying between Sicily and Tunisia. Ju.52s, Fiat G.18s and SM.82s were viable targets for the squadron, which continued its successful career by putting several examples of these types out of action.

A new CO, Sqdn. Ldr. W. A. Smith DFC, took over in January 1943 but did not stay long before being replaced by Sqdn. Ldr. H. F. O'Neill. Little action was seen by 1435 Squadron during the spring of 1943, and the squadron moved to Safi on 10 June to make way for the expected build-up of squadrons at Luqa.

227 Squadron

Formed at Luqa on 20 August 1942 from a nucleus of 235 Squadron, 227 Squadron was commanded by Wg. Cdr. D. R. Shore AFC and operated Beaufighters.

On the day of formation, twelve of the squadron's aircraft took off to bomb a cruiser and to give protection to 39 Squadron's Beauforts, which had arrived at Luqa that day, while carrying out a torpedo attack. From this mission two of 227 Squadron's aircraft did not return, an inauspicious start; one of them was seen to crash into the sea off

Kalafrana. A similar mission was mounted next day. Eight aircraft, three of which carried bombs, provided an escort for Beauforts on 24 August and one Ju.88 was destroyed, the new squadron's first 'kill'. On 27 August another escort mission by eight aircraft resulted in the destruction of a Cant Z.1007, but two more Beaufighters were lost, bringing an end to the first hard week of activity for the squadron.

More escort work was carried out over the next few weeks, but more of the squadron's aircraft were lost. The CO was convinced that crews under his command had not been trained adequately, and wrote to Coastal Command to say so. He was probably proved correct on 4 October, when a disastrous operation was mounted. After the tail-wheel of one Beaufighter had collapsed on take-off, the undercarriage of another would not retract and a third had crashed into the sea, the other five were recalled. A search was made for the dinghy containing the crew of the crashed aircraft, and it was located next day by Sqdn. Ldr. Wigmore, who attempted to guide a HSL to the scene. One of his engines then failed and his aircraft also went into the 'drink', luckily with no loss of life.

The situation did not improve immediately, although a new CO who took over on 12 October was on the scene. Three aircraft took off on 14 October to attack merchant vessels, one of which was destroyed by a Beaufighter which then crashed into the sea. On the way home another one found itself in difficulties and also ditched, while the third aircraft, suffering from flak damage, crash-landed at Luqa. The squadron was now down to six aircraft, and it was not until 6 November that 14 replacement aircraft and 29 aircrew and extra

X8077 [F] a Beaufighter VIc of 227 Squadron, seen at Luqa not long before it ditched 70 miles east of the island on 28 January 1943.
[via A. Thomas]

ground crews arrived from the Middle East.

November 1942 was the month the tide turned for 227 Squadron, which began to see some success. On 13 November eight aircraft took part in an offensive sweep over the sea between Tunisia and Sicily and found sixteen Ju.52 transport aircraft and about thirty SM.81s. Running fights ensued, during which four Ju.52s, two SM.81s and a Do.24 flying boat were destroyed and several others damaged. Next day another sweep was carried out near Pantellaria to prevent the reinforcement by air of the enemy forces in North Africa, but from this mission two of the Beaufighters failed to return.

Similar sweeps were made from Luqa during the next few days, but on 25 November 1942 227 Squadron moved to Takali.

113 Squadron detachment

During September 1941, five Blenheims of 113 Squadron operated for a week from Luqa on convoy patrol duties. On 28 September two of them strafed the E-boat base at Pantellaria, badly damaging two vessels for the loss of one Blenheim, T1821. Two other aircraft patrolled, and one was hit by AA fire but survived. The detachment returned to Bagush on 30 September.

From the middle of September 1942, two Wellington aircraft of 113 Squadron operated for periods of time from Luqa on radar investigation missions. They were instrumental in confirming the existence of long- and short-range radars on Pantellaria, Cape Passero and Agregento, and also carried out a few offensive operations. During May and June 1943 a Blenheim Mk.V was also used, for calibration duties, but early in September 1943 the final sorties were flown before the small detachment left for Benina, to where the squadron's HQ had moved from Bilbeis during the interim period.

23 Squadron

While flying Mosquitos in an intruder role from Bradwell Bay on the east coast of England, 23 Squadron pilots were told on 6 December 1942 of an imminent move to the less severe climate of Malta. Next day ten of them collected new aircraft from St. Athan and Shawbury and long-range fuel tanks were fitted. The ground crew personnel, meanwhile, left to board HMS *Argus* at Glasgow for a rough voyage to Gibraltar, where they spent

an enjoyable Christmas. The aircraft were at the jumping-off point, Portreath in Cornwall, by 23 December but were delayed by bad weather, the first six not leaving Gibraltar to fly via Maison Blanche in Algeria to Luqa until 27 December. At Luqa the ground crews, who had flown from Gibraltar in a Liberator and a Hudson, awaited them.

On 29 December 1942 23 Squadron, the first Mosquito fighter squadron to be based in Malta, carried out its first operation from Luqa — an intruder mission over Sicily. The squadron was inspected by AVM Sir Keith Park on 1 January 1943, and on 7 January its first enemy aircraft was downed, during a night patrol over Comiso in Sicily. A flurry of intense activity occured on 19 January, when a report was received that Rommel's forces were retreating, so all available 23 Squadron aircraft were called on to attack the long columns of vehicles and troops west of Tripoli. Great damage was done that day, and on the following day a similar if smaller operation was staged, at the cost of one Mosquito which failed to return.

During February 1943 four Ju.88s were destroyed, twenty-seven locomotives were put out of action and another twenty-five slightly damaged, and similar results were obtained in March.

The CO, Wg. Cdr. P. G. Wykeham-Barnes DSO DFC, was replaced in April 1943 by Wg. Cdr. J. B. Selby DSO DFC. That month saw the figure of enemy aircraft destroyed by Malta-based aircraft reach 997, and an island-wide sweepstake was held on who would reach the magic 1000. 23 Squadron got its chance on 26 April, when Flt. Lt. A. J. Hodgkinson shot down two Ju.88s, but the squadron was not successful in the final countdown. During May 23 Squadron, although badly depleted in number of aircraft, continued to raid Sicily and the toe of Italy, claiming sixty-five trains and six aircraft destroyed, for the loss of seven Mosquitos and crews.

The aircraft situation eased early in July 1943 when the first Mosquito Mk.VI arrived. On 9 July the squadron was brought to readiness to provide overall intruder cover of the airfields in Sicily during the invasion of that island. A further development occurred on 17 July, when two of the new aircraft, fitted with long-range tanks, attacked airfields in the Rome area. Another six aircraft

23 Squadron Mosquito II DZ228 [YP:D] over Malta in 1942. This aircraft is recorded as 'missing off Malta' on 21 January 1943 *[IWM]*

were similarly fitted on 19 July but a raid on Malta that night, quite an unusual occurrence by then, prompted the removal of bomb racks and a return to intruder missions. It realised that until a forward operating base was available in Sicily the squadron could not cover central Italy effectively.

The invasion of Sicily having been carried out successfully, 23 Squadron commandeered Malta ASR & Communication Flight's Harvard aircraft on 28 July and flew it to Castel Vetrano, the first Allied aircraft to land there. By the end of August it was decided that the squadron would have to become mobile, and, the day after 23's thousandth sortie from Malta, plans were made on 31 August for a detachment of ground crew personnel to go to Sicily. The Mosquitos would fly there each day to refuel, carry out their missions at night and return to Luqa at dawn. On 3 September the thirty men left Luqa in a Dakota for Sigonella, where they found conditions very poor and had to scrounge tents and other supplies.

Most 23 Squadron personnel left for Alghero on 29 November, but the squadron HQ remained at Luqa until 7 December 1943 before following. The forward detachment had meanwhile moved to Gerbini Main on 5 October and to Pomigliano on 1 November.

458 Squadron, RCAF, detachment
Four Wellingtons of 458 Squadron arrived from Shallufa in Egypt on 6 January 1943 and began night shipping strikes. One of the Wellingtons was lost next day, but on 16 January another seven arrived to boost the squadron's efforts. Another aircraft was posted as 'missing in action' on 25 January, but the detachment was kept up to strength at all times.

In April 1943 the squadron began to receive the Mk.VIII version of the Wellington, but by 22 May the squadron had left for Protville in Tunisia.

683 Squadron
One of the results of the expansion of photographic reconnaissance activities in the Mediterranean area in 1943 was the formation of 683 Squadron on 8 February 1943 from 'B' Flight of 69 Squadron, which had outgrown itself. Ground crew personnel numbering fifty-two were posted from 69 Squadron, which was commanded by Wg. Cdr. Adrian Warburton DSO DFC, the renowned PR expert who had already made a considerable name for himself.

The Spitfires Mk.IV of the new squadron carried out PR work over airfields, ports and other installations in Sicily and southern Italy, and before

Seen at Ponte Olivo, Sicily, after leaving Malta, this Spitfire XI, EN657, served only with 683 Squadron.
[H. Levy, via A. Thomas]

long information was required about the island fortress of Pantellaria. To obtain the photographs, Wg. Cdr. Warburton ('Warby') himself carried out four or more sorties, and flew so low that he was fired on by anti-aircraft guns from above! Following the successful reconnaissance, Pantellaria was 'softened up' by the bomber force and surrendered.

By June considerable demands were being made on the squadron in connection with the forthcoming invasion of Sicily, and a Mosquito was also in use. When the invasion at last took place, patrols over the beaches were added to 683 Squadron's tasks, and a record number of sorties were flown. Wg. Cdr. Warburton, who by now had downed eleven aircraft in all, was awarded a second Bar to his DSO. On 6 July, taking off from La Marsa in Tunisia in a war-weary P-38 Lightning borrowed from friends in the USAAF, he crashed, and the aircraft was destroyed by fire. Unhurt, he walked away from the aircraft, borrowed another one and left for Malta, returning next day to collect his Spitfire which had been repaired.

The invasion completed, airfields were captured by the advancing troops, and 683 Squadron began to make use of airstrips at Lentini and Francesca. Photographic cover of Albania and north-west Greece was now required, and the squadron complied. On 17 September, however, it was learnt that a reduction was to be made to seven Spitfires, with a corresponding decrease in personnel. Almost all the much-reduced number of sorties that month were over the Adriatic area.

The CO was posted on 1 October 1943 and Flt. Lt. H. S. Smith took over. Only sixteen sorties were flown in October, some from Montecorvino in cooperation with the 5th Army. 683 Squadron's

time in Malta was coming to an end, and on 7 November 1943 an advance party left for El Aouina in Tunisia, followed on 20 November by the main group, which embarked on an LCT in Sliema Creek.

3rd Photographic & Mapping Group, USAAF

As part of the build-up to the invasion of Sicily, much greater effort was put into photographic reconnaissance of the island. To this end, six F-4 and F-5A Lightning aircraft of the USAAF's 3rd P&MG were detached from their base at Algiers at the end of March 1943 to operate from Luqa. No sooner had they arrived than one of the Lightnings was written off when it taxied too quickly along Luqa's somewhat rough taxitrack. On 28 March, the detachment's CO, Capt. Richardson, crash-landed his aircraft in Sicily while on the first PR sortie, and he was replaced by Lt. Joe Scalpone. The pilots were somewhat inexperienced, and the CO of 683 Squadron, Wg. Cdr. Adrian Warburton, flew one of the Lightnings on the next sortie to demonstrate the necessary techniques. Wearing US junior officers' uniform, he brought back his usual high-quality photographs! The Group continued to fly missions over Sicilian harbours and airfields before leaving some time after 19 June for their new base at La Marsa, Tunisia.

Known serial numbers for the aircraft used by the 3rd P&MG in Malta are: 41-2366 (F-4); 42-13071, 42-13082 and 42-13089 (F-5A).

108 Squadron

108 Squadron had been operating from Malta from time to time, but on 27 May 1943 a signal was received at squadron HQ at Bersis ordering a move

Seen in a stone block revetment at Luqa in the early summer of 1943 is F-5A Lightning 42-13071 of the 3rd Photographic & Mapping Group, which sent several such aircraft to Malta to carry out reconnaissance of Sicily in advance of Operation Husky. *[via Roger A. Freeman]*

to Luqa, a second Flight being put on standby. Four Hudson aircraft carried the ground crews and equipment on 2 and 3 June, and eight of the squadron's Beaufighters Mk.VI equipped with AI made the journey. The squadron was detailed to provide four aircraft at readiness each night, and on 5 June practice interceptions on Maltese radar stations began.

The invasion of Sicily was imminent, and sorties over that island began on 8 June with attacks on a road convoy and a railway line. A few days later, three US paratroop officers were flown over their designated dropping zone at Gela so that they could judge what had to be done. Offensive patrols continued, although on 1 July the nightly readiness state had to be reduced to two Beaufighters to conserve flying hours.

A new task was given to 108 Squadron when six Mosquitos belonging to 256 Squadron were attached to 108 for operations. These aircraft were fitted with AI Mk.VIII, as were eight Beaufighters Mk.VI which arrived for 108 Squadron a few days later. To make them operational and to maintain the Mosquitos, two weeks' work, it was said, had to be done in 36 hours!

It was revealed on 9 July that 108 Squadron, with 256 and 600 Squadrons, would be responsible for the defence of the armada of vessels to be used

in the invasion of Sicily. 108 Squadron's strength was now ten Beaufighters, eight of which carried AI Mk.VIII; these aircraft were not, however, allowed to cross the enemy coast, for security reasons. The nightly state of readiness was six aircraft. It was also revealed that six fighter direction ships would lay off the Sicilian coast and as soon as beaches were no longer being shelled mobile GCI Stations would be shipped ashore and set up.

On the night of 9/10 July patrols were made as ordered, but due to mis-identification as friendly aircraft about 25 Ju.88s were able to attack Malta. 108 Squadron was too late to intercept, and it was decided that in future standing patrols would be mounted. A Cant Z.1007 and a Ju.88 were shot down during the night of 10/11 July, but next night one of 108 Squadron's aircraft was destroyed by the debris of a disabled enemy aircraft.

By 13 July the GCI equipment on the Sicilian beaches was operating well, enabling the squadron to destroy fourteen enemy aircraft during the first week of the invasion campaign. A great strain was put on the ever-willing ground crews, particularly those dealing with the new AI Mk.VIII.

Enemy aircraft attacked shipping off Malta on 26 July, but this time 108 Squadron was ready, and bagged two of the thirty or so attackers. Patrols over Sicily were now discontinued, and the squadron concentrated on the defence of Malta, but approval was given on 26 July for the squadron to operate over liberated areas of Sicily. By the end of the month 23 enemy aircraft had been destroyed, with four damaged and six probably downed.

From 12 August, two Beaufighters were sent every night to newly-liberated Cassibile to augment 600 Squadron against enemy aircraft attacking Allied shipping. Only four aircraft were destroyed that month, as there was not so much opportunity for combat. Thereafter, the pressure lessened considerably. Standing patrols ceased on 5 September, and a period of training began, although the arrival of part of the surrendered Italian fleet in Grand Harbour on 10 September prompted a period of readiness against possible German reprisals.

In October 1943 there was no operational flying, and the squadron was adjusted to have two Flights at Luqa, the section remaining at Bersis being absorbed into 46 Squadron. November and December saw nothing but training flights, but on 28 December Beaufighter ND205 suffered hydraulic failure on take-off, and spun in 4 miles from the end of the runway. In doing so the aircraft hit a sheep pen, killing a Maltese shepherd.

Production of Beaufighter night-fighters ceased in January 1944, and all squadrons were told that they would gradually convert to other types. Meanwhile, all unnecessary flying was to be curtailed. This was unwelcome news for 108 Squadron, as a large number of aircrew needed practice. In February, during which month convoy patrols were being flown, the first Mosquitos arrived for 108 Squadron, and Hurricane Mk.IIc KX945 was received for drogue-towing duty. Beaufighters were not replaced entirely for some time, however. One of the new Mosquitos, KW157, was destroyed by fire on 8 March when the cockpit canopy flew open on take-off, and the aircraft swung, hitting a fuel bowser and Wellington HZ880 of 221 Squadron before cartwheeling.

Two Beaufighters flew to Catania on 20 March to take over 256 Squadron's night commitment, and on 22 April a detachment went to Naples to work with the USAAF's 416th Night Fighter Squadron. Another detachment was planned for six aircraft to go to Alghero on 10 May, but when the ground crews had boarded two Dakotas at very short notice

the task was cancelled, leading, no doubt, to allegations of SNAFU! Next day, however, an He.111 was destroyed in the Montpelier area—the squadron's first kill since September 1943. On 13 May a Hudson did take a few men to Alghero for a mission by three aircraft, and at the end of the month four aircraft were stationed there semi-permanently. Aircraft of the squadron were, by 31 May, operating from Alghero, Catania, Idku and Grottaglie as well as Luqa.

Consideration was being given by the end of May to moving the squadron to Hal Far, but an inspection of the buildings there, many of which were in a poor state, caused such a move to be delayed. Aircrew NCOs moved, meanwhile, from Balluta Buildings to the Poor House, not a popular idea. A second inspection of Hal Far was made on 23 June, and a date was set for moving, if the AMWD could work faster on the improvements. This plan was adhered to, and 108 Squadron duly found itself at Hal Far on 1 July 1944.

272 Squadron

By 13.00 on 4 June 1943 272 Squadron had completed its move to Luqa from Takali, without a break in operational efficiency. There were no offensive operations that month, however, the squadron devoting its time to convoy escort work and continuation training. Practice low-level bombing of Filfla Island claimed more victims on 6 June, when an aircraft crewed by men who had joined the squadron just a week before crashed into the sea.

On 1 July the squadron was ordered to send a detachment to Libya, and arrangements were made for thirty-two aircrew and forty-eight ground personnel to move. The men were flown to Gardabbia West in Wellingtons of 221 Squadron on 4 and 5 July, and fifteen Beaufighters also made the trip. Ground crews left in Malta were temporarily absorbed into other squadrons. All aircraft and crews returned to Luqa on 17 July, the ground crews in the comparative luxury of three Lodestar aircraft, probably those of 117 Squadron.

272 Squadron then began a new period of offensive operations with sweeps along the Greek coast on 22 July, during which a Ju.52 was shot down and a Do.18 destroyed at a seaplane base. Another Do.18 and two He.115s were destroyed

Two somewhat mangled Spirfire IXs of 1 Sqdn, SAAF (one coded AX:A) which flew briefly from Luqa during the Sicilian invasion period.
[S. M. Coates via A. Thomas]

during a similar sweep on 30 July. Greece continued to be the main object of the squadron's attentions during August, when 600 operational hours were flown and news of an impending move from Malta was received.

The CO and adjutant flew to Borizzo in Sicily on 2 September to inspect the squadron's new base, and as transport became available the squadron personnel made the move, the last men leaving Luqa on 11 September 1943.

244 Wing

The five squadrons of 244 Wing, all flying Spitfires, 92, 145 and 601 Squadrons RAF, 1 Squadron SAAF and 417 Squadron RCAF, arrived at Luqa from Ben Gardane in Tunisia on 7 June 1943. Once settled in, the Wing carried out island patrol sorties and offensive patrols over Sicily before the invasion of that island.

In readiness for the invasion, an advance party of the Wing left Luqa on 1 July for the marshalling

area at Tigne, but 1 Squadron SAAF, at least, was still active, flying top cover to B-26s and P-38s of the USAAF raiding Gerbini airfield on 5 July. By 16 July, six days after the Allied landings on Sicily, the Wing's aircraft had departed for newly-captured airfields at Pachino and Cassibile, the main ground party having left on LCTs from Msida Creek on 13 July. 417 Squadron, however, sent its ground crews by LST from Customs House, Valletta, on 19 July.

40 Squadron, SAAF

The personnel of 40 Squadron SAAF arrived in Grand Harbour from Tripoli on 16 June 1943, having previously been stationed at Ben Gardane. Having disembarked they were split up, the officers going to the Imperial Hotel in Sliema, the SNCOs to the Poor House and the other ranks to tents set up at Luqa. Sixteen Spitfires arrived on 23 June and four days later joined in the large number of sweeps being carried out over Sicily at the time.

This 145 Squadron Spitfire Vb, EN355 [ZX:O] based for a short time at Luqa, eventually met its match.
[via R. C. Sturtivant]

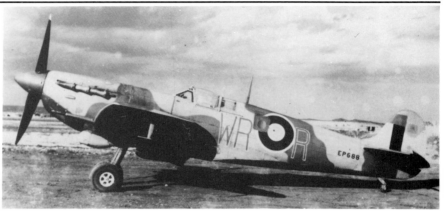

Code WR on Spitfire Vb EP688 indicates that the aircraft belonged to 40 Squadron SAAF, which lodged at Luqa for a few weeks in the summer of 1943 and took part in Operation Husky. *[via R. C. Sturtivant]*

Between 1 and 8 July there was surprisingly little activity, and the opportunity was taken to indulge in some swimming, dancing and drinking.

Two aircraft failed to return from a sortie on 10 July, one having been shot down by another Spitfire, but luckily its pilot was rescued. Another aircraft was shot down over Sicily on 12 July when it was jumped by three Reggianes. That day, twelve mechanics and armourers left for Sicily to assist Servicing Commandos in the event of 40 Squadron aircraft landing there before the squadron itself had moved. In fact it was 15 July before the first 40 Squadron aircraft made the journey to Pachino, its new home, the main party having left via Grand Harbour two days earlier.

600 Squadron

Previously based at Setif in Algeria, the ground party of 600 Squadron left the Tunisian port of Sousse on 24 June 1943 and the squadron's twenty Beaufighters flew across from Bone next day. Two days later, six aircraft at a time began day and night patrols, and over the next few days the squadron shot down a Ju.88 into Augusta harbour, a He.111 near Syracuse, two Ju.88s, an He.111 and a Cant Z.1007 in one combat, a Do.217 near Catania, an He.111 and, on 17 July, six aircraft in one day.

However, 600 Squadron was very mobile, and on 25 July an advance party left for Cassibile in Sicily in a Dakota, followed next day by the Beaufighters and on 29 July by the rear party, which embarked in an LCT at Marsa.

256 Squadron

Six crews of 256 Squadron, based at Ford on the south coast of England, heard on 1 July 1943 that

they were to go on attachment to Luqa, and after hurried preparations the six Mosquitos left next day to fly via Gibraltar. Arriving safely in Malta on 5 July, they spent a few days on local training, and after joining in patrol work they soon had great success. On 15 July the 256 Squadron crews shot down no less than four Ju.88s and a Cant Z1007 during one patrol, and in the first six nights eighteen enemy aircraft were claimed.

The remainder of the squadron, having moved back to Woodvale from Ford, were notified on 25 August that they, too, were to move to Malta. The main party and HQ sailed on 15 September to Bone in Algeria under "awful" conditions, and the aircraft flew out on 27 September. After over three weeks at sea, the main party arrived at Bone and transhipped to a small French vessel on 9 October, arriving in Malta four days later to find that the squadron's equipment was held up somewhere for lack of shipping space. Ground crews settled in at Safi Camp, but very little could be done due to the continued non-arrival of the 'gear', and it was not until 27 December that at last unloading began.

Convoy patrols began in January 1944, but an influx of new crews demanded considerable training effort. Some of the ground crews went to Alghero in Sardinia on 7 February to service aircraft which were to carry out intruder missions from there, but snow prevented any such activity and everyone returned to Luqa ten days later. On 7 March, however, a detachment was sent to Pomigliano in a Dakota and a Wellington of 221 Squadron, and on arrival work with the 416th Night Fighter Squadron of the USAAF began. Another detachment was at Catania in Sicily.

The Pomigliano detachment returned suddenly

256 Sqdn. Mosquito XII HK128 coded JT:G at Luqa. The contents of the mule-drawn wagon are a mystery!
[J. Betts]

on 21 March and packing began for a planned move to La Seina. The advance party left in Dakotas on 27 March, but three more 'Daks' which arrived on the same day to take the squadron to Borrizzo had to leave empty when the pilots were told that 256 Squadron knew nothing about it! The squadron's main party left by ship on 30 March.

73 Squadron detachment
A transient unit, 73 Squadron sent nine Hurricanes to Luqa from La Sebala 2 in Tunisia on 8 July 1943. They carried out intruder patrols over Sicily for three nights over the invasion period, during which the Hurricanes strafed MT vehicles and railway lines, but returned to La Sebala 2 on 13 July.

239 Wing
In support of the invasion of Sicily, the four Kittyhawk-equipped squadrons of 239 Wing came together at Luqa on 14 July 1943. From Takali came 3 Squadron RAAF, from Hal Far 250 Squadron, and 260 Squadron arrived from Zuara in Libya with 450 Squadron RCAF. These movements were carried out to consolidate the Wing, which, after bombing targets in Sicily, moved to Pachino on 18 July to take up residence on that newly-captured airfield.

1437 (Strategic Reconnaissance) Flight
Probably the only Mustang aircraft to operate from Malta were those of 1437 (SR) Flight, which arrived from North Africa on 16 July 1943. Under the command of Lt. McLaren, the Flight managed to carry out a dozen reconnaissance sorties before moving to Lentini in Sicily on 31 July 1943. The Flight's Mustangs were Mk.III aircraft, probably those in the HK serial range taken over from the USAAF in the field, officially in August 1943.

232 Wing
Two units of 232 Wing, 55 and 223 Squadrons, both equipped with Baltimores, arrived at Luqa from Reyville in Tunisia on 20 July 1943 under the command of Gp. Capt. Roulston. While in Malta, the squadrons carried out attacks on tactical targets in the occupied parts of Sicily before moving to the island on 10 August.

219 Squadron detachment
On 26 July 1943 219 Squadron, based at Bone in Algeria, began sending weekly detachments of its Beaufighters Mk.VIF to Luqa. This promised to be a welcome change for the crews, who had heard stories of greater activity there, and of well-stocked shops. They were wrong on both counts, but being in Malta was better than being in Algeria, even allowing for attacks of the dreaded 'Malta Dog'.

Ground crews were flown to Luqa on 28 July to service the aircraft, and the squadron began to fly patrols every night, regardless of the weather. Little enemy air activity was seen, however, apart from an He.111 which was chased away on 6 August. One of the Beaufighters, V8871, caught fire and crashed into the sea two miles (3km.) north of Gozo on 13 August, but that was the only loss.

After flying final sorties, the 219 Squadron detachment left Luqa on 27 August 1943 for La Sebala 2, to where the sqaudron HQ had recently moved.

38 Squadron
Tasked with taking over the full air-sea rescue function for Malta, 38 Squadron sent its advance party from Falconara in Italy to Luqa on 5 July 1945. The men quickly settled in, and the squadron's nine Wellingtons Mk.XIV and the main party of seven officers, 52 SNCOs and 205 other

Warwick I BV387 of 38 Squadron at Luqa in 1945. No individual letter is carried by this aircraft, but vestigial code S2, probably locally-allocated, can be seen.
[via R. C. Sturtivant]

ranks arrived between 11 and 13 July. It was some time before, on 24 August, a policy on ASR in the Mediterranean was promulgated, and 38 Squadron was instructed to arrange a detachment of four Wellingtons, with ground crews, to Elmas in Sardinia. Two days later, the squadron became operational, taking over the air-sea rescue commitment from 283 Squadron, and the detachment left for Elmas, where the men soon remarked that they liked life better than in Malta, even though facilities were lacking! Three Warwick aircraft were received in August to begin replacing the Wellingtons.

The squadron's services were used on 16 September, when a Ju.52 carrying 18 people from Luqa to Ajaccio in Corsica crashed into the sea. One of 38 Squadron's Wellingtons carried out an intensive search but found no trace of the aircraft or survivors. The first operational lifeboat drop by 38 Squadron was not made until 4 June 1946, however, when a Wellington and a Warwick scrambled to rescue the crew of an Anson of 284 Wing Communications Flight which had come down in the sea near Castel Benito. The last Wellington on the squadron left for disposal that month and Warwicks Mk.I formed the squadron's

Two Lancasters of 38 Squadron flying westward over Marsaxlokk Bay. Kalafrana is visible at centre left of the picture and St. Lucian's Tower in the bottom right-hand corner. *[F. D. Sheppard]*

Lancaster GR.3
RE123 [R] of 38
Squadron, based at
Luqa.
[NWMA]

equipment. However, more changes were in the air, as the first Lancasters Mk.III arrived on 15 July and were taken to 137 MU at Safi for attention before being issued for use.

To deal with the problem of shipping carrying illegal immigrants to Palestine, 38 Squadron was involved in sea searches, and set up a detachment of Lancasters at Ein Shemer in Palestine in September 1946, where they remained for some eighteen months.

Routine ASR work and illegal shipping patrols continued over the next few months, but the squadron was strengthened in July 1947 by the addition of two Lancasters for Naval cooperation tasks. A second detachment to facilitate searches for illegal immigrants was established at Ramat David in Palestine at the end of March 1948, but this party and the Ein Shemer detachment left by 15 May with the withdrawal of British troops from what was about to become the State of Israel.

During July 1948 the squadron, now with its full complement at Luqa, took part in Exercise 'DXM 48' to test the defences of Malta. Soon after this, on 3 September, one of the Lancasters, TX269, using radio call-sign MBWYN, was lost tragically when it crashed on Monte Christo Island, off Italy at night; the wreckage was found next day by a Firefly from Hal Far.

Over the next few years, 38 Squadron's activities centred around the maintenance of ASR facilities, interspersed with periodic exercises, detachments to such RAF bases as Negombo in Ceylon, where six aircraft spent time in May 1952, and training exercises carried out by the Joint Anti-Submarine School in Northern Ireland, for which the 38 Squadron aircraft flew to Ballykelly.

By January 1953 only five aircraft were available to the squadron, but in April two were sent to Habbaniya in Iraq, where trouble was brewing. They returned in July to find the squadron at a low ebb, three Lancasters being struck off charge due to detereoration of airframes. However, the first of the new Shackleton MR.2s arrived in October and conversion training was under way by the end of the month. By January 1954 all eight Shackletons had arrived, but on 12 February one of them, WL794, was lost during an exercise with a submarine, HMS *Tudor,* all ten on board losing their lives.

For several years 38 Squadron continued with a

The result of a short-circuit during maintenance to a Lancaster at Luqa c.1953.
[R. Robinson]

Seen at Luqa in 1965 is Shackleton MR.2 WR963 [X] of 38 Squadron. With much up-dating, this aircraft remained in service another 27 years!
[via A. Thomas]

routine of maritime patrols, enlivened by patrols off Mozambique during the Rhodesian UDI crisis and periodic detachments in the Persian Gulf area and to Ballykelly for training at the Joint Anti-Submarine School. The squadron left Luqa, however, on 30 October 1965 to become the RAF presence at Hal Far when that airfield was handed back by the Fleet Air Arm.

728 Squadron
Equipped with a motley collection of Beaufighters, Martinets, Baltimores, Seafires, Mosquitos and Walrus amphibians, 728 Squadron moved from Takali to Luqa on 1 January 1946. The Mosquitos were used for converting pilots onto twin-engined types and for radar calibration duties, work which 728 Squadron took over from 255 Squadron, which had recently left Malta for Egypt. 728's stay at Luqa was, however, destined to be a short one, as on 5 May 1946 a move was made to Hal Far, where the squadron would spend the rest of its long and useful life.

185 Squadron
As the first stage of a move to Idris in Libya, 185 Squadron's sixteen Vampires and one Meteor arrived at Luqa from Hal Far on 23 July 1952, along with first-line servicing personnel. The squadron appears not to have flown much while at Luqa and left for Idris on 14 August 1952.

AHQ Malta Communications Flight / Malta Communications & Target Towing Flight / Squadron
Having moved from Hal Far on 4 January 1946, the AHQ Malta Communications Flight suffered a reduction in work-load when, on 8 January, the daily meteorological flight which had been performed for just over a year was withdrawn. In February two of the Ansons were disposed of and in April the Expeditor aircraft left for Austria to be returned to the USAAF, so that by March 1946 the Flight's strength was two Wellingtons and three Ansons. However, although the ground staff was greatly depleted, the Flight was able to do everything demanded of it, including several casualty evacuation flights from Sicily to Malta.

The Flight's first accident, luckily not a fatal one, occured on 31 August 1946 when Wellington Mk.X LP805 crashed on take-off after the throttle lever had broken in the pilot's hand. Commanded by Flt. Lt. Morgan, the unit now used three Wellingtons and an Anson, and ten aircrew and nine ground crew men were on the 'staff'. One of the 'Wimpeys' left in October, as did the Anson, but in November three Wellingtons were in use.

The Flight played its part in the reduction of RAF commitments then taking place, making the final evacuation of RAF Catania just after Christmas 1946 and helping to close RAF Elmas in January 1947. During the spring, however, the Flight's aircraft, down to two in number, were both

LP805 [M] was a Wellington X of AHQ Malta Communications Flight.
[A. Thomas via R. C. Sturtivant]

Beaufighter TT.10 RD802 was at the end of its delivery flight from the UK on 20 October 1954 for use by Malta C&TT Sqdn. when it swung on landing and its undercarriage collapsed, causing it to be struck off charge.
[P. M. T. Green collection]

grounded as being beyond repair, but an Anson arrived in May and another in June, although there was only one pilot! It was November before the Flight was up to full peacetime strength, flying two Ansons Mk.XIX. In December 1947 a Proctor aircraft was added for the benefit of staff officers. One of the Ansons, VL306, force-landed on the beach at Homs, Libya, in January 1948, but was not badly damaged, although it did not return to the Flight. At about this time a Dakota Mk.IV, KN279, came into use by the Flight for transporting VIPs, being allocated to the MEDME (VIP) Flight.

By October 1953, the Malta Communications Flight had two Valettas on charge (VX575 and VX580) and one Dakota (KN647). Sadly, VX575, which was named *'La Valette'*, suffered an overspeeding propellor on 16 December and crashed near Qormi, with the loss of the navigator's life. In February 1954 an Anson, VM338, and Valetta VX574 were added to the Flight, but more significant was the establishment of a target-towing Flight using a Beaufighter TT.10 and the upgrading of the unit to Squadron status during May of that year.

A further severe loss was suffered by the squadron on 21 June 1954 when Dakota KN647 crashed near Nairobi while on its way to Durban,

South Africa, in support of three Shackletons of 37 Squadron. All seven men on board the Dakota lost their lives, a sad event.

Two 'new' aircraft arrived for the squadron in November: Dakota KK129 and Pembroke WV733, the first of its type in Malta. A second Pembroke was added in the following January. At the end of March Dakota KN645 left for the UK, ostensibly for disposal, but this venerable aircraft spent time on the Queen's Flight and with the RAF element in Norway before ending its days in the RAF Museum at Hendon, where it is preserved for posterity. The replacement aircraft was another Dakota, KN598.

Anson TX172 left for the UK on 13 August 1955, and spent a further 13 years in RAF service, ending its days in 1968 as one of the last of its type. The squadron's original Beaufighters, RD761 and RD867, returned to the UK for disposal at the end of 1955 and were replaced by similar aircraft, RD850 and SR914. A third 'Beau', RD754, was replaced by SR919 in February 1956.

The first jet aircraft on the squadron, Meteor T.7 WG964, which had previously been used by Malta Sector staff, was transferred to Malta C&TTS in April 1956, and two similar aircraft were taken on charge in July. Dakotas KK129 and KN598 returned to the UK early in August and

Valetta C.2 VW856 of Malta Communications & TT Flight, seen on the rainy Lyneham apron in 1958.
[A. Thomas]

were replaced by Valetta VW831.

During the Suez crisis in November 1956 the squadron stood by to evacuate RAF families from Idris in Libya but seems not to have been needed. Soon afterwards, Beaufighter SR914 left for the UK and arrived at Tangmere three days later on one engine! There were still three Beaufighters in use, however, with three Valettas, two Pembrokes, a Meteor T.7 and a Meteor F.8, WH401. By June 1957, when the Beaufighters returned from a six-week detachment in Cyprus, another Meteor F.8, WH256, had arrived.

By now, the squadron's equipment comprised three Beaufighter TT.10 target-tugs, two Meteor F.8s and one T.7, two Valettas and two Pembrokes. The Beaufighters were, by now, elderly, and were often unserviceable, but on 19 November all three took to the air together for the first time for eighteen months! Next day two of them had once more developed problems. Towing was taking place, however, for the benefit of the Army, the Royal Navy and the Indian Navy. One of the drogue operators, LAC Brown, was given a Queen's Commendation For Valuable Service In The Air after the drogue cable had fouled part of the aircraft. LAC Brown, on his own initiative, leaned out of the Beaufighter, his legs grasped by a passenger who was along for the ride, and cut the offending cable away.

At about this time, a period was spent by the squadron at Takali, but the exact dates are in question, and it is not clear whether the squadron HQ moved. It is known that all elements were back at Luqa by 7 October 1957.

The squadron's first trip behind the 'Iron Curtain' was made on 2 September 1957, when Pembroke

WV734 flew to Split and Gorizia in Yugoslavia for an unrecorded purpose. Soon after this trip, all the communications aircraft on the squadron were unservicable for one reason or another, and the Beaufighters were pressed into service instead! Fitted with special VIP seats consisting of packing cases and rubber cushions, the 'Beaus' flew far and wide carrying important personnel. One went to Athens on 26 September carrying spares for a Valiant grounded there! In addition, the squadron's Target-towing Flight was asked by the Fleet Air Arm to carry out all the target-towing tasks for the Navy between 24 and 28 September, as 728 Squadron's Sturgeons were all grounded!

Now that Takali was under-used, the decision was made to relieve some congestion at Luqa, and the Malta Communications & Target Towing Squadron was the unit involved, making the short move on 25 February 1958.

1357 (Pampa) Flight

Formed at Luqa under the command of a Flt. Lt. Smith on 1 February 1946, this unit, which would have had a meteorological task, never received any aircraft and was disbanded on 10 April. This was a great disappointment to the Met. Office, which had hoped to be able to provide more accurate forecasts based on the Flight's work.

37 Squadron

Having arrived from Ein Shemer in Palestine on 1 April 1948, 37 Squadron, equipped with Lancaster MR.3s, continued a routine of training for air-sea rescue duties. A detachment was left behind, however, and another at Ramat David, to maintain anti-immigrant patrols until the final British

Lancaster ASR.3 SW287 of 37 Squadron carrying a Lindholme lifeboat *[R. Robinson]*

Lancaster ASR.3
RE159 of 37
Squadron climbing
away from Luqa.
[R. A. Waller]

withdrawal from Palestine on 15 May. One aircraft was also sent to Shallufa to carry out ASR duties there. An early task for 37 Squadron was to search for a DC-3 of BOAC which had been on the way from Luqa to Marseilles on 14 July, and the wreckage of this aircraft was duly found on a beach near Toulon, a discovery the Lancaster crew would rather not have made.

At the end of September the responsibilty for ASR around Malta was taken over from 38 Squadron for a month, during which an aircraft was scrambled on 30 September to assist the crew of a Mosquito airborne from Luqa to Germany which suffered an engine fire, causing it to dive into the sea off Gozo. Next day the Gozo ferry overturned in a heavy swell with nineteen on board, and 37 Squadron was scrambled to look for survivors.

During the next few years detachments to Gibraltar and to Ballykelly in Northern Ireland for the Joint Anti-Submarine School were frequent, and the squadron participated in the annual defence exercises in an anti-submarine role. Something

much more unusual came about in April 1951, when a familiarisation flight was made to an oasis known as Kufra, 450 miles (720km.) south of El Adem, where the crew took part in exercises with the French Foreign Legion! None of them wanted to join!

After searching for a Hunting Airways Viking and finding its remains in the Sicilian mountains on 16 February 1952, 37 Squadron took part in exercise 'Grand Slam', in which the fleets and air forces of Great Britain, the United States, France and Italy were involved. The squadron's particular function was convoy escort work, but this was hampered by the strike of workers in Malta, which meant that airmen had to carry out domestic duties as well as their operational tasks.

Detachments to Ballykelly continued, and in July 1952 seven aircraft, complete with ground crews, spent three weeks at Idris. The year was spoiled for 37 Squadron, as for everybody at Luqa, by the crash of Lancaster SW344 in Luqa village on 30 December after suffering engine failure on take-

Possibly RF308 of 37 Squadron, this Lancaster looks distinctly down in the mouth after a take-off crash at Luqa.
[R. Robinson]

off. Three of the four crew were killed, as was a Maltese lady, and two civilians were injured.

By February 1953 only five Lancasters of 37 Squadron were serviceable after two had been declared u/s by the Avro representative. Nevertheless, two aircraft went to Habbaniya in Iraq with two of 38 Squadron on 1 April to carry out operations over the desert in the Qatar Trucial Coastal Territory following violation of an agreement with Saudi Arabia. Subsequently, the two Lancasters were repositioned at Sharjah in what is now the UAE, and returned to Luqa on 28 June. By March 1953 the Lancaster conversion unit, 236 OCU at Kinloss, had closed, new crews then being trained on Shackletons. They then had to be converted to the more elderly Lancaster on arrival in Malta!

Tension in the Canal Zone resulted in 37 Squadron carrying the men of the Marine Commando Brigade in five flights to Fayid on 14 May, and this turned out to be the final operation of any scale by the Lancasters, as the first two of the squadron's new Shackletons arrived at the end of July. By the end of September conversion to the new type was complete, and six of them were sent to Aden on a ten-day detachment. The Shackletons were generally liked at this point, although one or two pilots preferred the Lancasters, the last of which left for the scrapyard in the UK early in October.

Another unpleasant task for 37 Squadron came about on 9 April 1954 when Shackleton WL793 was scrambled to look for BOAC Comet G-ALYY, which had gone down near Elba. The wreckage was eventually found by a BEA Ambassador and was marked by WL793.

Anti-smuggling patrols kept the squadron busy in 1955 and 1956, but in 1957 there was talk of a possible disbandment. However, the squadron was reprieved, and a move to Aden was ordered, the reduced squadron, of five aircraft only, making the move at the end of August.

39 Squadron
Equipped with Meteor NF.13s, 39 Squadron, no stranger to Malta after spending time there during the Second World War, arrived at Luqa on 10 January 1955 from Kabrit in Egypt. Navigational, instrument flying and interception training occupied the squadron during the spring, and on 7 April there was participation in Exercise 'Easter Egg' designed to practice protection of Hal Far airfield against air attack. In June, however, unserviceability became a problem, but towards the end of July there were enough aircraft for the squadron to take part in the annual defence exercise at night. Later in the year detachments went to Idris for air-to-ground firing practice.

Seven of the Meteors went to Nicosia as a detachment in August 1956 in response to the growing tension in the Middle East. There, defensive patrols over the island became the routine, as did interception patrols against aircraft dropping supplies to EOKA terrorists on Cyprus. The main part of the squadron returned to Luqa on 23 March 1957, leaving two aircraft behind in case trouble brewed again.

Practice interceptions, including many on civilian aircraft, occupied 39 Squadron during 1957, but it seems that airline pilots did not appreciate being intercepted, and the order to desist was given on 10 September, apart from interceptions of any aircraft failing to comply with the special regulations in force over Cyprus. The Nicosia detachment was in fact increased to four aircraft on 4 November due to fresh tensions in the area, this time between Turkey and Syria. This problem was soon over, however, and two Meteors returned to Luqa.

By May 1958, 39 Squadron was back at Nicosia

Carrying Suez invasion stripes, Meteor NF.13 WM339 awaits business at Luqa in November 1956. *[via A. Thomas]*

in strength, eight aircraft being sent there in view of the state of emergency in the Lebanon. The detachment then took part in ensuring that British civilians were evacuated safely from that country. This task complete, the squadron regrouped at Luqa on 18 June after being relieved in Cyprus by 153 Squadron. However, plans were afoot to disband the squadron, and after due ceremony 39 Squadron disbanded on 31 July 1958, to reform the following day when 69 Squadron, which had also just disbanded (at Laarbruch in Germany) became the new 39 Squadron at Luqa, equipped with ten Canberra PR.3s and a T.4.

The new squadron's task consisted of mapping survey work, mainly over East Africa and the Arabian peninsula, and photo-reconnaissance flying as part of a commitment to NATO, which included keeping an eye on the growing Russian presence in the Mediterranean Sea. The PR.3 aircraft were replaced by PR.7s in October/November 1962 and the squadron was able to extend its survey operations to the Far East. In addition, it participated in many NATO exercises and continued to carry out low-level PR missions.

After 15 years in Malta, 39 Squadron left for Wyton in the UK on 30 September 1970 to continue its role in northern latitudes.

Valiant Wing

Four Valiant aircraft, three from 214 Squadron and the other one from 207 Squadron, arrived from Marham on 24 September 1956 to complete the preliminary deployment ordered under Operation 'Albert', the precautions being taken in anticipation of trouble brewing up in the Suez Canal Zone. Another Valiant, from 49 Squadron at Wittering, turned up on 1 October but left again after four days.

The main force of what was to be known as the Valiant Wing arrived on 26 October and comprised eight aircraft of 214 Squadron, two of 207 Squadron and two of 148 Squadron, another Marham-based unit. Finally, on 30 October, the last two Valiants, from 138 Squadron at Wittering, flew in.

On the last day of October the Valiants, with Hal Far- and Cyprus-based Canberras, raided Abu Sueir, Kabrit, Almaza and other Egyptian Air Force airfields, most of which were former RAF Stations. Little damage was done, however, and only one Egyptian Meteor fired on a Valiant. Further raids followed, but by 8 November a truce had been declared, and the Valiant crews were able to relax. By 17 November it was judged that it was safe to release the Valiants, and that day all eighteen of them took off on their homeward journey

13 Squadron

A unit which had spent its time in the Middle East since the end of 1942 with but one short break, 13 Squadron, flying Canberra PR.9s, moved to Luqa from Akrotiri in Cyprus on 1 September 1965. After settling in, the squadron carried on with its reconnaissance tasks over the central Mediterranean, keeping watch in particular on the increasing numbers of Russian naval vessels in the area.

On 6 January 1972 13 Squadron returned to Akrotiri when the political situation in Malta was causing problems, but came back to Luqa on 10 October of the same year. Examples of the Canberra PR.7 were then added to the squadron's inventory and gradually replaced the PR.9s, which had all been disposed of by October 1976.

13 Squadron, which had the distinction of being the last squadron to leave Luqa when the RAF vacated the airfield, departed for Wyton in the UK on 3 October 1978.

Valiant B(PR).1 WZ395 of 214 Squadron is typical of the aircraft of this unit which formed part of the Valiant Wing at Luqa during the 1956 Suez campaign.
[via A. Thomas]

A Shackleton of the MR.3 nose-wheel variety, WR974 [H] of 203 Squadron, on approach to Luqa c.1969.
[via A. Thomas]

203 Squadron

203 Squadron's first postwar move overseas, apart from short detachments, was made on 1 February 1969, when the squadron's Shackleton MR.3s flew from Ballykelly in Northern Ireland to Luqa. 203's main task was now to intercept the submarines of the Russian Black Sea Fleet, then in the process of building up its presence in the Mediterranean area. From July 1971, Nimrod MR.1 aircraft began to replace the Shackletons, the last of which departed in January 1972.

When a delicate political situation arose in Malta in January 1972, 203 Squadron left, transferring to the US Navy base at Sigonella in Sicily on 12 January in order to maintain its NATO responsibilities, but returned to Malta when the problem eased.

Disbandment of 203 Squadron took place on 31 December 1977, toward the end of the RAF tenure of Luqa.

A nice view of Nimrod MR.1 XV228 of 203 Squadron over Grand Harbour in 1977.
[Flt. Lt. D. McCormack via A. Thomas]

Chapter 3
HAL FAR

The birth of an airfield.

The long history of Hal Far, the first permanent airfield to be built on the island of Malta, goes back to the early nineteen-twenties, when construction of a shore base for carrier-borne aircraft of the Fleet Air Arm began. Initially attached to the Malta Naval Air Station at Calafrana, the airfield at Hal Far was officially opened on 16 January 1923 by His Excellency Field Marshal Lord Plumer, the Governor and Commander-in-Chief, who was accompanied by the Premier of Malta and Ministers of the Legislative Assembly and senior Naval and Army officers. A short flying display of aircraft from Calafrana then took place.

Just over a year later, on 19 February 1924, another flying display was arranged, at the wish of Lord Plumer, who, with certain members of the Maltese Government, wanted to see some of the first flights of service aircraft from Hal Far. Aerobatics were performed by a number of Fairey Flycatchers, which had been sent to Malta and erected at Calafrana the previous month.

HMS *Eagle* arrived off Malta on 7 June 1924 and three of its four Flights flew off to Hal Far, where two Bessoneau hangars had been erected for them. These Flights were 402 Flight with six Flycatchers, 422 Flight with six Blackburns and 460 Flight with Blackburn Darts. All three Flights then proceeded to carry out deck-landing trials and

other exercises with HMS *Eagle,* rejoining the ship but returning to Hal Far on 20 October for the winter. The first torpedo-carrying exercise from Hal Far was carried out on 28 November 1924, when Darts made a mock attack on HMS *Queen Elizabeth.*

1925 and 1926 saw a steady stream of disembarked naval aircraft at Hal Far, and at the end of 1926 civilian aircraft began to appear. De Haviland DH.66 Hercules G-EBMY of Imperial Airways brought the Director of Civil Aviation on 22 December on its way to Khoms and a week later came a similar aircraft, G-EBMX, carrying the Secretary of State for Air, Lord Hoare, and his wife, with AVM Sir Geoffrey Salmond, on an inaugural flight between Croydon and India. Two more Hercules aircraft staged through Hal Far on delivery to the Middle East early in 1927.

On 29 March 1929, Hal Far was upgraded to become an RAF Station in its own right. The RAF Base Miscellaneous Flight (or Station Flight, as it would have been called in later years) was formed on 1 April, and on the same day a corporal and four airmen arrived from Calafrana for guard duties. The first Station Commander, Wg. Cdr. C. W. Nutting OBE DSC, did not, however, arrive from the UK until 10 May.

An air display was held at Hal Far on 18 May 1929; taking part were Fairey IIID floatplanes from

Hal Far's hangars from the air in 1929, with a variety of aircraft in attendance.
[via R. C. Sturtivant]

Hangars at Hal Far under construction in March 1929; standing by with engine running is Vickers Vellore G-EBYX, in transit to Australia via Marseilles, Rome, Hal Far and Benghazi (although a forced landing was made at Mersa Matruh, where damage was sustained). The crew was Flt. Lt. Moir and Fg. Off. Owen.
[P. H. T. Green collection]

Letting their hair down at Hal Far on an unrecorded date between the wars were these RAF men, with their less innovative compatriots looking on.

Hal Far from the air
c.1931.
[Maj. Gen. Moulton
via R. C. Sturtivant]

481 Flight at Calafrana, Avro Bisons of 423 Flight from HMS *Eagle,* Blackburn Darts of 463 Flight from HMS *Courageous*, and Fairey Flycatchers of 402 Flight, also from *Eagle*. There were also dummy parachute drops and aerobatics and a mock attack on an 'enemy' headquarters. A relay race over a four-mile triangular course, starting from Hal Far and turning round Delimara lighthouse and Ta'Silch wireless station was also included.

Later that year, history was made when a Fleet Air Arm pilot from HMS *Courageous,* Owen Cathcart-Jones, made the first landing of a fighter aircraft on an aircraft carrier at night. Flying a

Fairey Flycatcher from Hal Far on 25 November, he landed without difficulty on the deck of *Courageous* while she was at anchor in Grand Harbour, demonstrating the possibilities of, in modern parlance, an 'extended operational envelope'.

The busy 'thirties.
The carrier-based Flights continued to come ashore at Hal Far over the next few years, but by 1934 they had generally been absorbed into larger Squadrons. The first of these to arrive at Hal Far was 812 Squadron, which flew off HMS *Glorious*

The aircraft of the RAF Base Miscellaneous Flight, with some visitors, seen over Hal Far about 1931; note the landing circle roughly central to the airfield [P. H. T. Green collection]

Blackburn Ripon S1265 [75] lets go its torpedo off the Maltese coast in 1933. Note the swastika emblem on the wheel disc. *[J. W. Parsons]*

in April 1934, equipped with Blackburn Baffins. It also spent time on other carriers before returning to Hal Far on 22 March 1935 along with 825 Squadron, which flew Fairey IIIFs. Other FAA squadrons which used Hal Far for short periods during the mid-thirties were 800 Squadron from HMS *Courageous* with Hawker Nimrods in January and December 1935; 801 Squadron from HMS *Furious,* also flying Nimrods, in July and August 1934 and January 1935; 802 Squadron, flying Nimrods and Ospreys from HMS *Glorious,* on many occasions from April 1933 onwards; 810 Squadron from HMS *Courageous* in December 1935, flying Baffins; 811 Squadron in January 1935, flying Baffins from HMS *Furious;* 812 Squadron from HMS *Glorious,* flying Blackburn Ripons, many times from April 1933; 813

Squadron Swordfish from HMS *Eagle* in March 1937; 821 Squadron's Fairey Seals from HMS *Courageous* in March and December 1935; 822 Squadron, flying Fairey IIIFs, later Fairey Seals, and from July 1936, Swordfish, from HMS *Glorious* on many occasions; 824 Squadron from HMS *Hermes* with Seals in November 1934 and from HMS *Eagle* in March 1937; and 825 Squadron flying Fairey IIIFs from HMS *Eagle* and HMS *Glorious* in 1935 and 1936 and Swordfish from HMS *Glorious* from July 1936.

1934 was a year of increasing activity at Hal Far. On 16 April Wg. Cdr. R. L. G. Maris DSO took over from Wg. Cdr. E. R. Prettyman DFC as Station Commander, and on the very next day the Station was inspected by the Chief of the Air Staff, ACM Sir Edward Ellington. Not content with this,

The NAAFI building at Hal Far, seen from the married quarters. *[J. Ward]*

A slight mishap to Nimrod S1580 at Hal Far in 1934. The crew of Osprey I S1681 from HMS Glorious passing takes no notice. *[J. W. Parsons]*

the AOC, Air Cdre. C. E. Rathbone, made another inspection on 25 April. Building work on the Station was also in hand; in September seven airmens' married quarters were taken over from the builders and a grocery shop and beer store were added to the NAAFI facilities.

Civilian aircraft also appeared in small numbers during 1934. On 4 September Sir Alan Cobham's Airspeed Courier force-landed at Hal Far while attempting a non-stop air-to-air refuelling flight to India and on 13 October DH.84 Dragon G-ACOR *"Fiona"*, owned by Graham McKinnion, arrived from Catania in Sicily, leaving for Tripoli next day. DH.86 VH-OSG of Qantas Airways arrived on 3 November 1934 from Rome and left for Benghazi and 11 December saw Imperial Airways HP.42 G-AAXE staging through on the way to Australia.

By February 1935 the activity generated at Hal Far by the aircraft carriers of the Mediterranean Fleet came to a head when HMS *Courageous, Furious* and *Eagle* were all at Malta at the same time, creating an unacceptable number of movements to and from the airfield. The Rear-Admiral in command of carriers, the Rt. Hon. Sir Alexander Ramsey, visited Hal Far on 5 February and was apparently able to sort things out, relieving

the load on Hal Far's hard-pressed ground crews.

The Jubilee of His Majesty King George V was celebrated in Malta by a review held at Marsa racecourse on 6 May 1935, and the Hal Far-based units, 447 Flight, 812 Squadron, 825 Squadron and Station Flight, took part. 812 Squadron excelled by carrying out illuminated night-flying, while two Avro Tutors, presumably belonging to Station Flight, performed illuminated aerobatics.

In June 1935 the night-time theme was continued when Hal Far aircraft took part in night bombing exercises for the benefit of army searchlight operators. This activity may have taken place just at the right time: in the autumn of that year, Italy's dictator, Mussolini, renewed Italian attempts to conquer Abysinnia (now Ethiopia), and Great Britain sent two RAF squadrons to Malta as a precautionary measure. 74 Squadron, equipped with Hawker Demons, was shipped to Malta on HMS *Neuralia*, arriving at Hal Far on 11 September 1935, while 22 Squadron, with Vildebeestes, arrived from Donibristle in Scotland on 10 October. Their stay was quite lengthy, 74 Squadron's dismantled Demons leaving for Hornchurch in July 1936 and 22 Squadron returning to the UK the following month.

Wg. Cdr. W. L. Taylor AFC took over from Gp.

A Blackburn Baffin on somewhat low finals at Hal Far. *[J. Ward]*

Capt. Maris as Station Commander on 29 April 1936, and at the end of July the Station returned to its normal function as a Fleet Air Arm base. However, another unit which was to make its home at Hal Far for a lengthy period, 2 Gunnery Cooperation Flight, arrived from Alexandria on 7 April 1936. This unit was split between Hal Far, where it operated remote-controlled Queen Bee and Swordfish target aircraft for gunnery practice, and Calafrana, where the same types of aircraft, but equipped with floats, were used. The Flight was re-titled 3 Anti-Aircraft Cooperation Unit on 1 March 1937, the new unit's 'A' Flight being at Hal Far.

A tornado which struck Malta on 24 November 1936 demolished three hangars at Hal Far, damaging all the aircraft of 802 and 812 Squadrons, which were on a period of temporary disembarkation. Seven of 812 Squadron's Baffins were so badly damaged that they had to be Struck Off Charge. His Excellency the Governor of Malta visited the site next day, as did the AOC on 26 November, but all the AOC could do was to issue instructions for rebuilding to begin.

By July 1937 the personnel strength of RAF Hal Far was 75 officers, 72 NCOs and 342 other ranks. All the FAA carrier-based squadrons had left Malta in April to take part in the Royal Review of the Fleet at Spithead, leaving just 3 AACU, of which detachments were regularly sent to Alexandria and Gibraltar, and Station Flight. FAA squadrons began to re-appear after the Royal Review, and on 28 December 1937 were visited by the Inspector General of the RAF, Marshal of the RAF Sir Edward Ellington GCB CMG CBE.

During 1938 new buildings to replace those destroyed in the tornado of November 1936 were completed, and included a Bellman hangar. Heightened awareness of the ominous situation in Europe prompted the use, from July 1938, of a Fairey Seal aircraft to carry out spotting tasks as part of a coastal defence programme. This aircraft was attached to Hal Far's Station Flight. A period of emergency was recorded at Hal Far between 21 September and 6 October 1938, and soon afterwards a flow of RAF aircraft in transit began. Five Ansons on their way to Abu Sueir (4 FTS) in

Osprey I, S1686 [549] of 802 Squadron, HMS Glorious, at Hal Far in 1934. *[J. W. Parsons]*

An 802 Squadron Nimrod fighter at Hal Far in 1933.
[J. W. Parsons]

Egypt arrived on 22 October and another five four days later, while on 24 October five Wellesleys of the Long Range Development Flight, Upper Heyford, arrived on their way to Ismailia, leaving next day.

Tension in Europe steadily increased, and at Hal Far on 8 April 1939 another period of emergency began. Defence posts were manned and respirators issued. Sqdn. Ldr. W. L. Houlbrook, formerly CO of 3 AACU, took over from Wg. Cdr. J. S. Fall as Station Commander on 29 August, and 3 AACU became an operational unit, carrying out anti-submarine and close reconnaissance patrols. Station Flight and SHQ personnel were absorbed into 3 AACU.

Hal Far awaits hostilities.
After the outbreak of war on 3 September 1939 and the lack of any immediate action on Malta, 3 AACU resumed its training role on 3 October. Sqdn. Ldr. Houlbrook relinquished his post of Station Commander to Wg. Cdr. O'Sullivan on 1 January 1940 and returned to 3 AACU. During March, intensive operational training by aircraft from HMS *Glorious* took place at Hal Far, while 3 AACU carried out target shoots and Station Flight put up coastal patrol aircraft. A number of Bristol Blenheims bound for 203 Squadron at Heliopolis staged through Hal Far from Marseilles (Marignane) during March, as did Lockheed F-ARPP carrying General Weygand, which came in from the same place on 28 March.

On 18 April 1940 3 AACU was again put on an operational basis as relations with Italy were becoming strained. Next day, four Sea Gladiators were issued to Station Flight as equipment for a Fighter Flight to be set up at Hal Far. Meanwhile, on 19 April, a detachment of the King's Own Malta Rifles had taken over duty as airfield guards from Maltese auxiliaries.

Anxiety over Italy's intentions caused most of April's training programme to be cancelled and instead operational training was given to pilots totally unused to it. Two Seal spotter aircraft were available at 20 minutes notice from 1 May, and 3 AACU again became operational, its training commitment being cancelled. Two of its aircraft were to be available at 30 minutes notice, one armed with four 250lb. (115kg.) GP bombs and one for reconnaissance. Practice blackouts were ordered every night, and on 4 May preliminary plans for the evacuation of RAF men's families were drawn up.

An interception exercise was held on 8 May in cooperation with the Mediterranean HQ War Room, and Station defences were tried out. Three days later, after the authorities had learned of the use of troop-carrying aircraft and paratroops by the Germans in Holland, Hal Far airfield was blocked by motor vehicles except for one landing strip which could also be blocked in an emergency. By 20 May small arms had been issued to officers and SNCOs, gun posts were fully manned and RAF Hal Far was at full readiness. Three of the Gladiators were at 2 minutes' notice between 04.00 and 19.30 and one of 3 AACU's Swordfish could be in the air within 15 minutes, day or night.

Compulsory evacuation of the RAF dependents to Parisio Palace, Naxxar, began on 20 May, but some elected to return to the UK on the SS *Oronsay*. Five days later, however, the evacuation was discontinued and the families returned, remaining on 12 hours' notice of further evacuation. To complete Hal Far's preparations, a curfew was imposed on 27 May between the hours of 23.00 and 05.00, anyone breaking the curfew without good reason being likely to be shot at.

Attacked!

Italy joined Germany in the Second World War on 10 June 1940 and next day ten aircraft raided Hal Far. One or two were shot down by anti-aircraft fire, but sixteen 250lb bombs were dropped, causing little damage. More Italian aircraft were over Malta during the afternoon, and one was shot down by one of Hal Far's Gladiators. On 13 June there were raids all day, and two men of the Devonshire Regiment were killed.

Reinforcements arrived on 20 June in the shape of 36 men of 767 Squadron, and the squadron's Swordfish aircraft flew in from Medjaz-el-Bab two days later. The only other aircraft present at Hal Far at the time were four Swordfish of 3 AACU and the four Sea Gladiators of Fighter Flight. Meanwhile, enemy air raids continued, the Officers' Mess receiving a direct hit on 26 June and 18 bombs falling without damage on 30 June. Fighter Flight personnel were very pleased that four Hurricane aircraft arrived on 28 June to boost their capabilities.

767 Squadron was renumbered 830 Squadron on 1 July 1940 and the Swordfish began a period of offensive operations from Hal Far against targets in Sicily. Raids on Hal Far continued during July and August, several of 830 Squadron's Swordfish aircraft being damaged. The Fighter Flight was upgraded to become 261 Squadron on 1 August 1940, and next day 418 Flight arrived, its Hurricanes being absorbed immediately into 261 Squadron. It was now managing to intercept the

Italian raiders more effectively, and protracted dog-fights took place. However, on 15 September, twenty Ju.87s with CR.42s and Macchi 200s in attendence managed to get through to drop delayed-action bombs on Hal Far.

During the early part of 1941 the raids, mostly small-scale, continued, but on 5 March a major dive-bombing attack by over sixty aircraft took place. Severe damage was caused to buildings, all the barracks being made uninhabitable. Three Swordfish and a Gladiator were destroyed on the ground, but there were no casualties. On 2 April, amid constant raids, ten Hurricanes and an escorting Blackburn Skua arrived, and on 27 April another fifteen Hurricanes and two Fairey Fulmars reported for duty. Three more Fulmars flew in from HMS *Formidable* on 9 May. On 16 May Sqdn. Ldr. A. C. Martin took over as Station Commander from Wg. Cdr. J. E. Allen, who had been in the position since 8 November 1940, but Sqdn. Ldr. Martin was himself replaced on 3 June by Gp. Capt. M. L. Taylor.

Aircraft strength was now building up, fourteen Hurricanes and four Fulmars arriving on 21 May, another seventeen Hurricanes on 6 June and yet another eleven on 14 June. The enemy must have spotted these movements, as at 05.30 on 7 June Italian fighters machine-gunned Hal Far. On 11 June 185 Squadron Hurricanes intercepted Macchi 200s over Hal Far, and shot several of them down, losing one Hurricane in the process. This aircraft was being flown by a pilot of 46 Squadron, which was in transit to the Middle East at the time without aircraft of its own. The Fleet Air Arm, meanwhile, had disembarked 800X Flight of nine Fulmars from HMS *Furious* to Hal Far on 21 May 1941 to add to Malta's defence capability.

Wg. Cdr. R. H. Harris took over command of

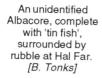

An unidentified Albacore, complete with 'tin fish', surrounded by rubble at Hal Far.
[B. Tonks]

An example of the devestation inflicted on Hal Far in 1942 by the seemingly unstoppable Luftwaffe.
[Sqdn. Ldr. P. H. Roberts via A. Thomas]

the Station on 26 July 1941 but relinquished it on 26 September to Wg. Cdr. R. I. MacDougall. Raids on Malta continued, but Hal Far-based aircraft were able to carry out a few aggressive sorties against targets in Sicily. Further capacity came on 18 October 1941 with the arrival of the Albacore and Swordfish aircraft of 828 Squadron from HMS Ark Royal, but 800X Flight was disbanded on 13 November 1941.

The year 1941 ended with a night raid on Hal Far by three Ju88s of the Luftwaffe, which had recently entered the war in the Mediterranean, having previously entrusted matters to the Italian Air Force. During this raid a Swordfish was badly damaged but no buildings were affected.

January 1942 saw raids on Hal Far continue, mainly on a smaller scale, but during the month a Hurricane, two Skuas and two Swordfish were destroyed and fifteen Hurricanes, three Swordfish and a Fulmar were damaged. The raids then intensified, and on 6 February four Ju.88s dropped fifteen bombs, destroying a hangar, the 830 Squadron armoury and an 828 Squadron Albacore.

On 22 February there were seven raids between 10.15 and 18.10, and severe damage was caused. The cinema and MT yard were demolished, a bus, two cars, two tractors and a bowser destroyed and three Albacore and two Swordfish aircraft written off. The enemy campaign continued during March, but on 9 March a Ju.88 was shot down by AA and the crew of two taken prisoner. A hangar was destroyed on 18 March and during an afternoon raid by 30 Stukas (Ju.87s) on 24 March the naval wing of the Officers' Mess and some barracks were destroyed. During this raid six airmen, three soldiers, and two civilians were killed and twelve airmen, three naval ratings, a Maltese auxiliary and two civilians were posted as missing. The last day of March saw a raid by twenty Ju.88s during which an Albacore and a Swordfish were destroyed and a Mosquito from Luqa crash-landed and burst into flames; luckily the crew escaped. Reinforcements in the shape of 229 Squadron's Hurricanes arrived on 28 March, but the squadron disbanded on 29 April.

So life under extreme conditions continued for

Typical of the many buildings at Hal Far which were severely damaged during the siege is this one, probably a barrack block.
[R. A. Powell]

those at Hal Far. Four raids by Ju.88s took place on 1 April and eight Hurricanes, among others, were damaged. On 17 April Gp. Capt. J. G. H. Thomas DFC took over as Station Commander from Wg. Cdr. C. Ryley DFC, who had only held the position since 6 March. The NAAFI, the Sergeants' Mess and a stores building were wiped out in raids on 26 April and other buildings were badly damaged. To inspect all this chaos HE the Governor, Field Marshal Viscount Gort VC, visited on 29 April.

Better news cheered those at Hal Far a little on 9 May 1942, when the first eleven Spitfires for 185 Squadron arrived after flying off the American carrier USS *Wasp*. By the end of that month, during which Wg. Cdr. J. F. Griffiths became Station Commander, raids on Hal Far had diminished and the squadrons were able to lick their wounds.

During the autumn of 1942 there was little enemy activity at Hal Far, but there were movements of Station Commanders, many of whom seem to have been anxious to be elsewhere. Wg. Cdr. H. L. Dawson DFC, who had replaced Wg. Cdr. Griffiths, left on 16 December and was succeeded by Wg. Cdr. J. M. Thompson DFC. By this time Hal Far squadrons were back on the offensive. Another squadron of Albacores of the Fleet Air Arm, 821 Squadron, arrived from Berka on 30 November 1942, and on 9 February 1943 a Supermarine Walrus amphibian flew in from Castel Benito in Libya for air-sea rescue duties. Twelve more Albacores, this time 826 Squadron aircraft, arrived on 15 February from Misurata, but they were purely in transit to Bone.

Once the siege of Malta was over, things could settle down a little at Hal Far. Defence capability was supplemented by a detachment of the RAF Regiment on 14 March 1943, replacing 'A' Company of the Devon Regiment, which left the island after three years of valuable service. However, for the first time in several months a daylight raid was made on Hal Far on 21 May. Thirty-six aircraft, Fw.190 fighter-bombers escorted by Fw.190 and Bf.109 fighters, made the attack and although only six 550kg bombs were dropped three Albacores and a Spitfire were destroyed. One Fw.190 was shot down on the edge of the airfield by AA fire and an unexploded bomb was found on top of a revetment wall.

In June 1943 radical changes to Hal Far's

complement took place. 821 Squadron's Albacores left for Tunisia on 4 June, followed next day by 185 Squadron, which moved the short distance to Qrendi, and on 8 June 828 Squadron took its Albacores to Takali. In their place came four squadrons of Spitfires forming 324 Wing — 43, 72, 93 and 243 Squadrons — which arrived from Mateur between 9 and 12 June. The ground crews came in on 9 June under the command of Gp. Capt. G. K. Gilroy DSO DFC+Bar, with Wg. Cdr. H. S. L. 'Cocky' Dundas as Wing Commander Flying. One of 243 Squadron's aircraft crashed into a wall while landing and was written off, the pilot being badly hurt. The fifth squadron of 324 Wing, 111 Squadron, went to Safi but operated with the others.

An ASR Swordfish took off on 12 June to search for a German dinghy but itself failed to return after its maximum endurance of seven and a quarter hours. A Beaufort and a Wellington then began a search, but it was later discovered that the Swordfish had landed, lost, at Lampedusa, which was still in Italian hands and being bombed by the Allies at the time. The pilot, Sgt. Cohen, was offered the surrender of the island between raids. He was delighted to fly to Sousse in Tunisia to announce his single-handed defeat of the Italian garrison!

Hal Far begines to develop.
By the end of June 1943, a 3000ft (915m.) paved runway (runway 13/31) had been completed, extending from the original grass field to form a runway of 6000ft. (1830m.) total length, and the construction of runway 09/27, 4800ft. (1465m.) in length, had been commenced. Extra aircraft pens, an underground operations room and a protected control tower were also put into use at this time.

RAF Hal Far was very pleased to receive a visit from His Majesty King George VI on 20 June 1943, accompanied by Lord Gort, after the King had arrived from Tunisia in HMS *Anson*. Another important visitor was Field Marshal Montgomery, who was present on 4 July, six days before the invasion of Sicily began. Two other visitors on 4 July were B-17 aircraft of the 20th and 96th Bombardment Squadrons of the USAAF, which landed after being damaged in a raid on Catania.

In connection with the Sicily campaign, many squadron movements took place at Hal Far. 828

Either a Boston of the RAF or a USAAF A-20 being refuelled at Hal Far in 1943. The two pieces of ordnance in the foreground look ominous!
[P. H. T. Green collection]

Squadron's Albacores returned on 8 July and next day 250 Squadron arrived from Zuara with Spitfires. Walruses of 284 Squadron flew in (very slowly!) from Algiers to add to Hal Far's air-sea rescue capabilities on 12 July, and three fighter squadrons of the USAAF, the 64th, 65th and 66th, comprising the 57th Fighter Group, arrived from Tunisia, flying P-40 Kittyhawk aircraft, on 5 July. The invasion completed, the four squadrons of 324 Wing left for Sicily between 14 and 17 July, 250 Squadron moved to Luqa on 13 July and the American squadrons moved to Pachino on 19 July. The vacancy created by the departure of 324 Wing was filled on 21 July by the arrival of the three squadrons of 3 (SAAF) Light Bomber Wing — 12 and 24 Squadrons flying Bostons and 21 Squadron with Baltimores. The Wing carried out several missions before leaving on 19 August for Gerbini. Just before they left, 284 Squadron had taken its

Walruses to Casablanca and for a short time Hal Far's only resident was the ASR & Comms. Flight, which moved to Takali on 25 August.

The Officers' Mess closed down on 30 August and the officers moved into billets at Birzebugga, but before long flying activity recommenced. Between 24 and 30 September 1943 all three squadrons based at Qrendi — 185, 229 and 249 — moved to Hal Far and continued their training programme, though 249 Squadron soon left for Grottaglie in Italy.

From 23 November 1943 the Station Commander was Wg. Cdr. J. M. Thompson DSO DFC+Bar, who was at the presentation of a Station Crest by AVM Sir Keith Park KBE CB MC DFC on 27 December. At a ceremonial parade the AVM expressed his congratulations to Wg. Cdr. Thompson for a fine turn-out. A few days later, AVM Park left in a Mosquito for Cairo to take up

BR495, the Spitfire Vc used in 1943 by the Wing Leader, Wg. Cdr. Percy Prosser Hanks, carried his personal code.
[Sqdn. Ldr. P. H. Roberts via A. Thomas]

his new post as AOC-in-C Middle East and was succeeded as AOC Malta by Air Cdre. J. R. Scarlett-Streatfield CBE. His tenure did not last long, as by the time the 'top brass' visited Hal Far on 2 February 1944 to inspect the rebuiding and extension work he had been succeeded by AVM A. H. Wann.

'A' Flight of 229 Squadron left Hal Far for Catania in Sicily on 30 January 1944 to join 'B' Flight, which was already there on detachment. Reconstruction work continued, but was hindered on 5 February by a fierce gale which caused part of one of the new buildings to take to the air. One Sqdn. Ldr. Wilmott complained that he should have been scrambled to shoot it down! Although the new Officers' Mess was incomplete, a great trek of inmates from Birzebugga began on 17 February, the officers bedding down wherever they could while things were sorted out. The SNCOs were now able to occupy the vacated building at Birzebugga.

Yet another Station Commander, Wg. Cdr. Ogden, took over on 18 February 1944 and, with the AOC, conducted a rigorous inspection of the new buildings on 24 February. The new facilities were particularly important as the idea was mooted that Luqa airfield should be handed over to BOAC, the prospect of which prompted large numbers of officers from Luqa to inspect Hal Far's new buildings.

On 1 March 1944 the Air Sea Rescue & Communications Flight, which had returned from Takali on 1 February, was renamed Air Headquarters Malta Communications Flight, and two Avro Ansons arrived next day for use on a twice-weekly service to Sicily. The first Vickers Warwick for ASR duties with 283 Squadron arrived on 4 April 1944 from Sardinia, and three more came in on 9 April. It was 28 April, however, before Dakotas brought the squadron's ground crews in. 'Air Force Day' was held for the first time on 21 June 1944 in perfect weather, soon after the completion of runway 09/27. There was a ceremonial parade and an inspection by the Governor, Lord Gort, followed by a march-past of all RAF units on the island. Static displays of aircraft and equipment were presented and 185 Squadron returned to give an aerobatic display. To round off the day there was a dance in the Officers' Mess.

The SNCOs moved their Mess from Birzebugga to Kalafrana on 1 July and three days later yet another Station Commander, Gp. Capt. F. H. Tyson, took up residence. There then began another series of squadron movements. The Beaufighters of 108 Squadron arrived on 1 July, but stayed only until 27 July before moving on. On 25 July 185 Squadron ceased operating and left next day for Perugia, where it was joined by its Grottaglie detachment. In its place a detachment of 255 Squadron, flying Beaufighters, arrived from Foggia Main for night patrol work, and they were joined on 16 August by the Lockheed Venturas of 27 Squadron, SAAF. After doing some useful work, 255 Squadron left on 25 August, and Gp. Capt. Tyson followed three days later, to be replaced by Wg. Cdr. J. H. Gaynor.

Visitors of a more unusual nature arrived on 11 September 1944 in the shape of two US Navy Catalina amphibians with Free French crews. One of them flew with a number of Royal Navy officers on board who were sceptical about aerial mine-spotting (although such methods had been used for many years); they returned wiser men, as, sixteen miles south of Malta they had located five German mines. The Catalinas carried out further sorties before leaving on 9 October.

Work had been proceeding on the construction of a new Operations Room to replace the one underground, and it came into use on 6 October 1944, by which time the nearest conflict was 600 miles away! The new building was doubtless inspected by yet another Station Commander, Gp. Capt. A. W. Bates, when he took over on 20 October. A Station cinema was by now functioning in the airmen's dining hall, and although it was said to lack the comfort of the Odeon cinemas back home it was better than nothing.

The end of the war was, it was devoutly hoped, now in sight, and steps were taken to provide help for the large proportion of RAF personnel who would be leaving the Service as soon as they could. On 12 October 1944 an inaugural meeting was held at Hal Far to discuss post-war careers, but although the decision was made to set up a formal scheme, little was done for several months.

Some more construction work was begun in October 1944, principally on a number of Nissen huts located near the barrack blocks, to be used as reading rooms and rest rooms as well as spare sleeping quarters. Unfortunately, the worst storm Malta had experienced for forty years hit the island on 28 December, and torrential rain and gales hit Hal Far for four days, causing severe damage to buildings and aircraft and not helping the work being done at the time.

The SAAF Venturas of 27 Squadron left for La Seina on 8 November 1944 and were not replaced. Little flying was done by 283 Squadron or the Communications Flight during December 1944 or January 1945, but towards the end of January the prospect of great activity caused by the forthcoming tripartite conference at Yalta in the Crimea became apparent. It was planned that the Prime Minister of Great Britain, the President of the United States and others would stage through Malta, requiring considerable air support to counter a possible enemy attack. Thus, on 27 January 1945, nine Spitfires of 1435 Squadron, based at Grottaglie, and six Mosquitos of 256 Squadron from Foggia arrived. Two of the Mosquitos duly intercepted the Prime Minister's York aircraft north-west of the island on 29 January and escorted it to Luqa. During the early part of February all the attached aircraft were busy shepherding VIP flights in and out of Malta and providing ASR cover.

At 20.05 on 1 February 1945 a York of 511 Squadron, MW116, sent a 'Mayday' message reporting that it might have to ditch near Lampedusa. Ten minutes later a Mosquito was airborne from Hal Far but had to return due to generator trouble. Warwick 'M' then took to the air, and a final message was received from the York stating that it was ditching. High Speed Launch 2617 and Pinnace 1263 were searching the area by 21.20 and at 21.35 Warwick 'G' joined in. A US Navy Catalina, one of two on detachment at Hal Far (one being 02962), left Hal Far and at 06.58 next day reported spotting wreckage in the sea. By 07.13 it was confirmed that of the 15 people on board the York eight were dead and seven were in hospital on Lampedusa. All in all, a sad day's work.

During February 1945 hurried arrangements were made to deal with the arrival of four squadrons of the Fleet Air Arm. Sites were cleared and marked for new buildings and for large dispersals on the south side of the airfield. The AMWD was very busy providing more Nissen huts for sleeping accommodation and two Double Iris dining halls.

The expected influx of FAA squadrons on temporary attachment for training began on 8 March 1945 with the arrival of personnel. The aircraft flew in on 20 March — 48 Fairey Barracudas of 812 and 814 Squadrons, 47 Chance-Vought Corsairs of 1850 and 1851 Squadrons and three Supermarine Seafires of 736B Flight. These aircraft flew from the carriers HMS *Venerable* and HMS *Vengeance* and apart from one bent tail-wheel on a Corsair all went well.

Aircraft movements at Hal Far during April 1945 - 4700 - were high due to the presence of the FAA squadrons, but tailed off in May, when only 930 movements were recorded. On 11 May the squadrons carried out a large-scale dummy attack on Tripoli, Operation 'Sling', before leaving Hal Far on 20/21 May at the end of their training period.

Peacetime routine.

May 1945 included, of course, VE Day, celebrated at Hal Far by a Christmas Day routine. The thoughts of all personnel must then, notwithstanding the continuing war in the Far East, have turned to their future lives as civilians. The Educational & Vocational Training scheme (EVT) planned some months previously now began, and 664 people requested EVT in one or more of 94 courses. 205 more sought information on specific occupations, and 120 asked for career advice, so that by the end of May Hal Far was very much involved in the EVT Scheme.

To assist in the calibration of Mediterranean Fleet aircraft carriers, a Flight of Mosquitos, said to be from 614 Squadron, arrived on 1 May 1945. Ten days later eight Spitfires of 682 Squadron flew in from San Severo in Italy to do similar work with HMS *Duke of York, Anson* and *Cleopatra* but were found to be unsuitable and returned to base on 20 May.

Next to arrive at Hal Far was a detachment of 624 Squadron to assist in mine-spotting duties. A ground party turned up on 29 June 1945, and before long the detachment's Walruses were carrying out tedious searches based on information provided by the beaten German authorities. Little success was achieved, and doubts were raised about the authenticity of the information. Then came 73

A USAAF P-40 coded 2:7, probably from the 57th Fighter Group, visiting Hal Far in 1945.
[via R. C. Sturtivant]

Squadron, ground crews of which arrived on 2 July to take up temporary residence in the Nissen huts on the erstwhile Naval site.

The Warwicks of 283 Squadron ceased operating from Hal Far on 26 August 1945 and left for Maison Blanche in Algeria. Further changes to units at Hal Far were in the offing; the first of eight Supermarine Sea Otters of 1702 Squadron, FAA, arrived on 20 September from HMS *Trouncer* via Cape Bon to take over mine-spotting duties from 624 Squadron, which left for Littorio on 30 September. In October 728 Squadron at Takali was able to take over fleet requirements and radar calibration work from the 255 Squadron detachment, which remained at Hal Far for the time being.

Meanwhile, EVT courses were in great demand, and language courses and building trade work were particularly popular. Several RAF men were, by September, working at civilian concerns in Valletta such as the 'Times of Malta' newspaper and photographic shops.

Development work at and around Hal Far continued during the early post-war period. A new Station Church, St. Christopher's, was dedicated on 1 July 1945 by HE the Governor and C-in-C Malta and Lady Schreiber, with AVM K. B. Lloyd CBE AFC. This building doubled as a gymnasium. To modernise air traffic control procedures, it was recommended that either a Beam Approach Beacon System (BABS) or Ground Controlled Approach (GCA) should be installed.

October 1945 saw the arrival of the three Wellingtons of 765 Squadron, FAA, from Lee-on-Solent on 3 October and the departure for Hassani in Greece of 624 Squadron on 1 October and 1702 Squadron on 16 October. In January 1946, 892 and 1792 Squadrons of the FAA arrived for short stays and 255 Squadron finally left for Gianaclis.

More and more personnel were leaving Hal Far for demobilisation by January 1946 and were not replaced. Although Hal Far was an RAF Station, by now most of the personnel were from the Fleet Air Arm, and the end of its time under RAF control, at least for many years, was now in sight. A date for handing over to the FAA was set for the end of March but then revised to mid-April. 73 Squadron was to remain as a lodger unit, occupying the domestic site on the north-west side of the airfield. Of the two radar units, 502 AMES (now established on Gozo to provide better coverage on that side of the island) and 501 AMES, were to be transferred to the operational control of RAF Luqa. Also to remain at Hal Far were the Sector Operations Room and AHQ Malta Photographic Section.

The Navy takes over!

At sunset on 14 April 1946 the RAF ensign was lowered for the last time and next day Hal Far was placed under FAA command as HMS *Falcon*. Over the next nineteen years, Hal Far would see many squadrons come and go, mainly those of the Fleet Air Arm but also some RAF units and a considerable US Navy presence.

On the day of the handover, two flying units were present at Hal Far — 765 Squadron, which would disband at the end of April, and the RAF's 73 Squadron, now a lodger unit. On 5 May, 'new blood' arrived in the shape of 728 Squadron, the Fleet Requirements Unit, from Luqa, and this squadron was destined to make its home at Hal Far for over twenty years. As the Station became busier, a Station Flight was formed in March 1947, working closely with 728 Squadron, the pilots of which seem to have flown for both units as required.

During the late 1940s, Hal Far provided shore

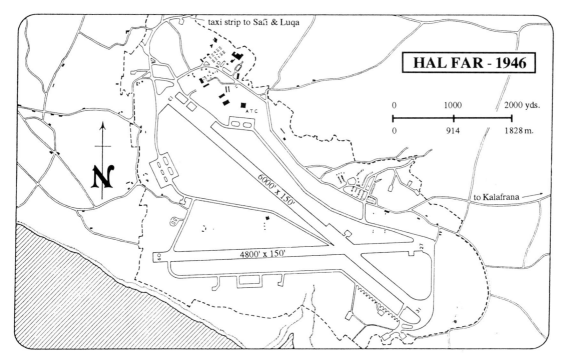

taxi strip to Safi & Luqa

HAL FAR - 1946

| 0 | 1000 | 2000 yds. |
| 0 | 914 | 1828 m. |

ATC

N

6000' x 150'

4800' x 150'

to Kalafrana

facilities for many carrier-based squadrons of the Mediterranean Fleet as well as a longer welcome for several other FAA squadrons. In addition, the first of a series of summer camps for UK-based RNVR squadrons was held at Hal Far in August 1950, although no more took place until May 1952. These two-week training camps carried on until the Suez crisis of 1956, and after that, in March 1957, the RNVR squadrons were disbanded.

The RAF established another lodger unit at Hal Far in September 1951, when 185 Squadron was re-formed to fly Vampire FB.5s. Among the many units moving in and out at that time were two squadrons, 75 and 76, of the Royal Australian Air Force, which replaced 185 Squadron at the end of July 1952 when it moved to Luqa. After spending a short period at Nicosia in January 1953, the Australians left for the UK in May 1953 to take part in the Coronation Review.

Although detachments of US Navy patrol squadrons had visited Hal Far on detachment on several occasions before, a much more important USN presence began at Hal Far late in 1953 with the establishment of FASRON 201 Special, a large

Over the cliff near Hal Far into the Mediterranean goes a surplus-to-requirements 728 Squadron Seafire in about 1946.
[R. G. Harrington]

Left: Coded O5:D, an 805 Squadron Firefly being towed to Hal Far's scrap area, c.1946.
[R. G. Harrington]

Right: Seafire F.47 VP465 [136:O] of 804 Squadron at Hal Far in 1948.
[P. Cook via R. C. Sturtivant]

Left: Turkish Air Force Oxfords 105, 122 and another staging through Hal Far c.1946.
[R. G. Harrington]

Right: Firefly FR.1 PP596 [282:P] of 827 Squadron taking off from Hal Far in 1948.
[Rogers via R. C. Sturtivant]

Left: Two Firefly FR.1s of 805 Squadron, PP470 [O5C] and PP594 [O5D], over Malta in 1946, during a time when several periods were spent ashore from HMS *Ocean*.
[Lt. Cdr. P. J. Hutton via R. C. Sturtivant]

Right: US Navy F6F-5P Hellcats of VF-9A (Fleet Fighter Squadron 9A) from the carrier USS *Phillipine Sea* visiting Hal Far, probably in 1947.
[R. A. Waller]

The signals square at Hal Far, c.1946 *[R. G. Harrington]*

Left: Along this line-up of aircraft from HMS *Ocean* at Hal Far c.1946 can be seen Firefly I PP543 of 816 Squadron coded O6 and Seafires of 805 Squadron coded O5:G and O5:H.
[via R. A. Waller]

Right: A carrier-based Fairey Barracuda operating from Hal Far c.1946.
[via R. A. Waller]

Left: A US Navy target-towing JD-1 Invader of VU-4 (Fleet Utility Squadron 4) at Hal Far during an exercise during the late 'forties.
[R. A. Waller]

Right: Firefly I PP549 [O5:W] of 805 Squadron at Hal Far c.1946.
[R. G. Harrington]

Visiting Hal Far on an unknown date in the early 1950s was this Corsair of the US Navy.

aircraft-servicing unit. To enable the airfield to cope with the additional traffic caused by visiting USN aircraft, improvements to facilities were put in hand, some at least, including a large new control tower, being funded by the US Government. Also supplied from US Navy stocks was a set of GCA (Ground Controlled Approach) equipment, which went into sevice in April 1954. In addition to the servicing facilities, two USN squadrons were now based at Hal Far — VW-2, which flew WV-2 Warning Star airborne early warning aircraft, and VR-35, which used R4Q Packets ('Boxcars') for general transport work.

As an exercise to determine ways of protecting Hal far against possible air attack, Exercise 'Easter Egg' was held on 7 April 1955 involving simulated combat between Seahawks, Avengers, Wyverns, Skyraiders, Meteors and Shackletons, the latter presumably pretending to be heavy bombers!

By now a very busy airfield, Hal Far continued to receive FAA squadrons on both short and long-term visitations. One important aircraft present for three weeks in August was the prototype Blackburn NA.39, the foreruner of the Buccanneer, which was carrying out hot weather trials. Additionally, 208 Squadron of the RAF based its Meteor FR.9 reconnaissance aircraft there between January and March 1956. The Suez campaign in the autumn of that year made life even more hectic, as Hal Far was the temporary home of the Binbrook Canberra Wing. The Canberras returned home by December, however, and the situation at Hal Far eased a little.

During March 1958 a notable arrival was 728B

Hal Far's control tower in 1946. *[R. G. Harrington]*

Squadron, which was dedicated to flying pilotless aircraft as part of the operational trials of the Seaslug guided missile. The Whirlwind helicopters of 728C Squadron also arrived that spring, as did a detachment of Sea Venoms of 751 Squadron, an electronic counter-measures unit, to carry out trials with the Fleet. Further ECM aircraft arrived in July when 831B Squadron brought Sea Venoms, Avengers and Gannets for a four-month stay.

Left: Coded 109:R, this F2H Banshee of the US Navy, ∞1249, is seen on a visit to Hal Far.
[NWMA]

Right: 820 Squadron Firefly AS.6s from HMS *Theseus* lined up at Hal Far in 1953.
[B. Lowe via R. C. Sturtivant]

Left: Firefly AS.5 WB260, seen at Hal Far during an open day on 28 August 1954. Three days later it was allocated to 1841 Squadron RNVR at the squadron's summer camp, and returned to the UK. [Flt. Lt. B. A. Pendlebury via R. C. Sturtivant]

Right: On show at the air display at Hal Far on 28 August 1954 was Attacker FB.2 WP277 [145:J] from HMS *Eagle*.
[Flt. Lt. B. A. Prendlebury ia R. C. Sturtivant]

Left: Another aircraft at Hal Far's display on 28 August 1954 was Sea Fury FB.11 VX639.
[Flt. Lt. B. A. Pendlebury via R. C. Sturtivant]

Right: Carrying Suez invasion stripes, Avenger AS.5 XB389 [982:B] and XB374 [981:B] of Ship's Flight, HMS Bulwark are seen here at Hal Far.
[via R. C. Sturtivant]

Left: P2V-5 Neptune 128396 of US Navy Squadron VP-24 (not VA-HM-13 as marked) at Hal Far in August 1958.
[via G. Cruikshank]

Right: 'Super-Connie' WV-2 of US Navy Squadron VW-2 on a visit to Hal Far in August 1958.
[via G. Cruikshank]

Left: Hal Far's massive post-war control tower, construction of which was financed by the US Navy, is (in 1992) in use by the Malta Fire Dept., who have built a practice building alongside.
[author]

Right: Gannet WN407 of 847 Squadron, coded 088:HF, was not based at Hal Far but at Nicosia, hence the Cyprus map on the rudder. Administration of the squadron was, however, carried out at Hal Far, which explains the code letters.
[via R. C. Sturtivant]

Left: Visiting Hal Far from HMS *Ark Royal* in 1960/61 were Whirlwind HAS.7s coded 90:R and 95:R.
[A. E. Hughes via R. C. Sturtivant]

Visiting Hal Far from HMS *Victorious* in 1960 was Gannet AEW.1 XL495 [425:V] of 849 Squadron.
[A. E. Hughes via R. C. Sturtivant]

FASRON 201 Special was disbanded in October 1959 and 728 Squadron moved into the vacated buildings. A new arrival at Hal Far that month was 750 Squadron, an observer training unit from Culdrose, where weather conditions for such work were deemed less than suitable.

At the end of 1959, therefore, four units were based at Hal Far: the long-resident 728 Squadron, flying a variety of aircraft; 728B Squadron, using Fireflies and Meteors; 750 Squadron with Sea Princes; and Station Flight. It was another two

years before this situation altered when 728B Squadron disbanded in December 1961, its task complete.

Repairs to the main runway during March 1962 caused 728 Squadron to operate from Takali for a few days, leaving 750 Squadron to use Hal Far. Reduced activity caused a reversion to 0800-1700 working hours on 1 January 1963, and at the same time the airfield's GCA approach system was withdrawn.

One event which caused some amusement at

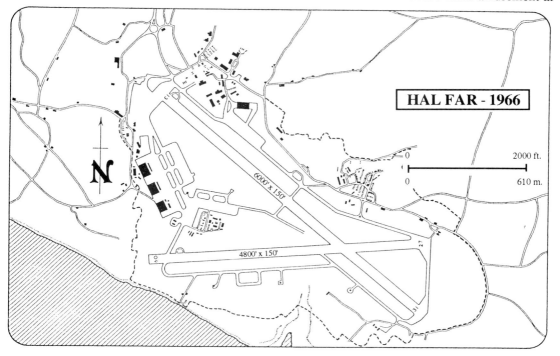

HAL FAR - 1966

2000 ft.

610 m.

Hal Far in its final form, seen from the air in 1973. *[P. H. T. Green collection]*

Hal Far in 1964 was the theft of a Dutch Navy Tracker by an electrician, who was also an unqualified pilot, of that service. Operated by 2 Squadron, the aircraft, serialled 153, lifted off the Hal Far runway at 06.55 on 7 March. Shackletons of 38 Squadron, Sea Venoms and Whirlwinds of 728 Squadron and the boats of 1151 MCU were scrambled to search for the Tracker, which it was thought would inevitably crash. At 11.55, however, controllers at Benina reported an aircraft circling, and twenty minutes later stated that an aircraft had landed at a disused airstrip known as

Merryfield. What happened to the pilot, referred to as the 'Flying Dutchman', is not recorded, but a message of thanks was received at Hal Far from the CO of Netherlands Task Group 1.

The beginning of the end...

In line with the gradual run-down of British naval activity in the Mediterranean, the other units at Hal Far went into slow decline in numbers of aircraft and personnel, but not of course in quality of performance. No longer required, the Station Flight disbanded in 1965, and 750 Squadron

In a sorry state is Firefly AS.5 VT423 after a crash-landing following a mid-air collision with similar aircraft WB418 of 812 Sqdn. on 6 October 1950 *[J. Betts]*

Empty now, this barrack building at Hal Far stands as a reminder of all the airmen and naval ratings who passed through it over the years.
[author]

returned to the UK in June of that year, leaving 728 Squadron, in reduced form, in splendid isolation as the only inhabitant.

Hal Far, for nearly twenty years under FAA control as HMS *Falcon*, reverted to RAF 'ownership' on 1 September 1965 after an impressive ceremony the previous day, and 38 Squadron moved its Shackletons in from Luqa. Only eighteen months later, however, this squadron disbanded, and when long-term resident 728 Squadron followed suit at the end of May 1967 Hal Far's 43-year active life as home to a huge number of flying units came to an end.

Subsequently, Hal Far was placed on a 'care & maintenance' basis as a satellite of Luqa for a time, followed by a period of intermittent use by civilian aircraft. In 1978 the site was used temporarily by the helicopters of the Armed Forces of Malta before being officially handed over to the Maltese Government in January 1979. Nowadays, some light industrial buildings are in use on the site, and car racing takes place on part of an old runway. The area around the control tower is in use by the Maltese fire authorities for training purposes, and the remains of a number of aircraft used for rescue training could until recently be seen.

Hal Far's early postwar control tower, replaced during the 1950s by the much larger structure, seen disused but in surprisingly good condition in the 1970s. *[Paul Francis]*

Flying Units at Hal Far

Summary					
Unit	From	Date in	To	Date out	Aircraft Types
422 (FS) Flt.	HMS Eagle	6.24	HMS Eagle	2.26	Blackburn I
402 (FS) Flt.	HMS Eagle	6.24	Gosport	4.29	Flycatcher
460 (FT) Flt.	HMS Eagle	10.24	HMS Glorious	10.32	Dart; Ripon
403 (FF) Flt.	HMS Hermes	11.24	HMS Hermes	8.26	Flycatcher
441 (FR) Flt.	HMS Hermes	12.24	HMS Hermes	5.25	Fairey IIID (note E)
440 (FR) Flt.	HMS Eagle	5.25	HMS Eagle	6.26	Fairey IIID (note E)
423 (FS) Flt.	HMS Eagle	2.26	HMS Eagle	3.29	Bison II
401 (FF) Flt.	HMS Eagle	2.26	HMS Hermes	9.26	Flycatcher
441 (FR) Flt.	HMS Eagle	3.26	HMS Eagle	2.27	Fairey IIID (note E)
421B (FS) Flt.	HMS Eagle	4.27	HMS Eagle	4.28	Bison II
463 (FT) Flt.	HMS Courageous	5.28	HMS Courageous	1.30	Dart
407 (FF) Flt.	HMS Courageous	6.28	HMS Courageous	8.29	Flycatcher
446 (FR) Flt.	HMS Courageous	6.28	HMS Courageous	1.30	Fairey IIIF (note E)
404 (FF) Flt.	HMS Courageous	9.28	HMS Courageous	8.29	Flycatcher
445 (FR) Flt.	HMS Corageous	10.28	HMS Courageous	1.30	Fairey IIIF
464 (FT) Flt.	HMS Courageous	10.28	HMS Courageous	1.30	Dart
RAF Base Misc. Flt.	(formed)	1.4.29			Fairey IIIF; Avro 504N; DH.60
402 (FF) Flt.	HMS Eagle	6.29	HMS Eagle	5.31	Flycatcher
448 (FR) Flt.	HMS Eagle	8.29	HMS Glorious (note F)	3.4.33	Fairey IIIF
461 (FTB) Flt.	HMS Glorious	7.30	HMS Glorious (note G)	3.4.33	Ripon
462 (FTB) Flt.	HMS Glorious	7.30	HMS Glorious (note G)	3.4.33	Ripon
447 (FSR) Flt.	HMS Glorious	7.30	(became part of 701 Flt.)	7.36	Fairey IIIF (note E)
405 (FF) Flt.	HMS Glorious	7.30	HMS Glorious	9.32	Flycatcher
406 (FF) Flt.	HMS Glorious	7.30	HMS Glorious	1.32	Flycatcher
408 (FF) Flt.	HMS Glorious	7.30	HMS Glorious	3.31	Flycatcher
441 (FSR) Flt.	HMS Glorious	7.30	HMS Glorious (note F)	3.4.33	Fairey IIIF
450 (FSR) Flt.	HMS Courageous	1.32	HMS Courageous	2.32	Fairey IIIF
445 (FR) Flt.	HMS Courageous	1.32	HMS Courageous	2.32	Fairey IIIF (note E)
446 (FR) Flt.	HMS Courageous	1.32	HMS Courageous	2.32	Fairey IIIF
408 (FF) Flt.	HMS Glorious	2.32	HMS Glorious (note H)	3.4.33	Nimrod I
409 (FF) Flt.	HMS Glorious	1.33	HMS Glorious (note H)	3.4.33	Nimrod I
812 Sqdn.	HMS Glorious	11.4.34	HMS Furious	26.6.34	Baffin
812 Sqdn.	HMS Furious	13.10.34	HMS Eagle	11.2.35	Baffin
812 Sqdn.	HMS Eagle	22.3.35	HMS Glorious	2.9.35	Baffin
825 Sqdn.	HMS Eagle	22.3.35	HMS Glorious	2.9.35	Fairey IIIF
74 Sqdn.	abd. HMS Neuralia	11.9.35	Hornchurch	7.36	Demon
22 Sqdn.	Donibristle	10.10.35	Donibristle	8.36	Vildebeeste III
825 Sqdn.	HMS Glorious	23.12.35	Aboukir	5.2.36	Fairey IIIF
2 Gun. Coop. Flt.	Alexandria	7.4.36	(became 3 AACU)	1.3.37	Queen Bee
825 Sqdn.	HMS Glorious	27.7.36	HMS Glorious	4.1.37	Swordfish I
823 Sqdn.	HMS Glorious	30.10.36	HMS Glorious	30.1.37	Swordfish I
3 AACU 'A' Flt.	(ex 2 Gun. Coop. Flt.)	1.3.37	(disbanded)	19.9.40	Queen Bee; Swordfish
Fighter Flight	(formed)	19.4.40	(disbanded)	29.4.40	Gladiator
Fighter Flight	(re-formed)	2.5.40	(became 261 Sqdn.)	1.8.40	Gladiator; Hurricane
767 Sqdn.	Medjaz-el-Bab	22.6.40	(became 830 Sqdn.)	1.7.40	Swordfish I
830 Sqdn.	(ex 767 Sqdn.)	1.7.40	(disbanded)	31.3.42	Swordfish I
261 Sqdn.	(formed)	1.8.40	Takali	20.11.40	Gladiator; Hurricane I
418 Flt.	(UK)	2.8.40	(absorbed into 261 Sqdn. on arrival)	2.8.40	Hurricane I
185 Sqdn.	(formed)	12.5.41	Qrendi	5.6.43	Hurricane I, IIa, IIb; Spitfire Vb, Vc
800X Flt.	HMS Furious	21.5.41	(disbanded)	13.11.41	Fulmar
828 Sqdn.	HMS Ark Royal	18.10.41	(disbanded)	31.3.42	Albacore I
605 Sqdn.	(in transit to FE)	10.1.42	Takali	12.1.42	Hurricane
229 Sqdn.	El Firdan	28.3.42	(disbanded)	29.4.42	Hurricane
RNA Sqdn.	(merger of 828 and 830 Sqdns.)	31.3.42	(disbanded)	end of '42	Albacore; Swordfish
821 Sqdn.	Berka	30.11.42	Monastir	4.6.43	Albacore
828 Sqdn.	(re-formed)	12.42	Takali	8.6.43	Albacore
ASR & C Flt.	(formed)	3.3.43	Takali	25.8.43	Walrus
43 Sqdn.	Mateur	9.6.43	Comiso	14.7.43	Spitfire Vb, Vc (note J)
72 Sqdn.	Mateur	10.6.43	Comiso	15.7.43	Spitfire Vb, Vc, IX (note J)
243 Sqdn.	Mateur	9.6.43	Comiso	20.7.43	Spitfire Vb, Vc, IX (note J)

Unit	From	Date in	To	Date out	Aircraft Types
93 Sqdn.	Mateur	10.6.43	Comiso	19.7.43	Spitfire Vb, Vc, IX (note J)
828 Sqdn.	Monastir	8.7.43	(disbanded)	1.9.43	Albacore
250 Sqdn.	Zuara	9.7.43	Luqa	13.7.43	Kittyhawk III
284 Sqdn.	Algiers	12.7.43	Casablanca	15.8.43	Walrus
65th FS, USAAF	Takali	15.7.43	Pachino	19.7.43	P-40
12 Sqdn. SAAF	Ben Hagan	21.7.43	Cuticchi/Gerbini	19.8.43	Boston III (note K)
21 Sqdn. SAAF	Ben Hagan	21.7.43	Cuticchi/Gerbini	19.8.43	Baltimore (note K)
24 Sqdn. SAAF	Suliman North	21.7.43	Cuticchi/Gerbini	19.8.43	Boston III (note K)
229 Sqdn.	Qrendi	25.9.43	Catania	30.1.44	Spitfire Vc, IX
249 Sqdn.	Qrendi	24.9.43	Grottaglie	27.10.43	Spitfire Vb, Vc, IX
185 Sqdn.	Qrendi	30.9.43	Grottaglie	2.44	Spitfire Vb, Vc
ASR&CF	Takali	1.2.44	(became AHQ M CF)	1.3.44	Anson; Wellington X
AHQ Malta CFlt.	(ex ASR & CF)	1.3.44	Luqa	4.1.46	Anson; Wellington
283 Sqdn.	Borgo	6.4.44	Maison Blanche	27.8.45	Warwick I
108 Sqdn.	Luqa	1.7.44	Idku	27.7.44	Beaufighter VI
255 Sqdn. det.	Foggia Main	26.7.44	?	4.9.45	Beaufighter VI; Mosquito
27 Sqdn. SAAF det.	La Seina	16.8.44	La Seina	8.11.44	Ventura V
614 Sqdn. det.	Amendola	1.5.45		28.6.45	Mosquito XXV
682 Sqdn. det.	San Severo	10.5.45	San Severo	20.5.45	Spitfire XI, XIX
624 Sqdn. det.	Falconara	29.6.45	Littorio	30.9.45	Walrus I
73 Sqdn.	Brindisi	3.7.45	Takali	17.7.46	Spitfire IX
255 Sqdn.	Rossignano	4.9.45	Gianaclis	1.2.46	Mosquito XIX, XXX
1702 Sqdn.	HMS Trouncer	22.9.45	Hassani	16.10.45	Sea Otter I
765 Sqdn.	Lee-on-Solent	6.10.45	(disbanded)	30.4.46	Wellington X, XI
2 OATS	(formed)		(disbanded)		Anson (note L)
728 Sqdn.	Luqa	5.5.46	(disbanded)	31.5.67	(various)
Station Flight	(re-formed)	3.47	(disbanded)	.65	(various)
814 Sqdn.	HMS Vengeance	11.11.47	SS Otranto (no a/c)	16.3.48	Firefly I
802 Sqdn.	Abbotsinch	11.11.47	Takali	24.11.47	Seafire XV
812 Sqdn.	HMS Ocean	20.6.49	Culham	12.9.49	Firefly FR.5
804 Sqdn.	HMS Ocean	18.7.49	HMS Glory	20.12.49	Sea Fury FB.11; Firefly FR.5
812 Sqdn.	Culham	28.9.49	HMS Glory	11.11.49	Firefly FR.5
VP-20		.50			Privateer
VP-23		1.51			Privateer
827 Sqdn.	Ford	25.5.51	HMS Illustrious	12.10.51	Firebrand; Firefly FR.1
807 Sqdn.	HMS Ocean	3.8.51	HMS Ocean	12.9.51	Sea Fury FB.11
185 Sqdn.	(re-formed)	15.9.51	Luqa	23.7.52	Vampire FB.5
809 Sqdn.	Culdrose	18.1.52	Culdrose	19.3.52	Sea Hornet F.20, NF.21, PR.22
802 Sqdn.	HMS Theseus	4.2.52	HMS Ocean	4.4.52	Sea Fury FB.11, T.20
810 Sqdn.	HMS Ocean	9.4.52	HMS Glory	21.5.52	Firefly FR.5
898 Sqdn.	HMS Theseus	15.5.52	Kasfareet	23.6.52	Sea Fury FB.11
801 Sqdn.	Lee-on-Solent	24.6.52	HMS Glory	2.9.52	Sea Fury FB.11, T.20
821 Sqdn.	Ford	26.6.52	HMS Glory	2.9.52	Firefly FR.5
75 Sqdn. RAAF	Williamstown (Aust)	28.7.52	Nicosia	1.1.53	Vampire FB.9
76 Sqdn. RAAF	Williamstown (Aust)	28.7.52	Nicosia	1.1.53	Vampire FB.9
810 Sqdn.	HMS Glory	14.8.52	HMS Theseus	15.10.52	Firefly FR.5
807 Sqdn.	HMS Glory	15.8.52	HMS Theseus	15.10.52	Sea Fury FB.11
898 Sqdn.	HMS Glory	15.8.52	HMS Theseus	15.10.52	Sea Fury
807 Sqdn.	HMS Ocean	16.1.53	HMS Ocean	15.4.53	Sea Fury FB.11
849B Sqdn.	HMS Glory	16.1.53	Culdrose	2.11.53	
75 Sqdn. RAAF	Nicosia	9.2.53	Takali	9.6.53	Vampire FB.9
76 Sqdn. RAAF	Nicosia	9.2.53	Takali	9.6.53	Vampire FB.9
804 Sqdn.	HMS Theseus	18.2.53	HMS Indomitable	27.4.53	Sea Fury FB.11
FASRON 201 Spec.		.53	(disbanded)	9.59	(various)
849C Sqdn.	HMS Glory	16.12.53	Culdrose	8.4.54	Skyraider AEW.1
849E Sqdn.	Culdrose	7.4.54	Culdrose	16.9.54	Skyraider AEW.1
803 Sqdn.	HMS Eagle	14.4.54	Lee-on-Solent	13.8.54	Attacker FB.2
845 Sqdn.	HMS Eagle	3.5.54	HMS Eagle	19.8.55	Whirlwind HAS.22
803 Sqdn.	Lee-on-Solent	19.8.54	HMS Albion	11.11.54	Seahawk FB.3
849B Sqdn.	Culdrose	11.10.54	Karouba	26.3.55	Skyraider AEW.1
813 Sqdn.	HMS Albion	16.10.54	Karouba	9.3.55	Wyvern S.4
VP-11		.54			Neptune
849D Sqdn.	Culdrose	30.3.55	Culdrose	9.10.55	Skyraider AEW.1
VP-21		8.55			Neptune
809 Sqdn.	Takali	17.11.55	HMS Ark Royal	25.11.55	Sea Venom FAW.21
891 Sqdn.	Yeovilton	5.1.56	Yeovilton	26.3.56	Sea Venom FAW.21
208 Sqdn.	Abu Sueir	17.1.56	Akrotiri	25.3.56	Meteor FR.9

MILITARY AVIATION IN MALTA G.C. 1915-1993

Unit	From	Date in	To	Date out	Aircraft Types
751 Sqdn. det.	Watton	30.1.56	Watton	20.2.56	Avenger AS.4
892 Sqdn.	Yeovilton	9.7.56	HMS Eagle	14.8.56	Sea Venom FAW.21
812 Sqdn.	HMS Eagle	3.8.56	HMS Bulwark	9.12.56	Gannet AS.1, T.2
Canberra Wing	Binbrook	9.56	Binbrook	12.56	Canberra B.2, B.6
804 Sqdn.	HMS Bulwark	1.12.56	HMS Ark Royal	4.2.57	Seahawk FGA.6
893 Sqdn.	HMS Eagle	24.12.56	HMS Ark Royal	5.2.57	Sea Venom FAW.21
VP-21		12.56		5.57	Neptune
VP-24		.56			Neptune
VA(HM)-13		.56			Neptune
VW-2		.56		.59	Warning Star
VP-23		6.57		10.57	Neptune
804 Sqdn.	Lossiemouth	29.7.57	HMS Ark Royal	31.8.57	Seahawk FGA.,6
VP-11		.57		.58	Neptune
825 Sqdn.	Culdrose	15.1.58	Culdrose	21.4.58	Gannet AS.4, T.2
751 Sqdn. det.	Culdrose	19.2.58	Culdrose	20.3.58	Sea Venom ECM.21
728B Sqdn.	Stretton	6.3.58	(disbanded)	2.12.61	Firefly U.9; Canberra U.10; Meteor U.15, U.16
728C Sqdn.	Lee-on-Solent	7.2.58	(redes. 848 Sqdn.)	14.10.58	Whirlwind
831B Sqdn.	HMS Eagle	4.7.58	Culdrose	6.11.58	Avenger AS.6; Gannet AS.1; Sea Venom ECM.21
848 Sqdn.	(ex 728C Sqdn.)	14.10.58	Worthy Down	9.11.59	Whirlwind HAS.22
VP-23		11.58		5.59	Neptune
750 Sqdn.	Culdrose	13.10.59	Lossiemouth	23.6.65	Sea Prince; Sea Venom FAW.21, FAW.22
38 Sqdn.	Luqa	30.10.65	(disbanded)	3.67	Shackleton

Note E: some aircraft, fitted with floats, operated from Kalafrana
Note G: this unit became part of 812 Squadron
Note J: these four squadrons comprised 324 Wing
Note L: this unit had its HQ at Kalafrana

Note F: this unit became part of 823 Squadron
Note H: this unit became part of 802 Squadron
Note K: these three squadrons comprised 3 SAAF Wing
Note M: these five squadrons comprised 322 Wing

The Fleet Flights

During the nineteen-twenties and thirties a substantial number of independent Flights, each part of the Fleet Air Arm of the RAF, made their homes at Hal Far. Their work consisted of training for the functions for which they were designated. The Flights were numbered in the 400-series and subdivided into Fleet Fighter Flights numbered 401 to 419; Fleet Spotter Flights numbered 420 to 439; Fleet Reconnaissance Flights numbered 440 to 459; and Fleet Torpedo Flights numbered 460

onwards. The 460-series was abandoned in April 1929 and existing Flights in that group renumbered into the 440-series. At about the same time the 400-series Flights were renamed Fleet Torpedo Bomber Flights.

In April 1933 those Flights still in existence, including 408, 409, 441, 448, 461 and 462 Flights at Hal Far, were reorganised into new Squadrons numbered in the 800-series. 447 Flight, however, was not affected until it became part of 701 Squadron in July 1936.

A 405 Flight Fairey Flycatcher after a very heavy landing at Hal Far in July 1930. Note the remains of the engine off to the left!
[Sqdn. Ldr. Dawes]

Left: Flycatchers
S1066 [1] and S1070
[4] of 402 Flight
ready for launching.
[G. W. Jordan]

Right: Blackburn
Dart N9693 of 460
Flight at Hal Far.
[G. W. Jordan]

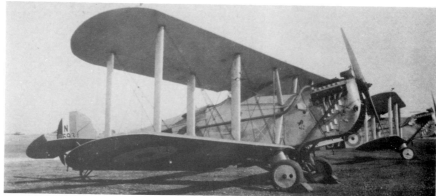

Left: Four Avro
Bisons II of 423
Flight over Malta in
the late 'twenties:
N9848 [24]; N155
[20]; N9594 [27]; and
another [25].
[G. W. Jordan]

Left: Fairey IIID
S1019 [40] of 440
Flight in about
1925/26.
[G. W. Jordan]

Right: An Avro Bison
II from 423 Flight at
Hal Far.
[G. W. Jordan]

Left: Blackburn
Ripon IIa S1469
[64], probably of 460
Flight, after coming
to earth somewhat
spectacularly!
[D. R. Neate]

Left: 402 Flight's
Fairey Flycatcher
N9892.
[G. W. Jordan]

Right: Blackburn
Ripon II S1364 [64]
of 461 Flight, HMS
Glorious,
photographed in
November 1932 at
Hal Far.
[J. W. Parsons]

RAF Base Miscellaneous Flight/Station Flight
Formed on 1 April 1929 (the 11th birthday of the RAF) to coincide with the formation of RAF Hal Far, this unit was in effect a Station Flight, in the terminology of later years. The first CO was Flt. Lt. Pickering, but he was replaced by Fg. Off. K. E. Parker on 17 July 1930 and he by Fg. Off. G. Francis on 27 March 1931.

Aircraft used initially by the Flight included an Avro 504N, a Gipsy Moth, a Fairey IIIF and probably an Avro Tutor, as one of the latter crashed into the sea on 15 July 1934 while being flown by Fg. Off. J. K. Castris.

Station Flight Hal Far was absorbed into 3 AACU on 29 August 1939, just before the outbreak of the Second World War. In effect, however, the

Flight came into being again on 9 October, when a Fairey Seal aircraft which had been used intermittently for coastal defence since July 1938 was again put into service. A similar aircraft was added later.

812 Squadron
Equipped with twelve Blackburn Baffin aircraft, 812 Squadron disembarked to Hal Far from HMS *Glorious* in April 1934 when that carrier returned to the UK for a refit. Apart from periods on HMS *Furious* between June and October 1934 and on HMS *Eagle* between February and March 1935, 812 Squadron operated from Hal Far until HMS *Glorious* returned to the Mediterranean in September 1935, when the squadron re-

Left: Avro 504N K1957, seen at Hal Far in 1933, was used by the RAF Miscellaneous Flight. Note the Maltese Cross on the front fuselage, just below the cockpit.
[J. W. Parsons]

Right: A Fairey IIIF of Hal Far Station Flight in the early 1930s.
[James Pickering]

Two aircraft of the RAF Miscellaneous Flight at Hal Far in 1933: DH.60 Gipsy Moth K1199 [4] and Fairey IIIF S1507 [3] *[J. W. Parsons]*

Right: A smart vic formation of nine Baffins of 812 Squadron, Hal Far, over the Maltese countryside in October 1934.
[Cdr. J. S. Stead via R. C. Sturtivant]

Left: The effect of the tornado of 24 November 1936 on some of the Baffins of 812 Squadron at Hal Far. Eight were struck off charge after this calamity.
[C. Bristow via R. C. Sturtivant]

embarked.

812 Squadron re-appeared at Hal Far several times up to the spring of 1940, by which time it was flying Swordfish aircraft, and several times postwar, when it operated Fireflies and Barracudas.

825 Squadron

On 22 March 1935 825 Squadron disembarked from HMS *Glorious* to Hal Far when the carrier left the Mediterranean for the UK. When *Glorious* returned in September the squadron's Fairey IIIFs rejoined it for further service aboard, but spent more time at Hal Far from Christmas 1935 to February 1936, when the squadron moved to Aboukir in Egypt.

In order to convert to Swordfish aircraft, 825 Squadron appeared at Hal Far again on 27 July 1936. By the end of October the conversion programme was complete and the squadron embarked on HMS *Glorious* for deck landing and stowage trials. These complete, 825 Squadron

returned to Hal Far on 9 November, remaining there until returning to HMS *Glorious* on 4 January 1937.

Over the next few years, 825 Squadron found itself at Hal Far many times on short-term disembarkations.

74 Squadron

Not many RAF squadrons were formed on board ship, but one of the few was 74 Squadron, created in the wake of the Italian campaign in Abyssinia in 1935. To man the new squadron, ten officers, eighteen SNCOs and 79 airmen were drawn from six other squadrons in the UK, and on 3 September 1935 they set sail for Malta on SS *Neuralia*. In charge was Sqdn. Ldr. H. G. Crowe MC, and the squadron officially came into being on the day of departure. The Hawker Demon aircraft, with stores and equipment, left England on board the SS *Maihar*.

Arriving at Malta on 11 September, the squadron personnel settled in at Hal Far. Three days later the SS *Maihar* arrived in Grand Harbour for off-loading. The aircraft, disassembled, were soon on shore, and their fuselages were towed to Hal Far, an hour's journey. By 20 September all but one of the Demons were available for service, although the armament equipment needed more attention. Three days later, the squadron, ready for action, was inspected by the Air Officer Commanding Malta.

A programme of training by day and night then began, the aircraft being progressively camouflaged. The activities included affiliation with the Scapa flying boats of 202 Squadron, practice interceptions, and simulated attacks on destroyers, while on 25 November 74 Squadron combined with 22 Squadron to make a mock attack on HMS *Australia*. After work, the ground crews found relaxation in Beppo's Bar, conveniently located next to the squadron's hangar!

Early in October, flotation gear was fitted and

Hawker Demons of 74 Sqdn. flying over typical Maltese scenery during the squadron's detachment to Hal Far in 1935. Below can be seen Marsa racecourse/polo ground and the Hospital of St. Vincent de Paule. Note the irregular positions of the roundels on the upper wings of the aircraft.
[J. Tufnail via Bob Cossey]

training began in earnest with 202 Squadron, based at Calafrana. This comprised low-level attacks on destroyers, AA guns and towed sea targets, and night flying with the aid of paraffin flares was also tried out.

Stone revetments had been built at Hal Far and on 18 December a war test was carried out. All the aircraft were taken from their hangars and installed in the pens in twenty minutes and later were removed and were airborne in five minutes. A further timed test on 7 January 1936 saw the squadron re-armed and refuelled in less than ten minutes.

One of the Demons made a forced landing on the uncompleted civil airport at Takali on 1 February 1936 after engine failure but appears to have survived the ordeal. During that spring training continued, and included the bombing of sea targets, low level attacks on Grand Harbour and bombing at Filfla Island. On 20 May the Governor, Sir Charles Bonham-Carter, visited the squadron and expressed his thanks for the task being carried out. The squadron suffered the loss of two of its personnel on 5 June, when Flg. Off. J. A. Sutherland and AC1 Chalk were killed in the crash of a Vildebeeste of 22 Squadron.

By July 1936, however, the Abyssinian crisis was over, and on 13 July orders were received for the Demons to be dismantled and taken to Calafrana for shipment to the UK. Between 24 and 27 July all personnel also moved to Calafrana on the first stage of the journey home on board the troopship HMS *Somersetshire*.

22 Squadron

The second of the two squadrons sent to Malta as a precautionary measure during the Italian campaign in Abyssinia, 22 Squadron left its UK base at Donibristle in Scotland on 3 October 1935. After passage from Glasgow on board SS *Cameronia*, the squadron personnel, under the command of Sqdn. Ldr. R. J. M. de St. Leger, arrived in Grand Harbour on 10 October and travelled to Hal Far.

By 21 October the squadron's Vildebeeste aircraft had been erected and tested, and the squadron was able to begin a programme of offensive training. Simulated attacks on destroyers in the Malta area formed the main part of this task, which continued, interspersed with periods of

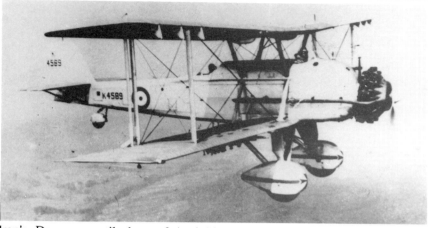

Although seen over English countryside, this Vildebeest III of 22 Squadron, with a Maltese cross on each wheel spat, clearly served with the squadron's detachment at Hal Far during the Abysinnian crisis.
[P. M. T. Green collection]

work with 74 Squadron's Demons, until the following July. On 20 July 1936 the order was received for the Vildebeestes, apart from K4608, which had been destroyed in a fatal crash on 5 June, to be dismantled for return to the UK. By 24 July the aircraft had been moved to Calafrana and before long the personnel followed, finally embarking in HMS *Somersetshire* on 21 August for the homeward voyage.

823 Squadron

From its formation in April 1933 to January 1940, 823 Squadron spent many periods of time ashore at Hal Far after disembarking from its parent carriers, HMS *Courageous* and HMS *Glorious,* but the most significant period was between 30 October 1936 and 30 January 1937. During this spell ashore the squadron was converting from Fairey Seal aircraft to the then modern Swordfish I to enable it to take up a torpedo-spotting role. This completed, the squadron re-embarked on *Glorious.*

2 Anti-Aircraft Cooperation Flight/ 3 Anti-Aircraft Cooperation Unit.

This somewhat nomadic unit arrived from Alexandria on 7 April 1936 and began to provide radio-controlled de Havilland Queen Bee target aircraft for the benefit of gunners in Malta. On 1 March 1937 the unit was retitled 3 AACU and was then under the command of Sqdn. Ldr. G. C. Shepherd. Detachments were sent to Gibraltar and Alexandria from time to time, and in September 1938, during the emergency period, the unit's stores were embarked on HMS *Glorious,* only to be hastily returned to Hal Far when the panic had subsided.

A red-letter day in the usually mundane annals of 3 AACU was 14 January 1939, when the first recorded pilotless take-off and landing was carried out at Hal Far. The aircraft involved was Queen Bee K4229, and the historic event was witnessed by the AOC Mediterranean Command, Air Comm. Leckie.

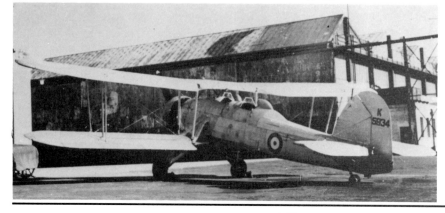

Swordfish I K5934 of 3 AACU's land-based 'B' Flight at Hal Far.
[R. C. Sturtivant]

Sqdn. Ldr. W. L. Houlbrook took over as CO of 3 AACU on 8 July 1939 and some of the unit's personnel left for Alexandria on 29 August. On that day 3 AACU became an operational unit, using seven Swordfish aircraft for anti-submarine patrols and close reconnaissance. The unit also absorbed the remains of Station Flight on that date. The Queen Bees left for Alexandria on 2 October, and next day 3 AACU resumed training duties with the seven Swordfish, two of which were drogue-towing machines. Seven Blackburn Skuas were received during October to boost the unit's strength.

Training continued until 18 April 1940, when 3 AACU was again put on a temporary operational basis. This was probably the status of the unit when it disbanded, a shadow of its former self, on 19 September 1940.

Fighter Flight Malta.

In April 1940, with an attack on Malta by the Italians anticipated, no fighter aircraft were based on the island, as all available Hurricanes and Spitfires were needed for the defence of Great Britain and on the Western Front. However, when the AOC Malta, Air Comm. F. H. Maynard, heard that eight crated Sea Gladiators which had been left behind by HMS *Glorious* were stored at Kalafrana he asked the C-in-C Mediterranean, Admiral Sir Andrew Cunningham, for them to be made available to form a local defence unit. This request was granted, and on 19 April 1940 Flg. Off. Mick Collins and a team of fitters and riggers began to assemble and rig four of the Gladiators, the other four being retained for HMS *Eagle*. The work took

two days, after which the aircraft were towed along the road to Hal Far and taken on charge by the newly-formed Fighter Flight. As soon as they had been flight tested, R/T and armament trials began. Six pilots — Sqdn. Ldr. A. C. 'Jock' Martin, Flt. Lt. G. Burges (Air Comm. Maynard's personal assistant, a flying-boat pilot), Flt. Lt. P. G. Keeble, Fg. Off. J. L. Waters, Fg. Off. W. J. Woods and Pt. Off. P. B. Alexander — were allocated to the Flight, but on 29 April the Flight was disbanded, as the Fleet Air Arm had decided it needed the Gladiators in Alexandria, and the aircraft were returned to Kalafrana. This move was again reversed on 2 May, when the Gladiators came back to Hal Far, and they were servicable next day. The six pilots, lacking fighter experience, then began training and by 11 June, when the first raid on Malta took place, the Fighter Flight was ready and waiting.

Two formations, each of five SM.79 Sparviero (Sparrow) three-engined bombers of the Regia Aeronautica, approached Malta that day. These raiders were intercepted by the Gladiators, and in the course of the air battle one of the Italian aircraft was shot down into the sea, the first of hundreds of enemy aircraft to be destroyed over and around the island during the course of the war. Many more raids followed during the next few days, but by 16 June the three serviceable Gladiators of Fighter Flight had compelled the Italians to maintain thirty-strong fighter escorts for their bombers. It was realised, though, that the venerable biplanes could not be expected to keep up the pace for long, neither could the (now) seven pilots, who took turns in sitting ready for action in the cockpits for

Gladiator N5519 [R] of the Fighter Flight in 1940. The pilot, Flt. Lt. G. Burges, is seated in the cockpit ready for the 'off' if a raid develops. Note the three-bladed propellor on this aircraft.
[After The Battle magazine]

Gladiators 'Faith', 'Hope' and 'Charity' in the dark days of 1940. The closest two aircraft bear no markings other than roundels; the Gladiator to the rear appears to be addorned with an 'S' that is mostly obscured by the fin of the machine in front. *[James Pickering]*

four-hour stretches covering the daylight hours. There were two mishaps in June; in one, Sqdn. Ldr. Martin was unhurt when his Gladiator crashed on take-off, and in the other Flt. Lt. P. W. Hartley was slightly injured when his aircraft crash-landed after its undercarriage was damaged on take-off. Another Gladiator collided with a Queen Bee of 3 AACU while landing on 23 June, but the pilot, Fg. Off. Woods, was not hurt.

Ground crews worked long hours to keep the Gladiators, now by common consent among the pilots named *'Faith'*, *'Hope'* and *'Charity'*, airworthy. Bristol Mercury XV engines from Blenheims, with three-bladed propellors found in a store, replaced the original Mercury IX engines to give greater power and to obviate the use of maximum boost during the climb to height which was so essential to the Flight's operations.

After claims had been made on 22 June 1940 by Berlin Radio to the effect that the Italians had totally destroyed the dockyard in Malta, a SM.79 flew over the island to photograph the scene. The Fighter Flight was ready for it; diving from nearly 20000ft (6000m.), Flt. Lt. Burges in *'Faith'* and Flg. Off. 'Timber' Woods in *'Hope'* succeeded in shooting the Italian aircraft into the sea. Two of its crew baled out and became the first prisoners of war taken on the island.

The AOC was pressing hard for replacement or supplementation by Hurricanes, and on 28 June four of these more modern aircraft arrived in Malta. In fact they were in transit to Egypt, but the AOC obtained permission to retain them and they were taken on charge by Fighter Flight. At once they took over the main responsibility for defence from

the Gladiators, but together the two types continued to perform sterling work up to and beyond 1 August 1940, when Fighter Flight was upgraded to form 261 Squadron. On that day, only one Gladiator and one Hurricane survived. During its brief but hectic life, the Fighter Flight had intercepted 144 Italian bombers, shot down five (ground gunners downing the other ten), and damaged many more.

Later, the Chief Justice of Malta, Sir George Borg, said that the three Gladiators of the Fighter Flight had been *"like rays of light in our darkest hours"*. When he accepted *'Faith'* on behalf of the people of Malta on 3 September 1943 Sir George remarked *"This aeroplane will always remind us of the gratitude my countrymen owe to the Royal Air Force"*. Today, *'Faith'* stands on display in the National War Museum in Valletta, a fitting memento of those dark days and the men who flew in the Fighter Flight.

830 Squadron

During the spring of 1940, 767 Squadron of the FAA carried out training at Hyeres, in the south of France, but by mid-June the powers that be had decided that France was not the place to be, and on 18 June the squadron's Swordfish aircraft flew out, six to Gibraltar and twelve bound for Malta. These staged through Bone in Algeria, from where on 21 June they flew to Malta after refuelling at Medjez-el-Bab and Timimi, finally landing at Hal Far with some difficulty due to the runway obstructions.

Once arrived, 767 Squadron was immediately transformed into 830 Squadron, a first-line unit, under the command of Lt. Cdr. F. D. Howie, and began working-up, which included dive-bombing on Filfla Island early each morning before any enemy raids took place.

830 Squadron's first mission was a dive-bombing attack on the oil refineries at Augusta in Sicily at dusk on 30 June, but little damage was done. In July nine Swordfish bombed a hangar at Catania on the 6th, scoring a direct hit, and on 19 July the squadron attacked a submarine. A night raid on 13 September by nine aircraft proved something of a disaster; the target was again Augusta, which was dive-bombed, but one Swordfish, L2854, was shot down into the harbour, L9741 crashed in Italy and another ditched off Malta on the return flight. Two crews were lost, and the only reward was damage to one ship. After this, raids on Sicily and solo sweeps were ended as being too dangerous.

Late in September 1940 six new Swordfish were flown off HMS *Illustrious* for 830 Squadron, and long-range tanks were fitted to all the aircraft. Blind-flying panels were also received but not fitted. By this time, 830 Squadron was the only British anti-shipping squadron in the central Mediterranean, and thus bore a heavy burden.

During October and November 1940, 830 Squadron practiced dive-bombing and formation flying by day and night, culminating in an attack on Tripoli harbour on 10 December by eight Swordfish which dropped four tons of bombs. Bad weather prevented further missions until 21 December, when Tripoli was again raided, this time by six aircraft carrying torpedoes and four carrying bombs. Of these raiders, K8866 was lost.

In January 1941 raids on Sicily were again sanctioned, and ten Swordfish of 830 Squadron took off on the 10th to attack shipping at Palermo with bombs and torpedoes. Four of them aborted with engine trouble, but the others attacked, without much success. Better results were achieved on 27 January, when, after being spotted by a Sunderland flying boat of 228 Squadron from Kalafrana, a small enemy convoy 180 miles from Malta making for Tripoli was attacked by seven of 830 Squadron's aircraft. Two Fulmars of 800X Flight provided top cover and 830 Squadron was able to sink one merchant vessel and damage others in its first torpedo attack on shipping at sea. At the end of the month the squadron began carrying out 'rat hunts' along the coast of Tunisia.

Tripoli harbour again felt the effects of 830 Squadron's efforts on 8 February, when ten aircraft sowed mines in the port area ready for the arrival of a German convoy carrying troops and supplies for the Afrika Corps. Nevertheless, as 830 Squadron was still the only anti-shipping sqaudron in Malta, the enemy could send convoys in the knowledge that they stood a very good chance of reaching North Africa. The job of keeping the elderly Swordfish aircraft in the air became harder all the time. Daily inspection and servicing were carried out in the open at Hal Far, while major servicing was done at Kalafrana. The number of patches visible on the Swordfish grew daily, but all flyable aircraft stood by, fully armed, to attack any suitable target on demand. The Air Ministry decided that constant mining of Tripoli harbour was the top priority, but Admiral Cunningham disagreed; he laid down that 830 Squadron's main function was

A Swordfish I of 830 Squadron, Hal Far, visiting Takali.
[via R. C. Sturtivant]

to be torpedo-dropping on enemy shipping at sea, a task at which the squadron's lack of success was giving concern. Mining continued, however, five sorties to Tripoli being made early in May for the loss of one aircraft, P4232, which was shot down in shallow water.

The remnants of 829 Squadron personnel from HMS *Formidable* were absorbed by 830 Squadron early in June 1941, easing the workload a little. On 8 June eight of the Swordfish accompanied Wellingtons on a raid on Tripoli, each carrying two flame floats and two 25lb. (11kg.) bombs. The squadron was further reinforced on 25 July by six more Swordfish aircraft and crews which made a 4 hour 30 minute flight from HMS *Ark Royal*. Two of the new aircraft carried ASV radar, which was first used on a raid on a convoy on 31 July, with no results. Fitting of the blind flying panels received some time before now began.

A night raid on Catania on 16/17 August caused a good deal of damage, but probably the squadron's most rewarding effort so far came on 2 September, when nine Swordfish carrying torpedoes made an evening attack on five large merchant vessels with destroyer escort which were on the way to Tripoli. One ammunition ship blew up, and another was seen to return to port in Messina. Large quantities of supplies, particularly fuel and ammunition, were thus prevented from reaching Libya.

A few clandestine operations were flown by 830 Squadron at this time to deposit agents behind enemy lines. On 16 September, on such a mission, the pilot of a Swordfish attempting to land in a dry lake bed near Sousse in Tunisia found it to be muddy and crash-landed. The agent escaped, but the two crew members, Lt. C. B. Lamb and Sqdn. Ldr. J. M. Robertson, were captured and tortured by the Vichy French Deuxieme Bureau.

Early in August the CO, Lt. Cdr. Howie, had been posted, and his replacement, Lt. Cdr. J. G. Hunt, took over on 1 October, just before the campaign of attacks on Libya-bound shipping increased in intensity. Eight aircraft took off to attack one such convoy off Pantellaria on 11 November, but three aborted with engine trouble. All the others, K5945, K5979, K8405, V4295 and V4421, were shot down off Sicily and the crews lost — a terrible day for 830 Squadron. However, between May and November 1941 the squadron had sunk 110000 tons (112000 tonnes) of shipping and damaged another 130000 tons (132000 tonnes), a creditable performance in the circumstances.

Mine-laying in Tripoli harbour continued, now sometimes in conjunction with the Albacores of 828 Squadron, a new arrival in Malta. At the same time, 830 Squadron's five or so serviceable aircraft carried out torpedo attacks on ships at sea as targets presented themselves. The renewed blitz on Malta early in December 1941 did not help matters, but the squadron, now under the command of Lt. Cdr. F. H. Hopkins DSC, survived.

By early January 1942 only two serviceable aircraft could be provided, but bad weather allowed work to proceed on the ground, and on 6 January four aircraft, including one with ASV, went to Luqa for a night operation against a large vessel. On 12 January eight Swordfish formed the entire strength of 830 Squadron, but two new aircraft arrived on 19 January via Benina, landing during an air raid on Hal Far, one of the two being damaged in the process.

March 1942 saw 830 Squadron in great difficulties. Due to enemy raids on Hal Far, shortage of spares and losses in combat, the squadron was down to six aircraft, all of them out of action. Two aircraft being ferried to the squadron from El Adem on 2 March disappeared on the way, adding to the difficulties. To create, therefore, a unit of reasonable strength, 830 and 828 Squadrons were combined on 31 March 1942 to form the Royal Naval Air Squadron Malta, though each retained its identity on paper.

261 Squadron

When it was known, late in July 1940, that reinforcement Hurricanes were on the way to Malta, the decision was taken to form a new squadron to accommodate them. On 2 August, twelve Hurricanes of 418 Flight, escorted by two Skuas, flew off HMS *Argus* as part of Operation 'Hurry' and on arrival at Hal Far were at once combined with those of Fighter Flight Malta to form 261 Squadron.

For the next nine months, 261 Squadron formed the mainstay of the aerial defence of Malta, operating initially from both Hal Far and Luqa, but on 20 November 1940 a move was made to newly-opened Takali.

A weary airman rests on the mudguard of a printers and stationers truck which had been commandeered for the use of 261 Squadron's armourers.
[James Pickering]

185 Squadron

On 12 May 1941, 185 Squadron was re-formed at Hal Far from part of 261 Squadron and 1435 Flight, and Sqdn. Ldr. Mould DFC was appointed as the new squadron's CO. 185 Squadron's Hurricanes went into action at once, but the four aircraft which took off on the first operation were unable to locate their target. Three more sorties that day were also inconclusive, but at 18.00 hours four of the Hurricanes, flying above 261 Squadron aircraft, spotted six Bf.109s about 6000ft. (1800m.) above them. However, the Bf.109s did not attack and left the area.

Next day, four Hurricanes on patrol were attacked by bomb-carrying Bf.109s but managed to evade them, although one pilot lost control and baled out. During the second patrol of the day on 14 May, the 185 Squadron Hurricanes were set upon by a large force of Bf.109s, but again managed to evade them. A patrol that afternoon was set upon by Bf.109s and the patrol's leader, Pt. Off. Hamilton, was shot down.

Success began to come 185 Squadron's way on 6 June 1941, when an He.111 was severely damaged. That day, the squadron began to operate after dark, but reverted to day fighting on 1 July,

when new pilots arrived to strengthen the squadron. There were now twelve Hurricanes on charge, some of which were able to intercept a formation of Macchi 200s on 4 July and destroy two and damage three of them. This was the first opportunity in which the squadron Hurricanes equipped with cannon were used.

Beginning to take the offensive, 185 Squadron carried out two sweeps over the coast of Sicily on 6 July, and on 9 July two aircraft strafed the seaplane base at Syracuse, destroying six flying boats and damaging four more, as well as generally upsetting everyone in the area. It is said that on the way home to Hal Far, Sqdn. Ldr. Mould broke the world low-flying record by cruising at 4 inches (10cm.) above sea level!

A raid on Luqa by over forty Italian Macchi 200 aircraft on 11 July was intercepted by 185 Squadron Hurricanes, which shot down three and claimed nine probables. There was , however, a degree of frustration due to lack of early warning of raids. Further Italian attacks followed. On 25 July a large number of enemy fighters escorted four reconnaissance aircraft over Malta, and 185 Squadron was successful in destroying one SM.79 and a Br.20.

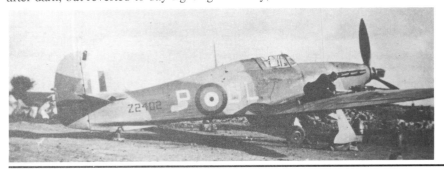

Hurricane IIa Z2402 [GL:P] of 185 Squadron at Hal Far.

Apparently undergoing major repairs is Hurricane IIa Z2982 of 185 Squadron. On 27 May 1942, after the squadron had re-equipped with Spitfires, this aircraft disappeared while on a ferry flight.
[R. A. Powell]

All these operations were as nothing, however, compared with the onslaught mounted by the Italians on 26 July. 185 Squadron was scrambled at 05.20 to find an attack on Grand Harbour by E-boats guarded by Macchi 200 aircraft under way. Attacking, 185 Squadron destroyed four E-boats and a Macchi, but one of the Hurricane pilots had to bale out. He swam to an E-boat, which contained eight dead Italians, captured the flag as a souvenir, and was soon back at Hal Far.

During the rest of the summer and autumn, 185 Squadron carried out many routine patrols and provided cover for Beaufighters attacking targets in Sicily on a number of occasions. Early in November, 185 Squadron mounted a few fighter-bomber sorties over Sicily, shooting up trains and other targets but later in the month reverted to defensive operations. These continued during the early part of 1942. Some successes were made and a few aircraft lost; particularly sad was the loss of Sgt. Choffe on 22 February, only six days after his first sortie with the squadron.

Throughout the spring and summer of 1942, 185 Squadron was kept busy on scrambles and interceptions, losing a few aircraft but destroying many, mainly Ju.88s and Bf.109s taking part in the intensive raids being mounted all day and every day against Malta. Reinforcements in the shape of eleven Spitfires were flown off the carrier USS *Wasp* for 185 Squadron on 9 May 1942 and next day the squadron's first Spitfire sorties were flown — a patrol over Grand Harbour by four aircraft. The summer wore on, and on 6 August the CO, Sqdn. Ldr. New, was posted, his successor being Lt. C. J. Swales of the South African Air Force, who was promoted temporarily to Captain. The tide of battle was now turning, and 185 Squadron began to go onto the offensive by attacking, in particular, targets in Sicily. During one 'rhubarb' to Comiso on 27 August, led by Capt. Swales, 185 Squadron caught Ju.88s and Bf.109s in the act of taking off, and were able to destroy five of them and claim another four as probables. Seven of the Spitfires carrying out another sweep over Sicily on

The mortal remains of Spitfire Vc BR294 [GL:E] of 185 Squadron after crash-landing at Hal Far on 2 July 1942
[R. A. Powell]

185 Squadron
Spitfire IX MH704
[GL:H] at Hal Far.
[F. E. Wattam]

9 September met eight Macchi 202s, of which they destroyed two, but Sgt. Weaver, one of the successful pilots, was himself damaged and had to force-land on a Sicilian beach.

During the autumn routine patrols continued, little resistance being met. Christmas Day that year was treated as a rest day, but on 31 December six Spitfires attempted to bomb the airfield on the island of Lampedusa, without success due to heavy and accurate flak. Offensive sweeps over Sicily continued in the early days of 1943, the targets including Ragusa and Licata railway station and the power station at Porto Empodocle. 250lb. (115kg.) bombs were used during these 'softening-up' missions.

In April 1943 185 Squadron began to fly missions in cooperation with the USAAF bomber force, carrying out diversionary sweeps or acting as escort to B-24s bombing such targets as Catania. A further change of command came on 1 June 1943, when Sqdn. Ldr. H. A. Crafts, who had taken over from Capt. Swales, was posted and Sqdn. Ldr. L. N. MacDougall arrived from 1435 Squadron. Just after that, 185 Squadron moved the short distance from Hal Far to Qrendi to carry on the good work from there.

185 Squadron returned to Hal Far at the end of September 1943 but did not carry out any more offensive operations. Instead, the squadron made courier flights to Italy and maintained a state of readiness in case of any enemy retribution. The AOC visited the squadron on 6 December and expressed his great satisfaction at the good condition of the aircraft and at the fact that he had survived a crash on take-off from Catania. There was a scramble on 7 December but the plot turned out to be five Dakotas. The more relaxed atmosphere encouraged the arrangement of a Christmas party on 22 December, at which the CO reported that he would soon leave the squadron.

At the end of 1943, the 185 Squadron scoreboard recorded the following figures:

Enemy aircraft destroyed	135
Enemy aircraft damaged	144
Enemy aircraft probably destroyed	66
Submarines sunk	1
Motor torpedo boats sunk	4
Trains destroyed	7

In February 1944 most of the squadron left Malta for Grottaglie in Italy to carry out defence duties, and the small remaining party followed in August, ending 185 Squadron's long involvement in Malta's history.

800X Flight
When 47 Hurricanes were flown off HMS *Furious* to Hal Far on 21 May 1941, the four Fairey Fulmars belonging to 801 Squadron which accompanied them were retained in Malta as 800X Flight. They took part in patrols over the island as required, and on 16 July one of them caused a stir in the enemy camp by circling Gerbini airfield in Sicily with its landing lights on as if preparing to land. Given permission by the Italian controller to do that, the Fulmar's pilot flew low over the airfield and bombed two aircraft, setting one on fire. Later, however, on the night of 7/8 October, one of 800X Flight's aircraft was shot down while patrolling the same area of Sicily, and its crew was taken prisoner. 800X Flight was disbanded on 13 November 1941, and the two remaining Fulmars, N1931 and N4001, were flown away.

828 Squadron

Eleven Fairey Albacores and two Swordfish of 828 Squadron flew off HMS *Ark Royal* on 18 October 1941 en route to Hal Far, where the squadron would join in the anti-shipping operations being conducted so valiantly by 830 Squadron. Unfortunately, one of the Swordfish failed to arrive, but the bulk of the squadron settled down to a short training programme before carrying out its first mission from Malta — a raid by seven Albacores on Comiso airfield in Sicily on 28 October, from which one aircraft did not return.

Three days later, another raid on a variety of Sicilian targets was mounted, and for a time Sicily was the regular destination for 828 Squadron, the submarine pens at Augusta being given particular attention. On 20 November, however, six of the squadron's Albacores joined 830 Squadron Swordfish in a mining raid on Tripoli harbour, 828 Squadron's first such mission. Next day came the squadron's first attack on shipping by torpedo-carrying Albacores, the target being a convoy heading for Benghazi. Then followed more mining trips and attacks on Libyan airfields, during which one aircraft was lost on 28 November.

By January 1942 the Albacores, less reliable than the Swordfish, were beginning to feel the effects of intense use, and at the end of the month only five were serviceable. On 31 March the squadron was merged with 830 Squadron to form the Royal Naval Air Squadron Malta, but retained its identity on paper.

828 Squadron regained its full status in December 1942 when 830 Squadron's last aircraft was struck off charge. The squadron continued its anti-shipping duties, which culminated at the end of May 1943 in Operation 'Corkscrew', the campaign to capture the island of Pantellaria. 828 Squadron Albacores took part by dropping flares and spotting for a naval bombardment, and on 11 June both Pantellaria and Lampedusa surrendered.

828 Squadron moved to Takali on 8 June 1943 but returned to Hal Far on 8 July, eventually being disbanded there on 1 September 1943.

229 Squadron

A detachment of 229 Squadron Hurricanes arrived at Hal Far on 28 March 1942 from El Firdan via Takali, where the aircrafts' long-range tanks were removed. As no ground personnel had made the journey, fifty airmen were attached to the squadron from HQ reserves.

Daily scrambles and interceptions were the routine during April, but after losing a number of aircraft to enemy action and accidents the detachment ceased to function on 29 April 1942.

Having re-formed at Takali in August 1942 and subsequently spent some time at Qrendi, 229 Squadron returned to Hal Far on 25 September 1943. At first little operational flying took place; instead, the pilots indulged in intensive practice in

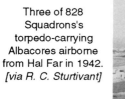

Three of 828 Squadrons's torpedo-carrying Albacores airborne from Hal Far in 1942.
[via R. C. Sturtivant]

An Albacore of 828
Squadron, Hal Far,
carrying code S5:H.
[B. Tonks]

formation flying, air-to-ground and air-to-air firing, dog-fighting, dive-bombing and aerobatics. On 26 October, sadly, one Spitfire was lost and its pilot, Flt. Sgt. D. Ripper, was killed when it crashed at Tal Pitfalli, near Dingli, when the aircraft's wings broke off at low level. While on a weather flight, the aircraft had become iced up, causing instability, and a rapid dive had been impossible to overcome.

Shipping escorts were resumed in November, and on 22 November eight of the squadron's Spitfires joined four Hurricanes of 87 Squadron, based at Borizzo, and eight Spitfires of the USAAF's 4th Fighter Squadron in such an escort. Another one on 25 November involved just two of 229 Squadron's aircraft with three Mosquitoes of 256 Squadron and fourteen Spitfires of the USAAF's 2nd FS.

Patrols over Sicily were resumed during the second week of December, but something unusual came 229 Squadron's way on 8 December, when four of the Spitfires flew out to meet a C-54 transport aircraft and several P-38 Lightnings thirty miles west of Gozo and to escort them to

Luqa. The C-54 carried President Roosevelt of the United States and his entourage.

On Christmas Day 1943, after an enormous dinner, a number of the ground crews left in a Dakota for Catania in Sicily, followed by eight of the Spitfires. At Catania they began to operate as a detached Flight. Meanwhile at Hal Far there were a number of scrambles during January 1944, but it became clear that the squadron would leave the island shortly. On 30 January, after some difficulties with Maltese personnel who did not want to move, the remainder of 229 Squadron joined the detachment at Catania.

Royal Naval Air Squadron Malta
On 31 March 1942 the two FAA squadrons in Malta, 830 Squadron flying Swordfish and 828 Squadron with Albacores, combined to form the RN Air Squadron Malta. In command was Lt. Cdr. Hoskins, until on 7 June he was posted and succeeded by Lt. Cdr. A. J. Roe. During July a brief respite from constant air raids allowed the squadron's ground crews to make all its aircraft serviceable, but shortages of fuel, spares and

Hurricane IIc Z2481
of 229 Squadron
was struck off
charge after damage
suffered in the air
raid on Hal Far on 29
April 1942.
*[P. Hands via R. C.
Sturtivant]*

The 229 Sqdn. operations board, showing the code latters of thirteen aircraft, the pen in which each one was located, and the pilots' names. *[D. R. Neate]*

aircraft and lack of targets within range did nothing to boost morale.

In August another CO, Lt. Cdr. Lashmore, took over, and found that only two torpedo-carrying Albacores, one similar Swordfish and one ASV-equipped Swordfish were available. With these the RNAS pressed on, with some success. Some of 826 Squadron's Albacores were absorbed in

December, when the two remaining Swordfish were cannibalised to create one floatplane for use by the ASR Flight at Kalafrana.

The RN Air Squadron Malta, never a fully-fledged unit, faded away on the demise of 830 Squadron and the resurgence of 828 Squadron at the end of 1942.

821 Squadron
Equipped with Albacore aircraft, 821 Squadron moved to Hal Far on 30 November 1942 from Dekheila, and then concentrated on attacking enemy shipping supplying North Africa. One Flight, Detachment 4, moved to Castel Benito in mid-March 1943 to provide illumination for RAF aircraft bombing nearby Tripoli at night, but returned to Hal Far a month later.

Its services needed elsewhere, 821 Squadron left for Monastir in Tunisia on 4 June 1943.

Air Sea Rescue & Communications Flight
In order to create a fully-fledged air/sea rescue unit for Malta, with a secondary role of communications, two Blenheim aircraft arrived at Hal Far from El Adem in Libya on 3 March 1943. They spent the rest of the month carrying VIPs between Malta and North Africa, probably in connection with the imminent invasion of Sicily, but on 6/7 April one of them flew to Heliopolis to escort the unit's third aircraft, a Harvard Mk.II, to Hal Far via Mersah Matruh and Castel Benito. This Harvard was to be a very useful part of the Flight's equipment for the next two years.

The next stage in the ASR&CF's development was the arrival from Luqa on 21 April of its ASR section, which had been operating on an ad hoc basis for some time. This gave the Flight the use of

Three Albacores of 821 Squadron, Hal Far, BF710 [S5:L], BF712 [S5:B] and BF574 [S5:M], seen over the island. *[via R. C. Sturtivant]*

two Walrus amphibians for picking up ditched aircrews, and practicing for this task was soon commenced. While taking off from the sea east of Malta on 12 May one Walrus, P5718, suffered damage to a float, and had to taxi to Kalafrana, proving the adaptability of the already-ageing Walrus.

Orders were received on 14 May that the Flight was to concentrate on ASR work at the expense of communications flying, but this edict seems to have largely been ignored. Larger aircraft in the shape of two Wellingtons arrived on 1 June, and later in the month the Flight's practice ASR flying was put into action in searches for a Spitfire pilot ten miles (16km.) from Filfla Island and for a ditched Wellington. The Flight's own Wellingtons were taken to Safi for alteration of the front turret to make them more suitable as observation platforms. The Harvard, meanwhile, was in demand as a training aircraft for less-experienced pilots of 1435 Squadron at Safi and others at Qrendi. On 1 July it was flown to the new and very temporary airstrip at Xewkija on Gozo by AVM Sir Keith Park, the AOC, and then to Qrendi. Two days later, a less potent aircraft, Proctor P6116, arrived for Sir Keith's personal use.

During July 1943 the arrangements for handling transit aircraft at Luqa became overcrowded, and the ASR&CF offered to handle some aircraft at Hal Far. Whether this actually happened is not known. The Flight was expanding rapidly itself: on 3 July it was learnt that six more Walruses and ten crews would be allocated to it, which would bring the total number of aircrew to fifty. One of the original Walruses left that day for Monastir to escort four Stinson aircraft to Hal Far via Lampedusa, a trip of less than a hundred miles (160km.) on each leg.

Another of the Walruses searched on 4 July for the crew of a B-17 Fortress aircraft which had ditched, but was recalled when it was found that the men had been picked up by a German boat. The first two of the additional Walruses arrived on 5 July in poor shape, with threadbare tyres and no ASV equipment. Two more which flew in on 9 July were in better condition but had no VHF radios.

By now it was realised that there was a singular lack of customers to be picked up from the sea and it was recorded that even Germans would have been welcome! A search for a ditched Halifax on 18 July was abortive, as was a search for a Mosquito five miles (8km.) off Sicily on 21 July.

Three Fairchild Argus aircraft arrived from Monastir on 19 July to be added to the Flight's inventory, but three Piper Cubs escorted by a Walrus from Monastir via Lampedusa to Xewkija on 23 July probably belonged to the US Army and were destined for Sicily.

The first search by the ASR&CF which was successful in the sense that bodies were found was on 26 July 1943, when the crews of a Mosquito and a Beaufighter were located and later picked up by HSL. On 7 August came the Flight's first rescue, when a 185 Squadron pilot was picked up, but a heavy swell prevented the Walrus's take-off. Not to be beaten, the Walrus pilot taxied for 4 hours 20 minutes all the way to Kalafrana!

Malta ASR&CF's first spell of duty at Hal Far ended on 25 August 1943 when a move was made to Takali. However, the Flight returned to Hal Far on 1 February 1944 with a modified task pending. A Magister aircraft was taken on charge on 8 February, and on 12 February the last of the ancient Walrus amphibians departed. Two more Wellingtons arrived on 21 February.

On 1 March 1944 the Flight was renamed AHQ Malta Communications Flight. Its aircraft at that time comprised three Arguses, an Anson and two

One of the speedier aircraft used by AHQ Malta Communications Flight was Spitfire Vc JK777 [P], here seen at Hal Far in 1946. *[D. J. Dilworth via R. C. Sturtivant]*

Probably the only Baltimore used by Malta ASR & Communications Flight was this Mk.Vc, FW811.
[D. J. Dilworth via A. Thomas]

Spitfires for communications work; two Wellingtons Mk.X fitted with Lindholme rescue equipment for constant ASR standby; a Wellington Mk.Ic which had been out of action for several months; and a Proctor which was in Sicily in unserviceable condition. Another Anson, a Wellington and a Hurricane were received during April, but on 16 April 283 Squadron took over all ASR duties from the Flight, and all the Wellingtons departed. The communications flying at this time comprised daily trips around Sicily, usually calling at Borrizzo, Palermo and Catania, but on 6 June this schedule was reduced to every other day, soon altered again to a daily run to Catania only. By the end of June two Ansons, two Hurricanes and a Magister formed the stock of the 'Malta airline', but on 17 August a Wellington was collected from Heliopolis to handle longer distance runs to Italy, Algeria and other Western Mediterranean locations. Two Spitfires Mk.Vc arrived in

September, and in October a Baltimore Mk.V and a comparatively luxurious Expeditor Mk.II were taken on charge to supplement the Wellington.

On 12 December 1944 the Spitfires began daily early-morning meteorological flights, during which they climbed to about 24000ft. (7300 m.), allowing the pilot to assess upper air conditions which would enable the forecasters to provide more accurate reports. These flights continued for just over a year and were much appreciated by the Met. Office staff.

Four more Ansons arrived for the Flight in February 1945, as well as another Hurricane, and although there were several changes of aircraft during the rest of 1945 the establishment remained much the same. At the end of that year the Flight was ordered to vacate Hal Far as part of the handover to the Fleet Air Arm, and accordingly on 4 January 1946 a move was made, this time to Luqa.

Expeditor HB270 of AHQ Malta Communications Flight was eventually returned to the USAAF.
[D. J. Dilworth via R. C. Sturtivant]

SN:A, a Spitfire Vc, was the mount of Sqdn. Ldr. E. D. Mackie of 243 Squadron. one of the units which spent a short time at Hal Far during the invasion of Sicily.
[Sqdn. Ldr. E. D. Mackie via A. Thomas]

324 Wing

Four squadrons of Spitfires comprising 324 Wing, 43, 72, 93 and 243 Squadrons, arrived in Malta on 9/10 June 1943 to take part in the 'softening-up' of Sicily in advance of the invasion of that island. Settling in, the ground personnel, who had travelled by sea from Sfax in Tunisia, found conditions at Hal Far much more civilised than they had experienced at their previous base, Mateur. The Wing's aircraft flew in soon afterwards, but one flown by a 243 Squadron pilot was written off during its landing.

Offensive sweeps over Sicily began on 15 June and carried on for a few days, and enemy defences were found to be light.

Ten of 72 Squadron's Mk.IX Spitfires were exchanged with 243 Squadron Mk.Vs on 21 June and 72 Squadron, at least, was split into three self-supporting fully mobile Flights to prepare the personnel for the time when they would reach the Italian mainland.

Early in July the squadrons of 324 Wing switched to providing top cover for B-17s of the USAAF raiding targets in Sicily such as Catania and Comiso airfields, for B-25 medium bombers attacking Gerbini and Biscari and for P-40 fighter-bombers.

Three of the squadrons flew patrols over the invasion beach-heads on 10 July, while 72 Squadron stood by until escorting a raid during the afternoon. Highly successful operations during the next few days resulted in the destruction of several MC.200s on 11 July and at least eight more, with five Bf.109s and two Ju.52s, next day.

Only four days after the landings, 324 Wing HQ left Malta in two Dakotas to 'set up shop' on the newly-captured Comiso airfield, which had been heavily bombed by the Allies just a few days

previously. The four squadrons very soon followed, and by 20 July all had settled into their new, if temporary, home.

250 Squadron

The twelve Kittyhawks Mk.III of 250 Squadron, led by Sqdn. Ldr. Johns, arrived at Hal Far from Zuara on 9 July 1943 to play a part in the invasion of Sicily. Operations began two days later when all the aircraft bombed a bridge and road south of Catania with no opposition. Later the same day the squadron was unable to find a suitable target and so brought the bombs back, not a pleasant task for the armourers who had to defuse them. All twelve Kittyhawks again raided Sicily on 12 July, but on this occasion two of them collided, one pilot being killed and the other successfully baling out.

Following a raid by ten aircraft on horse-drawn transport in Sicily on 13 July, the squadron's aircraft landed at Luqa, to which the ground crews had moved during the mission, and from where a few more missions would be flown.

284 Squadron

Another of the many units destined to spend only a short time in Malta, 284 Squadron began to arrive at Hal Far on 9 July 1943, when the NCO aircrew, who had flown from Bizerte to Kalafrana in a Sunderland, appeared. As this was the day before the invasion of Sicily, one imagines that yet another group of airmen to swell the large numbers already on the scene would not have been too welcome! Nevertheless, by 12 July the squadron's Walrus amphibians were practicing sea landings, and the CO was anxious to work off Sicily, where he knew there would be a demand for ASR services.

It was not to be long before the CO's wishes

would come about, but before leaving Malta the squadron sent a Walrus to Monastir in Tunisia on 22 July to escort three L-4 Cub aircraft of the US Field Artillery to Lampedusa and thence to Xewkija and on to Sicily. On 25 July one of the Walruses was at Pachino on search and rescue tasks, and two days later the squadron, comprising five pilots, four WOps and eight ground crew borrowed from the Malta Communications Flight, left for Cassibile.

3 Wing, South African Air Force

Comprising three light bomber squadrons — 12 and 24 Squadrons with Boston Mk.III aircraft and 21 Squadron with Baltimores, 3 Wing SAAF arrived from Ben Hagan and Suliman on 21 July 1943 under the command of Col. J. T. Durrant DFC. Next morning they carried out their first operation from Malta, 12 and 24 Squadrons dropping 96 250lb. (115kg.) bombs on communications targets near Catania in Sicily. That afternoon, 12 of 21 Squadron's Baltimores joined 24 Squadron in a raid on a road junction at Palermo, meeting a moderate amount of flak which hit a Boston and caused it to ditch off Malta.

Next day 12 and 21 Squadrons carried on the job of bombing road targets in Sicily, but one of the Bostons, HK873, crashed on take-off from Hal Far, killing two of the crew. Seventy-two sorties were made on 26 July by the three squadrons, and next day thirty-five aircraft attacked the seaplane jetty and oil tanks at Milazzo, three Baltimores being damaged by AA fire.

Another tragedy occured on 9 August, when a Baltimore of 21 Squadron, AH173, leaving Hal Far for a routine inspection at Castel Benito, crashed on take-off, with the deaths of all three crew members.

The Wing's final operation from Hal Far was on 17 August, when eleven Bostons and five Baltimores raided transport targets in the toe of Italy. One of the Bostons of 12 Squadron, HK869, returning early with engine trouble, crashed at Luqa and all aboard lost their lives. Two days later, the Wing left Hal Far and moved to Gerbini/Cuticchi in Sicily.

283 Squadron

An advance party of 283 Squadron arrived at Hal Far on 2 April 1944 from Borgo in Corsica and two days later the first batch of ground crew members flew in in a 293 Squadron Warwick. Having flown Walrus amphibians until recently, the squadron was now in the process of re-equipping with Warwicks, and three new aircraft arrived on 9 April, the day before the squadron's main party left Borgo by sea.

Set the task of providing air-sea rescue facilities for Malta, 283 Squadron quickly settled down to training with three Warwicks fitted with airborne lifeboats. These aircraft were first called out in earnest to look for a P-40 which had disappeared on a flight from Sicily to Tunis on 1 May. Little then occurred until 22 July, when, twelve hours after the event, 283 was scrambled to look for the passengers of a USAAF B-17 who had all baled out

Although not photographed in Malta, this Boston III, Z2279 [OZ:C], is typical of the aircraft flown by 24 Sqdn., SAAF. [via A. Thomas]

BV458, a recently-acquired Warwick ASR.1 of 283 Squadron at Hal Far in the summer of 1944.
[R. C. Woolven via A. Thomas]

between Tunis and Sicily when an engine caught fire, several losing their lives in the process. Ironically, the B-17 landed safely back at Tunis, but 283 Squadron managed to find four survivors after a good deal of technical difficulty with the Warwicks.

During August a York carrying VIPs was escorted from Pomigliano to Cap San Vito and from Cap Blanc to Tunis, but on 24 August one of the Warwicks, BV280, was lost when it ditched 400 yds. (360m.) off shore at the mouth of Kalafrana Bay after both engines failed. One airman lost his life in this incident. Searches for a Mosquito, a Boston and a Ventura of the SAAF occupied the squadron in September and a Beaufighter was successfully located off Corfu in October.

A detachment of 283 Squadron at Grottaglie was moved to Kalamaki near Athens on 24 October, and during the same month a somewhat dangerous task, ferrying fifteen diphtheria patients, BOAC personnel, from Djerba to Tripoli, was undertaken.

December's work included the provision of two aircraft to cover the rescue of the passengers and crew of the MV *Kumonova,* a 1400-ton Yugoslavian vessel which plied between Malta and Catania. On 27 December, leaking badly and with engines stopped, the *Kumonova* sent an SOS and 283 Squadron dropped two lifeboats close to the stricken ship. These enabled most of those on board to reach safety, while a few more were picked up by small boats. Only two of the 190 people involved were lost, and the AOC Malta, AVM K. B. Lloyd, later sent a message of congratulation to the squadron.

At the end of January 1945 two Warwicks were detached to Saki in the Crimea to provide ASR facilities for aircraft carrying VIPS to the Yalta conference.

After the conference, the two aircraft escorted VIPs to the next stage of the proceedings, which were held at Cairo, before the detachment returned to Malta. Another detachment followed, this time to Blida, to where three aircraft and ground crews reported on 4 March 1945. While there, one of the Warwicks, BV472, engaged on SAR duties, suffered engine trouble and ditched 10 miles (16km.) west of Algiers, but luckily the crew was rescued.

A revised establishment for 283 Squadron was announced on 18 May: ten Warwicks and five Walruses or Sea Otters, but it is doubtful whether the extra aircraft ever appeared in fact. Soon, the twin problems of under-manning due to demobilisation and poor aircraft serviceability began to affect the squadron's performance.

All RCAF and RAAF personnel left in June, while in July the wings of all the Warwicks had to be removed and checked, due to a spate of ruptured fuel and oil tanks. On the lighter side, Sqdn. Ldr. R. B. Crampton, an Australian who had been the squadron's CO since its formation, married Wren Kathleen Sherwin at Sliema, but was soon posted, to be replaced by Sqdn. Ldr. P. R. Ellison.

However, the end of 283 Squadron's days in Malta was in sight, and on 26 August its ASR responsibility was handed over to 38 Squadron. After a farewell party, personnel for two new detachments, at Istres and Elmas, left on 28 August in Dakotas, while the main party set sail for Maison Blanche aboard the Italian cruiser *Duca d'Aosta* in Algeria on 31 August 1945.

108 Squadron

On moving the short distance from Luqa on 1 July 1944, 108 Squadron's officers left the Meadowbank Hotel in Sliema for the Officers' Mess at Hal Far. The NCO aircrew had to put up with the Poor House, while ground NCOs were billeted at Birzebugga and airmen were moved from the Poor House to Marsaxlokk. The squadron's stay was not destined to be a long one.

Little activity in the air was enjoyed, apart from an abortive scramble on 8 July, the first for a long time. There was a sad accident, however, when Beaufighter Mk.VI KW202, practicing firing on Filfla Island on 13 July, hit the water, the crew of two losing their lives.

Detachments which had been at Alghero in Sardinia and at Catania in Sicily were recalled on 25 July, much to their displeasure, as it had been decided that the squadron would disband, to reform at Idku. On 27 July two C-46s and four C-47s arrived to transport ground crews and equipment and by 30 July the move was completed. One of the Beaufighters, however, ND201, crashed at Safi while on an air test and was destroyed by fire.

249 Squadron

As the first stage of a move to Italy, 249 Squadron began to leave Qrendi for Hal Far on 24 September 1943. No operations were carried out from Hal Far; instead the squadron perfected its already efficient fighting techniques. Those in command being satisfied, the ground personnel embarked for Taranto, and thence to their new base at Grottaglie, on 19 October 1943. On 27 October the squadron's sixteen Spitfires took off from Hal Far and set course for Grottaglie, at the end of two and a half eventful years on the island of Malta.

255 Squadron

A detachment of Beaufighters of 255 Squadron, based at Foggia Main in Italy, arrived at Hal Far on 26 July 1944 and began flying patrols at once. On 30 July three of the aircraft intercepted an intruder eighty miles (130km.) east of Catania, and such operations were the order of the day for some time. A change of equipment came in January 1945 with the arrival of Mosquitoes Mk.XIX. The detachment was still present when, on 4 September 1945, the squadron HQ moved from Rossignano, its base during the previous few months, to Hal Far. There the squadron took over 283 Squadron's dispersal area, but the air and ground crews found that life on a Station occupied by other units was not a welcome change.

One of 255 Squadron's tasks was to mount a flypast over Gozo on 16 September 1945 to mark VJ-Day, after which the crews settled down to a peacetime routine of training, with some calibration work for the Navy. Problems with personnel soon occurred; most of the long-serving ground crews had been left in Italy for early repatriation and their replacements had little Mosquito experience and needed training. In addition, leave to the UK and Sicily had begun. These factors meant that flying had to be restricted to 200 hours per month.

Wg. Cdr. J. R. H. Lewis DFC took over from Gp. Capt. A. W. Bates as CO on 20 November 1945, after which the squadron seems to have achieved little before moving to Gianaclis in Egypt in January 1946.

27 Squadron SAAF detachment

Twelve Ventura V aircraft arrived at Hal Far from La Seina on 16 August 1944, followed by three Dakotas which carried ground crews and

Mosquito XIX TA437 [YD:S] of 255 Squadron at Hal Far in 1945.
[D. J. Dilworth via R. C. Sturtivant]

Walrus I amphibians of 624 Squadron, detached to Hal Far from Falconara in 1945, but here seen earlier that year at Grottaglie. The aircraft in this picture are Z1769 [A], L2201 [B] and W2741 [E]. *[via A. Thomas]*

equipment. On this day the squadron was recognised as being the only fully operational general reconnaissance unit covering the Mediterranean between Malta and Oran, so no time was wasted in getting down to business. The first operation from Hal Far, a shipping sweep, was mounted on 19 August, and the squadron settled down to the routine. One of the Venturas, JS891, however, swung violently on take-off on 21 August, ground-looped and burst into flames, but luckily the crew was rescued by young Maltese men who happened to be nearby.

Seven new RAF crews arrived on 22 August but proved a mixed blessing as they were poorly trained and prone to making two-wheel landings instead of the three-pointers favoured by the squadron! One of the newcomers wrote off Ventura FP639 by doing this and swinging on landing on 27 August, and he and all his colleagues were then subjected to further training.

Other detachments of the squadron at Bone and Reghaia came to Hal Far during September, and the complete operational strength of the unit was then in Malta, totalling 14 aircraft. Although it was believed that only one or two German submarines were still at large in the Mediterranean, convoy escorts were flown just in case. Early in October one of the submarines was reported east of Malta but 27 Squadron searched for four days without finding it.

The final operation by 27 Squadron SAAF from Malta was flown on 17 October 1944, and a farewell party was then held. The squadron began to leave for La Seina on that day, but the promised assistance of seven Dakotas was later cancelled, and over the next week or so the ground crews and their gear had to be flown out by the squadron's own Venturas.

682 Squadron detachment

In order to carry out the calibration of radar equipment for part of the Mediterranean Fleet, eight Spitfires Mks.IX and XII were sent to Hal Far from San Severo in Italy on 10 May 1945, complete with ground crews. The detachment succeeded in carrying out only part of this task before being recalled to base for the squadron's disbandment. The Spitfires thus flew out on 20 May, but the ground crews were stranded due to lack of transport, not leaving until 26 May.

624 Squadron detachment

'B' Flight of 624 Squadron arrived at Hal Far aboard four Dakotas from Treviso on 25 June 1945 and the Flight's four Walrus amphibians left Treviso next day via Falconara and Foggia, where three of them were delayed for 48 hours. The last one arrived on 4 July and mine reconnaissance missions began two days later. The month of August was something of a waste of time, and it was decided that the squadron should move on.

A certain amount of work was done in the early part of September, but on 30 September two Dakotas took the ground crews and equipment to Hassani in Greece, the aircraft, W2263, W2704, W2797 and W3020, following next day.

73 Squadron

Comfortable billets and beds awaited the personnel of 73 Squadron when they arrived from Brindisi on 21 July 1945, conditions which the men had not experienced for some time. After a couple of days spent sorting out equipment, four of the unit's Spitfires Mk.IX began training by practicing strafing attacks on the cruisers HMS *Belfast* and *Ontario* and the destroyers HMS *Avondale*, *Myngs* and *Cavendish* and practice interceptions

73 Squadron Spitfire IX
MJ238 [X], based at
Hal Far in early
post-war days.
[via R. C. Sturtivant]

on Mosquitoes of 255 Squadron. Formation flying also took up some of the squadron's time.

The prospect of remaining in Malta seems to have pleased the airmen, as did the regular hours which it was now possible to work. The main complaint was of being 'broke' after years of being able to buy cheap cigarettes and drink in Italy and elsewhere, prices being higher in Malta. Morale was high however, and when the CO, the Station Commander and the Naval Commander inspected the aircraft on 18 August the removal of a cowling revealed a gleaming engine, prompting expressions of surprise and appreciation from these officers.

A full programme of training continued during the autumn of 1945, and as an extra task the squadron began in September to fly meteorological missions. Victory celebrations on 16 September included nine of 73 Squadron's Spitfires flying with nine of 255 Squadron's Mosquitoes over Gozo, a sight much appreciated by the citizens of that quiet island. Demobilisation of personnel began to take its toll in October, and over the next few months proved to be an increasing problem, although the 'Met' flights were continued. In connection with the demobilisation, MRAF Lord Trenchard, visited the squadron on 3 April 1946 and gave an informal talk about conditions in Great Britain and in Germany. The acute shortage of ground personnel was relieved a little on 22 April when fifteen new 'bods' arrived.

The developing emergency in Palestine gave rise to an order received by 73 Squadron on 22 April 1946 to the effect that eight of the Spitfires were to be made ready to leave for that country at 48 hours notice. This order was modified to six aircraft, which left, carrying 90-gallon (400-litre) drop tanks, for Benina on 2 July. Benina airfield was found to be out of action, so the Spitfires returned to try again next day. While the Palestine detachment was away, a start was made on 15 July on a move to Takali, and all personnel were settled in there within two days.

1702 Squadron

After a short voyage in September 1945 from Scotland, where they had been based at Abbotsinch, 1702 Squadron's six Sea Otter

Sea Otter JM963
[O2:A] of 1702
Squadron touches
down at Hal Far
c.1946.
[R. G. Harrington]

A Fleet Air Arm
Wellington X, HZ470
[B] of 765 Squadron,
based at Hal Far in
1945/46.
[via R. C. Sturtivant]

amphibians arrived at Hal Far on 22 September. While there, the squadron devoted its time, under the command of Lt.(A) O. G. Hutchinson, to air-sea rescue duties before leaving for Hassani in Greece on 27 October 1945.

765 Squadron

The only Fleet Air Arm squadron to fly the Wellington Mk.X, 765 Squadron's main task while at Hal Far, where it arrived on 6 October 1945, was to carry troops from several points in the Mediterranean area to Malta for homeward embarkation. For this purpose, the squadron's aircraft, which included some Mk.XVI aircraft, were equipped with bench seating - not very comfortable, but few of the passengers would have minded, as they were on their way home!

Two of the Mk.X Wellingtons were lost to accidents while flying from Hal Far. On 26 March 1946, HZ470 crashed after engine failure on take-off, while on 5 April HE274 failed to pull out of a dive during a fighter affiliation exercise with a 73 Squadron Spitfire. The Wellington crashed into the centre of the ancient town of Rabat, causing the

deaths of the four crew members and twenty civilians and wrecking many houses.

Its work complete, 765 Squadron was disbanded at Hal Far on 30 April 1946.

2 Officer's Advanced Training School

Although based at Kalafrana, 2 OATS stationed its two Anson aircraft, NL170 and PH603, at Hal Far for the use of the unit's staff officers. The dates of the unit's presence are not clear, but can be assumed to have covered most of 1945.

728 Squadron

The final sojourn of 728 (Fleet Requirements) Squadron, and by far the longest, began on 5 May 1946, when it moved into Hal Far from Luqa. A motley selection of aircraft on charge at that time included examples of the Baltimore V, Beaufighter X, Martinet TT.I, Mosquito XXV, Oxford I and Seafire III, and these were used until more modern equipment became available. Due to the reduction in size of the Mediterranean Fleet, the squadron was by now working at a lower strength, but by no means less intensively. The squadron's

Not many Ansons were
ever based in Malta;
this one, PH603 [R]
was used by AHQ
Malta Communications
Flight and 2 Officers'
Advanced Training
School.
*[D. J. Dilworth via
R. C. Sturtivant]*

Left: A 728 Squadron Martinet goes about its target-towing business over Malta.
[R. A. Waller]

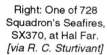

Right: One of 728 Squadron's Seafires, SX370, at Hal Far.
[via R. C. Sturtivant]

Left: Mosquito B.25 KB649 of 728 Squadron, Hal Far, carrying code M8:O.
[via R. A. Waller]

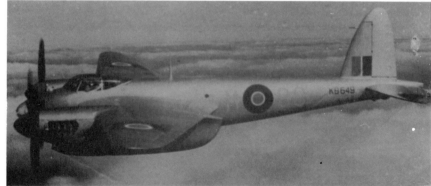

Right: Baltimore IIIa FA435 [801] of 728 Squadron, Hal Far, c.1946.
[R. G. Harrington]

Sturgeon TT.2 TS476 of 728 Squadron, with no code marked. It is seen at the August 1954 air display, alongside a Seahawk and a P2V Neptune of the US Navy coded HC.
[via R. C. Sturtivant]

CO was Lt. Comm. E. M. Britton, replaced on 3 June by Lt.(A) P. J. Cruttenden RNVR and on 21 October by Lt. Cdr.(A) J. R. Groves.

For general passenger and cargo transport work, two Expeditor C.2s were received in March 1948, and Mosquito PR.16s and Seafire F.17s arrived in May. Three of the Seafires were, however, written off in crashes at Hal Far in 1949, SX224 on 26 July, SX226 on 28 September and SX241 on 24 November when its engine failed on take-off. One of the Mosquitoes, NS531, also came to grief when, on 26 March 1949 it ditched half a mile off Delimara Point after suffering engine trouble on the return mail run from Bone in Algeria. Sea Otter ASR.2 JM880 landed in rough water to attempt to rescue the Mosquito's crew but was itself damaged and driven onto the rocks, where it broke up. Not a good day for 728 Squadron! The by now obsolete Martinets were replaced in March 1949 by Mosquito TT.39s to carry out the target-towing commitment, supplemented by Beaufighter TT.10s for a short time that autumn. At the end of December 1950 the aircraft on 728 Squadron charge comprised four Seafire F.17s; three Mosquito PR.16s; six Mosquito TT.39s; and two Expeditor C.2s. Apart

from the task of providing targets for Navy gunners, a similar requirement from Army gun batteries on the island was now being handled. One of the Mosquito TT.39s, PF482, was lost on 24 May 1951 when it crashed a mile from Castel Benito in Libya after severe rudder flutter developed; luckily two of the crew baled out and the pilot walked away from the wreck, which had touched down at 200 miles per hour!

The first two Short Sturgeon TT.2 high-speed target-towing aircraft arrived on the squadron on 17 August 1951, followed shortly by the first jet aircraft, a Sea Vampire F.20. The Seafires and Mosquitoes continued in use, however, until being gradually phased out during 1952, when they were replaced by Sea Hornet FR.20s, which began to arrive in February of that year. On 728 Squadron's books at the end of May 1952 were five Sea Hornets, five Sturgeons, two Vampires and the two ever-faithful Expeditors. A helicopter section was added to the squadron when Dragonflies arrived in December 1952, and this was to become, in effect, the mainstay of Malta's air-sea rescue service.

A variation to the usual Fleet requirements and other routine tasks was enjoyed in June 1953, when Exercise 'Retex' was held when the Mediterranean

The beautiful lines of the Sea Hornet F.20, seen here in 728 Squadron's VR848 [532:HF] being worked on in 1954.
[via R. C. Sturtivant]

A fine shot of 728 Squadron Sea Hornet F.20s VR856[534:HF], TT1•4 [531:HF] and VR848 [533:HF] flying from Hal Far in 1952. 533 still carries pre-1946-type roundels and fin flash. *[via R. C. Sturtivant]*

Fleet returned to the UK. 728 Squadron was used as a strike force, and the two Expeditors took off at dawn to act as decoys for three Sturgeons and three Sea Hornets which made strikes on vessels of the Fleet. Later in the morning the Sea Vampires joined in, as did two Sea Furies borrowed by 728 for the occasion. At the end of the day the verdict was that the exercise had been very worthwhile from the squadron's point of view, all crews having taken part. Another exercise, 'Summex 2', was held in July, involving attacks by 728 Squadron aircraft on Neptune patrol aircraft of the RAF.

At the end of 1953 the aircraft state remained essentially the same: Sturgeon TT.2s, Sea Hornet FR.20s and Sea Vampire F.20s, plus at least one Expeditor, an aircraft now decidedly 'long in the tooth' but a favourite with the Fleet Air Arm.

728 Squadron operated from Takali for a time during the summer of 1954, but returned to Hal Far on 9 October. On 29 November, the squadron took over part of the duty previously carried out by 78 Wing RAAF from Luqa of providing aircraft for the RAF's Sector Operations. Sturgeon TT.3s had arrived in July, and in November a further Expeditor, HD775, flew in from the UK for 728 Squadron's use.

The departure from Malta of Admiral Lord Mountbatten on 10 December 1954 was marked by Exercise Famous, a farewell flypast of 80 aircraft, of which 728 Squadron provided six — three Sturgeons and three Vampires. Eight other FAA squadrons and 78 Wing RAAF were the other units which mounted this salute to a great Commander-in-Chief.

By January 1955 the squadron's inventory comprised five Sea Hornet F.20s; eight Sturgeon TT.2s and TT.3s; five Sea Vampire F.20s; two Expeditor C.2s and three Dragonfly helicopters. On 8 February, however, the Admiralty established the squadron's future strength at eleven Sturgeons, seven Meteors and five Sea Hornets, and the first two Meteor T.7s duly arrived that day to replace two Sea Vampires, which left for the UK. In addition, Hal Far Station Flight, an

A Sea Vampire F.20 of 728 Squadron, VV146, at Hal Far in 1954. *[A, Greenhalph via G. Cruikshank]*

Sea Devon C.20 XJ319 of 728 Squadron at Hal Far in 1965, its front end shielded from the glare to allow work to be carried out.
[via G. Cruikshank]

unofficial unit regarded as part of 728 Squadron, was to be equipped with two Dragonflies, a Sea Fury and an Expeditor. Due to repairs on Hal Far's main runway from 1 April, the new Meteors flew as a detachment from Luqa for a six-month period.

Expeditor FT995 was lost on 28 May 1955 when it ditched 80 miles (130km.) north-east of Malta after suffering engine failure while returning from Istanbul. The crew and passengers were soon picked up by a Whirlwind helicopter of 845 Squadron and brought to Hal Far little the worse for wear.

During 1956 a detachment was maintained at El Adem, and daily trips were made between there and Hal Far. All remaining stores were collected from El Adem on 21 December, however, although one Petty Officer was said to be reluctant to return

to Malta as he wanted to 'go native'!

To add to the transport element, Sea Devon C.20s came into use by the squadron in August 1956, and Whirlwind HAR.3 helicopters supplemented the Dragonflies in the SAR role from June 1957 to November 1958. The earlier Sturgeons left in January 1956 and the Sea Hornets in February 1957, no doubt mourned by those who flew them. Meteor TT.20 target-tugs, which would form the basis of the squadron's equipment for the next nine years, began to arrive in March 1958 and by the end of the year had replaced the Sturgeon TT.3s, the last of which made its final flight on 1 October, suffering an undercarriage collapse as it taxied in at Hal Far!

728 Squadron's test pilot, Lt. Bernard, was sadly posted 'missing' on 5 December 1958 after

Right: 728 Squadron Meteor T.7 coded 571:HF waits for its next sortie from Hal Far.
[A. E. Hughes via R. C. Sturtivant]

Left: A Meteor of another Mark, a TT.20 displaying its serial, WD785, in an unusual place on its fin, and coded 582:HF, belonged to 728 Squadron.
[via R. C. Sturtivant]

failing to return from a sortie in Meteor T.7 WS106. Eleven sorties were flown to try to locate the missing aircraft, and Shackletons from Luqa and US Navy P2Vs joined in, but to no avail. Later, on 28 January 1959, the squadron took part in a search for a 500-ton boat reported missing between Malta and Tripoli, and the crew were eventually found in a dinghy by a USN aircraft.

The Expeditors were finally sent to the breakers' yard in June 1959, and the Dragonfly helicopters were withdrawn in October, so that at the end of that year 728 Squadron's 'fleet' consisted of Meteor TT.20s and T.7s for target-towing and training duties and Sea Devon C.20s for transport tasks, but no helicopters.

Another sad loss to the squadron occurred on 10 June 1960, when a Meteor flown by Lt. Pyke, who when attempting a single-engined practice landing, found that the engine would not restart. The aircraft came down just south of the old Safi airfield and Lt. Pyke lost his life. More fortunate were the two pilots aboard Meteor T.7 WA600, which was destroyed by fire after an aborted take-off on 12 October 1961; they escaped with burns.

The larger four-engined Sea Heron replaced the Sea Devons from March 1963, the last Sea Devon, XK896, leaving for the UK on 7 March. That month helicopters returned in the shape of Whirlwind HAS.22s for ASR work. One year later, on 4 March 1964, two mercy missions were efficiently handled by the Whirlwinds: in one an injured seaman was lifted off a liner near Grand Harbour and flown to Floriana parade ground to be taken to King George V hospital, and in the other mission a steward was lifted off RFA *Wave Ruler* and flown to RN Hospital Bigli. The Whirlwinds were withdrawn in August 1965. By the end of 1964 there was a shortage of pilots, reaching the point where there were two aircraft to each pilot!

One of the Herons was disposed of to the UK at the end of July 1965, leaving one, XR443, to carry

A nice formation of aircraft of 728 Squadron in August 1961, led by Sea Devon XJ348 coded 795. The Meteors are T.7 WL353 [574:HF] and TT.20 WD643 [585:HF], but the Seahawk, a visitor from another squadron, is not identifiable. In the top right-hand corner of the picture part of the remains of Safi airstrip can be seen, while below the nose of the Seahawk Hal Far's 1950s control tower is visible.

out the squadron's transport function, and the remaining Whirlwind HAS.22 departed in the same direction on 30 August. The detachment at Gibraltar was maintained, but there was a decreasing amount of work for the squadron to carry out, a reflection of the reduced British naval presence in the Mediterranean. This situation continued during 1966, and it gradually became clear that 728 Squadron's days were numbered. The sole Heron left for the UK on 28 March 1967, and the whole of April was spent in preparing the Meteors for ferrying. A farewell flypast was staged on 7 April, the five remaining Meteors taking part along with three Buccaneers, a Sea Vixen and two Gannets from HMS *Hermes*.The aircraft then departed, and after a cocktail party on 11 May 728 Squadron went into its terminal period before disbanding on 31 May 1967, after 24 years service to the Mediterranean Fleet.

Station Flight
Probably formed in March 1947 to service the requirements of the Station administration, Hal Far Station Flight was an offshoot of 728 Squadron. Its first aircraft seems to have been one or more Harvard T.3s, one of which, EZ406, was the ill-fated aircraft which collided with a 73 Squadron Vampire on 25 October 1948, crashing two miles west of Takali with the loss of the pilot's life. Also used during the early days was a Sea Otter, RD885, which porpoised and sank while alighting on the sea on 14 April 1948.

Subsequently, the Flight used examples of the Expeditor C.2 from 1950 to 1955, after which there was a gap in the transport capacity until February 1958, when a Sea Devon C.20 came into use. This smart little aircraft was disposed of in August 1959, however, and was not replaced until September 1964, when the larger Sea Heron C.2 arrived. Smaller piston-engined aircraft flown by

the Flight included Sea Furies between October 1952 and April 1954 and Fireflies between November 1950 and January 1955.

Jet aircraft arrived on the scene in April 1954, when a Meteor T.7 joined the Flight. It was replaced by a Hunter T.8 in April 1957. A Seahawk FB.5 was in use from August 1958 to July 1960, and during the same period a Sea Vampire T.22 was also in evidence.

Helicopters used by the Flight carried out an air-sea rescue role, and the first to be taken on charge, in December 1952, were Dragonfly HR.3s. These were replaced in 1959 by the HR.5 variety, and Whirlwind HAS.22s were added at the same time. The Dragonflies lasted until the end of 1962, when they were replaced by Whirlwind HAS.7s.

The Station Flight at Hal Far lasted until some time in 1965, the last aircraft in use being the Sea Heron, the Whirlwind having left the previous October.

814 Squadron
814 Squadron, using Firefly FR.1s, embarked in HMS *Vengeance* in September 1947 and joined the 15th Carrier Air Group in the Mediterranean. On 11 November the squadron came ashore at Hal Far, under the command of Lt. Cmdr. F. A. Swanton DSO DSC+Bar. There the usual naval fighter routine was followed until 16 March 1948, when the personnel embarked in SS *Otranto* for the UK to re-equip, leaving their aircraft behind.

It was several years before 814 Squadron was seen at Hal Far again. Now equipped with Avenger AS.5 anti-submarine aircraft, 814 flew to Hal Far from Eglinton in Northern Ireland on 7 February 1955, but stayed only a week before embarking in HMS *Centaur*. A further period at Hal Far between 7 and 26 April 1955 was the last before the squadron disbanded.

A third aircraft type, the Gannet AS.4, was used

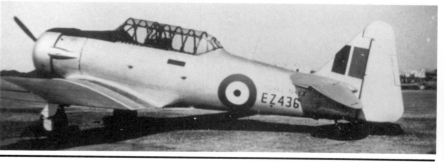

Harvard III EZ436 of Hal Far's Station Flight; this aircraft was later coded HF:913.
[R. A. Waller]

Meteor T.7 VW446
[412:HF] of Hal Far's
Station Flight at
altitude.
*[B. B. Evans via R. C.
Sturtivant]*

by 814 Squadron after its next re-formation, and these appeared at Hal Far from HMS *Eagle* on 26 August 1958, returning on 29 September. They were back on 31 October, staying until 2 December, when they flew off to Eglinton.

During its next reincarnation, 814 Squadron was a helicopter unit, flying Whirlwind HAS.7s on anti-submarine duties, and these 'choppers' came to Hal Far during an exercise with the US 6th Fleet in July 1960. Later that year, Wessex HAS.1s replaced the Whirlwinds, and these more modern aircraft were seen at Hal Far as a detachment in September 1962.

Even more modern equipment, Sea King HAS.1s, supplemented the Wessexes and visited Hal Far from HMS *Hermes* in October 1975.

802 Squadron

Commanded by Lt. Cdr. M. Hordern DFC, 802 Squadron arrived at Hal Far with 814 Squadron from HMS *Vengeance* on 11 November 1947. Possibly due to overcrowding the squadron moved its Seafire F.15s to Takali after a few days.

By 4 February 1952, when 802 Squadron was next at Hal Far, Sea Fury FB.11s and T.20s had replaced the Seafires. On that occasion, the

squadron disembarked from HMS *Ocean,* but on 4 April left for HMS *Theseus.* With the same aircraft, 802 was back at Hal Far between 6 and 27 August 1953. After that, the squadron re-equipped with Sea Hawk F.2s and FGA.4s and brought them as a detachment to Hal Far between 24 June and 18 July 1955. Later marks of the Seahawk, the FB.3 and FB.5, were operated from Hal Far by 802 Squadron for short periods in October and December 1956, when the squadron took part in the Suez campaign; in February, March and October 1958 and in February 1959, after which the squadron returned to the UK to disband.

812 Squadron

After several short-term periods of disembarkation at Hal Far from HMS *Ocean* post-war, 812 Squadron began a longer stay on 20 June 1949. Under the command of Lt. Cdr.(A) D. M. Roberts, the squadron flew twelve Firefly FR.5s carrying HMS *Ocean's* code letter O. These were soon supplemented by four Firefly NF.1 night fighters, taken over from 816 Squadron, and they were operated as 'Black Flight' until being transferred to 827 Squadron in June 1949.

812 Squadron left Hal Far in September 1949 to

Seen over typical
Maltese terraced fields
is Whirlwind HAS.22
WV205 [962] of the
Search & Rescue
section of Station
Flight, Hal Far.
*[B. Lowe via R. C.
Sturtivant]*

Biting the dust on Hal Far's runway was Sea Fury FB.11 VX628 [100:R] of 804 Squadron, which based this type there in the spring of 1953.
[via R. C. Sturtivant]

re-equip with modernised Firefly FR.5s before returning at the end of the month. However, life at sea beckoned, and the squadron embarked in HMS *Glory* on 11 November 1949, although several short visits to Hal Far were made up to March 1951. It was during one such visit that, on 6 October 1950, Fireflies VT423 and WB418 collided in mid-air; VT423 was able to land safely but WB418 ditched in deep water off Gozo.

Now equipped with Gannet AS.1 and T.2 aircraft in the anti-submarine role, 812 Squadron disembarked from HMS *Eagle* to Hal Far on 3 August 1956. Most of that year was occupied by the squadron, then commanded by Lt. Cdr. G. D. Luff DFC, in Fleet exercises, until on 9 December 1956 812 Squadron embarked in HMS *Bulwark* for the voyage to the UK to disband.

804 Squadron

Flying a mixed bag of Sea Fury FB.11s, Firefly 5s and Seafire FR.47s, 804 Squadron disembarked from HMS *Ocean* on 18 July 1949, although short periods ashore had been spent already at Hal Far during the previous few months. The Seafires were soon relinquished, the squadron carrying on its duties with the other two types until embarking in HMS *Glory* just before Christmas 1949.

After serving in Korean waters, 804 Squadron returned to Hal Far from HMS *Theseus* on 18 February 1953, still flying Sea Furies. This stay ended after ten weeks when the squadron embarked in HMS *Indomitable*.

Over the next few years, 804 Squadron continued to make use of Hal Far's facilities for short detachments. More modern aircraft appeared from March 1955, by which time the squadron was flying Seahawk FGA.4s. By the time a return was made to Hal Far for a longer period, when 804 flew off HMS *Bulwark* in December 1956, eleven of the later FGA.6 version of the Seahawk were being used. These aircraft had recently been flown in the Suez operation.

804 Squadron embarked in HMS *Ark Royal* in February 1957, bound for the UK, but the Seahawks were back at Hal Far at the end of July after flying out from Lossiemouth in Scotland. A month later came another move to *Ark Royal*, after which there were a few more short visits to Hal Far, though none by the Scimitars with which 804 Squadron was finally equipped.

827 Squadron

One of only two first-line FAA squadrons to operate the not entirely successful Firebrand TF.5 aircraft, 827 Squadron flew out to Hal Far from Ford on the south coast of England on 25 May

Although here not seen at Hal Far, Firebrand TF.5 EK780 [121:FD] illustrates the aircraft of 827 Squadron based there between May and October 1951.
[via R. C. Sturtivant]

1951. After routine torpedo strike exercises in the Mediterranean the squadron, led by Lt. Cdr. R. D. Henderson, embarked in HMS *Illustrious* on 12 October 1951 to return to England.

807 Squadron

Another of the many Fleet Air Arm units which spent significant periods of time in Malta post-war was 807 Squadron. Equipped with Sea Fury FB.11s in the early 1950s, 807 Squadron first appeared at Hal Far (apart from one earlier flying visit) on 3 August 1951 from HMS *Ocean*, to which a return was made on 12 September. On 17 October the squadron was back, but left again on 12 November, and was not seen as a full squadron again until 9 April 1952, by which time its allegiance had been transferred to HMS *Theseus*. Shorter spells at Hal Far followed, with a longer one between 15 August and 15 October 1952, and a final visit from 16 January to 10 April 1953, when the squadron sailed for Korea in HMS *Ocean*.

By the time 807 Squadron visited Hal Far next, in April 1960, re-equipment with Scimitar F.1s had taken place, following a period with Seahawks. After a few more short appearances, 807 Squadron left the Mediterranean on 30 April 1962 aboard HMS *Centaur* for disbandment.

185 Squadron

Re-formed at Hal Far on 15 September 1951, 185 Squadron was equipped with Vampires FB.5, five of which had arrived by the end of the month. The squadron's CO was Sqdn. Ldr. R. A. Innes, who took up his post on 2 October and led the squadron in Exercise 'Centaurus', a naval cooperation task, on 25 October. Low-level radar attacks on HMS *Magpie* followed.

The early part of 1952 saw the squadron making practice interceptions on Washington bombers on long-range navigational trips from the UK and in cross-country flights to El Adem and Castel Benito.

Mock attacks by carrier-based aircraft in March gave the 185 Squadron crews good practice in ground-controlled interception. The squadron's stay at Hal Far was destined to be short, however, as on 23 July all 16 Vampires and the one Meteor flew to Luqa as a temporary base before a more permanent move to Idris. First-line personnel also went to Luqa, leaving the remainder at Takali until about 14 August, when they left for Idris.

809 Squadron

Equipped with three marks of the beautiful twin-engined Sea Hornet, the F.20, NF.21 and PR.22,

Two Vampire FB.5s of 185 Squadron, WA442 [K] and WA387 [E], on a sortie from Hal Far in 1951.
[D. Lister via P. Porter]

185 Sqdn. Vampire FB.5 WG794, based at Takali, was written off in a dead-stick landing at Hal Far on 31 January 1952.
[J. Betts]

809 Squadron flew from Culdrose to Hal Far on 18 January 1952, but stayed only two months before returning to England.

810 Squadron

No stranger to Malta after a number of short visits since the War, 810 Squadron began a longer period ashore at Hal Far on 9 April 1952 after disembarking from HMS *Ocean*. Equipped with twelve Firefly FR.5s, the squadron carried on its fighter reconnaissance tasks until leaving to join HMS *Glory* on 21 May 1952.

From HMS *Glory,* 810 Squadron was back at Hal Far on 14 August 1952, but left again on 15 October to fly onto HMS *Theseus*. Several further short periods up to mid-1959 were spent at Hal Far by 810 Squadron, which later flew Sea Fury FB.11s, Seahawk FGA.4s and FGA.6s and finally Gannets AS.4 in the anti-submarine role.

898 Squadron

898 Squadron spent many periods ashore at Hal Far between August 1951, when it was equipped with Sea Fury FB.11s, and December 1954, by which time the Sea Furies had been replaced by Seahawk F.1s and FB.3s. The two longest spells were from 15 May 1952, when the squadron flew off HMS *Theseus,* and 23 June 1952, when a move was made to Kasfareet in Egypt, and between 15 August and 15 October 1952, when the squadron re-embarked in HMS *Theseus*.

801 Squadron

Twelve Sea Fury FB.11s of 801 Squadron flew to Malta from Lee-on-Solent on 24 June 1952 and carried on with routine fighter tasks with the Mediterranean Fleet until embarking in HMS *Glory* on 2 September that year.

821 Squadron

Operating as a strike squadron with ten Firefly FR.5s, 821 Squadron arrived at Hal Far from Ford on 26 June 1952, under the command of Lt. Cdr. B. H. Notley. Stores and ground personnel were carried on board HMS *Vengeance*. After nine weeks or so in Malta, however, reinforcements for the Korean conflict were required, and 821 Squadron embarked in HMS *Glory* on 2 September for the voyage to the Far East.

78 Wing, RAAF

Comprising two fighter squadrons, 75 and 76, 78 Wing RAAF was formed at Williamtown, New South Wales, in May 1952 specifically to supplement the RAF presence in the Mediterranean area during a time of poor east/west relations. The advance party of 78 Wing arrived in Malta on 9 July 1952 and the main group at the end of the month.

Once established at Hal Far, the two squadrons received Vampire FB.9s from RAF Safi and settled down to a routine of exercises and armament training, much of which was carried out at Idris in Libya. In order to spend time at an Armament Practice Camp, the two squadrons left for Nicosia on 1 January 1953 but returned on 9 February.

In May 1953 the Coronation Review of the RAF was staged, and twelve of 78 Wing's Vampires, led by Wg. Cdr. Brian Eaton DSO DFC, flew to Horsham St. Faith to prepare to take part. While in the UK, the detachment was also involved in Fighter Command exercises and in a major NATO exercise in Germany, for which the Vampires were based at Wahn from 26 July. While these events were taking place, the Wing HQ moved on 9 June to Takali, to where the detachment returned on 3 August 1953.

The Vampire FB.9s of 78 Wing RAAF at Hal Far ready to take part in the Battle of Britain flypast over the island on 15 September 1952.
[NWMA]

849 Squadron

An airborne early warning unit equipped with the Skyraider AEW.1, 849 Squadron split itself into five Flights which operated more or less independently, plus a HQ Flight at Culdrose in Cornwall. Detachments to Hal Far were common in the 1950s and can be summarised as follows, the more significant periods being marked *:

'A' Flight: 14 - 27 April 1954
                24 June - 23 August 1955
                29 June - 17 July 1956
                1 - 22 May 1960
                18 December 1960 - 6 January 1961
                28 April - 8 May 1961
'B' Flight: *19 January - 2 November 1953
                14 - 27 April 1954
                *11 October 1954 - 26 March 1955
                20 - 31 January 1956
                5 - 15 November 1960
                12 - 27 June 1962
                5 - 18 September 1962
                23 April - 11 May 1965
'C' Flight: 23 October - 30 November 1953
                *16 December 1953 - 8 April 1954
                12 - 16 December 1954
                25 April - 3 May 1957
                28 July - 4 August 1958
                15 December 1961 - 2 January 1962
'D' Flight: *30 March - 9 October 1955
                22 August - 23 September 1959
                11 - 21 March 1960

Gannet AS.4s began to replace the Skyraiders from September 1959, supplemented by AEW.3s from February 1960, and the last Skyraider left 'D' Flight at the end of that year. In February 1961 Gannet COD.4 'carrier on-board delivery' aircraft and T.5 trainers were added to the squadron.

803 Squadron

The Attacker FB.2s of 803 Squadron came ashore to Hal Far from HMS *Eagle* on 14 May 1954, but these were the last of the type seen in Malta, as they were flown to Lee-on-Solent on 13 August for withdrawal from service. They were replaced by new Seahawk FB.3s, which arrived from Lee-on-Solent on 19 August. After a period of working-up, the squadron embarked in HMS *Albion* on 11 November, but returned to Hal Far on 12 December before finally departing on 14 February 1955 to re-embark on HMS *Albion*.

By June 1958, 803 Squadron was equipped with Scimitar F.1s, embarked in HMS *Victorious,* but a short visit to Hal Far was made in November/December that year and another in November 1960. Two detachments were also made in 1962.

845 Squadron

Soon after re-forming as a helicopter unit, 845 Squadron found itself, on 3 May 1954, at Hal Far. Using Whirlwind HAS.22s, the squadron's main task was to evaluate the use of sonar equipment and to perfect navigation techniques. On 1 October, however, the squadron embarked in HMS *Eagle* to act as an assisting force for the victims of an earthquake in Greece, but on 27 October was recalled.

Detachments were made to HMS *Centaur, Triumph* and *Albion*, and on 18 January 1955 four Whirlwinds flew onto *Centaur* and four onto *Albion* for a visit to Toulon, returning to Hal Far on 14 March. The squadron left on HMS *Eagle* on 19 August 1955 for Gibraltar and the UK.

813 Squadron

Commanded by Lt. Cdr. C. E. Price AFC, 813 Squadron flew the Wyvern S.4 naval strike aircraft, and after teething troubles were overcome in the UK the squadron arrived at Hal Far on 16 October 1954 from HMS *Albion*. The Wyverns were not in evidence for long, however, as the squadron left for the UK via Karouba in Tunisia on 9 March 1955.

Seahawk FB.3 WM977 [146:C] of 803 Squadron visiting Hal Far from HMS Centaur in 1955.
[via R. C. Sturtivant]

A smart line-up of 813 Squadron Wyvern S.4s, which flew from Hal Far between October 1954 and March 1955. *[via R. C. Sturtivant]*

There was, though, a detachment, again from HMS *Eagle*, at Hal Far in June/July 1955.

891 Squadron

Flying Sea Venom FAW.21 all-weather fighters, 891 Squadron arrived at Hal Far from Yeovilton on 5 January 1956 and, apart from a couple of days on HMS *Ark Royal*, remained in Malta until leaving for the UK on 26 March that year.

In 1958, by which time later FAW.22 variants of the Sea Venom were being used, 891 Squadron staged through Hal Far on the way home from the Far East and Aden and in 1959 in the reverse direction.

208 Squadron

After moving to Hal Far from Abu Suier on 17 January 1956, 208 Squadron's Meteor FR.9 photo-reconnaissance aircraft were soon busy on such tasks as providing targets for USAF F-86 Sabres flying from Wheelus Field in Libya and on Naval cooperation work.

During February the opportunity was taken to use the facilities of 26 APC at Takali, but 208's time at Hal Far was short, as a move was to be made to Akrotiri in Cyprus as the second squadron to take up residence at that then-new airfield. The ground crews left Malta on 20 March 1956 by sea, and the aircraft followed five days later.

Meteor FR.9s WX956 and WX969 of 208 Squadron arriving at Hal Far from Egypt in January 1956. *[via A. Thomas]*

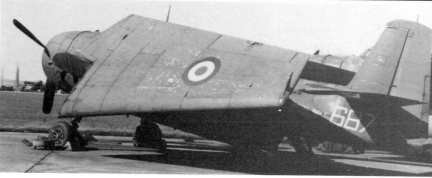

Wings folded, 751 Squadron Avenger AS.5 XB357 [687], seen here at its home base, Watton, operated from Hal Far for a short time early in 1958.
[via R. C. Sturtivant]

751 Squadron detachment

Operating as a dedicated Radio Warfare Unit, 751 Squadron, based at Watton in Norfolk, sent a detachment of Fireflies and Sea Furies to Hal Far from 30 January to 20 February 1956 and another, its 'B' Flight flying Avengers, between 19 February and 20 March 1958.

892 Squadron

892 Squadron's first appearance at Hal Far was on 4 January 1946, when Hellcat night fighters were still being flown. After that visit the squadron left on 18 February on the way home to disband.

Several years went by before 892 Squadron was re-formed, now flying Sea Venom FAW.21s. With these, it flew from Yeovilton to Hal Far on 9 July 1956 and took part in the Suez operation from HMS *Eagle* in November before returning to Hal Far. After that excitement, 892 Squadron embarked in HMS *Eagle* on 11 December to merge with 893 Squadron.

Over the next few years, 892 Squadron, which was re-formed in July 1959 to fly Sea Vixen FAW.1s and FAW.2s, appeared at Hal Far on short disembarkations.

893 Squadron

After making its first appearance at Hal Far on 11 August 1956, when its Sea Venoms FAW.21 flew in from Yeovilton via Rome (Ciampino), 893 Squadron alternated between Hal Far and HMS *Eagle*. The squadron played its part in the Suez campaign from that carrier, and returned to Hal Far on 24 December after absorbing 892 Squadron. 893 Squadron remained at Hal Far until 5 February 1957, when it embarked in HMS *Ark Royal* for the voyage to the UK.

Over the next few years, 893 Squadron was seen at Hal Far on short detachments, flying Sea Vixens.

825 Squadron

Equipped with nine Gannet AS.4s, 825 Squadron arrived at Hal Far on 15 January 1958 from HMS *Victorious*. This was the squadron's first lengthy sojourn on Malta since the War, although short visits had been made in the early 1950s when Fireflies were being flown. However, the squadron was destined to have a short incarnation, as, after carrying out its anti-submarine duties around Malta for three months it flew back to the UK on 21 April 1958 to disband.

893 Squadron Sea Venom FAW.21 WW287 [467:O] seen in 1957 on board HMS *Ark Royal*. This squadron had spent time at Hal Far during the previous year.
[A. Pearcy via R. C. Sturtivant]

831 Squadron Gannet
ECM.6 XG831 [390].
[via R. C. Sturtivant]

Later, as an anti-submarine helicopter unit, flying Whirlwinds, 825 Squadron disemabrked to Hal Far from HMS *Victorious* for three weeks in November 1960.

831 Squadron

The four Sea Venom ECM.21s of 'B' Flight of 831 Squadron, an electronic warfare unit based at Culdrose in Cornwall, arrived at Hal Far on 4 July 1958 after flying off HMS *Eagle*. In Malta, the Flight participated in fleet exercises before returning to Culdrose on 6 November 1958.

Several times over the next six years the Flight visited Hal Far on short detachments, latterly using the updated ECM.22 variant of the Sea Venom.

'A' Flight of the same squadron was equipped with Gannet ECM.4s and ECM.6s also visited Hal Far, for short periods between November 1959 and October 1965.

848 Squadron

A helicopter unit from as early as 1952, 848 Squadron was re-formed at Hal Far on 14 October 1958 from 728C Squadron to act as the Amphibious Warfare Trials Unit. The new unit was the first operational Royal Marine Commando helicopter squadron, and flew five Whirlwind HAS.22s for 45 Commando.

After a year of pioneering rotary-wing activity, 848 Squadron left Hal Far on 9 November 1959 to re-equip with Whirlwind HAS.7s at Worthy Down.

848 Squadron returned to the Mediterranean aboard HMS *Bulwark* and came ashore at Hal Far for a few days in March and May 1960 before leaving for the Far East.

FASRON 201 Special

Late in 1953, the United States Navy, which had over several years sent deployments of aircraft to both Luqa and Hal Far, established a semi-permanent base at the latter airfield. This unit took the title FASRON 201 Special, and as a Fleet Aircraft Service Squadron base, Hal Far became widely used by USN carrier-based squadrons and by land-based patrol squadrons.

Permanently allocated to FASRON 201 were two squadrons: VW-2, flying WV-2 Super Constellations on airborne early warning duties, and US Marine squadron VR-35, operating R4Q Boxcars on logistical duties. Patrol squadrons using Hal Far regularly included VP-11, VP-21, VP-23 and VP-24, flying the P2V Neptune.

Three years of accident-free operation between 1956 and 1958 earned FASRON 201 a Citation from the Commander Naval Air Force Atlantic Fleet, but the end of the unit was not long postponed, disbandment taking place in September 1959.

Operated by FASRON 201 at Hal Far was R4D-8 'Super-Dak' 50812 carrying unit code FU when photographed in August 1958.
[via G. Cruikshank]

A US Navy JD-1 Invader target-tug seen at Hal Far and probably based there. [J. Betts]

Binbrook Canberra Wing

No strangers to Malta, having been involved in Exercises 'Medflex Dragon' and 'Volo Two' in March 1956, detachments from three of the Canberra squadrons based at Binbrook returned to Hal Far in the autumn of that year fully prepared to take part in any offensive operations which might arise as a result of the crisis then brewing in the Suez Canal Zone. The three squadrons came to Hal Far after a short stop at Luqa, 12 Squadron arriving on 25 September, 9 Squadron on 30 October and

101 Squadron later. Ground crews flew in from Binbrook in Hastings aircraft of Transport Command, and were billeted with the Navy at Kalafrana.

At first light on 30 October, four Canberras making reconnaissance flights over the Canal Zone were intercepted by Egyptian Air Force MiG-15s, and the decision was then made to delay the planned bombing raids on Egyptian airfields. The British and French governments gave ultimatums to both the Israelis and the Egyptians to withdraw

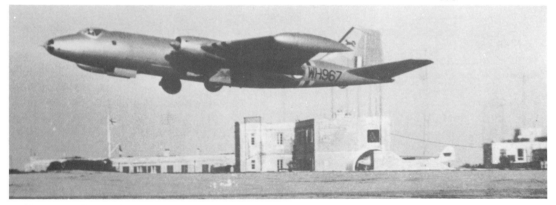

Above: Just lifting off from Hal Far at the time of the Suez campaign is Canberra B.6 WH967 of 12 Squadron, complete with the squadron's fox emblem on the fin and black/yellow campaign stripes. Partly hidden behind a wall is a Seahawk from HMS Eagle Below: Canberra B.6s of the Binbrook Canberra Wing (9, 12 and 101 Squadrons) lined up at Hal Far during the Suez crisis in late 1956. [via S. A. Scott]

Canberras B.2 and B.6 of 9, 12, and 101 Squadrons on the apron at Hal Far on 28 October 1956, during the Suez crisis. Note the black and yellow campaign stripes carried by all aircraft.
[P. Porter collection]

from the Canal Zone, even though the Israelis had not yet reached it! This act had little effect, and on 31 October the Canberras from Hal Far and others flying from Cyprus, together with Valiants from both islands, carried out strikes against Almaza, Abu Sueir, Kabrit and Cairo International airfields, with little opposition and without much damage being caused.

However, a truce brought about by political pressures came into effect on 8 November, although the Binbrook squadrons remained on standby for a time, 12 and 101 Squadrons beginning the homeward trip via Luqa on 29 November and 9 Squadron a couple of weeks later, probably spending the intermediate time at Luqa.

728B Squadron
After commissioning at Stretton in January 1958, 728B Squadron completed the move to Hal Far on 6 March. There the unit began at once to work up for the task of providing radio-controlled pilotless aircraft for the trials of 'Seaslug' surface-to-air guided weapons in conjunction with HMS *Girdle Ness*. Many modifications to the aircraft control systems were found to be necessary and were designed, installed, and tested by squadron personnel before optimum results were achieved. For this work twelve awards were made to members of the squadron, including the MBE to the CO, Lt. Cmdr. J. G. Corbett, who became the Navy's expert on the radio control of aircraft.

Four types of aircraft were used by 728B Squadron: initially Firefly U.9s were flown, and it was not until 10 July 1959 that the first Meteor U.15 arrived. Several Fireflies were retained, however, as the Meteors proved to be somewhat

troublesome in the 'drone' role. The unit's first Meteor 'drone' to be lost was shot down on 29 March 1960 by a Seaslug missile at 32000 feet (9700m) above the Mediterranean.

During the first two years of the unit's time in Malta, squadron pilots flew 687 hours in aircraft other than their own in order to help the Station fulfil its task. Types flown included almost everything on FAA strength, from Gannets to Dragonfly helicopters.

The first Canberra U.10 for 728B Squadron, and indeed the first in FAA service, WH921, arrived at Hal Far on 25 May 1961 and another one, WD941, soon afterwards. At the same time, Meteor U.16s were joining the Squadron, and the first one was flown pilotless on 11 October. The Seaslug trials were, however, drawing to a close, and the final sortie for HMS *Girdle Ness* was flown by Meteor U.16 WE932 on 13 November. On that date, there were also three Fireflies and five Canberras on the Squadron's strength. Two of the Fireflies were shot down on 23 November, one by a Scimitar from HMS *Centaur* and the other one by a Sea Vixen from HMS *Ark Royal*. The last one, which was also the last Firefly in FAA service, was destroyed by the gunners on HMS *Duchess* on 29 November. In all, 52 aircraft passed through squadron hands during its lifetime. The period when Canberras were flown was the most hectic, and several thousand extra hours were worked in order to adhere to the programme. During three years and nine months of its existence 728B Squadron never failed to launch a drone to meet the schedule, apart from during bad weather conditions. Its task complete, 728B Squadron disbanded at Hal Far on 2 December 1961.

Right: Two Firefly U.9s of 728B Squadron, WB257 [591] in the foreground, both minus wingtips, about 1960. *[A. E. Hughes via R. C. Sturtivant]*

Left: One of 728B Squadron's Firefly U.9s after a belly-landing at Hal Far. *[via R. C. Sturtivant]*

Right: Meteor U.15 target aircraft RA387 [658] of 728B Squadron at Hal Far. *[via R. C. Sturtivant]*

Left: Meteor U.16 WF716 [658] basks in the sun at Hal Far. *[A. E. Hughes via R. C. Sturtivant]*

All-white Canberra
U.14 drone aircraft
WH921 of 728B Sqdn.
at Hal Far in 1961.
[R. A. Walker]

728C Squadron

A short-lived and probably highly frustrated unit, 728C Squadron, another sub-unit of 728 Squadron, had been formed at Lee-on-Solent as the Amphibious Warfare Trials Unit to develop the use of helicopters in lifting Royal Marine Commandos from ship to shore in beach-head assaults. The squadron's four Whirlwinds were ferried to Malta on board HMS *Eagle* and HMS *Ark Royal*, and the squadron became established at Hal Far on 7 February 1958.

Within a few days, landing pads had been brought into use at Ghajn Tuffiela, Mtarfa barracks and St. George's, the HQ of 3rd. Commando Brigade, and by the end of the month most of the Marines on the island had been given air experience. During March, synthetic assault exercises were practiced, and by early April a good standard of operation had been reached.

On 7 April 728C Squadron joined HMS *Striker* for exercises with the Royal Marines at Tarhuna, south of Tripoli in Libya, but they were curtailed due to the political situation in Malta, and the squadron transferred to HMS *Ark Royal* to return to the island. After a short rest, however, 728C Squadron re-embarked on Ark Royal to go to Sardinia to take part in an exercise, after which the opportunity was taken to indulge in a 'jolly' at Civita Vecchia, but on the way the squadron was ordered back to Hal Far with all speed to play its part in the internal security of the island.

Following the subsidence of the problems on the island, 728C Squadron returned to its routine tasks. In June the squadron travelled to Cyprus on board HMS *Bermuda* with units of 45 Commando to help in the political situation there. The return trip was made on 26 July, and on 5 August the squadron took up its usual duties again. Later in the month amphibious assault exercises occupied the squadron, but in September two of the helicopters were detached to El Adem in Libya with half a troop of commandos.

By then fully competent in its task, 728C Squadron was upgraded on 14 August 1958 to become 848 Squadron.

750 Squadron

The Fleet Air Arm's Observer School, 750 Squadron had for several years been based at Culdrose in the extreme south west of England, but better weather conditions in Malta prompted a move to Hal Far in 1959. The nine Sea Prince T.1 aircraft left Culdrose on 12 October and after making an overnight stop at Orange in France arrived at Hal Far next day.

Routine training of observers continued, and it was quickly found that Idris in Libya was an attractive destination for navigational exercises. In

750 Squadron's Sea
Prince T.1 WP320
[669:HF].
[via R. C. Sturtivant]

Seen at Hal Far shortly before the Station's closure is Sea Venom FAW.22 XG721 [592:HF] of 750 Squadron.

addition to their normal tasks, squadron crews took part in search activities when required, as in March 1960, when two Sea Venoms from HMS *Albion* collided in mid-air and ditched. On that occasion, nothing was found.

Early in July 1960 the first jet aircraft for 750 Squadron — Sea Venoms — arrived for high-level navigation training, but the Sea Princes were retained, carrying out their navigational exercises to such destinations as Sigonella (Sicily), Palma (Majorca), Idris (Libya), Rome and Naples. By January 1961 a shortage of replacement fuel tanks for the Sea Princes curtailed operations, but in August the situation had improved, allowing five of them to fly to Rome on a land-away navigation exercise and 'jolly'. Low-flying over Sicily and radar homings took up much of the Sea Princes' time during the autumn, interspersed with sea searches for any fishing boats which might be in the way of the Sea Slug missile firings from HMS *Girdle Ness*.

Both types of aircraft made combined 'navexes' and social visits to such places as Pisa in Italy and Hyeres in the south of France during 1962, and it was during the return flight from Hyeres on 30 July

that one of the Sea Venoms experienced a flame-out at 40,000 feet (12200m.) altitude over Sicily, followed by a fire. Fortunately, the flames were put out, and the aircraft made an emergency landing on a disused airfield at Palermo. Another of the three Sea Venoms ran short of fuel and had to land at Sigonella, the US Navy base on Sicily.

Over the next three years, 750 Squadron continued with a similar work pattern, before leaving Malta in 1965. First to depart were the Sea Venoms, which left on 23 June, followed by the Sea Princes two weeks later, both making for the squadron's new base at Lossiemouth in Scotland.

38 Squadron

Following the transfer of Hal Far from the Fleet Air Arm back to the RAF, 38 Squadron arrived from Luqa on 30 October 1965 to be the sole RAF squadron, keeping company with 728 Squadron, which then became a lodger unit. The squadron's usual routine of maritime reconnaissance was undisturbed, and Shackleton MR.2s remained the unit's equipment until disbandment took place at the end of March 1967.

One of 1844 Squadron's Avengers was XB300, this shot illustrating the considerable size of the aircraft.
[B. W. Vigrass via R. C. Sturtivant]

While at summer camp at Hal Far in August 1956 (the last one held, as it turned out), 1844 Squadron from Bramcote flew these Avenger AS.5s.
[B. W. Vigrass via R. C. Sturtivant]

APPENDIX I : RNVR SUMMER CAMPS

Dates	Squadron	Home base	Aircraft used
1950			
30 July - 10 August	1830	Abbotsinch	Firefly FR.1
1952			
19 May - 30 May	1831	Stretton	Sea Fury FB.11
7 June - 12 June	1832	Culham	Sea Fury FB.11
1953			
23 Aug. - 4 Sept.	1843	Abbotsinch	Firefly FR.5, AS.6
24 Aug. - 5 Sept.	1830	Abbotsinch	Firefly FR.5, AS.6
1954			
8 May - 22 May	1842	Ford	Firefly AS.6
9 May - 23 May	1840	Ford	Firefly AS.6
20 Aug. - 3 Sept.	1831	Stretton	Sea Fury FB.11
22 Aug. - 5 Sept.	1841	Stretton	Firefly FR.1
4 Sept. - 18 Sept.	1833	Bramcote	Sea Fury FB.11
4 Sept. - 17 Sept.	1844	Bramcote	Firefly FR.5
1955			
8 May - 21 May	1830	Abbotsinch	Firefly FR.5, AS.6
8 May - 20 May	1843	Abbotsinch	Firefly FR.5, AS.6
31 May - 10 June	1841	Stretton	Firefly AS.6
22 Aug. - 2 Sept.	1844	Bramcote	Firefly FR.5
1956			
22 June - 6 July	1841	Stretton	Avenger AS.5
29 July - 10 August	1844	Bramcote	Avenger AS.5

Chapter 4

TAKALI

Origins.
The pre-war civilian airport at Ta Kali, used by Italian airlines until they moved to Luqa in April 1940, lay idle until the following October. On 30 October an instruction was sent to RAF Hal Far by HQ Mediterranean to form a small Headquarters at Ta Kali, where one fighter squadron would be based. Accordingly, Wg. Cdr. J. R. O'Sullivan and three SNCOs, 11 airmen and 17 soldiers for ground defence duties made the short journey and set up camp. Next day three SNCOs and 18 airmen of 261 Squadron arrived but until 20 November they were accommodated at Luqa.

During the first week of November several buildings were taken over as temporary accommodation, including The Pottery as barrack rooms and Institute, and Chateau Bertrand, which became known as the 'madhouse', as the NCOs' mess alongside that of the 8th Bn. Manchester Regiment. The original airport buildings were converted into offices, sick quarters and armoury, the Operations Room being sited in the prewar control tower. Two Imperial Airways employees, Mr. Ryan and Mr. Tomkins, acted as controllers. On 8 November the airfield officially became RAF Ta Kali (sic), with Wg. Cdr. O'Sullivan as Station Commander, and on 20 November 261 Squadron moved in from Hal Far.

In the new year, extra billets for officers were brought into use at 122 and 157 Eucharistic Congress St., Marsa. Raids on Ta Kali began on 9 March 1941, when a large number of enemy aircraft attacked, and a Hurricane was destroyed by fire and two others damaged. Three bombs dropped on the airfield on 30 March caused no damage, but small-scale raids in the middle of April were more effective. On 29 April the hangar and other buildings were damaged and several unexploded bombs were found.

In the thick of it.
Wg. Cdr. J. Warfield took over as Station Commander on 16 May 1941, and five days later 249 Squadron arrived from North Weald in the UK to replace 261 Squadron, which was disbanded. On 25 May the airfield was again shot up and two of 249 Squadron's Hurricanes were destroyed and another three damaged. By way of replacement and reinforcement, ten more Hurricanes arrived on 27 June from HMS *Ark Royal,* followed by another nine from HMS *Furious* and twelve from HMS *Ark Royal* three days later. More pilots also arrived

The sergeants' mess at Takali, Chateau Bertrand, better known as The Madhouse as it had attics on the ground floor and stables upstairs! It was later destroyed during a raid.
[James Pickering]

Takali from the air in February 1941. *[James Pickering]*

on 30 June from the UK: they were the personnel of 46 Squadron, which at the time had no aircraft of its own, and so the pilots flew with other squadrons as required. A new squadron, 126 Squadron, was formed at Takali on 28 June 1941 and added its weight to the growing defences.

The slackening of enemy activity (in relative terms) between April and November 1941 allowed some construction work to be carried out at Takali as elsewhere. Most important was the excavation of 'caves' to accommodate the operations room and power station, but above ground perimeter and dispersal tracks were laid down and many aircraft pens built. Subsequently, a 12000-gallon (26400-litre) fuel installation was also provided underground, and an attempt was made in December 1941 to construct underground hangars.

This project turned out to be unsuccessful, as the rock was found to be unstable for large-span tunnels and work was abandoned. However, the initial tunnelling work remained and old or unserviceable aircraft were put in them as decoys. Eventually, all administrative facilities were installed underground, as no buildings remained intact on the surface. Airfield lighting Mk.II was installed at about this time.

By now RAF Takali had become worthy of inspection by the 'top brass', and thus the Inspector General of the RAF, AVM Ludlow-Hewitt, arrived on 19 July 1941, followed a week later by the AOC Middle East, ACM Tedder. Air raids continued and casualties were sustained, including four airmen who were killed when a mine exploded during a monthly inspection on 2 September.

261 Squadron pilots at readiness in March 1941. *[James Pickering]*

Extract :- D.R.O's dated 14.5.41.
R.A.F. Station, Ta-Kali, Malta

A gibbet has been erected on the corner of the road leading to the caves. Any man, woman or child, civilian or service personnel, found guilty of sabotage, theft, or in any other way impeding the war effort and subsequently shot, will be hung from this gibbet as a warning to all others.

The gibbet erected at Takali in May 1941 as a deterrent against impeding the war effort.
[D. N. Enser]

A further influx of 344 airmen from the UK arrived on 28 September, and Parisio Palace, Naxxar, was taken over to house some of them, as was part of the Manchester Regt. barracks at Mtarfa. At the end of October, Xara Palace, Rabat, became another quarter for officers.

To relieve congestion at Luqa, 69 Squadron, flying Marylands, arrived on 31 October, but they found conditions at Takali unsuitable and returned to Luqa on 29 November. The Malta Night Fighter Unit, which appears to have been in unofficial existence, commanded by Sqdn. Ldr. G. Powell-Sheddon, since the end of July 1941, was reconstituted formally as 1435 Flight on 4 December. At the same time Sqdn. Ldr. Powell-Sheddon took over the role of Station Commander, but held it only until replaced by Wg. Cdr. W. A. Satchell on 20 December. He was there to welcome the AOC Malta, the GOC and HE the Governor when they visited Takali on Christmas Day to partake of dinner. The airmen were served a Christmas dinner in three sittings, waited upon by officers and SNCOs in the traditional way.

The year 1942 opened badly for those at Takali. There were several raids on New Years Day, and on 4 January two Ju.88s caused serious damage to roads and dispersals, a barrack block, six Hurricanes and a bowser which was burnt out. Next day there were six raids, during which 300 men of the Irish Fusiliers and the East Kents arrived to begin repairs. Also arriving that day was an advance party of 242 Squadron from Hal Far for temporary attachment to Takali for operations, although Takali was unserviceable from 5 to 9 and 11 to 13 January due to bad weather. The Hurricanes of 605 Squadron also moved in from Hal Far, on 12 January, but this squadron was disbanded on 27 February 1942.

Worse was to come...
More billets in Mosta were taken over on 8 January, and officers moved into Torre Combo, but on 19 January 122 Eucharistic Congress St. was destroyed in a raid and 9 Tower St. was damaged. Three airmen and a civilian were killed in this raid, during which Ju.88s made direct hits on rock shelters at Takali, damaging Hurricanes and Blenheims. Due to the damage to the airfield that day, the squadrons operated from Luqa. Raids continued through the month, and on 4 February a particularly heavy one was experienced, one large bomb falling close to the SHQ building, injuring ten people. Again the airfield was made partly unserviceable, and SHQ, the MT Section, Equipment and Parachute stores, 249 Squadron

offices and sundry other buildings all became unusable. The lesson learnt from this terrible raid was that SHQ should be located underground, and two days later this was put into practice, all ranks helping with the move.

Another heavy raid was inflicted on Takali on 9 February, causing severe damage to SSQ and killing three airmen and a soldier. By 18 February conditions on camp were said to be deplorable. March was no better: on 20 March nearly 75 Ju.88s raided Takali in what was regarded as the worst raid yet, causing great damage to barracks, roads and fighter pens. Again the airfield was heavily cratered and rendered useless, but even worse was to come next day, when almost a hundred raiders bombed Takali at 10.00, causing damage to three Beaufighters, two Hurricanes and a Spitfire and to the control van, and starting many fires. At 16.00 yet another raid, the third of the day, was suffered, and the Officers' Mess at Rabat was hit, six officers, including the Intelligence Officer, losing their lives. In 24 hours over 1500 bombs had been dropped on Takali and its environs, excluding incendiaries. The entire personnel was therefore evacuated to St. Edmunds College, Rabat, but, hardly surprisingly, there were a large number of absentees, for whom special police patrols searched. The equipment stores were now, not before time, established in underground caves.

By dusk next day, the airfield was serviceable once more, thanks to the large Army working party. Continuous raids were experienced for the rest of the month, and through April. An early morning raid by twelve Ju.88s which dropped sixty bombs put the airfield out of action for several hours, and later in the day 25 Ju.87 dive-bombers and four Ju.88s made another attack, destroying a Spitfire and damaging two more. By 6 April, when there were several raids on Takali, almost all the buildings had been destroyed, but equipment was being salvaged between raids in order to maintain some sort of life. The Orderly Room and Guard Room moved from St. Edmunds College, Mdina, to more secure habitats in caves, while Messina House was taken over as billets. Starting on 10 April, tents were erected in Boschetto Gardens, near Dingli, to accommodate Takali personnel. Added to these were sailors from HMS *Breconshire*, who arrived on 19 April for armament duties, and also the personnel of 603

Squadron, which arrived from the UK on 20 April. By 13 April a 300-strong Army working party was doing sterling work on runway repairs by day and night, while there was a brief respite from enemy attack. However, on 21 April the Ju.88s, 36 of them, returned to drop 150 bombs, destroying four Spitfires, followed by another raid, by Ju.87s, later in the day. On this day a cut in rations had to be imposed as it had become difficult to feed the personnel from existing stocks. Concerted attacks on Takali continued during the rest of April. The enemy was now concentrating on the underground hangars, but on 30 April a Bf.109 trying to intercept landing Spitfires was brought down by small arms fire, a cheering experience for the gunners, no doubt. Even more encouraging was the arrival on 9 May and 3 June of more Spitfires, flown off aircraft carriers.

The tented accommodation at Boschetto Gardens received a direct hit on 2 July, and seven airmen were killed, two more dying later of severe injuries, and another eleven were wounded. Fires started in the trees in this area (which is now known as Buskett Gardens) were soon put out.

...the worst is over.

Raids continued on a smaller scale during August, but all ranks worked from dawn to dusk, and sometimes longer, to provide aircraft to cover the arrival of a vital convoy. 229 Squadron was re-formed on 3 August, absorbing the personnel of 603 Squadron, Spitfires Mk.Vc being used by the new unit. Two Beaufighter squadrons, 272 and 227, arrived during November, and Takali airfield was an extremely busy spot. By the end of the year, however, the siege was over, and only spasmodic warnings of raids occurred. A new Station Commander, Gp. Capt. G. Y. Tyrrell MC, arrived on 2 February 1943 to take over from Wg. Cdr. W. A. Satchell DSO, and two weeks later the AOC inspected the Station and its aircraft, the first of a sequence of such inspections to ensure the Station's readiness for the forthcoming invasion of Sicily. There was, however, now time for sports, six-a-side football being popular, and in April a boxing tournament was held at Naxxar. The AOC, AVM Sir Keith Park KBE, returned on 12 April and accompanied ACM Tedder, the AOC-in-C, when he came to talk informally with pilots four days later. A further visit was made by the AOC on 21

April, when he inspected arrangements to house the personnel of the several extra squadrons expected to arrive in June. Yet another visit by the AOC was on 30 April, when he presented the Station crest and took a march-past. AVM Park must have liked Takali, as he came again, on 27 May, with Gen. Spaatz of the USAAF to view arrangements for American squadrons to use the airfield, and on 6 June, when he accompanied ACM Tedder again.

The expected extra squadrons then began to appear. First were the five Spitfire squadrons of 322 Wing, an advance party of which arrived on 3 June. The aircraft of the first two units, 81 and 154 Squadrons, flew in next day, and on 5 June 152, 242 and 252 Squadrons arrived. Conversely, 272 Squadron's Beaufighters left for Luqa on 4 June. Supplementing the squadron personnel were those of 3232 Servicing Commando, which arrived on 21 June. Sad to say, two airmen of this unit were killed by a small bomb which had lain undiscovered after being dropped during a raid some time before.

Enter the Navy!
Fleet Air Arm squadrons now began to appear at Takali. First to arrive was 828 Squadron, which moved from Hal Far on 8 June but left for Monastir three weeks later, and this was followed on 2 July by 815 Squadron, which disbanded at Takali on 24 July. Then came 826 Squadron, flying Albacores, which arrived on 10 July but was disbanded on 28 August. Lastly came 728 Squadron, the Navy's Fleet Requirements Unit, which moved in from Dekheila on 17 August to spend over two years at Takali. The Albacores of 820 Squadron also spent a few days at Takali in August after flying off HMS *Formidable,* as did the Seafires Mks.Ib and IIc of 885 Squadron and the Martlets Mks.II and IV of 888 Squadron's Detachment 8. From HMS *Illustrious* came the Seafires Mk.IIc of a

detachment of 894 Squadron, but all these naval aircraft had returned to sea by 20 September.

Several visiting aircraft, most of them damaged during the Sicilian campaign, landed at Takali during this crucial period, one being a B-25 of the USAAF which came in on 4 July with a dead first pilot. Four P-38s landed with minor problems on 6 July, while on 14 July three B-25s of the 21st Bomb Group appeared, one which was flak-damaged. On the same day a B-24 of the 389th Bomb Group, also damaged by flak, landed.

A unit of the Royal Australian Air Force, 3 Squadron, arrived at Takali on 9 July, bringing twelve Kittyhawk aircraft. However, this unit moved to Luqa four days later and was replaced by the first USAAF unit to be based at Takali, the 65th Fighter Squadron, equipped with P-40s. After two days, the Americans left for Hal Far, however, and by 20 July the Spitfires of 322 Wing had departed for newly-captured airfields in Sicily.

Takali was not ready to settle back and take things easy yet. No sooner had the Spitfires left than the A-20-equipped 47th Bomb Group arrived from Tunisia on 17 July, and over the next three weeks the four squadrons of this Group made several hundred sorties to targets in Sicily before moving into captured airfields on that island. After the A-20s had left, two squadrons of the Fleet Air Arm, 820 Squadron, equipped with Albacores Mk.I, from HMS *Formidable* and 810 Squadron with Barrucudas Mk.II from HMS *Illustrious,* arrived. Things at Takali then did begin to quieten down, the Fleet Air Arm units being the only ones present until the ASR & Communications Flight arrived from Hal Far on 25 August.

A quieter period.
Gp. Capt. G. Tyrrell MC, the Station Commander, was replaced by Wg. Cdr. J. Scoular DFC on 28 August 1943, but he in turn gave way to Wg. Cdr. F.

A Martlet II of the Fleet Air Arm's 888 Squadron (detachment 8), coded O7:K, seen at Takali while on detachment in 1943. *[NWMA]*

H. Tyson on 30 September. No operations were flown from Takali during the last three months of 1943, the beginning of a quiet period. By the end of the year, considerable construction work had been completed, the most important item being a 3300ft (1005m.) paved runway as an extension of the original 'grass' strip, thus forming a runway 6000ft. (1830m.) long. At the same time, a perimeter track was provided to the new runway and existing taxiways were widened. Extra aircraft pens and domestic accommodation were also built.

The ASR & Communications Flight did not stay long before returning to Hal Far at the end of January 1944, and during that year the only flying activity apart from, perhaps, a few visiting aircraft, were short-term detachments of FAA squadrons between July and September. Part of 888 Squadron from HMS *Formidable* arrived on 17 July, flying Martlets Mks.II and IV, and three units arrived together on 25 July: 800 Squadron from HMS *Emperor* with Hellcats Mk.I; 881 Squadron from HMS *Pursuer* with Wildcats Mk.VI; and Detachment 2 of 882 Squadron, which brought Wildcats Mk.V from HMS *Searcher*. 885 Squadron's Seafires appeared on 31 July from HMS *Formidable*, and during August and September the Seafires Mk.IIc of a detachment of

894 Squadron from HMS *Illustrious* were present. Then, on 1 November 1944, 727 Squadron arrived from Gibraltar, bringing its obsolescent Defiant Mk.I aircraft, only to disband on 7 December. All this Naval activity was under the control of HMS *St. Angelo,* the 'stone frigate' in Grand Harbour which housed Naval Headquarters. At the end of four and a half years of, at times, extremely tense, activity, RAF Takali was handed over to the Fleet Air Arm on 1 April 1945 to become HMS *Goldfinch.*

The Fleet Air Arm takes over.

Surprisingly little use appears to have been made of Takali by its new occupiers, probably due to the post-war severe cutbacks in flying affecting both services. A Communications Flight, also known as Station Flight, was formed in August 1945 and is known to have operated at least one Oxford (an unusual type in Malta) and a Tiger Moth, but it was the arrival of 73 Squadron RAF from Hal Far on 17 July 1946 to be a lodger unit which kept Takali alive. The Sea Otters of 1702 Squadron moved in two days later but left in September on disbandment. Apart from 73 Squadron's activities, 1947 was also a quiet year at Takali until the arrival on 24 November of 802 Squadron from Hal Far for

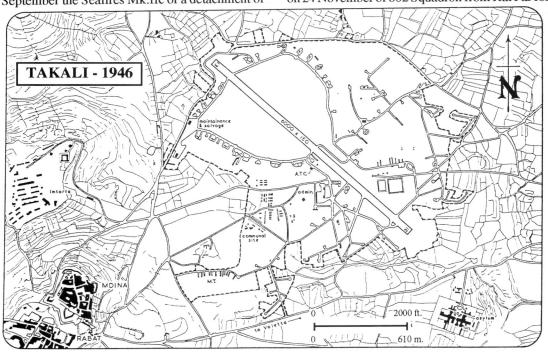

A view of Takali from the air in post-war days, the runway having been provided with Operational Readiness Platforms at each end. *[NWMA]*

a four-month stay. One interesting visitor that year was a US Navy F8F Bearcat from the USS *Leyte*; this aircraft, with a fouled drogue in tow, stalled from 20 feet (6 metres) when attempting to land and was completely wrecked.

During 1948 the peace of Takali was shattered at least four times by visits by F-47 squadrons of the USAF based at Neubiburg, near Munich. Usually accompanied by a B-17 'mother ship' and one or two C-47s, and sometimes by an A-26 target-tug aircraft, these squadrons used Malta for firing practice, but sometimes went on to the USAF base at Wheelus Field in Libya. On the occasion of the King's Birthday flypast on 8 June 1948 the F-47

pilots, having an hour to spare, were kind enough to join in the flypast before setting off 30 minutes later for Germany!

Just after 802 Squadron had left Takali to embark on HMS *Otranto* on 15 March 1948, the French Air Force C-in-C, North Africa, paid a visit, his aircraft being escorted to Takali by three Kingcobra fighters on 19 March. After a three-day stay, the entourage left for Bizerte on 22 March.

The year 1949 saw visits by the Sea Fury FB.11s of 807 Squadron and Fireflies FR. of 810 Squadron from Hal Far on 18 February, although these units stayed only a few days before embarking in HMS *Theseus* on 23 February. On 20 July, 32 Squadron arrived from Nicosia, bringing Vampire F.3s to take part in 'DXM '49', the Malta defence exercise. This squadron was back again in August 1951, by which time it was based at Shallufa and flying Vampire FB.5s.

Life at Takali began to become busier in 1952, an early indication of increased activity being the first of many summer camps held by UK-based squadrons of the Royal Auxiliary Air Force. First to arrive was 604 (County of Middlesex) Squadron from North Weald, then flying Vampire F.3s, and a further six camps were held at Takali that year. Two Vampires belonging to 608 Squadron did not survive to make the homeward journey: VX982 crashed on take-off on 8 September and VV526 stalled on take-off at El Aouina, Tunisia, four days later. In addition, other aircraft visiting Takali that year, mainly for gunnery practice, included four Meteor NF.11 night-fighters of an unrecorded unit for a week in July; four Vampires of the French Air Force from Bizerte to take part in Exercise 'DXM '52'; four Vampire NF.10 night-fighters of 23 Squadron, Coltishall, on 3 November for a week in the sun (or moon!); and, last but by no means least, forty F4U Corsairs of the US Navy which arrived

With Mdina in the background, two Vampire FB.9s of 213 Squadron, at Takali for an exercise, are prepared for another sorties *[B.A Crook, via P Green].*

Typical of the RAuxAF men who came to Takali during the early 1950s for two weeks' summer camp were those from 604 Squadron. Here, one of the squadron's Meteor F.8s forms a backdrop for a group photograph.
[J. Riordan]

to stay the night of 10/11 November.

Summer camps held by the RAuxAF continued in 1953, one Meteor, WE862 of 616 Squadron, being lost when it ditched off Valletta on 3 July. In addition, there were visits by four Meteor F.8s of 41 Squadron, Biggin Hill on 24 February for a few days; similar aircraft of 54 Squadron, Odiham, on 14 April; and yet more from 64 Squadron at Duxford on 20 April. Long-term resident 73 Squadron, however, left for Habbaniya on 4 May after nearly seven years at Takali.

Re-enter the RAF.

Takali was handed back to the RAF on 9 June 1953 and on that very day 75 and 76 Squadrons of the Royal Australian Air Force moved in from Horsham St. Faith, where their Vampire FB.9s had been based while taking part in the Royal Review of the RAF held at Odiham. Following the Aussies, 14 Squadron, Royal New Zealand Air Force arrived from Nicosia on 9 August with similar aircraft, but only stayed a week before returning to Cyprus. The squadron re-appeared, however, on 16 March 1954, for a seven-week stay.

Night-flying trials were carried out at Takali in December 1954 by four pilots from 29 Squadron, based at Tangmere in the UK. It was then decided that before general night-flying could be allowed the runway would have to be resurfaced to improve its somewhat poor condition. Consideration was also given at this point to a completely new runway, but nothing came of that idea.

For the first seven months of 1955 Takali was effectively on a 'care and maintenance' basis, and no RAuxAF summer camps were held that year, but on 1 August the Station once again became a self-accounting unit, under the command of Sqdn. Ldr. P. J. Jorden DFC until 19 September, when Wg. Cdr. R. Aytoun DFC took over. From that date, parenting facilities were provided for AHQ Malta; 100, 203, 447 and 840 Signals Units; 9 Police District; 52 Movements (Embarkation) Unit; and HQ Malta Sector. Runway resurfacing was carried out and completed by the end of August, but it was 13 October before the advance party of 32 Squadron arrived from Shaibah.

Flying activity at Takali gradually increased now that the 32 Squadron Venoms were present,

A line-up of 604 Squadron Vampire F.3s at Takali during the unit's summer camp in 1952. Rabat and Mdina are visible in the background.
[P. Howden]

604 Squadron
Meteors - two F.8s
and a T.7 - airborne
while at the
squadron's summer
camp at Takali in
1953.
[P. Howden]

and there were some visitors and short attachments. On 24 October Takali accepted a diversion from Luqa of Shackleton VP260 of 120 Squadron, based at Aldergrove in Northern Ireland. This aircraft had suffered hydraulic failure, but was safely put down at Takali, where it remained until being flown out on 6 February 1957. The Sea Venoms of 809 Squadron made use of Takali for a few days from 16 November, when they arrived from Yeovilton, as Hal Far's runways were being repaired, but crews travelled the short distance from Hal Far daily. Another Shackleton, WL797 of 38 Squadron, Luqa, diverted to Takali on 21 November after its tailwheel had collapsed while the aircraft was landing at its home base; this aircraft also stayed put for a long time, not being flown out until 28 June 1957.

The year of 1956 began at Takali with the opening on 9 January of the RAF Malta Recruit Training Unit, set up to provide an eight-week basic training course to locally-enlisted airmen. Thirty such men formed the first batch, and successfully 'passed out' on 3 March after inspection by Gp. Capt. E. J. Davy.

While 32 Squadron was detached to Idris in Libya for two weeks in February, 26 Armament Practice Camp arrived from Nicosia, and stayed until moving to Habbaniya in Iraq on 3 May. A week later, 32 Squadron followed them for a six-week detachment. In the interim period, one of the squadron's Venoms, WR320, crash-landed at Takali on 5 April 1956 after a flame-out, and the pilot, Plt. Off. K. M. Moore, was fatally injured; he lies buried at Mtarfa Cemetery. A few weeks later, on 3 May, a visiting Canberra from 101 Squadron, Binbrook, WJ762, overshot Takali after suffering hydraulics failure, but there were no injuries.

Crisis at Suez!

The Suez crisis prompted more activity at Takali during the latter part of 1956, the first new unit being 208 Squadron from Akrotiri in Cyprus,

equipped with photographic reconnaissance Meteor FR.9s, which arrived on 6 August. 32 Squadron was redeployed to Amman in Jordan on 28 August in order to have additional RAF presence on the eastern flank of the trouble area. Due to the crisis, the usual RAuxAF summer camps were cut short early in August and at least three squadrons had to make do with camps in England instead. In the event, no more RAuxAF squadrons ever appeared at Takali, as the flying units of the RAuxAF were disbanded on 10 March 1957. At the end of October, four Hunters of 111 Squadron, normally based in the UK at North Weald, were transferred to Takali from Luqa, where they had been on attachment, and, with 208 Squadron, were placed on dawn to dusk standby. Takali airfield remained open 24 hours a day as a diversion airfield, but in the event was not used. The 111 Squadron Hunters were relieved on 3 December by a detachment of 222 Squadron from Leuchars in Scotland, to which the Hunters were then transferred. The Whirlwind helicopters of 845 Squadron were also prominent at Takali between the end of October 1956 and 19 January 1957, when they finally departed on HMS *Albion*.

Back to normal.

The Suez crisis over, Takali returned to a quieter way of life, particularly after part of 208 Squadron left for Khormaksar in Aden on 12 January 1957 in connection with the Yemeni uprising there. Four Venoms of 249 Squadron from El Adem in Libya arrived on 30 March for a short period of armament training, and returned on 4 May for another month. With 208 Squadron, 249 took part in Exercise 'Medflex Epic' on 6 May by acting as part of the defending force. The annual Exercise 'Maltex' took place at the end of June, and this time twelve Hunter F.5s of 56 Squadron from Waterbeach were attached to Takali for two weeks.

An important technical unit, the Levant Canberra Servicing Unit, was formed at Takali on 1

De Havilland Devon
C.1 VP953 of Malta
Communications &
Target Towing
Squadron.
[R Robinson]

May 1957 to handle major servicing for all Middle East-based Canberra squadrons. This unit's presence ensured a steady flow of visiting Canberras for the rest of 1957, but in general the air traffic at Takali was quickly reducing in scale. For the first time, an 'At Home' day was held on 14 September 1957, a similar event in 1956 having been cancelled due to the Suez situation. A crowd of 10000 was expected; in fact three times that number turned up, causing the largest traffic jam ever seen on the island. The police soon lost control, and even the AOC Malta was obliged to abandon his car and walk across fields to reach the airfield. The sum of £388 was raised for RAF charities, and the figure would have been higher had not some cars been allowed in without paying in order to speed things up!

The beginning of 1958 saw the run-down continue. That part of 208 Squadron remaining at Takali was now doing little flying, and was preparing to disband. The Levant Canberra Servicing Unit left for Akrotiri in January, and 208 Squadron closed down on 28 February. On the credit side, Malta Communications & Target

Towing Flight was transferred from Luqa on 24 February, ensuring Takali's existence.

A new Station Commander, Wg. Cdr. G. S. Fry DFC, took over on 8 March 1958, and made his first flight as a passenger in a Meteor T.7 on 17 March, only to suffer the indignity of a tyre bursting on take-off, luckily without damage to himself or the pilot.

Seven Varsity aircraft from the School of Air Navigation at Thorney Island on the south coast of England arrived at Takali on 11 April 1958 as part of a long-range exercise, and stayed three days. Their presence caused feeding and bedding problems, but this was the first of many such visits. The work done by the trainee navigators cannot have been helped by the closure on 1 April of the Met. Office at Takali, however.

During April 1958 the political situation in Malta detereorated, and Takali provided guards to protect the AHQ building at Floriana against possible demonstrations. After a case of sabotage at Kalafrana, guards on the airfield were doubled. Riots were anticipated on May Day there was no trouble.

The latter-day Control Tower at Takali. The town of Mdina is on the horizion.
[P. J. Cooper]

Takali airfield from the air after the closure. The substantial Control Tower stands at the right of the picture. [*After the Battle magazine*]

Visiting aircraft on navigation exercises became a regular feature of Takali life during 1958. They were mainly Valettas and Varsities from 1 Air Navigation School at Topcliffe, but a few trips were made by Varsities from the Central Navigation & Control School at Shawbury, whose crews had no doubt heard of the delights of Malta! During November ten Seahawks of 898 Squadron from HMS *Eagle* spent nearly two weeks at Takali, and during the same month helicopters of 848 Squadron, Hal Far, used Takali intermittently for practice landings, as did some from HMS *Victorious* when that ship was in Grand Harbour during December. Two US Navy aircraft also put in an appearance, both believing they were landing at Hal Far: a P2V Neptune on 8 December and a Skyraider a week later.

Varsities from Topcliffe and from Hullavington, the latter operated by the Air Electronics School, continued to use Takali during the early part of 1959, but other than the activities of the Malta C&TT Sqdn. there was little flying, monthly air movements during the latter half of 1959 averaging only 250.

Between 25 May and 12 June fourteen Meteors and two Sea Devons of 728 Squadron operated from Takali while the runways at Hal Far were being repaired, while on 7 June a DC-4 of Lebanese Airlines put in an appearance when it landed with two engines cut due to shortage of fuel on a flight from Saudi Arabia to Tunis.

The first Maltese airman to reach Warrant Officer rank, W/O J. Galea, was presented with his warrant by the AOC Malta on 16 June 1959, testimony to the success of the local recruit scheme, which was still functioning as late as December 1959 and possibly later.

1960 saw the pattern of work at Takali continue, enlivened by the visit of HRH Prince Phillip on 27 April, when he flew to Gozo by helicopter as part of his visit to Malta, and by the Battle of Britain Open Day on 27 August, which nearly 15000 attended. As well as several Bomber Command and Transport Command aircraft visiting from the UK, five Hunters of 92 Squadron, four Canberras of 39 Squadron, four Shackletons of 38 Squadron, three Meteors and Valettas of Malta C&TT Squadron took part in the fly-past.

Helicopters were again seen at Takali between 29 July and 8 August 1960, when 820 and 824 Squadrons disembarked from HMS *Ark Royal* while the ship underwent servicing. 'Trade' at Takali in November that year was busier than for a long time, 387 movements being recorded.

By now, the only unit resident at Takali was the Malta Communications and TT Flight, which had been downgraded in December 1958. After this unit had been disbanded in 1963, RAF Takali was put onto a 'care and maintenance' basis and no further flying took place. The site was eventually transferred to the Government of Malta and since then has been used for a variety of light industrial purposes, many of the buildings remaining in surprisingly good condition.

Flying Units at Takali

Summary					
Unit	From	Date in	To	Date out	Aircraft Types
261 Sqdn.	Hal Far	20.11.40	(disbanded)	21.5.41	Hurricane I
249 Sqdn.	North Weald	21.5.41	Qrendi	23.11.42	Hurricane I, IIa, IIb
238 Sqdn.	UK on HMS Victorious	14.6.41	LG.07	15.6.41	Hurricane I
126 Sqdn.	(formed)	28.6.41	Luqa	1.5.42	Hurricane I
Malta NFU	(formed)	7.41	(became 1435 Flt.)	4.12.41	Hurricane
69 Sqdn.	Luqa	31.10.41	Luqa	29.11.41	Maryland I; Hurricane IIa
1435 Flt.	(formed ex NFU)	4.12.41	(disbanded)	7.42	Beaufighter; Hurricane
605 Sqdn.	Hal Far	12.2.42	(disbanded)	27.2.42	Hurricane IIb
603 Sqdn.	UK	20.4.42	(absorbed by 1435 Flt. and 229 Sqdn.)	3.8.42	Spitfire Vc
229 Sqdn.	(re-formed)	3.8.42	Qrendi	10.12.42	Spitfire Vc
272 Sqdn.	Idku	3.11.42	Luqa	4.6.43	Beaufighter I, VI
227 Sqdn.	Luqa	25.11.42	Idku	1.3.43	Beaufighter VI
81 Sqdn.	Utique	4.6.43	Lentini East	20.7.43	Spitfire Vc, IX (note M)
154 Sqdn.	Protville	4.6.43	Lentini East	20.7.43	Spitfire Vc, IX (note M)
232 Sqdn.	Protville	5.6.43	Lentini East	18.7.43	Spitfire Vb, IX (note M)
242 Sqdn.	Protville 3	5.6.43	Lentini East	22.7.43	Spitfire Vb, Vc, IX (note M)
152 Sqdn.	Protville	6.6.43	Lentini East	27.7.43	Spitfire Vb, Vc (note M)
828 Sqdn.	Hal Far	8.6.43	Monastir	28.6.43	Albacore
815 Sqdn. (Spec. Bomb. Flt.)	Dekheila	2.7.43	(disbanded)	24.7.43	Albacore
3 Sqdn. RAAF	Zuara	9.7.43	Luqa	13.7.43	Kittyhawk
826 Sqdn.	Tafaroui	10.7.43	(disbanded)	25.8.43	Albacore
65th FS, USAAF		13.7.43	Hal Far	15.7.43	P-40
47th BG, USAAF	Soliman (Tunisia)	21.7.43	Torrente Comminelli	9.8.43	A-20
728 Sqdn.	Dekheila	17.8.43	Luqa	1.1.46	(various)
ASR & CF	Hal Far	25.8.43	Hal Far	25.1.44	(various)
727 Sqdn.	Gibraltar	1.11.44	(disbanded)	7.12.44	Defiant I
728B Sqdn.	(formed)	1.45	(disbanded)	7.45	Martinet; Seafire
Comms. Flt. Malta	(formed)	8.45		8.46	
73 Sqdn.	Hal Far	17.7.46	Habbaniya	4.5.53	Spitfire IX, F.22; Vampire F.3, FB.5, FB.9
1702 Sqdn.	El Aouina (Tunis)	19.7.46	(disbanded)	12.9.46	Sea Otter I
802 Sqdn.	Hal Far	24.11.47	Lee-on-Solent	16.3.48	Seafire F.15
75 Sqdn. RAAF	Hal Far	9.6.53	Australia	24.1.55	Vampire FB.9
76 Sqdn. RAAF	Hal Far	9.6.53	Australia	24.1.55	Vampire FB.9
14 Sqdn. RNZAF	Nicosia	9.8.53	Nicosia	17.8.53	Vampire FB.9
14 Sqdn. RNZAF	Nicosia	16.3.54	Nicosia	9.5.54	Vampire FB.9
32 Sqdn.	Shaibah	15.10.55	Amman (Jordan)	8.56	Venom FB.1
APC Malta	(formed)	3.56	(disbanded)	2.57	Meteor; Vampire
208 Sqdn.	Akrotiri (Cyprus)	6.8.56	(disbanded)	28.4.58	Meteor FR.9
Malta Comms. & TT Sqdn/Flt.	Luqa	24.2.58	(disbanded)	4.63	various; see narrative

261 Squadron

After moving from Hal Far on 20 November 1940, 261 Squadron continued to act as the main defensive force covering the islands of Malta, but losses of aircraft and pilots were impossible to make good in those times of siege. Accordingly, on 21 May 1941, the squadron was disbanded, to be absorbed into newly-formed 185 Squadron at Hal Far, ground crews largely going to join 249 Squadron, which had arrived that day from the UK short of personnel.

249 Squadron

Previously based in England at North Weald, 249 Squadron, less ground personnel, was shipped to Malta by aircraft carrier, from which the squadron's Hurricanes were flown off to Takali on 21 May 1941. On the same day, ground crews from 261 Squadron were posted in to form the nucleus of maintenance staff of 249 Squadron.

Little is recorded of the details of 249 Squadron's activities during the rest of 1941: the intense enemy activity over Malta at the time may

A 261 Squadron Hurricane over a typical Maltese landscape in 1941. *[James Pickering]*

well have prevented the completion of even basic records. Takali airfield was being bombed very heavily in the early days of 1942, and part, at least, of 249 Squadron was sent to Luqa to operate from there. On 19 January four of the Hurricanes made a retaliatory attack on Comiso airfield in Sicily, each carrying 20lb (9kg.) bombs. No opposition was felt, and one aircraft on the ground was thought to have been destroyed. Several interceptions of Ju.88s and Bf.109s were made over Malta that day, 249 Squadron joining 126 and other squadrons in this seemingly never-ending task.

In February 1942, while the heavy raids on Malta, many on Takali, continued, 249 Squadron carried on with its job of intercepting and, if possible shooting down, the enemy raiders. On 4 February, while Takali was feeling the full force of the enemy's power, three of 249 Squadron's Hurricanes were shot down by Bf.109s. The disastrous effects of the constant bombardment prompted the move on 8 February of the squadron offices to a marginally safer location in Rabat, the ancient walled city on the hill overlooking Takali.

The first 15 Spitfires to reach the island arrived at Takali early in March and 249 Squadron began to re-equip. On the same day, Sqdn. Ldr. H. Beazley, 249's CO, relinquished command, to the great regret of the personnel. By mid-March the squadron had parted with its Hurricanes and was flying Spitfires on the never-ending interception sorties. A slightly different type of aircraft was found, taxiing on the water, on 8 April — a four-engined Do.26 flying boat, a rare bird indeed. Two Ju.88s and six Bf.109s were orbiting overhead, but 249 Squadron's three Spitfires repeatedly hit the Dornier, setting it alight and sinking it, and also dealt with a Ju.88 and a Bf.109.

The arrival on the island on 10 June of a number of Beaufort aircraft was covered by eight Spitfires of 249 Squadron, which managed to shoot down a RE.2001 and a Bf.109 which were attempting an attack. July 1942 saw continuing interceptions, and prominent among the pilots was Sgt. 'Screwball' Buerling, who destroyed several enemy aircraft. By the end of August, however, the RAF was beginning to take the offensive. Eight Spitfires went on a 'rhubarb' to Gela airfield in

Spitfire Vb BP845 just after flying off HMS Eagle to join 249 Squadron at Takali early in 1942. On 9 May that year the aircraft spun into the ground near Safi. *[Cdr. F. W. Baring via R. C. Sturtivant]*

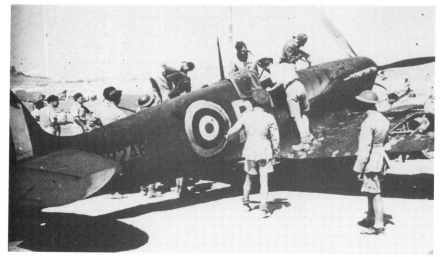

249 Squadron Spitfire V BR246, coded R, being worked on at Takali. This aircraft ditched off Malta when its engine failed during a convoy patrol on 13 August 1942. *[NWMA]*

Sicily on 27 August and apart from destroying a barracks and damaging several other buildings destroyed a Macchi 202 and probably Ju.87s and Bf.109s on the ground. Offensive reconnaissance of Sicily then became the order of the day, interspersed with shipping sweeps and patrols over Malta to deal with the much-reduced number of enemy intruders.

249 Squadron left Takali on 23 November 1942 to move to nearby Qrendi.

126 Squadron

126 Squadron was formed at Takali on 28 June 1941 under the command of Sqdn. Ldr. Rabaglati, and with a skeleton staff was able to mount an

attack on U-boats which were trying to penetrate Grand Harbour on 26 July, and a few more small-scale missions. It was early in August, however, before 183 NCOs and airmen arrived from the UK and the new squadron could regard itself as being at full strength and put its Hurricanes into full-scale combat.

This it did on 26 August, when 126 Squadron pilots engaged nine Macchis of the Italian Air Force and shot down three, with another as a probable. 16 aircraft raiding Malta from their base in Sicily were intercepted on 3 September and three shot down. The squadron then began to take the battle into the enemy camp by mounting surprise fighter-bomber attacks on Comiso on 16 October

Spitfire Vc BR458 of 126 Squadron flown by Wg. Cdr. P. P. Hanks, the Wg. Cdr. Flying at Takali, carried his personal code PP:H
[via R. C. Sturtivant]

and on Ragusa railway station on 23 October, before reverting to the main task of fending off raids on Malta. Four of the Hurricanes intercepted eighteen Macchis escorting four Cant 506s on 8 November, and shot down three of the enemy aircraft, and on 30 December took on and damaged many of a large fleet of Ju.88s raiding Luqa.

The new year saw concerted and prolonged raids on Malta, and 126 Squadron's base at Takali was badly hit, necessitating a temporary move to Luqa. From there, four Hurricanes set out on 19 January 1942 to bomb Comiso again, although two of them did not reach the target, dropping their bombs in the area of Noto instead.

At the end of February and early in March 1942, 42 Spitfires Mk.Vc arrived off Malta on aircraft carriers and were flown to Takali, some of them to re-equip 126 Squadron. Enemy raids on the island were by now at their most intense, and it was only just possible to keep 126 and the other Takali squadrons flying. The credit for doing so goes principally to the incredible efforts made by the ground crews, the hard work of whom is often overlooked. By 25 March the squadron had to move to Luqa again for a time. Next day a convoy reached the beleaguered island bringing desperately-needed supplies; the convoy was attacked very heavily by enemy aircraft, but all available fighters, including those of 126 Squadron, were used in a successful attempt to beat them off, in the course of which many of the raiders were shot down. Two days later, the Vice-Admiral Malta sent a message of congratulation to all the island's fighter squadrons, thanking them for their performance during the docking of the ships.

On 1 May the squadron's HQ moved to Luqa to rejoin the aircraft and personnel already there.

Malta Night Fighter Unit
Formed on 1 September 1941, this unit immediately began to use its Hurricanes on scrambles and dawn patrols. Initial success came on 5 September with the downing of a Cant aircraft of the Italian Air Force, and three days later a Cant 1007 was forced down, although next day its crew was rescued.

The Malta NFU was made more 'official' on 4 December 1941 when it was retitled 1435 Flight, under the command of Sqdn. Ldr. I. B. Westmacott.

69 Squadron
The island's specialist PR unit, 69 Squadron moved from Luqa on 31 October 1941 in a period of bad weather, which often caused Takali airfield to become unusable and thus inhibit operations. Some sorties were flown, however, and one, by the CO in Hurricane Z3053, ended in the aircraft crashing into the sea off the island. Wg. Cdr. Dowland was picked up none the worse after an hour by a Swordfish floatplane from Kalafrana. One Maryland was lost on 28 November while conducting a search south-east of Malta, and the following day, conditions having become impossible, 69 Squadron returned to Luqa.

1435 Flight
Formed on 4 December 1941 from the Malta Night Fighter Unit, 1435 Flight continued to use Hurricanes Mk.II as night fighters in a limited way. The Flight also began, on 24 January 1942, to mount intruder raids over Sicily, targetting such places as Gerbini, Catania and Comiso airfields. During the first such raid a Ju.88 fell prey to 1435 Flight. Little is known of the activities of the Flight until the Spring of 1942, when the night fighter task was taken over by radar-equipped Beaufighters of 89 Squadron, whereupon 1435 Flight disbanded.

However, the Flight seems to have been brought back to life for a short time to operate Beaufighters, one of which, X7642, shot down a Ju.88 on 7 July 1942, only to crash-land at Luqa five days later.

605 Squadron
A very short-lived resident at Takali, 605 Squadron brought its Hurricanes Mk.IIb from Hal Far on 11 February 1942 and carried out a few operations before disbanding on 27 February.

603 Squadron
Previously based at Peterhead in Scotland, 603 Squadron pilots found themselves at Takali on 20 April 1942, but contemporary records are very vague about their early activities in Malta. They were certainly active by 29 July, when the pilots of six of the squadron's Spitfires, airborne over St. Paul's Bay, spotted an enemy floatplane approaching. This aircraft landed on the water, and five crewmen climbed out onto the wings and waved white flags. Eventually the floatplane was

Beaufighter VI X8105 [S] of 272 Squadron at Takali; this aircraft was transferred to the USAAF in October 1943. *[A Tonks].*

taken in tow by a HSL.

On 3 August 1942 all 603 Squadron pilots were posted to join 229 Squadron, which was just being re-formed.

229 Squadron

229 Squadron was re-formed, this time with Spitfires, at Takali on 3 August 1942. Its routine until it moved to Qrendi on 10 December 1942 was one of scrambles, standing patrols and convoy guarding.

272 Squadron

Laden with some ground crew members, kit, food and drink, sixteen Beaufighters of 272 Squadron left Idku in Egypt on 3 November 1942 for Malta with the intention of taking part in the battle for Tunisia. Most of the ground crews were, however, left behind at Idku.

The squadron's first operation from Malta was on 10 November, when nine aircraft attacked the airfield at El Aouina, outside Tunis, very successfully. Two Ju.90s, five Ju.52s, a Ju.87, a large twin-engined aircraft and a big glider were left in flames and 16 more aircraft were damaged. One of 272's Beaufighters, however, had to force-land on the beach two miles (3km.) from the target. Apart from repeat performances of this attack, patrols of the Sicily/Tunisia channel and some shipping strikes were made in November. The final tally for that month was 21 aircraft destroyed in the air, twenty on the ground, nine damaged in the air and 23 on the ground, plus a 1000-ton motor vessel and two schooners damaged.

The same pattern continued during December, when the squadron had to use Qrendi airfield for a few days while Takali was out of action. It was during this month that German troops captured in North Africa told of the shattering effect that Beaufighter attacks had on them.

NE544 [B], a Beaufighter X of 272 Squadron, seen at Takali. *[A Tonks].*

January 1943 was occupied by the squadron in carrying out offensive sweeps with Spitfires of 229 Squadron west and south-west of Malta, over Pantellaria and Lampedusa, intruder patrols over Tripoli, a shipping strike off Sfax and an attack by five aircraft on motor transport on the Sfax to Gabes road. In addition, an Allied convoy was escorted into Grand Harbour on New Year's Day. February was a quieter month, taken up mainly with escorting friendly convoys, followed by intruder patrols, some over the toe of Italy.

During March 1943 HQ Middle East decreed that 272 Squadron was to carry out only convoy escort work, but the squadron got round that by recording a number of offensive sweeps as 'practice missions'. One such strike on 17 March was particularly rewarding when the enemy aircraft escorting a convoy, ten Bf.110s and Ju.88s, a Ju.52, a Cant 508, a Do.217 and a He.115, were attacked and several damaged. One Beaufighter failed to return, however.

Apart from a high-level dive-bombing attack on Lampedusa airfield with Spitfire escorts on 10 April, there were few offensive operations that month. May 1943 was not a good month for the squadron, and in fact 8 May was the blackest day in its history. Two aircraft were shot down by Macchi 202s off Cape Granitola, Sicily; a new Beaufighter being collected from the Middle East ran out of fuel and ditched; and an aircraft short of fuel crash-landed, with engines stopped, at Takali. Two days later an aircraft on a practice bombing run at Filfla Island was destroyed by the premature explosion of its bombs. Then, on 22 May, two Beaufighters were shot down by Bf.109s and another two landed, damaged, in Tunisia, so that by the end of the month six complete crews had been lost and nine aircraft written off.

At the end of May preparations were made for a move to Luqa. The ground crews still in Egypt were posted and new personnel taken on in Malta. A new CO, Wg. Cdr. W. A. Wild, was appointed to replace Wg. Cdr. J. K. Buchanan DSO DFC+Bar from 1 June and on 4 June 1943 272 Squadron left Takali.

227 Squadron

After arriving from Luqa on 25 November 1942, 227 Squadron's Beaufighters continued their offensive sweeps, shipping patrols and strikes on roads and railways in Tunisia. Several Ju.52 three-engined transport aircraft were destroyed during this period, as were at least one Bv.222 Wiking six-engined flying boat (the largest flying boat operational during the Second World War) and probably a Fw.200 Condor four-engined transport. The same pattern prevailed during January 1943, but in February no operations at all were carried out, and on 1 March the squadron moved to Idku in Egypt.

322 Wing

The advance party of 322 Wing, having arrived at Takali from Protville in Tunisia on 3 June 1943, was accommodated within three hours, a tribute to the organisation there. Next day, fifteen Spitfires of 81 Squadron and sixteen of 154 Squadron flew in, and on 5 June the Spitfires of the other three of the Wing's units, 152, 242 and 252 Squadrons, arrived. Over the next three days time was spent in familiarisation with the local area, but on 9 June 12 aircraft of the Wing were scrambled to intercept raiders which did not in fact appear. Next day 32 Spitfires took part in a sweep over Pozzallo, Sicily, eight of them carrying bombs, but one of the aircraft crashed on take-off and was destroyed by fire.

Sweeps over Sicily in preparation for the forthcoming invasion continued, up to 48 Spitfires of 322 Wing taking the air. Escort work was also carried out; 35 aircraft accompanied Mitchell medium bombers on a raid on Comiso airfield on 3 July, and next day twenty aircraft went to Catania with B-17s of the USAAF while another twenty made a return trip to Comiso. Over the next few days escort work kept the Wing busy, but on 9 July, D-1, 124 sorties were made to cover the invasion barges and other shipping leaving Malta for Sicily.

322 Wing Spitfires began to take to the air at 04.24 on 10 July, and soon five enemy aircraft were sighted and attacked, two bombers being destroyed. No more enemy aircraft were seen until 12.50, when eight Bf.109s were engaged. At 15.30 another eight Bf.109s were attacked, and one Spitfire, damaged in the fight, was forced to belly-land at Gela. Next day, operations by the Wing comprised beach and shipping patrols over the Sicilian beaches, and these continued until 19 July. Then, the immediate task complete, 322 Wing

A Kittyhawk III with code letters CV:Y obscuring the serial number, belonging to 3 Squadron RAAF, during Operation Husky in July 1943.
[NWMA]

began to pack up to leave Malta, and by 27 July all five squadrons had moved to their new base at Lentini East in newly-captured Sicily.

828 Squadron

A short stay indeed was made at Takali by 828 Squadron, which brought its Albacores from Hal Far on 8 June 1943, in the middle of the campaign to capture Pantellaria and Lampedusa Islands. This done, the squadron left for Monastir in Tunisia on 28 June before returning to Hal Far.

815 Squadron (Special Bombardment Flight)

Formed at Dekheila on 2 March 1943, the Special Bombardment Flight of 815 Squadron used three Albacores for fleet bombardment spotting, and moved from Dekheila to Takali on 2 July 1943, at the height of the preparations for the invasion of Sicily. Once this momentous event was over, the Flight was disbanded on 24 July, as was the main part of the squadron at Mersah Matruh.

3 Squadron RAAF

Another of the highly mobile units which camped almost overnight in Malta during the Sicilian invasion period, 3 Squadron RAAF flew its Kittyhawks from Zuara in Libya to Takali on 9 July 1943, the ground party having arrived in St. Paul's Bay five days earlier. The squadron was in immediate action covering the Allied landings, but once a bridgehead had been established it was time to move on. As the first stage of a move to Sicily, 3 Squadron left Takali for Luqa on 13 July 1943.

Albacores of 826 Squadron, based at Takali for a time in the summer of 1943, in formation off the coast of Malta.
[J S Houghton]

Seafire III NF521 of 728 Squadron, Takali, coded M8:L not as first appears M:8L!
[via R A Waller]

826 Squadron

Another Albacore-equipped unit, 826 Squadron arrived at Takali from Tafaroui in Algeria on 10 July 1943, the day of the invasion of Sicily. One can imagine the comments of the Station adjutant and his staff when confronted with the men of yet another squadron to house and feed! From Takali the squadron at once joined in the overall effort by providing anti-submarine support to the invasion shipping before disbanding on 25 August 1943.

47th Bombardment Group, USAAF

Soon after the invasion of Sicily, a four-squadron Bombardment Group of the USAAF, the 47th BG, under the command of Col. Malcolm Green Jr., took up residence at Takali. The ground crews of the first two squadrons, the 84th and 85th BS, arrived in no less than nineteen C-47s on 21 July 1943, and next day a similar number of C-47s brought in the men of the 86th and 97th BS. The aircraft used by the Group, A-20 light bombers, flew in on 23 July, and the Group's personnel were addressed by AVM Keith Park.

The Group began operations on 25 July with 33 sorties to targets at Troina in Sicily and next day mounted a massive 103-sortie operation to Regalbuto on the same island. One of the A-20s crash-landed at Takali on return and four diverted to Luqa, but there were no losses in action. Over the next two weeks up to 95 aircraft made concentrated attacks on such targets as Milazzo, Paterno, Santa Maria de Lacada, Adrano, Biancavilla, Bronte and Randazzo, the final mission being to the latter town on 10 August.

Between 10 and 13 August the large-scale movement took place again, when the Group moved on, to Torrente Comminelli, doubtless leaving Takali a much quieter place!

728 Squadron, FAA

After being absorbed into 775 Squadron at Dekheila (Egypt), a new 728 Squadron was quickly formed there on 14 August 1943 and moved to Takali on 17 August to act as a permanent Fleet Requirements Unit. The first aircraft used in Malta by this squadron were Defiant target-tugs, and sleeves were towed for the benefit of Navy gunners and for army gun batteries at Bahar-ic-Caghaq. Four of the Defiants went to Capodochino near Naples in January 1944 to tow targets for the US Navy and in March 728 Squadron sent aircraft to Catania in Sicily for a similar task.

New aircraft in the shape of Martinets, Swordfish and Beaufighters began to arrive in March 1944, and the Defiants were retired at the end of that year. Other types which joined the expanding squadron in small numbers in 1944 were Hurricanes, Beauforts and Baltimores, and with these the squadron worked closely with the Pacific Fleet, then 'working up' in the Mediterranean. During 1945 Seafires, Ansons, Marylands and Walruses joined 728 Squadron's inventory, but the Hurricanes, Swordfish, Ansons and Beauforts had all left by the time 728 Squadron moved from Takali to Luqa on New Year's Day 1946.

Air Sea Rescue & Communications Flight

Having moved from Hal Far to Takali on 25 August 1943, the ASR & CF continued its task, using Walrus amphibians and Wellingtons adapted for air-sea rescue work, Arguses for communications flights and a Harvard for anything which came its way. By October there was also an Italian aircraft on the Flight's strength — a Caproni 100 biplane which had been captured in the Western Desert by 450 Squadron.

This biplane, based on the DH60 Moth, is a Caproni 100 which was used by the Malta ASR&CF for a time. It carried the code GA-2, but no apparent serial number. *[NWMA]*

Early in October two Walruses were detached to Catania in Sicily to provide a local ASR service, but they returned on 18 November. Regular trips to Catania and Borrizzo in Sicily now occupied the Arguses and sometimes the Harvard, and it was becoming clear that more and larger aircraft were required. In January 1944 such a machine, Wellington Ic LB213, arrived, but before it could be used much the Flight was ordered to move back to Hal Far. This took several days, the last personnel leaving Takali on 1 February 1944.

727 Squadron

Some of the few Defiant target-tug aircraft to see service in Malta were those of 727 Squadron, a fleet requirements unit, which arrived at Takali from Gibraltar on 1 November 1944. However, there being little work to do, the squadron disbanded on 7 December.

728B Squadron FAA

In January 1945 728B Squadron was formed at Takali as a sub-unit of 728 Squadron. Initial equipment comprised five Martinet target-tugs

and three Seafires, and the Squadron acted as a Fleet Requirements Unit until disbanding in July of the same year.

Communications Flight Malta (FAA)

This Flight appears to have first seen the light of day in August 1945, and its initial equipment comprised Anson I, Beaufighter TT.I and Martinet TT.I aircraft. Between April and August 1946, Baltimores Mks. IV and V were added, but the Flight was then soon disbanded.

73 Squadron

Unknown to those involved, 73 Squadron, which completed its move from Hal Far on 17 July 1946, was destined to spend a considerable time at Takali. At first an acute shortage of personnel inhibited flying; there was, for example, only one electrician instead of the seven permitted, and he departed for demobilisation on 27 July! Three of the Palestine detachment's aircraft returned on 31 August, the other two having landed at El Adem in Libya with engine trouble, but in early September not one of 73 Squadron's Spitfires was serviceable,

One of the ASR&CF's earliest aircraft, Harvard IIa EX127, displaying the name *'Prunes Pride'* and some nose-art. Based at Takali, this aircraft flew into Xewkija on several occasions and this picture may have been taken there. *[NWMA]*

due to lack of ground crews. Six of the aircraft were then put into store at Safi. It was 17 September before two aircraft became serviceable, the first time for five weeks. By the end of December the situation had eased a little, as the squadron had come up to 70% of strength.

The year 1947 was taken up by a series of exercises with the Fleet. On 1 May all nine pilots were taken to Treviso in Italy by Lancaster to collect more Spitfires Mk.IX, and after acceptance checks they reached Takali a week later. Practice interceptions on Seafires and Fireflies from HMS *Ocean* and HMS *Triumph* then took up some time, and early in July a major exercise involving two Fleets was held, 73 Squadron again taking part.

August and September 1947 were prominent for the number of aircraft which had to be written off in crashes: six in four weeks. First, on 12 August, MJ891 flew into the ground on approach; three days later, MJ247 suffered engine failure on take-off; PT477 belly-landed on 19 August; on 1 September NH198 lost part of its propeller blade and had to force-land; MH979 belly-landed with a jammed undercarriage on 5 September; and finally the engine of MK158 failed on take-off on 8 September. These mishaps caused the remaining Spitfire IXs which had come from Treviso to be grounded , and thus no aircraft were serviceable, not even the squadron's Harvard, which was normally used for instrument training. In October the first Mk.XXII aircraft began to arrive as replacements, and by the end of November eight of the later model were on 73 Squadron strength.

The routine pattern of practice interceptions on such aircraft as Lincolns on the way from England to Egypt and on USAF B-29s practice-bombing Filfla Island continued during 1948, and the squadron was also involved in rather unsuccessful trials of radar control from ships. Small numbers of aircraft were detached to Castel Benito in Libya from time to time for army cooperation work, but otherwise the pattern of life varied little. By early April one Spitfire Mk.IX remained, all the others having been transferred to the Greek Air Force.

July 1948, however, saw the beginnings of modernisation for 73 Squadron with the arrival of the first two Vampire F.3s. After landing at Luqa, the first jet fighters ever to reach the island taxied to 137 MU at Safi, where they were at first used for technical instruction purposes. A week later, one of

them flew, presumably from Luqa, to Takali, the first jet aircraft ever to land there. When Exercise 'DXM '48' took place between 27 and 29 July, the two Vampires joined in, along with twelve of the squadron's Spitfires. Four more 'Vamps' arrived on 20 August, but the two original aircraft had to be grounded with wrinkled jetpipes. One Vampire stalled above the runway on 25 August and suffered a collapsed undercarriage, but the aircraft seems to have survived to fly again.

Six more Vampires arrived on 20 September 1948, and the last five Spitfires left for the UK on 18 October. Vampire VT808 was lost in tragic circumstances on 25 October, when it collided with FAA Harvard EZ406, belonging to Station Flight Hal Far, near Rabat; the Vampire was able to return to Takali, where it crash-landed and was destroyed by fire, but the Harvard crashed near Mtarfa.

73 Squadron was declared operational on Vampires on 1 November 1948 and a month later took part in an exercise with the USS *Franklin D. Roosevelt*, although no US Navy aircraft were seen on that day. Two days later four Corsairs were chased.

Between 21 April and 27 May 1949 the squadron spent time at armament practice camp at Nicosia and in July took part in the annual defence of Malta exercise. Five aircraft left Takali on 22 September for a tour of Italy, the ground crews travelling in two Dakotas. Unfortunately, no less than four of the Vampires, VT809, VT813, VT855 and VV204, force-landed, out of fuel, fifty miles south of Brescia next day and had to be replaced by other aircraft. Displays were then given at two airfields near Milan (Malpensa and Linate) and to high-ranking officers of the Italian Air Force at Rome (Ciampino) before the detachment returned to base on 29 September. On 17 October the squadron left for Kasfareet for an exercise, returning early in November, but by 5 December all the Vampires were grounded due to problems with wing rivetting, and remained so for the rest of the month.

Activities in 1950 included a visit to Nicosia for armament training in February and the beginning of re-equipment to the fighter-bomber FB.5 version of the Vampire in April. By June, a Meteor T.7 had been added to the squadron for instrument training, replacing the Harvard T.2b, FT155, which left on 12 September for transfer to 37 Squadron at

MILITARY AVIATION IN MALTA G.C. 1915-1993

A Vampire F.3 of 73 Squadron, VT809 [Z] seen at Takali in 1949; this was one of the ill-fated aircraft that ran out of fuel and force-landed in Italy on 23 September while on the way to a display. *[via A Thomas]*

Luqa. Two more Harvards used by 73 Squadron were TT.2b target-tugs, KF932, used between October and December 1949, and KF946 between January and August 1950. Both were struck off charge at the end of November 1950. The new Vampires were flown to England on 3/4 October 1950 to take part in the massive Exercise 'Emperor', staged to test the defences of the UK. Their route was via Istres to Odiham, and two Valettas from Kabrit provided the ground crew uplift. Return to Takali was made on 27 October.

After the usual training camp at Nicosia in February 1951, following which the ground crews, taken there in seven Valettas, were stranded due to lack of transport aircraft, further training was carried out at Castel Benito in May. As Takali's runway was being resurfaced, 73 Squadron moved completely to Castel Benito on 21 June, the ground crews going by sea, but were able to return a month later.

Back at Takali, 73 Squadron continued its routine training, but lost a Vampire on 13 August when it was damaged by debris caused by the collision of two US Navy Banshees. The Vampire pilot baled out and was picked up from the 'drink' two hours later.

That September, a potentially dangerous situation developed in Iran, and the British Government considered it prudent to make a show of force in the area. 73 Squadron was detailed to take part and left Takali on 17 September. Flying via Deversoir, Mafraq in Jordan and Habbaniya in Iraq, the sixteen Vampires and two Meteors soon arrived at Shaibah in southern Iraq, where they joined 249 Squadron, normally based at Deversoir. Six York aircraft carried the ground crews from Takali to Shaibah. Iranian troops seized control of the oil refinery at Abadan on 27 September, and on 7 October the Shah of Iran gave his approval to the 'nationalisation' of the refinery. Upon this, it was

decided to withdraw British forces, and 73 Squadron began to leave Shaibah on 9 October. On the homeward trip, the ground crews enjoyed the comparative luxury of Hastings aircraft!

During November 1951, the Vampire FB.5s were fitted with long-range tanks for the trip to the UK, as they were to be replaced by the more up-to-date Vampire FB.9, the first of which arrived on 24 November. Fourteen aircraft sent to Kabrit on 1 February 1952 to deal with unrest in the Canal Zone were a mix of the two Marks, but by the time the detachment returned on 29 February the last four of the new aircraft had arrived at Takali. The whole of April and May were also spent at Kabrit.

In August 1952 73 Squadron once again took part in the annual defence exercise, 'DXM '52', and carried out 'interceptions' on B-45s and Banshees at maximum speed and on Corsairs and Skyraiders of the US Navy at a somewhat slower pace! Afterwards, some of the squadron personnel visited USS *Wasp* to inspect the Banshees, which were generally considered about equal to the Vampires in performance.

73 Squadron's role was changed on 1 January 1953 from 'day fighter' to 'day fighter/ground attack', and this heralded a move from Malta. So it came that the squadron, after nearly seven years at Takali, moved to Habbaniya in Iraq, not by any means such an amenable spot, on 4 May 1953.

1702 Squadron

For its third period of service in Malta, 1702 Squadron flew its Sea Otter amphibians to Takali on 19 July 1946 from El Aouina, Tunisia, where they had been employed in mine-hunting duties. At Takali, 1702 Squadron maintained an air-sea rescue role until disbanding on 12 September 1946, when three of its Sea Otters embarked in HMS *Eagle* as a Ship's Flight.

802 Squadron

Equipped with Seafire F.15s, 802 Squadron moved from Hal Far to Takali on 24 November 1947 and continued its normal fighter tasks during the winter. However, in order to re-equip with Sea Furies, 802 Squadron left for Lee-on-Solent on 16 March 1948.

78 Wing, RAAF

While a detachment of Vampire FB.9s of the two squadrons, 75 and 76, which constituted 78 Wing was away in the UK, the Wing HQ moved to Takali from Hal Far on 9 June 1953. The detachment flew in from Wahn in Germany, where it had been taking part in a major NATO exercise, on 3 August, and a normal training routine was established.

The Wing was detached to Idris for the air-to-air firing range between 12 and 31 October 1953 and to Nicosia from 31 May to 5 July 1954, but by the end of that year the political situation was less sensitive and the Wing could think of leaving for home. Part of the Wing's personnel sailed for Australia on 4 January 1955 and by 24 January all the Australians had left.

14 Squadron, RNZAF

Part of a joint Commonwealth air force deployed in Cyprus, 14 Squadron of the RNZAF first came to Takali as a short detachment from 9 to 17 August 1953. At the time, the squadron was equipped with Vampire FB.9s, which appeared for a longer stay on 16 March 1954 to join the two RAAF squadrons at Takali.

14 Squadron left Takali on 9 May 1954 to return to Nicosia, but did not return to its homeland until June 1958, after spending three years in Malaya during the anti-communist campaign.

32 Squadron

Led by the CO, the advance party of six Venom FB.1 aircraft of 32 Squadron left Shaibah in Iraq on 12 October 1955 with Takali as their destination. The first ground party followed in a York aircraft two days later, and on 20 October it was possible to begin local flying in order to get to know the area around Malta. Initially at least, 32 Squadron was classed as a lodger unit at Takali, under the control of AHQ Cyprus.

By November the squadron was in its stride, and was carrying out practice interceptions on Canberras and on Lincolns which were jamming the GCI radio frequencies. Detachments to Idris for air-to-ground firing practice were made in the spring of 1956, and in March the squadron took part in Exercise 'Popsie Ten', during which numerous mock attacks were made on Canberras, Meteors, Vampires and French Air Force Mistrals. Armament Practice Camp at Habbaniya in Iraq occupied much of May and June, and between 16 and 20 July Exercise 'Maltex' was the main preoccupation, many 'attacking' aircraft being intercepted.

During the third week of August 1956 orders were received for part of the squadron to re-deploy to Amman in Jordan as part of the build-up to cope with the increasing tension in the Middle East. Eight Venoms and the squadron's Vampire T.11 left Takali on 28 August, ground crews followed on 3 September, further ground personnel went to Nicosia on 8 September, and the last remnants of 32 Squadron left Takali on 23 September 1956.

208 Squadron

As one of a number of movements of units in the Middle East prompted by the international situation, 208 Squadron, under the command of Sqdn. Ldr. J. N. Thorne, left Cyprus on 6 August 1956 and came to Takali. The squadron's new base was found to be more comfortable than Akrotiri had been, and morale improved when it was realised that 208 was the only operational squadron on the Station.

Soon after arrival, the squadron's Meteor FR.9 aircraft were used in practice strikes against ships in the area, while in September there were three exercises with the Navy, either strike practices or the defence of Malta against carrier-borne aircraft. It was noted at the time that the Malta GCI equipment was out of date, insufficient warning of approaching aircraft being given. In one extreme case an aircraft was vectored onto a destroyer steaming at five thousand feet! During one of these exercises, one of the Meteors, WB125, was destroyed when take-off was aborted and the aircraft was burnt out, badly injuring the pilot. Weapon training was carried out intensively, the air-to-ground firing practice at Idris due to lack of such facilities on Malta.

During the Suez crisis four of 208 Squadron's aircraft were designated as a Battle Flight, and stood ready from dawn to dusk to be scrambled by the Takali air traffic controller on instructions from Malta Sector. The GCI equipment was very quickly put right, and all aircraft approaching the island were identified. Eight other Meteors were made ready to move to Egypt at 24 hours' notice.

Another crisis arose in the early days of 1957 in Aden, where Yemeni tribesmen were agitating. Four of 208 Squadron's aircraft were sent there on 12 January, followed by two more two weeks later. At least one, WB138, force-landed in the Iraqi desert due to shortage of fuel, and this became the subject of a Court of Enquiry.

After a visit on 3 October 1957 by Members of both Houses of Parliament, none of whom made any comments about the squadron, favourable or otherwise, 208 Squadron learned that its days as a Meteor-equipped unit were numbered. In fact a new 208 Squadron was formed in the UK to fly Hunters early in January 1958, although the original unit still existed at Takali until 28 February.

Malta Communications & Target Towing Squadron.
A period of time had been spent by Malta C&TT Squadron at Takali during 1957, but the elements involved had returned to Luqa by 7 October. As there was spare capacity at Takali, however, the squadron, commanded by Sqdn. Ldr. N. W. Andrews, moved back from Luqa on 24 February 1958. Little flying was now being carried out by the Beaufighter target tugs, partly to conserve them and partly because there was only one drogue operator! By 1 April the target towing Flight was operating during mornings only, 728 Squadron of the FAA at Hal Far providing any afternoon target

requirements. The target-towing Flight was detached to Akrotiri in Cyprus at the end of May but this was to be its swansong, as on 7 August two of the Beaufighters, RD850 and RD867, were condemned. The first of two Devons to replace the unit's Pembrokes, VP953, arrived on 16 September, and on 29 September the very last Beaufighter, RD788, was grounded, to be flown to Luqa on 13 October and thence to Safi for breaking up. The squadron now had no target towing aircraft, and this duty was taken over by 728 Squadron for the time being. A second Devon, WB535, arrived on 2 November, and in December the Pembrokes left for the UK. At about this time the unit was down-graded to Flight status.

During 1959 converted Meteor F.8s were used for target-towing work, and one of them, WH256, was written off when the pilot abandoned take-off on 16 June and it crashed through a stone wall. The target Flight also undertook radar calibration work at Ta Silch and, in November, worked with the Army during exercises in Libya. The Flight's two Devons were VP953 and WB535, the Valetta was VW831 and the other Meteor F.8 was WG964.

Sqdn. Ldr. Andrews handed over the squadron to Sqdn. Ldr. P. Porter AFC on 16 July 1959 and he in turn to Sqdn. Ldr. P. J. Langley DFC in June 1960. On 13 November Dakota KN452 arrived as a replacement for the Valetta which had been allotted for VIP flights, but five weeks later it was sent back to the UK for use by the Queen's Flight. It was in turn replaced by Valetta VW836, which flew out from Benson.

The need for such a unit in Malta gradually diminished, and by April 1963 the Flight was disbanded, after many years of useful service under a variety of titles.

A typical shot of RAuxAF summer camp at Takali; this one shows Vampire F.3 VT793 of 601 Squadron, North Weald in June 1952. In the background is the 'silent city' of Mdina.
[via A Thomas]

APPENDIX II : RAuxAF SUMMER CAMPS

Dates	Squadron	Home base	Aircraft used
		1952	
31 May - 14 June	604	North Weald	Vampire F.3
14 June - 28 June	601	North Weald	Vampire F.3
28 June - 12 July	605	Honiley	Vampire FB.5
12 July - 26 July	612	Edzell	Vampire FB.5
26 July - 10 August	613	Ringway	Vampire FB.5
16 Aug. - 30 Aug.	501	Filton	Vampire FB.5
30 Aug. - 14 Sept.	608	Thornaby	Vampire F.3, FB.5
		1953	
13 June - 27 June	601	North Weald	Meteor F.8
27 June - 11 July	616	Finningley	Meteor F.8
11 July - 25 July	609	Church Fenton	Meteor F.8
25 July - 8 August	604	North Weald	Meteor F.8
5 Sept. - 19 Sept.	500	West Malling	Meteor F.8
		1954	
15 May - 29 May	615	Biggin Hill	Meteor F.8
29 May - 12 June	600	Biggin Hill	Meteor F.8
12 June - 26 June	601	North Weald	Meteor F.8
26 June - 10 July	604	North Weald	Meteor F.8
14 Aug. - 28 Aug.	611	Hooton Park	Meteor F.8
28 Aug. - 11 Sept.	500	West Malling	Meteor F.8
		1955	
(nil)			
		1956	
12 May - 26 May	500	West Malling	Meteor F.8
26 May - 8 June	609	Church Fenton	Meteor F.8
8 June - 22 June	600	Biggin Hill	Meteor F.8
22 June - 7 July	601	North Weald	Meteor F.8
21 July - 4 August	611	Hooton Park	Meteor F.8
4 Aug. - 11 Aug.	610**	Hooton Park	Meteor F.8

**advance party only; left for UK after 7 days due to Suez crisis.
604, 615 and 616 Squadrons were also due to be at Takali that summer but their trips were cancelled.

Above: Arming and re-fuelling a 604 Squadron Meteor F.8 during the squadron's summer camp at Takali in 1954. The squadron's scimitar emblem is visible on the nose-wheel door.
Below: RAuxAF Meteor F.8 of 616 Squadron, Finningley, at summer camp at Takali in 1953. [via A Thomas]

Chapter 5
SAFI

From dispersal to airfield

In the early days of the Second World War, the AOC Malta, Air Comm. Maynard, realised that the airfields on the island, and thus the aircraft on them, would be highly vulnerable to attack. He therefore ordered the conversion of a road which connected Luqa and Hal Far airfields into a dispersal track, and work commenced on the necessary widening and the provision of branch dispersals on which aircraft could be parked.

When extra facilities were required and sites for satellite airfields were being investigated, it was decided that a point about half-way between Luqa and Hal Far along this track would be suitable for development as an airfield, and by January 1941 the construction of a 3600ft. (1100m.) paved runway had started. In addition, the usual buildings such as control tower and crew rooms were erected. Even while the work was going on, Safi was used as a decoy for Luqa, and was attacked by five Ju.88s on 4 March 1942, when two Wellingtons on the dispersal track were destroyed and some offices

damaged. Several more Wellingtons were destroyed by fire on 9 March during a further raid. Some retribution was made on 7 April when a Beaufighter night-fighter shot down a Ju.88 which crashed on Safi strip.

The northwest/southeast runway was completed in February 1943, by which time No.1 Camp, with 'permanent' buildings, was well advanced and No.2 Camp, with Nissen huts, was under way. It was then decided that, as a matter of urgency, a second runway, in the east/west direction, was necessary, and to build it 5051 (Airfield Construction) Squadron, comprising 900 officers and other ranks, was drafted in from the Middle East to begin work on 1 March 1943. As no excavators or scrapers had arrived, just two grading machines were used, most of the work being done by locally-recruited hand labour, and almost every member of 5051 Squadron was used in a supervisory capacity. Part of Kirkop village was removed to allow for the runway, and after excavation, grading and consolidation three

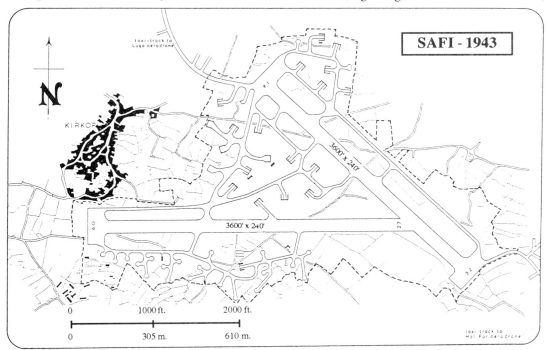

SAFI - 1943

KIRKOP

taxi-track to Luqa aerodrome

3600' x 240'

3600' x 240'

taxi track to Hal Far aerodrome

| 0 | 1000 ft. | 2000 ft. |
| 0 | 305 m. | 610 m. |

An aerial view of Safi airfield from the south-east. *[NWMA]*

applications of crude diesel oil were sprayed onto the surface to form a useable surface.

RAF Safi was formed on 20 March 1943 with Wg. Cdr. Innes B. Westmacott as Station Commander. Immense difficulties were found in obtaining supplies of many sorts, but they were overcome in time for a parade to be held on 15 May, when Field Marshal Lord Gort officially handed the Station to the AOC, AVM Keith Park.

The squadrons arrive...

Safi's first unit, 126 Squadron, arrived from Luqa on 7 June and 111 and 1435 Squadrons came in three days later. They carried on with their current tasks but broke off for an inspection by His Majesty the King, who arrived on 20 June along a road lined with African troops.

To relieve the pressure on accommodation, billets in Sliema were taken over, while the Station HQ was, for the time being, at 1/2 Don Rua Street in Sliema and the Officers' Mess at 70 Tower Road, along Sliema's seafront.

By the end of June, runway widening had been completed, giving runways 3600ft. by 240ft. (1100m. by 73m.). The signals section was also in use. The invasion of Sicily was now imminent, and Safi saw a string of VIP visitors, including General Montgomery on 4 July, Field Marshal Alexander on 7 July and General Eisenhower on 11 July. By that time, another squadron, 112 Squadron, flying Kittyhawks, had arrived, but it only stayed ten days. 111 Squadron departed at the same time.

Little flying took place from Safi during August 1943 apart from convoy patrols. Leave was granted to airmen, who were praised for the efforts they had put in during the recent Sicilian invasion period.

126 Squadron left Safi between 21 and 23 September 1943, leaving 1435 Squadron in sole possession. The CO of that squadron, Sqdn. Ldr. R. Webb, brought to Safi as a trophy an ex-Luftwaffe Bf.109G-2 fighter, captured in Sicily, which originally may have been Black 13 of 2/JG.27.

...and leave!

The short but busy life of Safi as an airfield was coming to an end, and between 15 and 19 October 1435 Squadron left for Italy. Flying ceased on 31 October and on 8 November RAF Safi was disbanded. Safi Camp, however, remained in use, and during August 1944 a Sergeants' Mess serving Luqa was transferred to it from the Poor House, as were some stores sections. Emergency landings were not unknown after its closure, an example being Beaufighter ND201 of 108 Squadron, which crash-landed on 28 July 1944 and was destroyed by fire after an air-test from Hal Far.

In January 1945 a new NAAFI was opened at Safi, replacing one with poor facilities. When 137 MU's HQ moved to Safi from Kalafrana on 27 June 1946 there was an influx of personnel, the sergeants taking up accommodation in No.1 Camp on 1 July, the MT and Fire sections moving in during July, and the officers on 23 August. The Station cinema, meanwhile, had re-opened at Safi and continued to give the usual programme of films of varying quality.

137 MU, whose CO was Gp. Capt. P. Bathurst, took over the administration of 1151 MCU, Kalafrana, on 1 October 1946 and continued this function for several years. By mid-1951 the MU was handling major work on Lancasters and Vampires as well as overseeing the operation of

397 MU, a subsidiary unit.

The first of a series of new Bellman hangars was completed in April 1953 for use by 397 MU, but was found to be less then waterproof! A second hangar was ready in June and the third in August, though it was not taken over until October. Heavy rain had again shown up the buildings' shortcomings, and more storms in November caused flooding.

Large stocks of barrack equipment held at 397 MU were released in November 1954 in a programme of up-dating the facilities at RAF Stations in the Middle East, but later that year and in 1954 a series of public auctions was held, and the sum of £43,891 was raised from the sale of domestic and other equipment to local buyers.

With the reduction of RAF presence in Malta, the need for the services of 137 MU diminished, and the unit closed down. The site, close to Luqa as it was, was eventually absorbed into the extended airfield, and it is now difficult to determine exactly where RAF Safi was located.

Flying Units at Safi

Summary						
Unit	From	Date in	To		Date out	Aircraft Types
126 Sqdn.	Luqa	7.6.43	Gerbini		23.9.43	Spitfire Vc, IX
111 Sqdn.	Mateur	10.6.43	Comiso		15.7.43	Spitfire Vc, IX
1435 Sqdn.	Luqa	10.6.43	Grottaglie		27.10.43	Spitfire Vb, Vc
112 Sqdn.	Zuara	9.7.43	Pachino		18.7.43	Kittyhawk III

126 Squadron

The first of the three fighter squadrons which occupied Safi airfield when it became an RAF Station in its own right was 126 Squadron, which brought its twelve Spitfires Mk.IX and four Mk.V from Luqa on 7 June 1943. Its task now became one of escorting bomber formations on daylight raids on enemy targets such as Comiso and Biscari airfields, to which B-24s of the US 9th Air Force were accompanied on 17 June.

On 24 July, escorts were provided for USAAF B-26s due to raid Gerbini, though in fact no rendezvous was made. Next day, B-17s bombing Gerbini were escorted to their target, and on 26 July Mitchells making for the same area were accompanied by 126 Squadron Spitfires. This type of work continued, and before long the squadron's aircraft could, if necessary, make landings on newly-captured airfields in Sicily.

After a few weeks, the squadron was notified of an impending move to the very place to which it had so often escorted bombers — Gerbini in Sicily. The first party flew out from Malta in seven RAF Dakotas on 21 September 1943 and the second group left next day in ten USAAF C-47s. On 23 September, when the squadron's Spitfires flew to their new base, the Safi Station Commander, Wg. Cdr. Westmacott, watched Sqdn. Ldr. W. T. Page lead the Spitfires off, and finally the rear party left in yet more Dakotas.

111 Squadron

Having arrived from Mateur on 10 June 1943 to take part in the invasion of Sicily, 111 Squadron spent a few days settling in and then, on 15 June, carried out an offensive sweep over Sicily with 93 and 72 Squadrons.

This type of operation was repeated two days later. On 20 June eight of the squadron's Spitfires mounted patrols over a cruiser bringing HM King

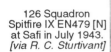
126 Squadron Spitfire IX EN479 [N] at Safi in July 1943. *[via R. C. Sturtivant]*

Flt. Lt. Green, CO of 126 Squadron's 'A' Flight, poses with ground crew in front of Spitfire VIII JF419 at Safi in July 1943. *[via R. C. Sturtivant]*

112 Squadron's Kittyhawks spent a few days at Safi in July 1943 before moving on to Pachino in Sicily, where this picture was taken. *[via R. C. Sturtivant]*

George VI to Malta and flew a series of island patrols. Next day, six Spitfires Mk.IX arrived to replace some of the Mk.Vc aircraft used up to that point, and for the next few days both defensive patrols over Malta and offensive sweeps over Sicily were carried out.

During the first week of July 111 Squadron concentrated on escort work. This enabled the pilots to get to grips with enemy aircraft, and on 3 July, while escorting 126 Squadron Spitfires bombing Biscari airfield, two Bf.109s were shot down, for the loss of one 111 Squadron aircraft. Next day, escorts were provided for B-26s attacking Gerbini, and this time heavy resistance by Bf.109s and Macchis was experienced.

Further escort jobs for B-24s, B-25s and Kittyhawks were flown until the invasion took place on 10 July, when the squadron patrolled over the beaches and covered landing craft and other shipping. One Spitfire, piloted by Sqdn. Ldr. Hill, was hit by flak and landed at Pachino, the first airfield on Sicily to be captured.

As soon as Comiso airfield was in Allied hands, 111 Squadron moved there, the better to continue its offensive operations against the rapidly-retreating enemy.

1435 Squadron

To allow space at Luqa for a large number of squadrons expected in connection with the invasion of Sicily, 1435 Squadron moved its 18 Spitfire Mk.Vs to Safi on 10 June 1943.

This was during a relatively quiet period, but escort work occupied the squadron for a time. The action rapidly built up in July, when 1435 Squadron was able to claim eight enemy aircraft shot down during Operation 'Husky'.

Subsequently there was a further slack period before the squadron moved to Grottaglie in Italy on 27 October 1943.

112 Squadron

Twelve Kittyhawk Mk.III aircraft comprising 'A' and 'C' Flights of 112 Squadron moved into Safi from Zuara in Tunisia on 9 July 1943, the day before Operation 'Husky', the invasion of Sicily. The squadron's first operation from Malta was carried out two days later, when all the aircraft attacked motor transport in Sicily. On 13 July, the Squadron's CO, Sqdn. Ldr. G. H. Norton, failed to return from a sortie, and two days later Sqdn. Ldr. P. F. Illingworth was appointed to replace him. However, 112 Squadron's stay in Malta was very short, as a move was made to Pachino on 17 July, the ground crews leaving by LST.

Chapter 6

QRENDI

Beginnings

Construction of a further fighter airfield in Malta, near the village of Qrendi, about three miles (five km.) south-west of Luqa, began in 1940. The new airfield was provided with two runways, one in an east/west direction 3300ft. (1000m.) long, the other running north-west/south-east 3543ft. (1080m.) long, and both were 150ft. (46m.) wide. Before these runways were finished, Qrendi airfield was used as a 'Q'-site with decoy lighting to divert some of the enemy's attention away from Hal Far. Near the latter runway was a large farmhouse which was taken over by the RAF; the ground floor was then used as a wireless operators' room and the upper floor as the airfield's control tower. Behind was a Nissen hut used as a rest room for ground crews and pilots. Other buildings were used as a guardroom, an airmens' mess and a sergeants' mess, the latter standing near San Niklaw Chapel. After considerable delays in construction due to lack of resources, the official opening 'ceremony' was performed on 10 November 1942 by AVM

Keith Park, who 'beat up' the airfield in his personal Hurricane, coded OK2, but Spitfire Vb EP546 of 126 Squadron had beaten him to it, having crash-landed on 17 August.

Ten months of activity

The first squadron to arrive was 249 Squadron, which transferred from Takali on 23 November 1942. The squadron's Spitfires continued their offensive operations and were joined by 229 Squadron on 10 December.

No more units arrived until 5 January 1943, when the third Spitfire unit, 185 Squadron, arrived from Hal Far. This squadron also concentrated on offensive patrols and reconnaissance over Sicily, with some escort work, until the end of September 1943. Photographic film brought back to Qrendi from these sorties was taken to the Central Photographic Section at St. John Cavalier in Valletta and thence to the Combined Operations Room at Lascaris for interpretation. By this time Qrendi had outlived its usefulness, and all three

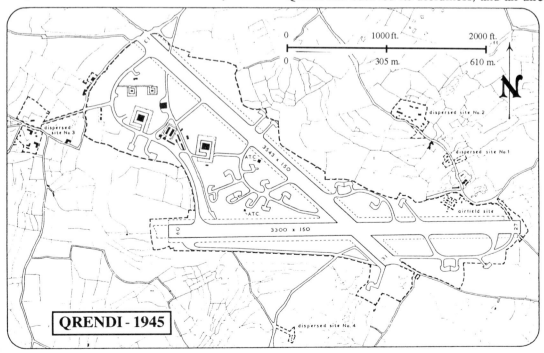

QRENDI - 1945

Sir Keith Park's Hurricane, with personal code OK:2, at Qrendi on the day of the official opening of the airfield by Lord Gort, 10 November 1942.

squadrons had left for Hal Far, where there was now less congestion, by 24 September 1943.

Rundown

Over a year later, on 28 December 1944, a York aircraft from Cairo landed on one of Qrendi's disused runways in very bad weather, the pilot believing himself to be at Hal Far. After three attempts, the York, minus its cargo, managed to take off next day.

A USAAF B-17 is also said to have made an emergency landing on one of Qrendi's runways during 1944. Certainly one of 73 Squadron's Spitfires Mk.IX belly-landed at Qrendi on 27 August 1945 due to hydraulic failure, and as late as 15 February 1949 a Firefly AS.5 of 812 Squadron,

The operations block at Qrendi. *[J. Betts]*

Above: Qrendi from the air in 1975. The control tower, a hangar and other buildings still stood at that time.
[After The Battle magazine]
Below: Seen from a great height in 1973: the remains of Qrendi airfield. *[P. H. T. Green collection]*

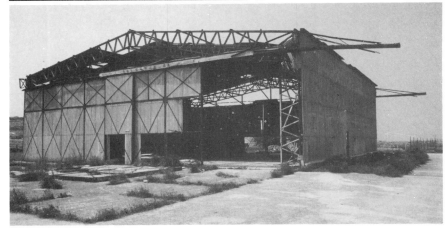

Left: Looking somewhat weatherbeaten when photographed in 1992 was this hangar at Qrendi. *[author]*

Right: Still standing in 1992 at what was the main entrance to RAF Qrendi are the former guardroom and dining hall, with the San Niklaw chapel in the background. *[author]*

Left: The view along the main runway at Qrendi in 1992, showing the 'central reservation' used for agricultural purposes. *[Emmanuel Muscat]*

Hal Far, VT366, force-landed on one of the obstructed runways after suffering engine trouble and caught fire.

After the war the airfield site was used as a camp site for regiments of the British Army, during the 1956 Suez crisis as a bomb store and until the mid-seventies as the site of a meteorological office.

Flying Units at Qrendi

Summary						
Unit	From	Date in	To		Date out	Aircraft Types
249 Sqdn.	Takali	23.11.42	Hal Far		24.9.43	Spitfire Vb, Vc, IX
229 Sqdn.	Takali	10.12.42	Hal Far		25.9.43	Spitfire Vc, IX
185 Sqdn.	Hal Far	5.6.43	Hal Far		30.9.43	Spitfire Vb, Vc

249 Squadron

After moving the short distance from Takali on 23 November 1942, 249 Squadron's Spitfires continued to carry out offensive sweeps over Sicily, particularly targetting Gela airfield. One aircraft was hit by AA fire on 30 November and was last seen preparing to land on the enemy airfield. Escorting 272 Squadron Beaufighters became a prominent feature of 249 Squadron's work during December 1942, even on Christmas Day, when trains near Kurst were attacked. Lampedusa Island's airfield also received 249 Squadron's attention that month.

January 1943 saw the campaign of interdiction by 249 Squadron continue. Targets in Sicily given

attention included a chemical factory at Pachino, the power station at Porto Empodocle, barracks at Licata and warehouses at Scicli. On 7 February two of the Spitfires set about a train near Gela, then spotted a Ju.52 transport aircraft and shot it down in flames. Next day a similar attack was made but this time the pilot of BR373 was not so lucky, as he was hit by flak while flying almost at ground level and had to force land. Continued sweeps over Sicily, some taking place while Allied heavy bombers were also raiding, prompted congratulations from the AOC on 15 February.

April 1943 was also a rewarding month for 249 Squadron. Four Ju.52s were shot down in flames off the north-east coast of Sicily on 22 April, while

A 249 Squadron Spitfire coded T:N, probably LZ889, on a Qrendi runway in May 1943.
[via R. C. Sturtivant]

Another 249
Squadron Spitfire,
JK803 [T:A] at Qrendi
in June 1943.
[via R. C. Sturtivant]

on the same day eight Spitfires from 249 and eight from 229 Squadron attacked the seaplane base and harbour at Syracuse. This was regarded as one of the most successful missions carried out from Qrendi, and was followed on 28 April by the downing of the thousandth enemy aircraft destroyed by Malta-based aircraft — another Ju.52 which Sqdn. Ldr. Lynch sent down five miles (eight km.) from Cape Cadafu. Yet another 'Tante Ju' went down a few minutes later. At the same time eight Spitfires of 249 Squadron made a sweep of the Syracuse area while Messina was being raided by medium bombers of the US 9th Air Force.

Offensive sweeps over Sicily continued during May and June with some success. Three Cant 506s and a Ju.52 were shot down by Sqdn. Ldr. Lynch and Fg. Off. Holmes on 10 May, and a Bf.109 damaged. Three days later, the squadron's aircraft escorted B-24s of the USAAF bombing Augusta as part of the final softening-up process before the Allies invaded Sicily on 10 July. Just after this momentous event, 249 Squadron was withdrawn from operations for three weeks and subjected to a period of intensive training to ensure its utmost efficiency. This was completed on 16 August, and four days later four of the squadron's Spitfires fitted with long-range fuel tanks flew to recently-captured Termini airfield on Sicily's northern coast to carry out patrols over Capri and Ischia.

Just visible on the original photograph are sixteen Luftwaffe crosses on the side of this Spitfire of 249 Squadron, which show the effectiveness of the pilot seated in the cockpit: Malta ace 'Screwball' Buerling.
[Norman Kingston]

QRENDI

BR566 [T:M] of 249 Squadron airborne from Qrendi in July 1943. *[via R. C. Sturtivant]*

Meanwhile, patrols over Malta continued on a much-diminished basis, and on 27 August a Ju.88 on a lone reconnaissance sortie was shot down into the sea 20 miles (32km.) east of Kalafrana, a result which seems to have pleased the AOC, who later complimented the squadron.

As the likelihood of enemy attack on Malta diminished with the Allied advance northward through Italy, Malta-based fighter squadrons became increasingly isolated, and a series of movements began. As part of the reorganisation, 249 Squadron left Qrendi on 24/25 September 1943 for Hal Far on the first stage of its eventual redeployment in Italy.

A Spitfire IX coded GL:V of 185 Squadron, Qrendi, stands in a revetment awaiting the next mission; July 1943.
[Sqdn. Ldr. P. H. Roberts via A. Thomas]

229 Squadron

Having moved from Takali on 10 December 1942, 229 Squadron carried on with its standing patrols over the islands and patrols to safeguard convoys at sea, but added attacks on power stations and ports in Sicily to the work-load. This routine formed the life of the squadron through that winter, but by April 1943 the squadron was frequently carrying out joint missions with 249 Squadron. On 19 April, however, a pair of 229's Spitfires sighted twenty or more Ju.52 troop-carrying aircraft at low level over the sea and were able to persuade two of them to 'ditch'.

Twelve of 229 Squadron's aircraft, with twelve from 249 Squadron, escorted B-24s raiding Gerbini on 15 June 1943. Enemy fighters were beaten off and the Liberators were escorted safely to the target and back.

Operational flying was much reduced over the next two or three months, until on 25 September 1943 229 Squadron left Qrendi for Hal Far.

185 Squadron

Following the move from Hal Far on 5 June 1943, 185 Squadron personnel settled in well at Qrendi, where the premises were in an old tower close to the runway. Patrols continued without a break, and escort duties were carried out for USAAF B-24s raiding Catania and other targets in Sicily. Four of the squadron's Spitfires, escorted by six more, dropped 250lb. (115kg.) bombs on Gela airfield on 10 June, and in July the squadron escorted B-17s to Gerbini and Mitchells to Palermo. Allied troops landed in Sicily on 10 July, and by early August the opposition had been eliminated. This enabled four 185 Squadron aircraft to land on the island for the first time on 20 August to refuel before making an attack on Capri. During this mission a Cant 536B flying-boat was sighted, attacked and destroyed near that scenic island. Similar sorties were carried out during the remainder of 185 Squadron's time at Qrendi, before the squadron moved back to Hal Far at the end of September 1943.

USAF C-47 0476412 after an emergency landing at Qrendi, being inspected by interested locals. The date must be after August 1955, for the records show that this aircraft was an ex-RAF Dakota (serial KN373) and was returned to the USAF on that date. The photograph shows a possible reason for the emegency landing; oil streaks on the top of the Port engine cowling and an undamaged vertical propeller blade on that engine indicates a possible in-flight engine shut-down. [J. Bezzina, via E. Muscat.]

Chapter 7

XEWKIJA

Built with all speed...

An exceptionally short-lived airfield by any standards, Xewkija airstrip, on the island of Gozo, was built to relieve anticipated congestion on Malta's five existing airfields during Operation 'Husky', the invasion of Sicily. Towards the end of May 1943 a party comprising the Governor of Malta, Lord Gort, AVM Sir Keith Park and a number of British and American military engineers visited Gozo and selected a site close to the villages of Xewkija, Ghajnsielem, Nadur and Xaghra. With the help of the Bishop of Gozo the local farmers were persuaded to part temporarily with 200 acres (80 hectares) of their land, which had constituted 400 separate plots in the most fertile part of the island, and after a rapid aerial and ground survey AMWD personnel quickly began clearance work.

With only limited hand equipment at their disposal, however, they soon fell behind schedule, and there were serious doubts about completing the job before the deadline at the end of June.

Fortunately the US Army Corps of Engineers came to the rescue and drafted in heavy plant, the first of which arrived on 6 June, and about 220 personnel. Included in the list of equipment used were four 12 cubic yard (9 cubic metre) scrapers, 24 dumpers, three graders, three bulldozers and several smaller items. Work on the site began in earnest on 8 June, and involved the demolition of a number of farm buildings and an ancient tower.

Apart from the British and American engineers, about 200 local people worked on the project, and on 23 June, fifteen days after construction work began, the first trial landings by Spitfires were made. Two landing strips had been provided, one in an east/west direction and the other running northwest/southeast, and there were

US Army gunners in an emplacement covering Xewkija airstrip.

Above: One of the Spitfires of the USAAF 31st Fighter Group's 307th Fighter Squadron, coded MX:H, undergoing servicing by a motley group of men, possibly including some from 3231 SCU of the RAF, in a very rudimentary shelter at Xewkija.. Below: The code letters HL:U signified a Spitfire of the 308th Fighter Squadron, USAAF, in an improvised pen at Xewkija. At least one of the ground crew is an RAF man.*[Photo's NWMA]*

XEWKIJA

From the appearance of the protective walls, this Martlet IV of 893 Squadron FAA, FN148, seems to have been a visitor to Xewkija. *[H. Newton via R. C. Sturtivant]*

standings of a sort for 76 aircraft. Dust presented a problem, but was cured by continuous spraying with salt water and rolling. After the American engineers left on 30 June, this task was performed by men of 5051 (Airfield Construction) Squadron who had been working at Safi.

Xewkija's assigned unit, the USAAF 31st Fighter Group, which comprised the 307th, 308th and 309th Fighter Squadrons, began to arrive from Tunisia on 30 June 1943, under the command of Col. Fred M. Dean.

The Group's Spitfires quickly began to take part in the run-up to the invasion of Sicily, and on 10 July, the day of the assault, added their weight to the Allied effort. Servicing facilities for the Group's aircraft were provided, in part, by the RAF's 3231 Servicing Commando, a highly mobile unit which was ready to move to Sicily when the time came.

On 10 July a P-40 of the USAAF created the first emergency at Xewkija by touching down at too high a speed and ground-looping. That evening a troop-carrying glider made a hasty landing on the airstrip after being cast adrift by a USAAF aircraft.

The troops aboard it had been destined to land behind enemy lines in Sicily, but, perhaps luckily, did not get that far. During the first three days after the invasion, C-47 aircraft landed at Xewkija with casualties from the invasion area, but to what hospital facilities such casualties were taken then is not recorded.

By 15 July it was possible to move the 31st Fighter Group to a newly-captured airfield in Sicily, and it is unlikely that Xewkija saw much more flying activity apart from US Army Piper Cubs (L-4s) crossing from North Africa to Sicily, and a little use by aircraft of the Fleet Air Arm. 3231 Servicing Commando left on 23 July, bound for Pachino South in Sicily. By June 1944 the site had been handed back to the owners, and reinstatement was under way. The identity of the land was, however, altered, and major claims for loss of soil and walls were received by the authorities.

The site of the short-lived airstrip at Xewkija seen in 1975. *[After The Battle magazine]*

Chapter 8

KALAFRANA

Beginnings: the First World War

Following the decision late in 1915 to construct a new seaplane base for Malta at Calafrana (sic), work began at once. Some materials originally intended for the construction of huts in the Dardanelles campaign were made available and a slipway and seaplane hangar were part of the scheme. At the end of July 1916, soon after completion of the new facilities, five Curtiss America flying boats arrived from Felixstowe carrying seven flying officers, two warrant officers and a number of mechanics, under the command of Flight Commander J. D. Maude.

In March 1917 three Short 184 seaplanes were sent out from Dundee in Scotland to replace the three remaining Curtiss Americas, and on 27 June two Italian-built FBA flying boats were added. One of these was forced to land on the sea on 8 July after warning a convoy of the presence of enemy submarines about 45 miles south-east of the island. The flying boat then drifted onto the north coast of Africa and the crew was captured by Arab tribesmen. Later in 1917 three more FBA boats and six more Short seaplanes were provided to cover losses.

Overall command of Calafrana and of the out-station at Otranto in Italy, which could be reinforced from Malta when necessary, was taken over by Comm. Murray F. Seuter in April 1917. Work that year for Calafrana-based aircraft consisted mainly of searching for, but not attacking, hostile submarines and mines, and escorting convoys, which were warned of the presence of any enemy vessels.

Construction of more hangars and accommodation for personnel was put in hand in February 1918, and that month Wg. Cdr. H. M. Cave-Brown-Cave took over command of Calafrana from Sqdn. Comm. Maude. The creation of the Royal Air Force from the Royal Flying Corps and the Royal Naval Air Service took place on 1 April 1918 and in August 268 Squadron was formed, comprising 433 and 434 Flights, to take over the Short 184 and 320 aircraft. 267 Squadron, which came into being in September 1918, comprised 360 to 363 Flights. This squadron flew F.2a and F.3 flying boats, the F.3s being some of those assembled in Malta dockyard. Soon, however, the first World War came to an end and there was little to occupy the squadrons. First to

An early view, about 1918, of the slipway at Calafrana, with a Curtiss 'Little America' flying boat apparently about to take to the water. *(via P Green)*

disappear was 268 Squadron, which disbanded in October 1919, but 267 Squadron hung on until August 1923, having initially concentrated on naval and army cooperation tasks, with some involvement in the emergency between Greece and Turkey in 1922/23.

Life between the wars

On 1 August 1923 RAF Calafrana became a self-accounting unit, comprising a Headquarters and 481 Flight, which was then on board HMS *Ark Royal.* 481 Flight disembarked at Calafrana on 28 August to take up long-term residence and was joined in June 1924 by 440 (Fleet Reconnaissance) Flight, flying Supermarine Seagull III amphibians. However, 440 Flight left on 9 December to join HMS *Eagle,* bound for England.

The even tenor of life at Calafrana continued through the late nineteen-twenties, enlivened by a visit late in 1928 by the Under-Secretary of State for Air, Sir Phillip Sassoon, accompanied by Air Commodore Sir Arthur Longmore. As part of a tour of many RAF Stations in the Middle East and Mediterranean, they arrived at Calafrana on 8 November in a Blackburn Iris flying boat from Benghazi and left two days later for Naples on their way home. No doubt everyone breathed a sigh of relief that the 'bull' was over!

On 1 January 1929 481 Flight was upgraded to become 202 Squadron, but still operated Fairey IIID floatplanes until July 1930, when a switch to Fairey IIIFs was begun. Sqdn. Ldr. R. H. Kershaw became Station Commander at Calafrana on 28 January.

During the autumn of that year there was some excitement when, on 29 September, three Farman Goliath floatplanes of the French Navy visited Calafrana on their way from Bizerte to Beirut. They left next day for Navarino Bay in Greece but returned on 25 October. Bad weather delayed their departure for Bizerte for four days, and they were then escorted to a point fifty miles beyond Gozo by 202 Squadron Fairey IIIFs. What a sight that must have been!

So the routine continued, enlivened by more visitors. Three Short Rangoon flying boats of 203 Squadron arrived on 25 February 1931 on their delivery flight to Basra in Iraq and they appear to have remained at Calafrana until 16 April. Air Chief Marshal Sir John Salmond, the Chief of the Air Staff, arrived aboard an Iris flying boat of 209 Squadron on 31 March 1931, inspected the Station next day (the 13th birthday of the RAF) and left for Sollum in Egypt. On 15 April an operation which was to become fairly commonplace took place when newly-assembled Fairey IIID aircraft flew off Calafrana's slipway to Hal Far.

Further visitors came and went in 1932, and included two Escadrilles of French Navy flying boats which arrived on 7 June. Each Escadrille, 3E1 from Berre in the south of France and 4E1 from Bizerte, comprised four CAMS 55 twin-engined biplane flying boats, and they stayed two days before leaving for Bizerte. Two Supermarine Southampton flying boats put in an appearance from 204 Squadron, based at Plymouth (Mountbatten) on 15 August and another one arrived next day. They all left for Naples on their way home on 22 August.

At the end of May 1932, after many experiments, night flying facilities were installed at Calafrana. The flarepath consisted of four floats

Calafrana's football field.

Rippon II [81] of 480 Flight lets go its torpedo off Calafrana in June 1931. *(Sqdn Ldr Dawes)*

from Fairey IIID aircraft, each fitted with an illuminating light, creating a path 250 yards (225m.) long. Henceforth, night flying became a regular practice.

Visitors during 1933 included Iris V flying boat S1593 *'Zephyrus'* from the UK via Berre and Naples on 10 June and Southampton S1648 from Gibraltar in 12 hours the same day. The Southampton left on 26 June for tropical trials at Port Sudan on the Red Sea, but the Iris stayed until 29 April 1934.

Short Scapa flying boats replaced the Fairey IIIFs on 202 Squadron in May 1935 and they were joined in April 1936 by 2 Gunnery Cooperation

An aerial view of Calafrana c.1936.
[A. H. Strudwick]

Above: Calafrana from the air in the 1930s, viewed from above Delimara Point. The north slipway and breakwater are on the right of the picture and the south slipway is approximately central. Hal Far is just visible in the top right-hand corner and the road connectijng the two Stations is plainly seen. The walled area on the extreme left of the picture is Fort Benghisa. Note the very spread-out layout of Calafrana. *[Sqdn. Ldr. C. B. Shore]*
Below: S.M. 66 I-NAVE of Ala Littoria after coming to grief in Marsaxlokk Bay in the 'thirties. *[A.H. Strudwick]*

Right: A Fairey IIIF floatplane lands alongside a Blackburn Iris at Calafrana in 1933. *[J. W. Parsons]*

Left: S1038, a Southampton I, at rest off Calafrana. Note the pith-helmeted gentleman in the dinghy and the RAF pinnace. *[NWMA]*

Right: Aquatic Sports day on the slipway at Calafrana 16 August 1935. *[J. Ward]*

Left: Short Singapore K3593 of 205 Squadron staging through Calafrana on the way to Singapore c.1936.

Right: On a hot summer day, Fairey IIIF Mk.II S1224 is prepared for duty at the top of a Calafrana slipway.
[NWMA]

Left: Fairy IIIF S1333 of 447 Flight.
(Sqdn Ldr Dawes)

Right: A Fairey IIIF of 825 Squadron in the workshops at Calafrana after a mishap on a carrier deck.
[Sqdn. Ldr. C. B. Shore]

Left: Two Blackburn Baffins from the batch K3546--K3559 being assembled at Calafrana before being flown off the slipway to Hal Far.
[J. W. Parsons]

Right: An unidentified Walrus on the slipway at Kalafrana.
[NWMA]

Below: The arrival of Sunderland I N9021 at Kalafrana in 1939 seems to have caused some interest among the airmen stationed there. The aircraft was on charge to the MAEE at Felixstowe at the time.
[P. H. T. Green colection]

Flight, which arrived at both Calafrana and Hal Far from Alexandria in Egypt. This unit's Calafrana element, flying pilotless Queen Bee floatplanes for gunnery practice purposes, became 'B' Flight of 3 Anti Aircraft Cooperation Unit on 1 March 1937 and moved to and fro between Kalafrana and Alexandria over the next three years. [Note: the spelling of the Station's name was altered to Kalafrana in December 1936, for reasons not known to this author.] Also based at Kalafrana at this time was 209 Squadron, which operated Short Singapore flying boats between September and December 1937, when the squadron returned to its UK base at Felixstowe. Other aircraft present at Kalafrana during the late prewar period included a detachment of five Supermarine Stranraers of 228 Squadron from Pembroke Dock, which arrived for a two-week stay on 4 September 1938.

In July 1936 four Catapult Flights formed at Kalafrana for operation from major ships of the Mediterranean Fleet. They spent periods of time on board but remained based at Kalafrana. By 1939 one Flight had moved away, but the others had been elevated to Squadron status, eventually being absorbed into other Squadrons in January 1940.

86 (General Reconnaissance) Wing was formed on 19 May 1939 to control 202 and 228 Squadrons, and the SS *Domana* was chartered to act as the Wing's mobile base. The ship sailed for the Middle East at the end of the month, just after a visit by two French floatplanes on 28 May. More French seaplanes were seen at Kalafrana on 19 July, when the French Air Staff made a visit, perhaps to judge the suitability of Malta in any future conflict.

Hostilities begin

RAF Kalafrana was raided by the Italian Air Force for the first time soon after hostilities began in June 1940, and suffered some damage to the northern slipway. The Station gunners were able to come into action on 4 July against enemy aircraft flying low overhead on their way to bomb Hal Far.

3 AACU remained at Kalafrana, on and off, until it was disbanded in September 1940, to be replaced in October by the Sunderland flying boats of 228 Squadron, which came out from Pembroke Dock. The squadron, which carried out anti-submarine patrols before leaving for Aboukir in March 1941, was the last major unit to be based at Kalafrana, which now settled down to a long period of acting as a staging post for flying boats passing along the Mediterranean on the way to more distant destinations. Much-needed pilots for the Malta-based fighter squadrons were sometimes flown in from the UK and elsewhere by Sunderland to Kalfrana. There were other activities, however. At one period two Latecoere 298B floatplanes with Free French crews operated from Kalafrana and carried out many reconnaissance missions over Sicily and North Africa before being grounded (or should it be 'watered'?) by shortage of spares. Much more interesting were the covert operations from Kalafrana carried out by an He.115A-2 seaplane in German markings. This aircraft had originally belonged to the Royal Norwegian Navy, carrying serial number 58. One of four such aircraft, it had been taken to Scotland by a Norwegian crew when their country fell to the Germans, and had been modified at Calshot by the removal of some of its canopy glazing and the installation of eight

Part view of BV185, the captured He.115 floatplane used for clandestine operations from Kalafrana.
[NWMA]

Browning guns in the wings. It was then allocated RAF serial number BV185 and was flown via Plymouth to Malta, probably early in November 1941, by Lt. Haakon Offerdahl of the Norwegian Navy. On its first clandestine mission, BV185 landed in Tripoli harbour to pick up British agents, but any subsequent missions are not recorded. Unfortunately, it was badly damaged and Struck Off Charge on 1 April 1942 when a hangar was wrecked.

During April 1942 there were several severe air raids on the Station. The Officers' Mess was badly damaged, as were the CO's house and Airmens' Married Quarters; the slipways and Sunderland hangar were hit and the gymnasium and grocery store were destroyed. A Walrus and a Swordfish were written off in one raid, during which four RAF personnel and two civilians lost their lives and nine RAF men and thirteen civilians were injured. Little flying activity was seen that month, the only movements being a Sunderland from Aboukir and a BOAC Catalina from Gibraltar, which each made two visits.

The Station Commander, Gp. Capt. C. H. Cahill DFC AFC, left on 2 May and was replaced by Gp. Capt. C. Greet, in whose damaged house Lord Gort, the new Governor General of Malta, was sworn in on 8 May after arriving by Sunderland. The Sunderlands and Catalinas continued their spasmodic visits during May and June, and in July and August Catalinas bound for 240 Squadron at Redhills Lake in India staged through. One of them, VA731, was left behind with mechanical trouble. Another notable arrival in August was a Cant Z.506B floatplane, serialled 139-10, which had been captured from the Italian Air Force and put into service as an air-sea rescue aircraft.

Gp. Capt. Greet left Kalafrana on 24 August 1942 and appears not to have been replaced for a time. No aircraft at all arrived at Kalafrana during September, October or November. However, in mid-December the situation changed when Sunderlands of 230 Squadron, based at Aboukir in Egypt, began to arrive at Kalafrana for overhaul. While in Malta, some of these aircraft carried out anti-submarine patrols. These comings and goings continued into 1943, when, in January, 230 Squadron's HQ moved to Dar-es-Salaam, while deploying detachments at Bizerte and Aboukir. One of the Sunderlands, JM673, took part in a

search on 13 June for the crews of two B-24s which had collided at position 3505N 1900E, without any recorded result.

During 1942 work in the Kalafrana machine shops became impossible due to the constant raids and it was therefore transferred to the 'caves' at Tal Handaq. The premises there, seven interconnected chambers, were originally intended to be the war headquarters but, not being required for that purpose, were put into use as an outstation of Kalafrana. Repair shops for engines and instruments were set up, with all the appropriate machine tools and a generating plant, were set up, and ventilation shafts 95ft. (29m.) deep and 3ft. (90cm.) in diameter, were driven down, each by one miner.

Present at Kalafrana during July 1943 were three OA-10 Catalinas of the USAAF, carrying 'tail numbers' 42-109021, 42-109024 and 42-109025. They came in from Bizerte and left after about two weeks for Protville in Tunisia. Visitors during August included a BOAC Sunderland, G-AGER, which arrived from Djerba on 10 August and left for Cairo two days later, and BOAC Catalina G-AGID, which came in from Gibraltar and left for Cairo on 17 August.

The time had now come for improvements to be made to both the working arrangements and the buildings on the Station. During August 1943 the Armament Repair Section moved from Gasan's Garage, Gzira, onto the Station and was replaced by the Propellor Repair Section, which had been working in Muscat's Garage, Gzira. The Equipment Branch then moved into Muscat's Garage. General Engineering and MT Repair Sections moved to a hangar on the north slipway, while the Engine Repair Section found itself back in its original workshop after working for some time in caves at Tal Handaq. Reconstruction and repair of buildings on the Station was made a priority, the aim being to restore to original condition the airmen's dining hall and barrack blocks, the Officers' Mess and the Aircraft Repair Section hangar. A corrugated iron building, formerly a briefing room, was allocated as a church.

Several times during October and November 1943 Curtiss SOC Seagull floatplanes of the US Navy used Kalafrana Bay as a mooring, but the squadrons to which they belonged are not known.

The Catalina which had been present at Kalafrana since the previous July had been repaired and used for a number of ASR missions, but on 29 October took off bound for the UK and its new unit, 131 OTU at Killadeas in Northern Ireland.

Bending and mending!

On 1 November 1943, Maintenance Wing Malta merged with RAF Kalafrana to form 137 Maintenance Unit, with headquarters at Kalafrana and commanded by Wg. Cdr. J. H. Gladstone. For administrative purposes, 137 MU was initially responsible for 204 and 205 ASR Units, but they were separated from 137 MU on 26 January 1944 to become known as 'M' ASRU. The Marine Section at Kalafrana, however, remained part of 137 MU.

The task of 137 MU was varied, ranging from the repair and salvage of motor vehicle and aircraft engines to the manufacture and repair of boots and shoes! Some of this work was carried out at out-stations at Tal Handaq and Fort St. Lucien, the latter site being devoted to ammunition storage. During the winter of 1943/44 several ENSA concert parties visited Kalafrana, three in January 1944 being entitled 'Six Bachelor Girls', 'Eastward Ho!' and 'Laughter and Rhythm', the latter featuring 'Stainless Stephen', a comedian well known at the time. Dances were also featured; at one, held in the NAAFI on 12 April 1944, the entire female population seemed to be present, some complete with babies, but the event was said to be a great success. The Station farm was also very active during this period; in January it provided 2.5 tons of potatoes and 3 tons of cabbages and cauliflowers, some of which were sold. Pigs and chickens were also reared.

There was, however, very little aerial activity by now. A Catalina, FP131, arrived from Gibraltar on 31 January and left next day for Cairo, and shortly afterwards a Cant floatplane paid a visit from Taranto and left for Augusta. The lack of 'trade' caused the closure on 5 February 1944 of the operations room at Kalafrana. During March there was only one movement, Cant HK976 with a mixed RAF and Italian crew which visited from Taranto. No more aircraft were seen at Kalafrana until 14 July, when two OS2U-2 Kingfisher floatplanes from US Navy Squadron VCS-8, 3116 and 3118, arrived for a two-day stay. A Cant Z.506 called briefly on 21 July, and two more US Navy aircraft came in on 30 July, but then there was another lull in activity.

Sqdn. Ldr. N. R. Mattingley had become CO of 137 MU and Kalafrana on 28 June 1944, but he was replaced on 28 July by Sqdn. Ldr. H. S. King OBE. On 31 August administrative control of Safi airfield, which had been vacated by fighter squadrons at the end of October 1943, was placed in the hands of 137 MU, but for the time being the work of the MU continued at Kalafrana, albeit on a reduced scale. Only one more visiting aircraft appears to have visited Kalafrana in 1944; this was Sunderland EK595, which stayed two nights in October on its way to the Far East. From that point, there was no aerial activity at all, at least until the end of 1945.

This three-engined Cant Z.506B floatplane was one of three captured intact from the Italian Air Force and used by the RAF for air-sea rescue duties. They carried serial numbers HK977--HK979, allocated in December 1943, and this example is seen at Kalafrana.
[D. N. Enser]

Seafire F.17s in the
Kalafrana scrapyard
in 1949
*[P. Cook via R. C.
Sturtivant]*

Post-war retrenchment

During 1945, at least, a unit devoted to the further training of administrative officers, 2 Officers' Advanced Training School, was active at Kalafrana, under the command of Air Comm. G. R. Lousada, a gentleman who had been prominent in Army Cooperation Command in the UK during the early days of the War. Two Anson aircraft were provided for the use of 2 OATS, but they were of course not positioned at Kalafrana, but at Hal Far. 137 MU's HQ left Kalafrana to move to Safi on 27 June 1946, by which time the site had been handed over to the Fleet Air Arm as an Aircraft Maintenance Yard (RNAMY). Other sections moved gradually, the sergeants taking up residence in No.1 Camp at Safi on 1 July , the MT and Fire section in July and the Officers' Mess in August. On 1 October 1946 137 MU, now under the command of Gp. Capt. P. Bathurst, took over the administration of 1151 Marine Craft Unit, which of course remained at Kalafrana. The MU's general work, though, involved such diverse items of equipment as oxygen, safety equipment, MT engines (which were dealt with at Tal Handaq), signals equipment, shoes, uniforms, lifeboats and armaments!

By 1952 137 MU, and therefore Kalafrana, where 1151 Marine Craft Unit was resident, had come under the control of RAF Luqa. Spasmodic flying still took place, most of the visitors being Sunderlands, some of them taking part in routine Coastal Command 'Fair Isle' detachments and

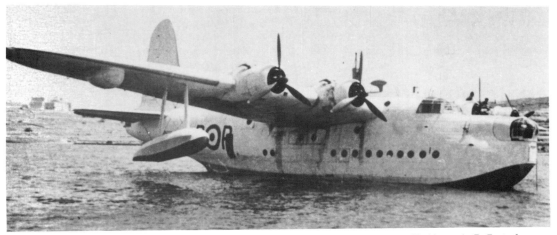

A Sunderland of 201 Squadron, Pembroke Dock, at rest at Kalafrana c.1951. *[D. Lister via P. Porter]*

201 Squadron
Sunderlands from
Pembroke Dock on a
'Fair Isle' detachment
to Kalfrana about
1952. The pinnace in
the foreground
belongs to 1151
MCU. *[D. Lister via P. Porter]*

some for exercises with the Mediterranean Fleet. Five Sunderlands belonging to 201 and 230 Squadrons arrived from Pembroke Dock on 12 May 1952 and stayed until 31 May, and other visitors that year included an Italian Air Force Cant floatplane serialled 83:4 on 24 July, Sunderland PP155 on the way to Pembroke Dock on 30 October and another Sunderland, EJ155, from Gibraltar on 2 December for engine repairs. Early in 1953 several more Sunderlands passed through, and in May six were present on a detachment from the UK, returning at the end of the month. During the summer a steady stream of RNZAF Sunderlands made use of Kalafrana's facilities while on their way to the Antipodes, while in the second half of August several Sunderlands flew airlifts to Greek islands, the first one carrying Lord Mountbatten. A different type of aircraft appeared on 12 and 16 November in the shape of an SA-16 Albatross of the US Air Force, which arrived from Wheelus Field in Libya to carry out 'circuits and splashes'.

Much the same pattern of occasional use of Kalafrana by flying boats, mainly Sunderlands, continued through 1954, varied by the arrival on 27 April of SA-16 Albatross 51-7255 to carry out night flying practice.

Control of 1151 MCU passed from 137 MU direct to RAF Luqa on 1 January 1955, although this modification altered nothing in practice. 1151 MCU's tasks remained the same — rescue, target-towing for air-to-sea firing, disposal of armaments

and anything else demanded of it. 1955 also saw a burst of activity by the flying-boats; the first one to alight was Sunderland GR.5 VB888 on 15 January, and four more touched down on 15 February from Pembroke Dock for a four-week 'Fair Isle' attachment. One of the RNZAF's Sunderlands, NZ4117, arrived on 20 April to stay four days, and in May four Coastal Command GR.5s, DP200, EJ153, ML817 and SZ567, called in on their way to the Far East. During the first week of July these all returned to the UK, calling in at Kalafrana for fuel. More unusual was an SA-16 amphibian of the USAF which had to be towed in to Kalafrana by HMS *Wakeful* on 5 July after making an emergency landing on the sea; this aircraft stayed a week for repairs before flying out. Two more Sunderlands made use of the facilities in October, two in November and just one, PP117, in December.

Another comparatively busy year for the servicing crew at Kalafrana was 1956, when there were flurries of activity in March and April. On 15 April, Sunderland RN299 decided that it preferred to touch down in St. Paul's Bay, to where the refuelling pinnace had to be sent from Kalafrana!

Civilian flying came to Kalafrana on 17 June 1956 when Short Solent G-AOBL of Aquila Airways arrived to refuel, followed by further visits on 29 June, 20 July and 27 July. Six Sunderlands of 230 Squadron, DP198 [A], DP200 [Z], EJ153 [R], JM718 [Y], PP117 [W] and RN284 [F] were present for four weeks from the end of June in order to take part in Fleet operations. Then came another Aquila Airways Solent, G-ANAJ, which touched down on 29 July, and Aquila was very active during August, when a third boat, G-ANYI, joined the other two. From 20 August flight numbers were being allocated to the service, but on 13 September, with the Suez crisis looming, the service was cancelled and the last boat returned to Southampton. After a short resurgence in November the Aquila service was not seen at Kalafrana again, or at St. Paul's Bay, where one of the aircraft touched down on 1 November!

The demise of the flying-boats

Only five Sunderlands appear to have made use of Kalafrana during 1957; although the type remained in RAF service until May 1959, the last recorded touch-down at Kalafrana was on 12 September 1957, when RN303 staged through on its way to Tobruk. Little, if anything, is recorded about the vacation of the Station buildings by the RAF and RN, but this probably took place in the 1956/57 period. Subsequently, the site has been much altered to become a fuel tank farm serving the islands' requirements.

Flying Units at Kalafrana

Summary					
Unit	From	Date in	To	Date out	Aircraft Types
267 Sqdn.	(formed)	9.18	(disbanded)	1.8.23	F.2a; F.3; Fairey IIIC
268 Sqdn.	(formed)	8.18	(disbanded)	11.10.19	Short 184, 320
481 Flight	HMS Ark Royal	28.8.23	(became 202 Sqdn.)	1.1.29	Fairey IIID
440 (FR) Flt.	HMS Eagle	6.24	HMS Eagle	12.24	Seagull III
445 (FR) Flt.	HMS Courageous	6.28	HMS Courageous		Fairey IIIF
202 Sqdn.	(formed ex 481 Flt.)	1.1.29	Alexandria	26.9.38	Fairey IIID, IIIF; Scapa; London
406 (FF) Flt.	HMS Glorious	27.5.31	HMS Glorious	21.9.31	Flycatcher
2 Gunnery Coop Flt.	Alexandria	7.4.36	(became 3 AACU)	1.3.37	Queen Bee
701 Cat. Flt./Sqdn.	(formed)	15.7.36	(became part of 700 Sqdn.)	21.1.40	Fairey IIIF; Shark; Seal; Swordfish
705 Cat. Flt./Sqdn.	(formed)	15.7.36	(became part of 700 Sqdn.)	21.1.40	Shark; Swordfish
711 Cat. Flt./Sqdn.	(formed)	15.7.36	Aboukir	19.8.39	Osprey III; Walrus
713 Cat. Flt./Sqdn.	(formed)	15.7.36	(became part of 700 Sqdn.)	21.1.40	Osprey; Seafox.
3 AACU (B Flt.)	(formed ex 2 GCF)	1.3.37	Alexandria	23.8.37	Queen Bee
209 Sqdn.	Felixstowe	19.9.37	Felixstowe	13.12.37	Singapore III
3 AACU (B Flt.)	Alexandria	19.10.37	Alexandria	3.10.38	Queen Bee; Swordfish
202 Sqdn.	Alexandria	13.10.38	Gibraltar	10.9.39	London II
3 AACU (B Flt.)	Alexandria	21.12.38	Alexandria	5.5.39	Queen Bee; Swordfish
3 AACU (B Flt.)	Alexandria		(disbanded)	19.9.40	Queen Bee; Swordfish
228 Sqdn.	Pembroke Dock	10.40	Aboukir	25.3.41	Sunderland I
ASR Flight					Walrus; Swordfish floatplane.

267 Squadron

Formed in September 1918 to take over the F.2a and F.3 flying boats at Calafrana, 267 Squadron comprised 360 to 363 Flights.

Following the end of the First World War, 267 Squadron remained at Calafrana as the sole occupant. Fairey IIIC floatplanes were added to the inventory in December 1920, and the F.3s were withdrawn in the following May. Sqdn. Ldr. W. G. Sitwell, who had been the squadron's CO since October 1920, when he took over from Sqdn. Ldr. E. Osmond, was himself replaced in May 1921 by Sqdn. Ldr. P. A. Shepherd. 267 Squadron's task was now one of Army and Navy cooperation, but on 23 September 1922 five of the Fairey IIICs were embarked in HMS *Argus* and one in HMS *Revenge* to deal with trouble brewing between Greece and

Turkey. Equipped with portable radio sets, the aircraft carried out aerial reconnaissance missions along the Greek and Turkish coasts to points up to 30 miles inland. Part of the detachment moved via HMS *Ark Royal* to the north end of the Bosphorus on 16 October and carried out more patrols from there. During November the remainder of the detachment joined *Ark Royal* at a point just off Constantinople (today's Istanbul).

The emergency over, 267 Squadron's detachment returned to Calafrana early in April 1923 aboard HMS *Ark Royal*, and its aircraft were replaced by new ones. However, further contraction of the RAF was now taking place and after the squadron's four remaining flying boats were scrapped, on 1 August 1923 267 Squadron was disbanded.

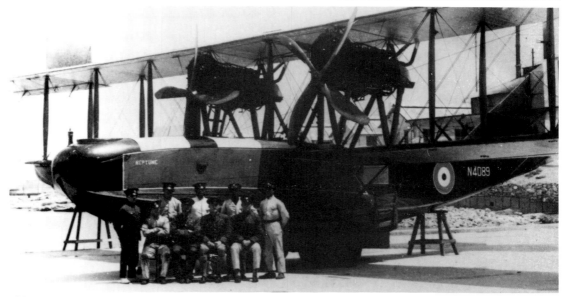

'Neptune', Felixstowe F.2A N4089, seen at Calafrana with air and ground crews; this aircraft was one of a batch of 20 built by Saunders. *[P. H. T. Green collection]*

268 Squadron

268 Squadron was formed in August 1918 to take over the Short 184 and 320 seaplanes already at Calafrana. The squadron comprised 433 and 434 Flights, and carried out cooperation tasks with the Navy and Army until becoming an early victim of post-war recession and being disbanded on 11 October 1919.

481 Flight

Formed on 1 August 1923 while on detachment aboard HMS *Ark Royal* from a much-reduced 267 Squadron, 481 Flight returned to Calafrana on 28

August of the same year. During that time the Flight was equipped with six Fairey IIID floatplanes and the unit had but a short life before being expanded into 202 Squadron on 1 January 1929.

440 (Fleet Reconnaissance) Flight

One of the many naval Flights which inhabited Malta (mainly Hal Far) during the 1920s and 1930s, 440 Flight came to Calafrana from HMS *Eagle* in June 1924. It operated Seagull III amphibians from there until returning to Eagle in December of the same year.

Malta-built Felixstowe F.3 N4370 of 267 Squadron, the last of a batch of 11, seen here on the slipway at Calafrana.
[via R. C. B. Ashworth]

445 (Fleet Reconnaissance) Flight
A small section of 445 Flight, equipped with Fairey IIIF floatplanes, operated from Calafrana for a few months from June 1928 before returning to HMS *Courageous*.

202 Squadron
202 Squadron came into being in January 1929 at Calafrana when 481 (Coastal Reconnaissance) Flight was upgraded to squadron status, although the establishment of Fairey IIID floatplanes, six, was not increased. Very gradually during that spring it was possible for the squadron, under its CO, Flt. Lt. C. Brumphrey DFC, to increase its flying hours, most of which were devoted to naval and army cooperation duties.

The new squadron took part in an air display at Calafrana on 25 May 1929, and the AOC, Air Comm. J. L. Forbes OBE, with HE The Governor and the C-in-C Mediterranean Fleet, attended. Other visitors, including airmen and their families, totalled 1700, but the event seems to have been somewhat tame by today's standards, particularly as the weather was not conducive to seaplane operations.

During June the squadron was successfully involved in submarine spotting exercises, involving flights of up to nine hours duration, and soon afterwards the CO was promoted to Sqdn. Ldr., befitting his status.

Routine flying occupied the squadron for the remainder of 1929, after which, on 28 January 1930, Sqdn. Ldr. R. H. Kershaw took over command. The squadron's first accident, sadly fatal for Flg. Off. R. F. Francis and his passenger, occurred on 5 June 1930, when Fairey IIID S1078 spun into the sea from about 3000 feet (900m.). Another tragedy took place on 7 July, when N9730 collided with an RAF dinghy while taxying, killing the boat's occupant.

In July, temporary re-equipment of the squadron began, with the arrival of Fairey IIIF S1374, but by the end of September not all the new aircraft had arrived due to a shortage. Gradually

A tidy line-up of 202 Squadron Fairey IIIFs at Calafrana: S1380, S1384, S1374, S1381, S1373, S1382 and one other. In the background is a Flycatcher floatplane. *[via P. H. T. Green]*

Dornier Super Wal I-RENE, seen in Marsaxlokk Bay, may have been one of those which had to be towed in to Calafrana when in difficulties. *[via R. C. Sturtivant]*

this was rectified, but in June 1931 corrosion of certain metal parts of the Fairey IIIFs was noted and this had to be corrected before the squadron departed on an autumn cruise to the eastern Mediterranean on 14 July. Ports of call were Corfu, Athens, Mirabella (Crete), Aboukir and Sollum. After take-off S1382 suffered engine trouble and had to put down in the Malta channel, from where it was towed back to Calafrana by RAF pinnace. Another aircraft, S1380, also experienced problems and stayed at Corfu to await the return of the others. All returned safely on 29 July, on which

day Sqdn. Ldr. H. W. Evans became CO of the squadron.

The tenor of everyday life was relieved on 16 February 1932 when an Italian-registered Dornier Wal flying-boat on the Malta to Tripoli service was forced to land fifty miles (eighty km.) south of Malta in rough seas. One of 202 Squadron's aircraft, S1384, found the Wal and signalled HMS *Brilliant*, which took the flying-boat in tow to Calafrana. Outside Marsaxlokk Bay the Wal capsized, but the passengers, on HMS *Brilliant*, were brought ashore. Next day two Fairey IIIFs

A formation of Fairey IIIFs from 202 Squadron. *[Sqdn. Ldr. C. B. Shore]*

Fairey IIIF S1517 of 202 Squadron, coded 4, taxies out at Calafrana in 1934. *[via P. H. T. Green]*

searched for the Wal, which had drifted 15 miles (24km.) and towed it to be beached on Calafrana's north slipway.

Similar search and rescue work was carried out by 202 Squadron on 13 May, when an Avro Avian with a woman pilot was very much overdue at Hal Far from Tripoli. No trace was found, and the search aircraft returned to Calafrana to learn that the Avian had bypassed Malta and landed at Catania in Sicily. Much better for crews' morale was the task they had on 29 May of escorting five new Moth aircraft of the Egyptian Air Force from Malta to Tripoli.

Another expedition took place on 20 June 1932, when four aircraft left for Khartoum via Aboukir. During the trip, valuable experience was gained in

beaching, mooring, picketing and refuelling, before the squadron returned to base on 15 July.

Later that year further anti-submarine exercises were held, with good results, and Sqdn. Ldr. A. H. Wann took command of the squadron. In 1933, apart from an annual cruise in June, little happened to break the squadron's routine work until 14 November, when another SANA Dornier flying-boat was in trouble. This time it force-landed 13 miles (21km.) north-north-east of the island and was towed to Calafrana by naval pinnace.

The annual cruise in 1934 was to Khartoum, with landings at Syracuse (Sicily), Corfu, Athens, Rhodes, Famagusta (Cyprus), Haifa (Palestine), Aboukir, Helwan and Luxor (Egypt), Wadi Halfa, Dongola, Merowi and Atbara. This elaborate trip

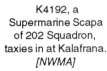

K4192, a Supermarine Scapa of 202 Squadron, taxies in at Kalafrana. *[NWMA]*

took five weeks but again a great deal was learned. Escort jobs which came 202 Squadron's way during the autumn included helping Valentias on the way to Baghdad to and from the island on 18 and 20 August and a Singapore flying-boat carrying Sir Phillip Sassoon inbound to Calafrana on 23 September and onward to Aboukir two days later.

Re-equipment with flying boats was announced on 16 October 1934, but it was to be some months before they arrived. Meanwhile, in January 1935, patrols and searches in cooperation with the Mediterranean Fleet and 812 Squadron from Hal Far intensified. The first Scapa flying-boat, K4142, arrived on 1 May 1935, but it was three months before the fifth one flew in. One Fairey IIIF was retained, and there was also a float-plane version of the Avro Tutor on the squadron strength. In charge of the new establishment was Wg. Cdr. J. H. Jones.

During the autumn of 1935 the conflict between Italy and Abbysinia was taking place, and steps were taken to impose a blackout on Malta. 202 Squadron aircraft carried numerous VIPs to view the result, and then took part in anti-submarine patrols and affiliation with the Vildebeestes of 74 Squadron, which was temporarily based at Hal Far. The patrols continued until the spring of 1936, many vessels being seen and reported. In August a night-time shadowing exercise with HMS *Queen Elizabeth* was carried out, and one aircraft took a doctor, an orderly and supplies to Mirabella in Crete to assist the passengers of Imperial Airways' flying-boat '*Scipio*', which had crashed there.

After a four-aircraft tour of the Adriatic and Aegean Seas in October 1936, two aircraft left on 12 December for Algiers on the first stage of a survey cruise of the west coast of Africa as far as Lagos, Nigeria. One aircraft, K4196, had engine trouble at Freetown in Liberia, but the other one, K4195, carried on to spend Christmas at Lagos. The two aircraft returned to Kalafrana on 23 January 1937, and a flight circumnavigating Africa was proposed for later in the year.

Before any such cruise could be made, however, the squadron re-equipped, in the autumn of 1937, with Saro London flying-boats. The shadow of a possible war prompted the continuation of intensive anti-submarine search and rescue and shadow exercises. By August 1938, St. Paul's Bay was in frequent use as an advanced base for 202 Squadron. On 22 September the squadron was ordered to reach a state of preparedness, and a mobilisation scheme was implemented. Three days later a movement order was received, and ground crews, stores and spares were embarked in HMS *Maidstone*, which then sailed for Alexandria. The six London aircraft had all followed by 27 September 1938, ending nearly ten years of residence by 202 Squadron at Kalafrana.

However, within a few weeks, 202 Squadron returned, and on 4 November two of the Londons carried the AOC and his staff to Alexandria, one of the aircraft making a surreptitious detour to take photographs of Mersa Matruh in north Africa. Live bombing practice on Filfla Island and searches for specified ships occupied the squadron during December, while in January 1939 two of the 'boats went to Casablanca via Gibraltar to carry out an exercise in the Western Approaches.

Italy annexed Albania on 6 April 1939, and 202 Squadron stood by in a state of readiness. As a

202 Squadron Saro London K6932 [B] becoming airborne from the waters of Marsaxlokk Bay. *[P. Arnold via R. C. Sturtivant]*

precaution, most of the squadron embarked in HMS *Maidstone* and sailed for the Middle East on 16 April and the remainder took to the water in HMS *Glorious* and HMS *Rutland* a week later. Nothing came of this expedition, and a return was made to Kalafrana.

News was received on 28 April that 202 Squadron was to re-equip with the much more modern Sunderland flying-boat, and on the same day the first. example, N6135, arrived. Two Londons left for the UK on 30 April, and a conversion programme began on 4 May. However, after the arrival of a second Sunderland, L5806, on 6 May, a high-level change of mind caused the re-equipment to be postponed and the conversion course ended. The two Sunderlands left for the Middle East and two Londons returned from England.

The ongoing threat of hostilities in the Middle East prompted a blackout exercise in Malta on the night of 19/20 May, and 202 Squadron carried out trials at altitudes, courses and times specified. The tension notwithstanding, four of 202 Squadron's Londons left for a flag-waving cruise to Greece on 19 June 1939, with visits to Corfu, Aristoli, Suda Bay, Athens, Volo, Mudros, Salonika and Navarin. While at Athens on 30 June, a Greek Dornier seaplane taxied into London K9684, which had to be beached while repairs were carried out. The other three aircraft returned to Kalafrana on 3 July.

Considerable night flying was carried out during July, and in the early part of August Exercise 'Xua' was featured. The political situation was now very tense, and in order to achieve maximum serviceability all personnel were recalled from local leave. Full war preparations were in force on 27 August, and on 2 September there was an air raid warning practice. By now, 202 Squadron was using a landing area at Marsa Scirroco as well as the one at St. Pauls Bay. Personnel were housed at various places: unmarried NCOs lived at the Teapot Hotel and other ranks in requisitioned flats at Marsa Scirroco.

The AOC visited Marsa Scirroco on 4 September and outlined details of patrols to be carried out if Italy entered the war, but five days later the squadron began to leave for Gibraltar, where it would spend the next five years.

406 (Fleet Fighter) Flight

Fairey Flycatcher floatplanes equipped this Flight, which came to Calafrana from HMS *Courageous* on 27 May 1931, staying less than four months before returning to the ship on 21 September.

2 Gunnery Cooperation Flight/ 3 Anti-Aircraft Cooperation Unit

In order to serve the requirements of the Mediterranean Fleet more precisely, 2 Gunnery Cooperation Flight moved from Alexandria to Calafrana on 7 April 1936. The Flight was equipped with Queen Bee pilotless aircraft, which served as targets for naval gunners on ships in the area. As part of an expansion scheme, the Flight

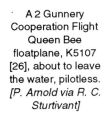

A 2 Gunnery Cooperation Flight Queen Bee floatplane, K5107 [26], about to leave the water, pilotless. [P. Arnold via R. C. Sturtivant]

L2194, a Walrus of 711 Squadron, coded 069, taxies onto the Kalafrana slipway.
[NWMA]

was upgraded to become 'B' Flight of 3 Anti-Aircraft Cooperation Unit on 1 March 1937, ('A' Flight being land-based at Hal Far), but continued its routine until 23 August of that year, when a return to Alexandria was made.

However, 3 AACU came back to Kalafrana on 19 October 1937, by which time some Swordfish aircraft had been added to the inventory. Two further periods were spent at Alexandria in 1938/39 before the unit was disbanded on 19 September 1940.

701 (Catapult) Flight/Squadron

Formed on 15 July 1936, this Flight inherited some of its Fairey IIIF aircraft from 447 (Catapult) Flight, a shipboard unit. Periodically the Flight embarked in the battleships HMS *Barham, Malaya, Valiant* or *Warspite*.

Shark, Seal and Swordfish aircraft were taken on charge later, and the Flight achieved Squadron status before the outbreak of war in September 1939. 701 Squadron disbanded into 700 Squadron on 21 January 1940.

705 (Catapult) Flight/Squadron

705 Flight was formed on 15 July 1936 from part of 444 (Catapult) Flight for use on board ships of the Battle Cruiser Squadron. Its aircraft were four Swordfish and two Sharks, but the latter were disposed of in June 1937. By the beginning of

1939, when the Flight became a Squadron, its aircraft were operating exclusively for HMS *Renown* and HMS *Repulse*.

The squadron disbanded into 700 Squadron on 21 January 1940.

711 (Catapult) Flight/Squadron

Primarily for deployment on ships of the 1st Cruiser Squadron, 711 Flight was formed at Calafrana on 15 July 1936 with Ospreys Mk.III as its equipment. These were superceded by Walrus I amphibians from October that year. Ships on which the Flight's aircraft were embarked included HMS *London, Devonshire, Sussex* and *Shropshire*. 711 Flight left Kalafrana on 19 August 1939 for Aboukir in Egypt.

713 (Catapult) Flight/Squadron

The fourth of the later Catapult Flights, 713 Flight was formed, with the others, on 15 July 1936 at Calafrana. The Flight was allocated to the 3rd Cruiser Squadron and operated Osprey aircraft between July 1936 and April 1938 and Seafox Is from November 1937 to January 1940.

713 Flight embarked periodically in HMS *Arethusa, Galatea* and *Penelope* and achieved Squadron status early in 1939. On 21 January 1940 it was, with the other two Kalafrana squadrons, disbanded into 700 Squadron.

228 Squadron
Sunderland I L5806
at its moorings next
to one of the
Latecoere 298
floatplanes.
[NWMA]

209 Squadron

After flying from Felixstowe on the east coast of England to Plymouth (Mountbatten) in four and a half hours on 17 September 1937 and from there to Berre via Hourtin next day, five Singapore flying boats of 209 Squadron arrived at Kalafrana on 19 September. Within a few days they were taking part in seven-hour anti-submarine patrols each day, but soon the Singapores left to carry out similar missions from Arzeu in Algeria. While there two aircraft went separately to Gibraltar to cooperate with destroyers and submarines in various exercises.

After returning to Kalafrana, the squadron carried on with its anti-submarine task until leaving on 13 December 1937 to fly back to England via Arzeu, Berre and Hourtin to reach Calshot on 16 December.

Sunderland I L5805 [BH:Q] of 228 Squadron alighting in Marsaxlokk Bay. *[via R. C. Sturtivant]*

A victim of an air raid on Kalafrana, 228 Squadron Sunderland L5807 burns fiercely. *[NWMA]*

228 Squadron

Sunderland aircraft of 228 Squadron had been attached to RAF Kalafrana on a number of different occasions before being based there. Two had arrived in May 1939 and another three in August from their base at Pembroke Dock in Wales, staying just a few days before returning home.

On 10 June 1940 (a most significant day in Malta's history), three of the squadron's Sunderlands had left Pembroke Dock to fly via Marseilles (Marignane) and Kalafrana to Alexandria, but one diverted to Bizerte and the others stayed overnight in Malta. Two of them returned on 9 July and carried out a dawn patrol of the Adriatic Sea during which the Italian Fleet was sighted and reported. An He.115 was engaged, but without visible result. Further dawn patrols were carried out until 13 July.

It is not clear when 228 Squadron moved officially from Pembroke Dock to Kalafrana, but it was certainly there by early October 1940. Although principally engaged in anti-submarine work, 228 Squadron also escorted Hurricane fighters into Malta from the aircraft carriers which had brought them to the Mediterranean. As a forward base, the squadron used St. Pauls Bay, and a French aircraft, probably a Loire 130, was used as a 'hack' between there and Kalafrana.

After continuing its anti-submarine role through the winter, during which, on 4 February 1941, permission was given for the squadron to violate Tunisian waters to attack any enemy shipping, 228 Squadron moved to Aboukir in Egypt on 25 March 1941.

AIR SEA RESCUE FLIGHT

At Kalafrana there was an Air-Sea Rescue Flight which flew Walrus amphibians and Swordfish floatplanes, but although dates and details of operations are not recorded it was certainly functioning by November 1941.

Chapter 9
THE AIR SQUADRON, ARMED FORCES OF MALTA

The Air Squadron of the Armed Forces of Malta had its origins in a decision made by the Labour Government of Malta in June 1971 to establish a coastal patrol service. Several patrol boats were obtained from the United States, and the West German Government offered to help in setting up a Flight of helicopters.

In October 1971 a number of Maltese soldiers and police personnel left for West Germany, where they received helicopter flying training. They returned to Malta in May with four Bell 47G helicopters for the new Flight, which was to form part of the 1st Regiment, Malta Land Force. West German Air Force technicians aided assembly of the helicopters, and an operating base was set up at St. Patrick's Barracks. Patrols started at once, and a search-and-rescue function was added, one of the Bells being fitted with floats for this purpose.

The MLF was re-titled Armed Forces of Malta in April 1973, in which year the Maltese Government made approaches to Libya, with whom close relations had been enjoyed during the previous two years, with a view to replacing the Bell 47s with more modern aircraft. As a result, an Agusta-Bell 206A Jet Ranger arrived at Luqa in June 1973 aboard a C-130 of the LARAF, complete with a Libyan flying instructor to provide conversion facilities. Larger helicopters arrived from Libya in January 1975, when two SA.321M Super Frelons were delivered, one of which was to remain on loan to the AFM. This aircraft, flown by Libyan crews with AFM observers, was also based at St. Patrick's Barracks, but had to visit Luqa between patrols for refuelling. The Super Frelon

and crew was exchanged every few weeks.

An aid agreement was signed with Italy in June 1975, allowing a military/technical presence on the island. Subsequently, the four Bell 47s and the A-B 206 were all sent to Italy for major overhauls, which were completed by June 1976.

When the RAF finally ceased flying at Luqa in October 1978 the Helicopter Flight moved from St. Patrick's Barracks to Hal Far for a short time. While there, three Alouette III helicopters were received from the LARAF, bringing the Flight's total strength to ten aircraft. The Flight moved to Luqa in March 1979 to take up the hangar, administrative and other buildings used by 13 Squadron in RAF days. On 1 April 1980 the Flight became part of a new division of the AFM entitled Task Force and was now involved in aerial survey and VIP-flying in addition to its routine work.

The ten-year political friendship between Malta and Libya ended in August 1981 when a dispute over marine territorial rights began. The Libyan mission was ordered out at short notice, and the three Alouette helicopters were left behind, subsequently being donated to the Task Force. Ever-closer relations with Italy then became possible, and during 1982 two Agusta-Bell 205-4B helicopters were provided by the Italian Air Force, although one soon returned to Italy.

Several years elapsed before the next alteration to the inventory took place. This was on 2 February 1992, when the TF's first fixed-wing aircraft arrived — five Cessna O-1E Bird Dogs donated by the Italian Air Force at Viterbo. Flying training and technical instruction was given at Viterbo by the

Mainstay of the AFM fleet for many years were four Agusta-Bell 47G-2 helicopters donated by West Germany in 1972. This one, 9H-AAG, (ex Luftwaffe 74+20), is seen in July 1992 wearing new-style roundels.
[D Pope]

Left: Hughes 369M 9H-ABY on floats and in the AFM markings. It is interesting to note that the floats bear the legend 'Air Cruisers Co."
[D Pope]

Right: One of the first fixed-wing aircraft obtained by the Armed Forces of Malta was this Cessna Bird-Dog, 9H-ACC, formerly Italian Air Force MM61-2986 coded EI-25. Now sporting its new insignia, ACC is seen here picketed at Luqa in July 1992.
[D.Pope]

Italians as part of the deal. Further helicopters were also donated by Italy when in June 1992 two ex-Guardia di Finanza Hughes 369Ms arrived. Yet more augmentation of the equipment is planned, as the three ex-Libyan Aloette III helicopters, which had been disused for many years were, in 1992, sent to France for refurbishment, after which they will be returned to use for SAR and offshore patrols.

The unit, commanded since 1989 by Maj. Joseph Smith, received a more appropriate title in July 1992, when it became known as Air Squadron,

Armed Forces of Malta. As such, the squadron now carries a revised roundel, a finely-detailed Maltese cross inside a broad red circle. More trainees are undergoing instruction in flying and technical subjects, and new hangarage at Luqa is planned. Malta's central position makes it a possible haven for illegal activities, and the Air Squadron plays a valuable part in preventing them. The aircraft are in radio contact with the AFM Operations Room at Luqa and with the Patrol Boat Squadron and the Maltese Police, enabling the Squadron to play a vital part in the AFM's activities.

Bell Jet Ranger 9H-AAJ, formerly 8185 of the Libyan Air Force.
[D. Pope]

Appendix III
UNITS AT UNKNOWN LOCATIONS

Summary					
Unit	From	Date in	To	Date out	Aircraft Types
86 Sqdn. det.	Thorney Island	21.7.42	(disbanded?)	8.42	Beaufort II
89 Sqdn. det.	Abu Suier	21.6.42	Abu Suier		Beaufighter
79th FG	(Tunisia)	4.7.43	(Sicily)	18.7.43	P-40

86 Squadron detachment
A number of Beauforts of 86 Squadron, based in the UK, arrived in Malta via Gibraltar on 21 July 1942 and went into action against shipping. Three of the aircraft, including AW355, were destroyed by flak on 24 July while attacking an Italian merchant ship, which was mortally damaged.

As the squadron HQ at Thorney Island was in the process of being reduced to a cadre, the detachment in Malta may also have been effectively disbanded by mid-August 1942.

89 Squadron detachment
Four Beaufighters of 89 Squadron left their base at Abu Suier in Egypt on 22 June 1942, probably as the squadron's 'C' Flight, and over the next few weeks succeeded in destroying a number of Ju.88s when 'scrambled' from the island. One of these 'kills' was the result of a fine effort by radar operator Sgt. D. Oxby in Beaufighter X7695. When the aircraft's radar failed, he took a small torch and screwdriver and stripped and repaired the set while in flight, enabling a Ju.88 to be downed. For this Sgt. Oxby was awarded the DFM.

The detachment returned to Abu Suier at an unrecorded date.

79th Fighter Group
Commanded by Col. Earl E. Bates, the 79th FG arrived in Malta from Tunisia on 4 July 1943 to take part in the Sicilian campaign. Consisting of the 85th, 86th and 87th Fighter Squadrons, the Group flew P-40s as part of the US 9th Air Force, and left for a new base in Sicily on 18 July.

The Siege Bell in its cupola overlooking Grand Harbour, Valletta - a fitting memorial to all the service men and women and civilians who gave their lives during the siege of Malta 1940 - 1942. *[D. Pope]*

Appendix IV
SUPERMARINE SPITFIRE EN199

The immaculate fuselage of Spitfire IX EN199, illustrating the main spar and under-carriage assembly and the Rolls-Royce Merlin engine on its bearers.
[D. Pope]

Displayed at the first Malta International Air Show on 26 September 1993 was partly-complete Spitfire Mk.IX EN199, which Mr. Ray Polidano, a banker and keen aircraft enthusiast, is restoring with the help and support of the National War Museum Association and Mr. Mike Eastman.

Salvaged from a Maltese scrap yard, the remains of this Spitfire were in poor condition, and the wingless restored aircraft contains a number of components from other Spitfires. The inhibited engine, for example, came from the Battle of Britain Memorial Flight, while the main spar and undercarriage were originally part of Spitfire EN976.

Vickers-Armstrongs built EN199 at Eastleigh, near Southampton, and it flew for the first time on 28 November 1942 before being delivered three days later to 12 MU at Kirkbride. It was transferred on 9 December to 47 MU at Sealand for packing, and on 20 December was shipped on board *SS Marsa* to Gibraltar, where the ship arrived on 13 January 1943. The Spitfire was then assembled and flown by 154 Squadron from two airfields in Tunisia before the squadron moved to Takali on 4 June 1943 in readiness for Operation 'Husky', the invasion of Sicily. When 154 Squadron left Malta for Sicily, EN199 was transferred to 1435 Squadron, but then joined 225 Squadron for a time during the Allied advance through Italy. Subsequently, EN199 returned to Malta to join Malta ASR & Communications Flight, which used it and a similar aircraft for high-speed communications work. Finally, EN199 found itself with 73 Squadron just after the end of the war, and it met its fate on 23 December 1946, when it was blown into a quarry adjacent to Luqa airfield during a gale, and was subsequently struck off charge.

One wing was obtained from a British source for this aircraft, arriving on board a Hercules aircraft of the RAF in November 1993. Two more wings have been located in the sea off Malta, thus allowing, it is hoped, a complete machine to be placed on display to represent the hundreds of Spitfires which flew from Malta's airfields during and after the Second World War.